DEDICATION

The phrase "behind every successful man is a woman" is an often repeated one. In my case, a more accurate rendering would be in front of every successful woman is a man taking the credit. Whatever seems good about this book is due in great part to my wife, Robin, whose tireless support, encouragement and love are responsible for its existence. If anything less remains, I must take responsibility.

Falls in Overland Basin

Nevada Wilderness Areas
and Great Basin National Park

A Hiking and Backpacking Guide

Michael C. White

WILDERNESS PRESS
BERKELEY

Photos and maps by the author
Design by Margaret Copeland
Cover design by Larry Van Dyke

Front cover photo © 1997 by Scott T. Smith
Back cover photos © 1997 by Michael White

Library of Congress Card Number 97-11921
ISBN 0-89997-194-6

Manufactured in the United States of America

Published by   Wilderness Press
                  2440 Bancroft Way
                  Berkeley, CA 94704
                  (800) 443-7227
                  FAX (510) 548-1355

                  Write, call or fax for free catalog

Front cover photo: Waterfall below Greys Peak, Humboldt National Forest.
Back cover photos: Liberty Lake from below Liberty Pass (top); Bristlecone pine, Great Basin National Park (bottom).

Library of Congress Cataloging-in-Publication Data

White, Michael, 1952-
    Nevada wilderness areas and Great Basin National Park : a hiking and backpacking guide / Michael C. White.—1st ed.
      p.   cm.
    Includes bibliographical references (p.) and index.
    ISBN 0-89997-194-6
    1. Hiking—Nevada—Guidebooks 2. Hiking—Great Basin National Park (Nev.)—Guidebooks. 3. Backpacking—Nevada—Guidebooks. 4. Backpacking—Great Basin National Park (Nev.)—Guidebooks. 5. Nevada—Guidebooks. 6. Great Basin National Park (Nev.)—Guidebooks. I. Title.
    GV199.42.N3W55 1997
    796.51'09793—dc21

                              97-11921
                                 CIP

Table Of Contents

TRAILS OF WESTERN & CENTRAL NEVADA

BEFORE YOU HIKE...

Hiking in the backcountry entails unavoidable risk that every hiker assumes and must be aware of and respect. The fact that a trail is described in this book is not a representation that it will be safe for you. Trails vary greatly in difficulty and in the degree of conditioning and agility one needs to enjoy them safely. On some hikes routes may have changed or conditions may have deteriorated since the descriptions were written. Also trail conditions can change even from day to day, owing to weather and other factors. A trail that is safe on a dry day or for a highly conditioned, agile, properly equipped hiker may be completely unsafe for someone else or unsafe under adverse weather conditions.

You can minimize your risks on the trail by being knowledgeable, prepared and alert. There is not space in this book for a general treatise on safety in the mountains, but there are a number of good books and public courses on the subject and you should take advantage of them to increase your knowledge. Just as important, you should always be aware of your own limitations and of conditions existing when and where you are hiking. If conditions are dangerous, or if you're not prepared to deal with them safely, choose a different hike! It's better to have wasted a drive than to be the subject of a mountain rescue.

These warnings are not intended to scare you off the trails. Millions of people have safe and enjoyable hikes every year. However, one element of the beauty, freedom and excitement of the wilderness is the presence of risks that do not confront us at home. When you hike you assume those risks. They can be met safely, but only if you exercise your own independent judgement and common sense.

General Information

Chapter 1
INTRODUCTION

To the uninitiated the state of Nevada conjures up two visions: vast open space devoid of life except for the ubiquitous sagebrush, or, in stark contrast, the glittering opulence of casino-style gaming on the neon-enriched Las Vegas strip. To people familiar with only these two visions, the idea of magnificent wilderness areas existing along the crest of Nevada's high mountain ranges seems as much of a contradiction as an ocean resort in the middle of the Sahara desert. Travelers on the major highways speed through the state, the vast landscape a mere obstacle to reaching their ultimate destination, unaware of what lies beyond the asphalt and sagebrush. And yet, fourteen sublime wilderness areas and one National Park straddle the highest elevations from one end of the state to the other, providing rich opportunities for recreationists to enjoy some of the most pristine and untamed lands in the lower forty-eight states. Almost too difficult to believe is that the most arid state in the entire nation has mountain ranges harboring lush wildflower-laden meadows, crystal-clear rushing streams and high alpine lakes.

When Congress passed the original Wilderness Act in 1964, Nevada was the beneficiary of only one designated wilderness—Jarbidge, an area of 64,667 acres near the Idaho border in the northeastern part of the state. Jarbidge was representative of much of the state itself: lonely, isolated, spectacular and a well-kept secret. Many hours away from any substantial population center, it remained a little known place, revealing its beauty and charm only to those with foreknowledge or an avid curiosity. Twenty-five years later, the Nevada Wilderness bill, signed by President Bush in 1989, incorporated thirteen new wilderness areas within the state into the national system, increasing its size in Nevada by approximately 733,400 acres. In addition, Great Basin National Park, including 13,063-foot Wheeler Peak as the centerpiece, became a reality in 1986 just a few years prior to the creation of the wilderness areas.

These new designations, coupled with the fact that Nevada has recently been the fastest-growing state in the union, have sparked an increased interest in the state's backcountry.

Most of the Nevada wilderness areas remain essentially as they always have been, thanks primarily to the major distances that visitors must overcome to reach them. Notable exceptions are the Mt. Charleston Wilderness outside Las Vegas and the Mt. Rose Wilderness near Reno-Sparks, Lake Tahoe and Carson City. Undoubtedly, the National Park designation has increased visitation at Great Basin, but it remains hundreds of miles from any population center. Outside of these popular regions, most of Nevada's wilderness areas are still rich in solitude and undefiled terrain. Even within the more heavily visited regions there are trails that see little use, providing many opportunities for hikers, backpackers and equestrians to get away from it all. Typically, visitor use is so light throughout the state that wilderness permits are not required in any of the wilderness areas, and voluntary registration is requested at only a few locations. Most areas do not even have stay limits or restrictions on party size, and the few that do have relatively liberal limits.

If you know anything at all about the topography of Nevada, the term "basin and range" should be familiar, although the fact that Nevada is the most mountainous state outside of Alaska is possibly a more obscure bit of information. A seemingly endless row of mountain ranges, separated by an equivalent number of basins or valleys, all trend almost exclusively along a north-south axis. These linear mountain ranges, with peaks as high as 13,000 feet, can be relatively short to fairly long north-south but seldom very wide. Most of the wilderness areas are correspondingly narrow, paralleling the crests of their ranges. As could be expected, the two longest trails in Nevada span the length of their respective ranges along the crests of the Toiyabe and the Ruby Mountains.

The ranges selected for wilderness protection in Nevada are island sanctuaries for diverse ecosystems that differ greatly from the surrounding basin environments. Whereas the basins can be extremely dry and somewhat inhospitable at certain times of the year, the ranges, thanks to greater precipitation and cooler temperatures, contain timber, meadows, streams and occasional lakes, providing safe havens for an abundance of wildlife. This contrast is so extreme that many residents who live in a valley are totally unaware of the diverse and rich environment that exists many thousands of feet above them in the mountains.

Probably the most famous inhabitant found in some of these island wildernesses is the bristlecone pine, the oldest living things on the planet. Other interesting residents of the Nevada mountains include mountain lions, bobcats, bighorn sheep, antelope, deer, elk, coyotes and a wide variety of game and nongame birds, including the majestic golden eagle.

Whether you travel to one of the wilderness areas or Great Basin National Park, the Nevada mountains have a lot to offer the adventurer willing to journey away from the more popular western mountain ranges.

Blue skies, clear air and stunning vistas are here in abundance. The only items lacking in these mountains are people—no standing in line to beat the quota for wilderness permits, no competition for the last available campsite at your favorite lake, and no shuttle-bus rides to trailheads through car-choked valleys. Much of the wilderness is so remote that, depending on circumstances, you may be able to do an entire trip without encountering another person. Since many of these areas are a considerable distance away from a community of any size, such potential for solitude may discourage those used to a more civilized wilderness experience. The land remains, for the most part, wild and untamed, a true representative of what wilderness should be.

FLORA

Any attempt to categorize the diverse vegetation of such a vast area as the Great Basin will ultimately result in an oversimplified description. Some generalizations, if not completely accurate, will help us classify the region into manageable groupings. Within the island sanctuaries of the Nevada mountain ranges a certain unique degree of biodiversity exists; however, the following classifications will aid recreationists understanding of the flora in the Nevada wilderness.

Shadscale Zone

Named after the principal shrub (*Atriplex confertifolia*), the Shadscale Zone occurs at lower elevations where soils are alkaline and precipitation is low. The mountainous areas of Nevada are all well above this zone, but chances are you will drive through much of this zone on your way to the trailhead. Although shadscale, one of the three most prolific plants in the Great Basin, is the dominant species in this zone, rabbitbrush, bud sagebrush, saltbush, spiny hopsage, greasewood and horsebrush may appear as well. Shadscale is an important winter forage, palatable to domesticated grazing animals as well as to rodents, rabbits and deer.

Sagebrush Zone

No plant is more associated with Nevada and the Great Basin than the big sagebrush (*Artemesia tridentata*). The yellow-flowering plant is honored as the state flower. The sagebrush zone receives a greater amount of precipitation, contains less salty soils and has a lower evaporation rate than the shadscale zone. Although the ubiquitous sagebrush seems to dominate everything within sight, before the advent of livestock grazing this zone was three-quarters covered with grasses. Since cattle eat grass and avoid sagebrush, a typical area today contains much less grass and much more sagebrush.

Most any drive to a trailhead in Nevada will pass through the sagebrush zone, and many hikes will actually begin and remain in this zone for an extended time. Under the right conditions this zone can occur all the way up to regions above 10,000 feet. Often this zone intermixes with the pinyon-juniper zone, with no clear-cut boundaries between the two.

A wide variety of shrubs can accompany the sagebrush, commonly including rabbitbrush, blackbrush, ephedra, bitterbrush, spiny hopsage and snowberry.

Pinyon-Juniper Zone

Above the sagebrush zone, the pinyon-juniper zone contains extensive woodlands of the single-leaf pinyon pine (*Pinus monophylla*) and the Utah juniper (*Juniperus osteosperma*). Beginning around 5,000 feet the zone often extends to 8,000 feet and sometimes beyond, thriving in locations receiving over 12 inches of annual precipitation. The woodlands of the pinyon-juniper zone form the largest forested zone in the Great Basin, exceeding all other forested areas combined. Rarely gaining a height over 30 feet, these two trees display rounded, spreading crowns—squat forms one would not associate with the perfect shape for a Christmas tree. Junipers sometimes appear in isolated groves at the lower elevations while pure stands of pinyon pine are common at the higher elevations.

Many of the trails in the Nevada wilderness areas spend much of their initial mileage passing through the pinyon-juniper zone. Roads to higher-elevation trailheads also pass through this extensive zone. In days gone by, Indians spent a great deal of time in this region collecting pine nuts from the pinyon trees, which were one of the few staples of their diets. A mutually beneficial relationship exists between the pinyon pine and the pinyon jay. The jay collects pine nuts from the cones and stores them in the ground for a springtime food supply, perpetuating the tree supply since the bird

Stephens Creek in the East Humboldt Range

does not collect all the stored seeds. Other animals dependent upon the vegetation of this zone are mule deer, bobcat, mountain lion and coyote.

Shrubs sharing this zone with the pinyon pine and juniper are big sagebrush, serviceberry, bitterbrush, snakeweed, snowberry, elderberry, rabbitbrush and wild rose. Scattered throughout the region, curlleaf mountain mahogany (*Cercocarpus ledifolius*) grows on rocky, arid slopes and ridges and is highly drought-resistant. Small stands of this tree appear periodically through and above the zone.

Riparian Zone

The thin, green strands of vegetation straddling the creeks, streams and rivers in the Nevada mountains form the riparian zone. Approximately 75% of the plant species in the state depend upon this zone for their survival, in spite of the fact that only 1% of the land is classified as riparian. Typically, these areas are dense with brush, flowers and trees, forming the most lush environments found in the Great Basin.

Many trails follow paths in or along riparian areas adjacent to waterways. Many thankful hikers have found relief from the glaring sun of a hot afternoon in the cool understory of the riparian zone. The refreshing environment along the streams and rivers of this zone attracts many animals as well.

Three species of cottonwood are the dominant trees along the lower riparian elevations, Fremont cottonwood (*Populus fremontii*) being the most common. At the upper elevations, between 6,000 and 8,000 feet, quaking aspen (*Populus tremuloides*) form well-defined groves of a few clumps to thousands of plants covering many acres. An extensive variety of plants occur within the riparian zone, including alder, willow, birch, dogwood, elderberry, serviceberry, chokecherry and wild rose. An almost equal number of wildflowers flourish in the moist conditions.

Mid-Elevation and Upper Elevation Forests

While the vegetation in lower elevations forms somewhat well-defined zones, the vegetation above the pinyon-juniper woodlands varies from range to range. The most biologically diverse ecosystems occur at the fringes of the Great Basin; as one travels toward the Basin's center the ecosystems in the mountains become less diverse. Some ranges within the Great Basin contain relatively dense mixed forests, such as the Jarbidge Mountains and the Snake Range, but the typical Nevada mountain range has rather sparsely wooded slopes of limited species.

Where soil conditions permit, the one species found throughout the Great Basin is the quaking aspen. The dominant tree in the upper elevations of the riparian zone, aspen intermixes with conifers in mid-elevation regions and exists in pure stands in canyons of many of Nevada's ranges. Most common between elevations of 6,000 and 8,000 feet, aspen may extend as high as 10,000 feet under the right conditions. For instance, extensive stands of the tree appear on the plateau of Table Mountain in

Table Mountain Wilderness as well as the slopes leading up to the crest. In the fall the brilliant yellow leaves lend a dramatic texture to the landscape in many of the canyons and upper slopes of the mountains.

The area in the Mt. Rose Wilderness is not a true Great Basin environment and is biologically distinct from its eastern neighbors. Located at the extreme western edge of the Great Basin within the Carson Range, a sub-range of the Sierra Nevada, the Mt. Rose Wilderness contains the most varied flora of any range in the state. Fifteen species of conifers occur within the region. Four species occur in the pinyon-juniper zone. Between 5,000 and 7,500 feet the forests consist of ponderosa, sugar and Jeffrey pine, white fir, and incense cedar. Douglas fir makes rare appearances between these altitudes. From 7,500 to 9,000 feet red fir is the dominant conifer, with smaller amounts of white fir, lodgepole, Jeffrey and western white pines and mountain hemlock. Above 9,000 feet whitebark pine mixes with lodgepole pine and mountain hemlock.

MID-ELEVATION FORESTS

A traditional mid-elevation forest is absent from the typical Nevada mountain range. Often the sagebrush zone extends above the pinyon-juniper woodlands all the way to the upper elevation forests. This is particularly true of the central Nevada mountains, such as the Toiyabe, Toquima and Monitor ranges. Aside from the presence of aspen and occasional groves of mountain mahogany, many of the upper hillsides are devoid of trees. Defying an across-the-board classification, however, some of the slopes of Nevada's mountains possess a varied mid-elevation forest.

The Snake Range, site of the Mt. Moriah Wilderness and Great Basin National Park, has the most diverse coniferous forest outside of the Mt. Rose Wilderness, seven species occurring in the mid-elevation and upper-elevation forests. Composing the middle region are Douglas fir, white fir, subalpine fir and ponderosa pine. The Jarbidge Mountains possess the most significant mid-elevation forests in the state, with densely covered hillsides of subalpine fir. The Spring Mountains, site of the Mt. Charleston Wilderness, has white fir and ponderosa pine comprising the forest of its middle zone.

UPPER ELEVATION FORESTS

At the higher elevations below timberline, a more definitive classification of conifers occurs in the upper-elevation forest. Three species, limber (*Pinus flexilis*), bristlecone (*Pinus longaeva*) and whitebark (*Pinus albicaulis*) pine, inhabit the semi-arid region of Nevada's mountains between 9,000 and 11,000 feet. Limber and bristlecone pine are the most dominant of the three, limber being most prevalent in the north and bristlecone in the south. Most of the wilderness areas possess two of the three species, but four have only one species. The Ruby Mountains contain all three. The only variant in this pattern occurs in the Snake Range, where Engelmann spruce mixes with limber and bristlecone pine at the upper elevations.

Although Great Basin National Park has a more famous reputation for the ancient bristlecone monarchs, the Spring Mountains, containing the Mt. Charleston Wilderness, have the most extensive stands of bristlecone pine in the Great Basin.

Alpine Zone

Above timberline the highest mountains possess limited alpine zones. Conditions in these elevations are extreme—intense sun, periodic drought, short growing season and high winds. Most plants never attain a height greater than a few inches, generally developing a mat-like structure. Where water is in greater supply, such as the Ruby Mountains, alpine flora thrive, producing nearly 200 plants classified as alpine. Many areas are too dry to sustain much of an alpine flora; others contain desert plants that have adapted to the high elevations. Wilderness Areas with a developed alpine flora include Mt. Charleston, Ruby Mountains, East Humboldt, Arc Dome and Alta Toquima.

FAUNA

The island sanctuaries of Nevada's mountain ranges hold an interesting and diverse population of animal species. The cooler temperatures and higher concentrations of water support a rich and varied concentration of mammals, birds and fish. Opportunities to view the wildlife in the wilderness areas of Nevada abound, although the populations tend to be wary of humans since contact has been historically low.

The one large mammal characteristically associated with mountain areas in the west is absent in the ranges of Nevada—the small part of the Sierra Nevada that extends into the state being the lone exception. Black bears, a species that thrives in many other mountainous regions, appear only in the Mt. Rose Wilderness. Whether they were never able to migrate from the Rockies or the Sierra to Nevada's interior ranges, or whether their populations were too small to sustain themselves, black bears are missing from the Nevada backcountry.

A seldom-seen predator is at the top of the food chain in the Nevada mountains—the mountain lion. Along with its smaller cousin, the bobcat, the mountain lion is thriving, so much so that a limited hunting season is in force. The elusive cats pose little threat to humans but remain mysterious and misunderstood inhabitants of the Nevada wilderness areas. On the canine spectrum of wildlife, the howls of coyotes can often be heard in the morning and evening hours.

The most mountainous state in the lower 48 harbors one of the most prolific populations of big game as well. Reintroduced to many of the ranges within the last couple of decades, bighorn sheep are making a recovery in many areas. Domestic sheep grazing in the mountains have been the biggest deterrent to their survival, as the domestic animals pass on fatal diseases to the bighorn population. Native bands occur in the Grant, Quinn Canyon and Currant Mountain regions. The sheep prefer the high country near rocky terrain and are rarely seen close up. Look for them in the upper parts of steep canyons. A few areas support small herds of mountain goats as well.

Rocky Mountain elk live in the Jarbidge, Table Mountain and Mt. Charleston wilderness areas. Elk are relatively easy to find during the rut of autumn, when bugling males inadvertently reveal their positions and the locations of their harems. The most prolific large mammal in the Nevada backcountry is the mule deer, and it provides the greatest opportunity to be seen. Given the protection of park designation, hiking within Great Basin National Park without seeing numerous individual mule deer is almost impossible. Antelope are common in the lower elevations, preferring the wide open sagebrush and grassland terrain.

Smaller mammals common in the backcountry include skunks, foxes, marmots, rabbits, pikas, chipmunks, squirrels and beaver. Bats often appear just after dusk patrolling the skies for insects, particularly near water sources. Although mice are common in many areas, they do not seem to present the same types of problems as they do in more popular western wilderness areas.

The clear skies of the Nevada backcountry provide the perfect opportunity for viewing many of the raptors that frequent the state. Golden eagles are by far the largest birds of prey, often seen in pairs rising on the thermal currents of the summer air above deep canyons. Many species of hawks and falcons appear as well, along with over 300 varieties of smaller birds. Chukar, partridge, Hungarian partridge, California quail, blue grouse, ruffled grouse and sage grouse are important game birds.

The lakes, rivers, streams and creeks of Nevada's backcountry provide sanctuary for a diverse population of fish. Due to the isolation of the vast majority of Nevada's waterways, 67 endemic species of fish occur within the state. Unfortunately, due in large part to the diversion of many of those water sources for agriculture, Nevada has the highest number of threatened and endangered fish species. Even so, within the wilderness areas anglers can test their luck on a wide variety of trout (See Appendix III).

GEOLOGY

Any attempt to generalize about the geology of an entire state as large and complex as Nevada results in gross oversimplification. Lay readers would appreciate the nontechnical description that John McPhee provides in his book *Basin and Range*. Probably no other phrase besides "basin and range" gives such an accurate idea of the state's topography: Rows of linear mountain ranges, separated by broad valleys, march in a continuous succession across the state.

According to geologic theory, approximately 40 million years ago extensional forces began to pull apart the crust of the Great Basin in the east-west direction. Vertical cracks perpendicular to these forces formed in the thin crust, and valleys formed where the land between cracks dropped, mountains where it rose. Over 200 ranges were created across the Great Basin, almost all of them trending in the north-south direction.

Erosional forces continued to shape the topography of the ranges. During the Ice Age glaciers sculpted the peaks and high canyons of the tall mountains. A remnant glacier is still visible below the steep eastern face of Wheeler Peak in Great Basin National Park. Many of the tallest ranges in Nevada show evidence of past glaciation in the form of cirques and classic U-shaped canyons.

Rock composition of the Nevada mountains is highly variable and often unique to a particular range. All three types of rock—volcanic, sedimentary and metamorphic—appear in various places throughout the state.

CLIMATE

Nevada is an arid state—the most arid of all the United States. Because of the great size of the state (7th largest at 286,367 square miles) the climate varies tremendously from one end of the state to the other, particularly from north to south. One thing remains constant, however—the relative lack of moisture.

The massive Sierra Nevada is the main reason that Nevada receives an average of less than nine inches of precipitation annually. As Pacific storms move east, their moisture-laden clouds rise, cool, and drop most of their water on the western slope of the Sierra before crossing into Nevada. Little parts of Nevada in the eastern part of the Sierra have the highest annual precipitation totals in the state. For instance, Marlette Lake, one mile east of Lake Tahoe at 7823 feet, receives 27 inches annually. Occasionally, the typical pattern of eastward-moving Pacific storms is interrupted as warm

Rainbow over Arc Dome, Arc Dome Wilderness

air from the south moves northward into the state along the eastern edge of the Sierra.

As Pacific storms move into the state, the rise-cool-drop-water process repeats itself, although on a much reduced scale. Whatever moisture remains from the trip over the Sierra is caught by a succession of high Nevada mountain ranges, leaving extremely small amounts for the intervening basins. While interior valleys in the central and southern regions may receive as little as 4 inches of precipitation per year, mountain areas above 7,000 feet may benefit from over 15 inches.

In the mountains most of the precipitation falls as snow from Pacific storms during the winter months. Locked into a virtual deep freeze, the mountains store moisture over the winter in their annual snowpacks. When warmer temperatures arrive, the snow melts, replenishing the drainages and soils with life-giving fluid. A smaller percentage of precipitation occurs in the form of thunderstorms during the summer months. Although infrequent, thundershowers can be intense, producing as much rain in minutes as normally occurs over several months.

The immense size of the state allows for significant variations in the climactic patterns. For example, the extreme northeastern part of Nevada benefits from a series of storms each winter that seem to dip down from the northwest, brushing the extreme corner while missing most of the state. The Jarbidge, East Humboldt and Ruby Mountains profit from the increase in moisture in this microclimate, which produces some of the most biologically diverse ranges in the Great Basin. At the opposite end of the state, the southern regions receive some of the least amounts of precipitation. While the town of Elko in the northeast has an annual total of 9 inches of precipitation, Las Vegas in the extreme south must survive with a mere 4 inches annually.

Anyone who has spent much time in the Southwest is familiar with the cycles of drought that periodically inflict extra-dry conditions upon the region. The recreationist must adapt to these dry periods just as the flora and fauna of the region have adapted for the sake of their own survival. During drought cycles trails in the mountains open earlier but require extra effort in finding water supplies.

As a desert, the Great Basin experiences wide variations in temperature, often within a 24-hour period. Abundant sunshine can produce extremely hot summer days, particularly in the valleys, while clear nights may see the thermometer drop by as many as 70 degrees. Temperatures vary considerably throughout the region as well. Daily July high temperatures in Las Vegas average 104 while in Elko the average is 90.

HISTORY

Exploration of Nevada

The mountains of Nevada are an important part of the history of the state. For the first pioneers they were obstacles to westward migration that had to be overcome, or more often circumvented. The fate of the Donner Party, although their disaster occurred in the Sierra just west of Nevada, is an epic struggle familiar to many. Once the various trails became well traveled, the mountains became focal points for a gold and silver rush that continues to this day in various, more sophisticated forms. In modern times, as the state increases rapidly in population, the ranges are receiving an increased focus for their recreational values.

The Great Basin, containing most of the state of Nevada, was the last area of North American exploration south of the Arctic. The interior drainage patterns, severe physical conditions and surrounding patterns of settlement bypassing the area all combined to discourage exploration until the middle of the 1800's. The resulting mystery that shrouded this huge area of land encouraged an erroneous belief in an inland waterway coursing through the area and connecting the Rocky Mountains to the Pacific Ocean. This riverine concept became known as the San Buenaventura, the hope and dream begun by cartographers and perpetuated by fur trappers.

As almost everyone knows, before the white man entered the Great Basin, the area was home to Native Americans, principally Paiutes, Washoes and Shoshone. Because of the harsh environment, these tribes never grew to the stature of the surrounding tribes, such as the plains and coastal tribes, who enjoyed much better concentrations of resources for their livelihood. Certainly these original residents sought the mountains for cooler climes in the hot summers, for perennial streams and for high concentrations of game. The discovery in 1978 of an archeologically significant encampment high on the tablelands of Mt. Jefferson in the Toquima Range underscores this idea. Certainly the natives knew what most people in the current age are unaware of—that the mountains of Nevada contain vital, thriving ecosystems above the sometimes inhospitable basins. On the whole, the Indians of Nevada were peaceful and not much of a deterrent to the eventual exploration of the area by Caucasians.

Alexander von Humboldt (1769-1859) was a famous statesman, explorer and cartographer who never visited the Great Basin but greatly influenced the physical conceptions of the region. He was in the New World between 1799 and 1804 and, among other things, he prepared a map of the western part of the New World. Humboldt incorporated two major errors into his map, which was used for decades as the basis for the topographic depiction of the Great Basin—Lake Timpanogos and the San Buenaventura River. Other influential explorers, such as Lewis and Clark and Zebulon Pike, would help to perpetuate the myths of an inland waterway and a vast, freshwater lake in the midst of the Great Basin.

Fur traders made the first serious excursions into Nevada. Having played out many of the prosperous rivers in the Rockies and the Pacific Northwest, they began the search for another area rich in pelts. Jedidiah Smith (1798-1831) became the first American to cross the Great Basin. After leaving California and scaling the Sierra Nevada, he made a lightning dash across the center of the state to the Salt Lake area in 1827. Due to the hurried nature of the trip, he obtained little geographical information about the Great Basin.

Peter Skene Ogden, working for the Hudsons Bay Company, took his Fifth Snake Country Expedition of 1828-29 into the northern part of the Great Basin, crossing the present-day boundary of Nevada near the town of McDermitt. Traveling south, the expedition reached the Humboldt River and followed it eastward. Leaving the river near Elko, Ogden crossed the Ruby Mountains over Secret Pass and over a southern spur of the East Humboldt Mountains before heading into the Snake River system for the winter. The following spring Ogden and his men returned to the Humboldt and followed a circuitous course to the Humboldt Sink. Heading back up the river, the party turned north and exited the state west of the Santa Rosa Range.

Ogden's Sixth Snake Country Expedition came back to the Humboldt Sink the next year and proceeded to the Walker Lake region. Heading southwest, the party passed the present site of Hawthorne before reaching Owens Valley. Winter weather forced the expedition south across the Mojave Desert to the Colorado River and into California. When Ogden left his post, John Work assumed his position, leading another expedition into similar terrain in 1831. The explorations of Ogden and Work proved to be invaluable in the initial understanding of Great Basin topography, but although they came to understand the true nature of the Great Salt Lake as possessing no outlet, the idea of the San Buenaventura remained alive and well.

The next few years saw a flurry of interest by the mountain men in searching out vast areas of the Great Basin looking for a major stream to keep their fur-trapping livelihoods intact. Exploration of most of the major streams of the Great Basin had found them wanting as sources for a prosperous fur trade. The British and American companies discovered the area to be inhospitable, suitable for only a subsistence level of existence.

As the Pacific Coast area began to prosper, an overland route to California became a necessity. In 1832-33 the Walker-Bonneville party established a large part of what would become the Overland Trail. Heading west from Salt Lake, the expedition crossed the East Humboldt Range, paralleling Ogden's route along the Humboldt River to the Humboldt Sink. Following a seasonal stream, they crossed into the Carson Sink and then headed westward over the Sierra Nevada into California. Crossing back over the Sierra, Walker and his men reentered the Great Basin near Owens Valley, eventually rejoining the approximate location of their previous route and returning to the Salt Lake area. Although Smith and Work had traveled the Humboldt River, the Walker expedition was the first group of whites to record their excursion into the Carson Sink, up the Walker River and over a pass through the Sierra.

In 1841 the Bidwell-Bartleson party became the first migrating group to employ covered wagons in the traverse of the Overland Trail as well as the first to bring white women into the region. Many more wagon trains

Old cabin near Baker Creek in Great Basin National Park

would follow as the westward migration came into full swing. Despite the increase in the number of people crossing the Great Basin, a complete understanding of the geography continued to elude the minds of men. It was not until John C. Fremont visited the area that the mystery was solved.

As more and more people were crossing the arid west heading toward California, the idea of a more practical route following a more pronounced system of rivers became increasingly appealing. Fremont headed up a series of expeditions that, among other duties, would make an extensive survey of the region in the hopes of locating a better route to California. In a number of wide-ranging explorations, Fremont discovered many areas previously untouched by Caucasians. On the Second Expedition, on May 23, 1844, John C. Fremont made the pronouncement that the vast area of the Southwest was an interior drainage, a "great basin." With the backing of the Federal government and the technical support of trained cartographers in his party, Fremont's discovery became the touchstone for the understanding of Great Basin geography.

Although hundreds of immigrants traveled across Nevada to reach California over the next fifteen years, few decided to remain within the Great Basin. In 1859 the discovery of gold and silver in the Comstock Lode was about to alter these migratory patterns. Thousands of people flocked into the Virginia City area to grab some of the vast wealth lying below the surface. The hills of the Tahoe Basin were practically denuded of timber to support the infrastructure of the mines and the burgeoning city. If you plan to hike within the Mt. Rose Wilderness, most of the trees you will see belong to second growth forests recovering from the wholesale cutting during the mining boom.

The immense wealth pouring out of the Comstock, coupled with the need for additional congressional votes in favor of the 13th Amendment abolishing slavery, pushed the Nevada territory toward statehood. On October 31, 1864, Nevada became a state. Although statehood had little effect on the mountainous areas within the new state, entanglement with the agencies of the Federal government would have profound implications for the administration of these areas for many decades, up to the present day.

14 Wilderness Areas and 1 National Park

The designation of 14 wilderness areas and Great Basin National Park has a long and difficult history. In the first wilderness bill passed by Congress in 1964, Nevada gained only one designated wilderness area, Jarbidge. Just under 65,000 acres in the original Jarbidge allotment remained Nevada's only protected land until 20 years later, when Great Basin National Park came into existence. The fight to establish the park began near the turn of the century, and the park became a reality only after economics turned the populace in favor of a designated national park.

Three years later, after much debate and compromise, on December 5, 1989, President Bush signed into law a bill creating 14 new wilderness areas and expanding the size of the Jarbidge Wilderness by 48,500 acres. Nearly 800,000 acres of untrammeled backcountry now lie in the Nevada wilderness system, along with an additional 77,000 acres of Great Basin National Park. Additional Wilderness Study Areas (WSA's) are in the review process, which may ultimately increase the amount of Nevada wilderness.

The compromises necessary for designation of these areas seemed to some to be unnecessary concessions to ranchers, mining interests and other commercial interests. Many other Nevada residents, sympathetic to the "Sagebrush Rebellion" (a very loose-knit grass-roots movement opposed to Federal jurisdiction over land within the states), were unhappy with any federal government control of land. Nonetheless, the 14 areas are wilderness and remain so, waiting for the recreationist to experience the many wonders of the rich and varied backcountry.

Modern Day Issues

Mining and ranching interests have had the most obvious effects on the mountains of Nevada. The discovery of gold and silver in the Comstock led to other pursuits of precious metals throughout the state. Hardly a range in Nevada was untouched by the various mining booms that have hit the region. Many of the wilderness areas retain remnants of a more prosperous, or at least more active, mining period. Whether it's a trail following an old mining road or a log cabin built by a long-deceased miner, visible evidence of mining activities is prevalent throughout the mountains, inside and outside the wilderness areas. Fortunately, in most cases, modern-day mining activities are typically confined to large-scale operations outside the wilderness boundaries. Unfortunately, if companies or individuals holding previous permits can jump through the governmental hoops, mining is allowed within wilderness areas under certain restrictions.

If the mining bug did not captivate the hearts of rural Nevadans, about the only other viable pursuit was ranching. Most of the early settlers favored the valleys at the base of the mountains for their homes, enduring the milder winters at the lower elevations. The raising of cattle and sheep, however, necessitated moving the herds up into the higher regions of the mountains during the hot summer months for grazing. This introduction of domestic animals into montane ecosystems decimated much of the native vegetation in the later part of the 19th century. Unlike the plains states, Nevada never supported a large herd of buffalo or other large mammal that survived on the native grasses. Introduction of cattle and sheep to the area destroyed the range lands. The areas that we see today as endlessly filled with sagebrush were in actuality composed of 75-90 percent grasses before the days of domestic livestock grazing. Since the mid-1930's the BLM and the Forest Service have attempted to regulate the grazing rights of ranchers in the interest of managing the resources more effectively.

As a compromise to insure passage of the 1989 Nevada Wilderness bill, Congress allowed the grazing rights of ranchers to continue in areas of previous use inside the wilderness-area boundaries. To have disallowed the practice would have ended or drastically reduced the cattle and sheep raising that families had carried on in the same locales for generations. Without the mountain ranges providing forage for the animals, according to the ranchers, there is no economically feasible alternative. Unfortunately, the grazing of cattle and sheep in these areas has many negative effects on the mountain ecosystems.

A hiker or a backpacker usually does not take long to see the harm that grazing does to riparian environments in the many canyons and meadows where it's allowed. Hooves trample moist areas, turning them into a muddy mess. Grassy areas near streams become gnawed down to the ground. Certain plant species are destroyed. Narrow, vibrant creeks become wide, shallow and unhealthy. Who knows what effect livestock urine and feces have on the water quality? Many a pleasing campsite becomes less than desirable amidst a field of cow pies and air filled with black flies.

Sheep do not treat the land much better than their bovine counterparts. In addition to their erosion, effect on water quality and destruction of habitat, domestic sheep carry diseases that devastate the bighorn sheep population that is native to the mountain ranges.

The dilemma is substantial. In the grand scope of things, all the millions of acres of grazing on public lands in Nevada produces no more beef than Vermont does. Should the government restrict an activity that ranching families have practiced for generations? Certainly not without compensation for their loss—but where does the money come from? At least in Great

Basin National Park a conservation organization is in the process of establishing a fund to purchase the grazing rights from the ranchers. However, it's fairly obvious that the continuation of grazing privileges in the wilderness areas is not in the best interest of the fragile ecosystems of the Nevada mountains.

The U.S. government owns Nevada—at least 86% of it. The BLM, Forest Service, Air Force, Army, Navy and Atomic Energy Commission oversee the bulk of land within the borders of the state. The 14 wilderness areas and the one national park occupy a very small fraction of that land, and yet there was, and still is, tremendous opposition to their creation. The fight to preserve the Nevada backcountry is not over. A number of wilderness study areas remain under review for potential wilderness designation in the future, and proper protection of the resources within already designated wilderness should not be ignored. The mountains of Nevada are a precious resource, providing many spectacular opportunities to enjoy the natural environments, deserving your respect and protection.

Chapter 2
ABOUT THIS GUIDE

Widely dispersed throughout the state of Nevada are 14 wilderness areas along with Great Basin National Park, each region unique in composition. With this book, the author has attempted to create a fairly comprehensive guide to the trails within these areas, omitting only those routes that are obscure or sorely lacking in favorable qualities. The trail descriptions, in many ways, are just basic introductions to these diverse areas, providing a starting point for further exploration. Much of the Nevada backcountry, including some very spectacular areas, remains inaccessible by trail. However, the outdoor enthusiast with the necessary off-trail skills will find relatively easy travel into virtually every corner of this rugged environment. If you are an experienced backwoods traveler, don't limit your hiking to the established trails, as the vast majority of the wilderness is open terrain well suited to direct cross-country travel. In other words, let this guidebook serve as a beginning for wider pursuits in the discovery of the Nevada mountains.

Each chapter of trail descriptions covers one of the wilderness areas or the Great Basin National Park (the lone exception is Chapter 13, grouping the Currant Mountain, Quinn Canyon and Grant Range wildernesses). Each chapter begins with a map of the area. Trip numbers on one of these maps correspond to trip numbers in the chapter, and the same for campground numbers. Trailhead letters on these maps correspond to letters after the boldface word "Trailhead" in the text. Each trip is shown on a topographic map in the back of the book. Within each chapter is general information about the area as well as specific trail descriptions. A brief summary of this information follows.

INTRODUCTION

Beginning each chapter are introductory comments regarding the general attractions and points of interest in the area, as well as brief discussions of climate, natural history and human history, and any specific conditions unique to the range.

LOCATION

Some very general descriptions give the location of the area within the state, along with the major highways and roads providing access.

CAMPGROUNDS

Developed campgrounds near the mountains are somewhat scarce in Nevada as compared to other western states, but so is the demand for their use. A large percentage of the trailheads described in this book have developed or primitive campsites, which appear in the individual trail descriptions.

If you do not mind primitive campsites with little or no services, almost the entire state is at your disposal. Since most land in Nevada is federally owned, theoretically that means that it belongs to the people. In addition to cities, towns and private ranch land, other areas to avoid are military reservations and land around active mining claims. If you use a primitive site as a camp, observe minimum-impact camping techniques and restore the site to its original condition.

Forest Service campgrounds and their services appear in this section. Many of the Forest Service campgrounds do not require a fee. A $ sign designates those that do. The more popular developed sites will accept reservations by phone or mail.

RESOURCES

The state of Nevada, fifth largest in area, has only one major city, one medium-sized city, and a handful of sizable towns. Many of the mountain ranges are hundreds of miles from any major habitation. A list of outdoor suppliers, if any, appears in the introduction to each area. However, unless you are close to Las Vegas, Reno or Elko, do not expect to be able to acquire much in the way of backpacking gear. Little more than the basic necessities of food, lodging and gasoline are available in the other towns—if there are any near your destination. Ironically, you may have to travel great distances to secure a replacement piece of outdoor equipment left at home on the kitchen counter, but usually close at hand are legalized gambling and prostitution, even in the most unlikely of places. Always carry extra water, a shovel and emergency items, and make sure your spare tire is fully pressurized before you need it.

OUTFITTERS/GUIDES

Many of the wilderness areas have guide and outfitting services that provide trips into the mountains for recreationists and hunters. The Forest Service authorizes these businesses to perform services on federal land, operating under permits that receive periodic review. Individuals or groups interested in obtaining more information about these services can contact the listed companies by mail or phone.

U.S. FOREST SERVICE

Compiled at the end of the introduction are the locations of headquarters and district offices of the Forest Service (the Park Service in the case of Great Basin National Park). Addresses and phone numbers appear for the offices that have jurisdiction over each particular area. Forest and Park Service personnel are typically congenial and ready to assist you in most any way. If you are inquiring about specific trails or other backcountry information, contact a wilderness ranger, if possible.

TRAIL DESCRIPTIONS

Following the introduction, individual trail descriptions provide a wealth of information about each particular trip.

Trip Type: Each trip is described as a dayhike, an overnight backpack or a multiday backpack. In addition, a trip is characterized as:

1. Out and Back: These travel to a specific point and return via the same trail to the same trailhead.
2. Shuttle: These begin and end at different trailheads, requiring the use of two vehicles or other arrangements for pick-up.
3. Loop: These begin and end at the same trailhead but minimize the distance one must backtrack by forming a full or a partial loop.

Estimates of days are for the average hiker and will vary between individuals and between groups. Estimates include some time for enjoying features of the trip.

Distance: This is the most accurate and up-to-date figure available.

Season: Winter snowfall is the main determinant of when a trail will be snow-free. The heavy winter of 1994-95 kept most of the ranges under snow until the end of July, but during some drought years in the 1980's and early 90's one could have hiked clear trails all year long. Every condition in between these two extremes occurs at one time or another in the Nevada mountains. On the average, season listings should be fairly reliable.

Since Nevada spans such a large area, conditions can vary considerably from one end of the state to the other. Check with the individual ranger stations to be sure about conditions.

Access: Just traveling to a trailhead can be an adventure. While paved roads will deliver you to a significant number of trailheads, many require journeys of considerable distance on dirt roads. Typical sedans can negotiate the approach to most trailheads in this guide, but some trips will require a high-clearance vehicle and a few trips will require a 4-wheel-drive. Where an approach requires travel on more than one type of surface, the least-developed surface appears in the heading. If a trip necessitates the use of a vehicle other than the average car, that is noted. Classifications of access include:

1. Paved road: Accessible to all vehicles
2. Gravel road: Improved gravel surface typically passable to sedans
3. Dirt road: Improved dirt surface passable to most sedans
4. Rough dirt road—high-clearance vehicle necessary: Unimproved dirt road with some sections requiring a durable, high-clearance vehicle
5. Rough dirt road—4-wheel-drive necessary: Primitive dirt road with sections requiring a high-clearance, 4-wheel-drive vehicle

Water: In the driest state, water is a precious commodity. This listing will provide some idea of the availability of water along the trail. Of course, water conditions vary from year to year and from the beginning of the season to the end. By fall some streams shown as perennial on maps may be running intermittently or not at all. You should always bring a good supply of water in your vehicle and begin your hike with full containers. The trail descriptions should help you plan your water supplies on the trail

Maps: The first entry under this heading is a reference number for trail maps, found in the back of the book. These maps, reduced copies of the USGS "quads," highlight the described trails and parts of the access road.

Following the number for the map(s) included in the trip are titles for USGS 7.5-minute quadrangles covering the trip, referred to as "topos" in the text. The ones that cover the trip are named under "Maps." These maps are relatively recent, and they offer the most detail at the best scale. These USGS "topos" are available at outdoor stores or directly from the government at:

US Geological Survey
Box 25286
Denver, CO 80225
Phone: 1-800-USA-MAPS

The Humboldt and Toiyabe districts of the Forest Service have published up-to-date maps at ½" = 1 mile, providing a good overall picture but at too small a scale to use as the sole reference for the backcountry. They are best for providing information about the roads approaching the trailheads. Humboldt National Forest has produced excellent, larger-scale maps with contours for the Jarbidge Wilderness and the Ruby and East Humboldt wildernesses. Purchase these maps directly from individual ranger stations or Forest Headquarters:

Humboldt National Forest
976 Mountain City Highway
Elko, NV 89801
(702) 738-5171

Toiyabe National Forest
1200 Franklin Way
Sparks, NV 89431
(702) 331-6444

Inyo National Forest
White Mountain Ranger Station
798 North Main Street
Bishop, CA 93514
(619) 873-2500

Private companies produce maps for some of the more popular areas. Where appropriate these maps are noted in the individual trail descriptions.

Introduction: Features and qualities of the trip appear in the introduction, providing the potential hiker, backpacker or equestrian with a general idea of the trip and its high points.

Trailhead: Most directions begin from the major town or highway closest to the trailhead. Many of the roads away from the highways are not clearly marked, so pay close attention to the directions and always have the right map available for verifying the route.

Description: Specific, although not detailed, directions are given for each trail. The author doesn't want you to keep your nose in the book and miss the whole reason you came to the mountains. Use this guide as a quiet shepherd pointing the way into the wilderness.

Chapter 3
TRAVELING IN THE WILDERNESS

SEASONS AND WEATHER

Guidelines about when to hike in the Nevada mountains are probably the most arbitrary specification in this book. Nevada weather can be widely variable from one season to the next, and from one year to the next. In years of little or no snow, one could travel across the mountains virtually unimpeded at any time of year. After winters of tremendous snowpack, hikers plagued with cabin fever must wait until midsummer to escape confinement. But usually the hiking season begins early in June and extends well into October, and prime time for outdoor recreation occurs between early July and late September.

All the hikes in the Nevada wilderness areas are in mountainous terrain and are subject to the whims and caprices of mountain weather. You doubtless expect to enjoy a bountiful supply of sunshine, but you must also prepare for thunderstorms during the summer months, as well as cold fronts that can create winter-like conditions at the higher elevations during spring and fall. A beautiful summer day filled with warm sunshine can suddenly turn cold, with a bone-chilling wind and pelting rain. Do not assume that the driest state in the nation never has inclement weather—Be prepared! Fortunately, thunderstorms resolve and cold fronts pass, returning favorable weather to the ranges. The proper equipment coupled with wisdom and proper judgment will enable you to ride out the worst of conditions until the return of better weather.

OBJECTIVE HAZARDS

Lightning

There are two aspects of lightning to avoid: the direct strike and subsequent ground currents. The best place to be in the mountains during a thunderstorm, other than behind the plate-glass window of a lodge next to a warm fire, is a broad valley near the shorter trees in a dense stand of timber. But with few dense forests, these mountain ranges offer little sense of safety from lightning. The best rule is to be lower than nearby projections. If you find yourself on top of a ridge when a storm is imminent, retreat immediately to lower ground. But avoid hollows, depressions, overhangs and small caves, as these areas increase your exposure to ground currents occurring after the initial strike.

Hypothermia

Hypothermia is the condition of the human body's core temperature dropping below normal in response to prolonged exposure to cold conditions. Air temperature is not necessarily the determining factor, as many cases of hypothermia occur when the thermometer registers above freezing. Wind chill, fatigue and wetness (from rain, melting snow, submersion or even excessive perspiration) can exacerbate the problem.

The best cure for hypothermia is prevention. Do not get too cold, too tired or too wet. Always be prepared with the proper equipment and knowledge of its use. Dress in layers and take the time to adjust your clothing when conditions change, preventing yourself from becoming too hot or cold as well as preventing excessive wetness, either from precipitation or perspiration. Refrain from pushing on toward exhaustion when tired and remember to drink plenty of fluids and eat plenty of energy-producing food. If you suspect one of your party may be experiencing the symptoms of hypothermia, handle the situation immediately. Due to loss of mental acuity, you will not be able to detect symptoms in yourself.

Altitude

The trails in the Nevada wilderness areas range in elevation from about 5,000 feet to 13,140 feet, altitudes high enough to bring on mountain sickness and its more serious counterpart, acute mountain sickness. Symptoms may include headache, fatigue, loss of appetite, shortness of

Thomas Creek Trailhead, Mt. Rose Wilderness

breath, nausea, vomiting, drowsiness, dizziness, memory loss and loss of mental acuity. Although rare at these altitudes, acute mountain sickness is possible. Such cases require immediate descent, and medical attention will likely be necessary.

To avoid this affliction, drink plenty of fluids, eat a diet high in carbohydrates and acclimatize slowly. Camping near your trailhead on the first night helps to avoid mountain sickness. If you live in Nevada, chances are you live at a significant elevation already, and so require less time to acclimatize.

Sun

High altitudes can turn one of the prime attractions of wilderness into a potential detriment—too much sun. Unprotected exposure to the sun at altitude for as little as one-half hour may be enough for some people to develop a sunburn. With less atmosphere above to absorb the sun's rays, you must use sunblock for the skin and sunglasses for the eyes. Light-colored, loose-fitting, lightweight clothing used in combination with a wide-brimmed hat will provide additional protection.

Avoid the potential for more serious sun-related problems such as heat stroke, heat exhaustion, dehydration and cramps by maintaining a proper intake of fluids and salts.

Water

Water is scarce in some areas of the Nevada wilderness—in some places completely unavailable. In dry years the situation can be even worse. Many of the trails require proper planning to assure that rest stops and campsites will have adequate water supplies nearby. Always bring plenty of water and start your trip with full water bottles.

The question of water quality in the mountains of Nevada has not gained much attention, unlike in some of the more popular areas of the West. Most government publications regarding the Nevada wilderness areas do not even mention the possibility of contracting giardia or other water-borne illnesses, despite the fact that virtually every area in the state supports cattle grazing during the summer months. The degradation caused by cattle combined with an increase in human visitation can only affect the water quality of lakes and streams adversely. Since giardia and other water-borne microbes are invisible to the naked eye, the only completely safe practice is to purify all drinking water by filtration, boiling or chemical means.

While most water-related problems have to do with its scarcity, too much water can be an infrequent but potentially dangerous problem as well. During a heavy thunderstorm, isolated flash flooding can occur. In such conditions you want to be away from any narrow canyons, safely on higher ground. Heavy winters can also produce heavy runoff during the spring and early summer, making stream crossings hazardous. You won't find many bridges over dangerous stretches of rivers and creeks as you do in other, less primitive wilderness areas of the West. Consider yourself fortunate if you happen to find a downed tree that spans the width of a turbulent stream. If traveling early in the season, check with the Forest Service for updates on fords and crossings.

Animals

Nevada is blessed with an abundant, diverse and thriving wildlife population, the mountainous areas providing suitable habitat. Only a few animals can be considered potentially dangerous to humans, and the actual chance of a negative encounter is extremely low.

The only Nevada wilderness area where bears exist is the Mt. Rose Wilderness, on the eastern edge of the Sierra Nevada, and they have yet to become a real nuisance. If you camp in the Mt. Rose backcountry, you probably do not even need to bear-bag your food.

The next largest predatory animal of any concern is the mountain lion, prolific enough in many of the areas to justify a limited hunting season. A sighting of one of these large cats is a rare experience, as they tend to avoid all human contact. They might see you, but you will almost never see them. If mountain lions concern you, avoid solitary travel—they do not like humans and prefer groups of them even less.

Found in virtually any environment in Nevada, rattlesnakes can be a potential hazard to the hiker. However, the chances of an encounter are fairly low. In two full seasons of hiking throughout the state's wilderness areas, I encountered only two rattlesnakes, neither encounter dangerous in the least. A watchful eye is the best defense against an unexpected encounter. Remember, the snake does not want to see you either, and will avoid human contact if at all possible. Rattlesnakes are most common at lower elevations near streams in dry areas.

Ticks would be considered just nasty blood-sucking pests except for their potential for infecting you with debilitating disease. The population seems to increase in the spring of wet years, and become much less noticeable by midsummer. You can inhibit their invasion by using insect repellent and wearing a long-sleeved shirt and long pants, with the cuffs stuffed into your socks. Daily self-inspection and examination by a comrade are wise practices. If a tick does attach itself, use tweezers to gently pull the pest out. Mosquitoes and black flies can also be a nuisance at certain times, but pose no significant danger to humans.

WILDERNESS ETHICS

Wilderness is designated primarily to protect land from the influence of man. The user is responsible for treating these pristine areas with the grateful respect of a visitor allowed into a natural treasure. Tenets of the environmental movement, well accepted by more cosmopolitan sectors of the nation, seem to have bypassed much of Nevada's backcountry. Therefore, your responsibility to practice minimum-impact camping is even more important in helping to protect this fragile resource in Nevada.

The overarching goal of the care of the wilderness is to leave the area in the same condition as it was found, or even better. Those coming after you should not be able to see that you were there. Your cooperation in maintaining the pristine nature of the Nevada wilderness insures the enjoyment of these mountains for generations to come.

If you are unfamiliar with the latest low-impact backcountry techniques, *Backpacking Basics* by Winnett and Findling, published by Wilderness Press, would be a welcome addition to your library. The Forest Service also has some helpful information about wilderness ethics available at the ranger stations.

Wilderness Permits And Other Restrictions

Currently, permits are not required for visits into the Nevada wilderness areas, because use is relatively light—with a few exceptions in the Mt. Charleston and Mt. Rose Areas. Some parts of the Humboldt National Forest have voluntarily registration, aiding the Forest Service in monitoring use patterns on certain trails. Group-size and limit-of-stay restrictions occur in only a handful of areas and are not very limiting.

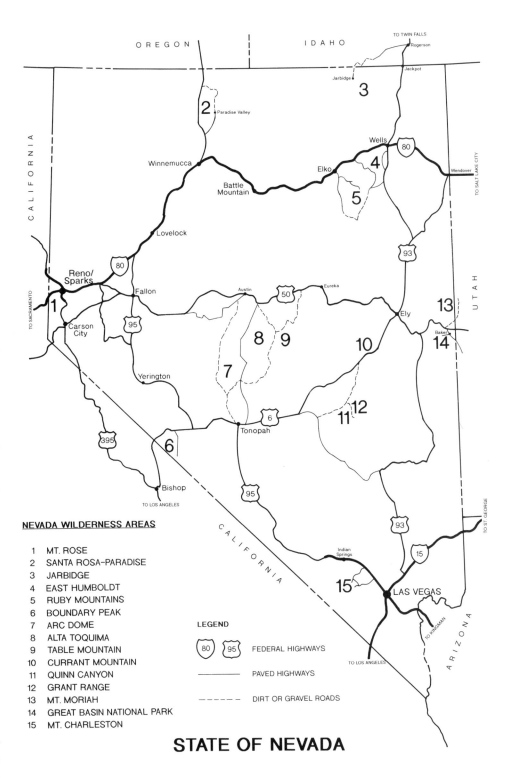

NEVADA WILDERNESS AREAS

1. MT. ROSE
2. SANTA ROSA-PARADISE
3. JARBIDGE
4. EAST HUMBOLDT
5. RUBY MOUNTAINS
6. BOUNDARY PEAK
7. ARC DOME
8. ALTA TOQUIMA
9. TABLE MOUNTAIN
10. CURRANT MOUNTAIN
11. QUINN CANYON
12. GRANT RANGE
13. MT. MORIAH
14. GREAT BASIN NATIONAL PARK
15. MT. CHARLESTON

LEGEND

80 95 FEDERAL HIGHWAYS

——————— PAVED HIGHWAYS

- - - - - - DIRT OR GRAVEL ROADS

STATE OF NEVADA

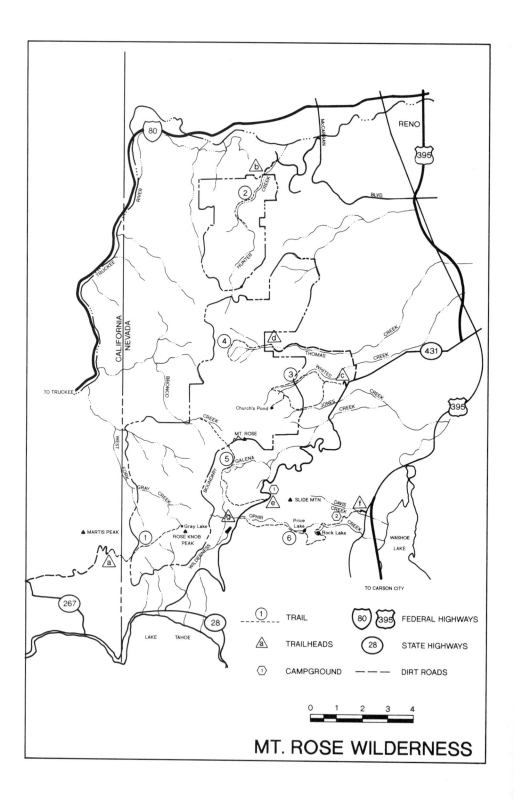

MT. ROSE WILDERNESS

Legend:

- ① TRAIL
- Ⓐ TRAILHEADS
- ① CAMPGROUND
- 🛡️80 🛡️395 FEDERAL HIGHWAYS
- 28 STATE HIGHWAYS
- — — — DIRT ROADS

Scale: 0 1 2 3 4

Map labels: RENO, TO TRUCKEE, TO CARSON CITY, CALIFORNIA, NEVADA, LAKE TAHOE, WASHOE LAKE, MARTIS PEAK, SLIDE MTN, ROSE KNOB PEAK, MT. ROSE, Gray Lake, Price Lake, Rock Lake, Church's Pond, GALENA, OPHIR, BRONCO, HUNTER, THOMAS, WHITES, JONES CREEK, DAVIS CREEK, GRAY CREEK, TRUCKEE RIVER, WEST FORK, BOUNDARY, WILDERNESS, BLVD, McCARRAN

Trails of Northwestern Nevada

Chapter 4
MT. ROSE WILDERNESS

The Mt. Rose Wilderness, located on the north-south trending ridge of the Carson Range above the eastern shore of Lake Tahoe, is a backyard playground for the residents of Reno/Sparks, Lake Tahoe and Carson City. The centerpiece of the wilderness is 10,776-foot Mt. Rose, a volcanic peak, third highest in the Lake Tahoe basin, offering commanding views of the surrounding terrain. On clear days, you can gaze northward from the summit all the way to snow-capped Mt. Shasta. The trail to the top of Mt. Rose is the most popular trail in the area and quite possibly the entire state. A typical summer weekend will see numerous cars lining the road at the trailhead while other trails around the flanks of Mt. Rose see very little use, offering the diligent hiker a chance to have a true wilderness experience within minutes of urban civilization—a rarity for cities of similar populations.

A transition zone between the vegetation of the Sierra Nevada and of the Great Basin, the Mt. Rose region contains plants and trees from both zones, making for a very rich and diverse environment. Elevations range from 5100 to 10,776 feet, furthering the biological diversity of the region. Dry, sagebrush-covered slopes, common to much of the Great Basin, are present throughout the wilderness, as expected, but so are lush streamside settings more reminiscent of coastal regions. Common in east-flank Sierra drainages as well are stands of quaking aspen that turn gold in the autumn, creating a spectacular display of color along many of the creeks. And of course, the wilderness is home to a varied display of wildflowers.

The 28,000-acre wilderness is split into two parts: the Hunter Creek unit, a 5,000- acre piece at the north end of the Carson Range containing only one trail along Hunter Creek, and the 23,000-acre Mt. Rose unit, containing most of the land and most of the trails. Separating the two areas is a jeep road that climbs to Hunter Lake and the crest of the Carson Range— a concession to off-road-vehicle users. Other than the trail along Hunter

Creek, the rest of the Hunter Creek unit is largely inaccessible. The Mt. Rose unit offers trails to the highest peak and the lowest canyons. Lakes, creeks, meadows and ridges await the traveler looking for adventure in the Mt. Rose Wilderness.

LOCATION
Mt. Rose Wilderness Area is approximately 15 miles southwest of Reno/Sparks and a little northeast of Lake Tahoe. This portion of the Carson Range is bounded by Interstate 80 on the north, U.S. Highway 395 on the east, State Route 431 (Mt. Rose Highway) on the southeast and State Route 28 around Lake Tahoe to the south.

CAMPGROUNDS
1. MT. ROSE CAMPGROUND—U.S. Forest Service $
   Open mid-June through September (weather permitting)
   Camping, Picnicking, Water
   Just west of the Mt. Rose Summit on State Route 431
      (Mt. Rose Highway)

2. DAVIS CREEK PARK—WASHOE COUNTY $
   Open all year
   Camping, Picnicking, Group Facilities, Water, Sewage Dump
   Lower Trailhead for the Ophir Creek Trail (See Trip #4)
   Off State Route 439 (Old U.S. Hwy. 395) south of Reno on the west
      side of Washoe Valley

RESOURCES
With a combined population of a quarter of a million people, the Reno/Sparks and Carson City areas offer everything the outdoor recreationist could possibly need, including a relatively inexpensive array of lodging, dining and entertainment.

OUTDOOR SUPPLIERS
MARK-FORE & STRIKE
SPORTING GOODS
490 Kietzke Lane
Reno, NV 89502
(702) 322-9559

KEVIN'S SKI & SPORTS
RENTALS
1941 N. Carson
Carson City, NV 89701
(702) 882-7779

RENO MOUNTAIN SPORTS
155 E. Moana Lane
Reno, NV 89502
(702) 825-2855

ONE MOUNTAIN SPORTS
4375 S. Carson
Carson City, NV 89701
(702) 882-9360

SIERRA MOUNTAINEER
1901 Silverada Blvd.
Reno, NV 89512
(702) 358-4824

SPORTING RAGE
3827 S. Carson
Carson City, NV 89701
(702) 885-7773

TWIN CITIES SURPLUS
1675 E. 4th St.
Reno, NV 89503
(702) 323-5630

FOREST SERVICE

Carson Ranger District
1536 South Carson Street
Carson City, NV 89701
(702) 882-2766

Toiyabe National Forest
1200 Franklin Way
Sparks, NV 89432
(702) 331-6444

Trip 1 🌲

GRAY LAKE

Trip Type: Dayhike or overnight backpack; Out and back
Distance: 6.6 miles round trip
Season: Early July to early October
Access: Rough dirt road—high-clearance vehicle necessary
Water: None until Gray Lake
Maps: #1
  Martis Peak 1955 (photoinspected 1973), *Mount Rose* 1992,
    7.5 minute quadrangles
  Mt. Rose Wilderness map, Toiyabe National Forest (to be
    released)

Introduction: If you have a high-clearance, durable vehicle and you do not mind using it you can get into the heart of the Mt. Rose Wilderness where few ever tread. Gray Lake lies land-locked 2 miles away from the steady stream of traffic along the Mt. Rose Highway, from which an easy trail could take you the short distance to the lake except that it is blocked to the public, lying on the private land of the Incline Lake resort. The rough drive and longer hike are well worth it, however, rewarding the diligent effort with lovely scenery around a delightful meadow-rimmed lake and grand views of Lake Tahoe from the 2-mile traverse of the high ridge between Mt. Baldy and Rose Knob Peak.

Trailhead: (a) Located almost directly on the California-Nevada border, the Gray Lake trailhead is close to the west edge of the Mt. Rose Wilderness.

In order to get there, however, one must first travel a great distance into California and then 5 miles along a rough dirt road.

Reach California Highway 267 from Interstate 80 in Truckee, or from Lake Tahoe off California Highway 28 in Kings Beach. Travel south from I-80 or north from Hwy. 28 on Hwy. 267 to Martis Peak Road, 0.4 miles north of Brockway Summit (9.1 miles from I-80 and 3.6 from Hwy. 28). Turn east onto Martis Peak Road. Travel through mixed forest of ponderosa pine and white fir up the well-graded, gravel road, continuing straight ahead at a major intersection with a road bearing left (north) at 0.25 mile.

At 1.3 miles turn right (southeast) onto a dirt road just before the main road bends north. Pass over the Tahoe Rim Trail 0.1 mile farther. At 0.7 mile from Martis Peak Road bear left at a "Y" intersection, following the more traveled path. Cross a seasonal creek around a broad sweeping curve and continue straight up the main dirt track, ignoring lesser side roads. Just after an open area, near a seasonal creek surrounded by aspens, the road reaches a "T" intersection at 2.3 miles from Martis Peak Road. Beyond this point the road gets rougher and steeper, making a high-clearance vehicle essential. Bear left and quickly come to another "T" junction, where you turn right (southeast). Stay on this rocky road as it climbs and winds another mile to the last road junction. A little over 0.1 mile from a hairpin turn the actual road to the trailhead turns right onto a primitive dirt track.

Parties without a penchant for extreme off-road travel will be happy to park their vehicles here and avoid the extremely steep and rocky jeep road ahead, preferring to walk the last quarter mile to the trailhead. Park your vehicle off the road in a small clearing 3.5 miles from Martis Peak Road and 4.8 miles from Highway 267.

Description: Hike up the steep road toward the top of a ridge, reaching a broad knoll with good views of Lake Tahoe. The jeep road ends on this knoll and at the far end is a trail marker and the beginning of the actual trail to Gray Lake. The path heads gently up through boulders and widely scattered firs and pines to the edge of a hillside where views of majestic Lake Tahoe's north and west shores widen and improve. The condition of the trail, well graded and well defined, seems somewhat strange in light of the poor condition of the road. The Forest Service maintains both the access road and the trail, but the California road is under the jurisdiction of Tahoe National Forest whereas the Nevada trail falls under Toiyabe National Forest. Traditionally, one agency knows little about what is going on with the other agency even when they share a border. Coupled with the fact that this is a rather obscure trail, do not expect either division to have much information on the road or trail conditions—unless you can talk to a wilderness ranger who has actually been to the area.

Just below the summit of 9,271-foot Mount Baldy you reach the Mt. Rose Wilderness boundary in a patch of scattered pines. From the boundary the trail traverses an open hillside covered with wildflowers in season. Now all of Lake Tahoe comes into view and you can see the upscale community of Incline Village, the ski slopes of Diamond Peak and the Mt. Rose Highway. Unobstructed views continue across the open hillside until a series of three very short switchbacks lead through a rocky section to the actual crest and then down the other side. The gentle uphill traverse resumes as the trail skirts the slopes below Rose Knob. If you desire even more spectacular views, you can easily ascend the 300 feet to the summit of Rose Knob.

Scattered whitebark pines greet you as the trail climbs away from Rose Knob toward a saddle along the top of the ridge. Just before the saddle the trail dips and then climbs to the top, which is a wonderful place to observe one of the many species of raptors that inhabit the area soaring on thermals high above the canyons. Leaving the superb views of Lake Tahoe behind, the trail begins a long descent into the West Fork Gray Creek basin. To the northeast, a mere half-mile away, Gray Lake remains hidden behind the shoulder of Rose Knob Peak. From the saddle the trail contours along the north side of the ridge through gray, rocky talus before descending amid more whitebark pines and occasional hemlocks to the lake, 3.2 miles from the parking area.

Gray Lake is a kidney-bean-shaped, shallow lake surrounded by green meadows. In the natural evolution of lakes and meadows, the shallow lake seems reasonably close to becoming part of Gray Meadow itself. Currently, a healthy stream flows in and out of the lake, although it appears just a matter of time before silt and debris fill the lake basin. By a human timetable, however, there are still many years left to enjoy this delightful little lake. The sparkling, spring-fed water of the inlet stream flows down from above the lake along a rocky channel softened by rich, green moss and brilliant wildflowers. At the head of the canyon the gray, volcanic rock of Rose Knob Peak forms a stark, contrasting background to the vibrant meadows rich with life. Through the years, avalanches have swept down the slopes of Rose Knob Peak, delivering a lot of timber along the slopes at the base of the peak.

Gray Lake seems devoid of any established campgrounds, probably due mainly to lack of use. Plenty of areas would be suitable for a camp if one wanted to spend the night, and firewood is plentiful. Swimming in the shallow lake seems to be less than desirable, but one may find the fishing to be good. The area is open to further exploration from an obscure trail junction in the trees above the northeast end of the lake. You can head northwest down Gray Creek or in the opposite direction one-half mile to aptly named Mud Lake. From the pass above Gray Lake one can easily ascend steep slopes to the top of Rose Knob Peak.

Retrace your steps to the trailhead.

Trip 2 ♤
HUNTER CREEK

Trip Type: Dayhike; Out and back
Distance: 7.0 miles round trip
Season: Late April to mid-November
Access: Dirt road
Water: Available in creek
Maps: #2
       Mt. Rose NW 1968 (photorevised 1982) 7.5 minute quadrangle
       Mt. Rose Wilderness map, Toiyabe National Forest (to be
       released)

Introduction: A short hike on the edge of Reno, relatively undiscovered, leads to some real surprises including a waterfall, lush green meadows and a forest grotto more reminiscent of a coastal hike than a foray into the eastern Sierra. If the handiwork of beavers interests you, the canyon is a veritable museum of their activity.

Shotgun shells and trash litter the trailhead. The first couple of miles are hot and dry, and rumors of rattlesnakes there abound. These factors combine to deter most of the city dwellers from discovering the wonderful treasures hidden above in Hunter Creek canyon. Ironically, one must drive right through one of Reno's poshest suburbs to the literal edge of town in order to reach the trailhead leading into federally designated wilderness. Currently, the access passes through the private land of an as yet undeveloped extension of the Caughlin Ranch subdivision. Once construction is completed, access will be cut off, and so far the Forest Service has no plans to alleviate the problem. A similar problem already exists regarding access for joggers and hikers to the nearby Steamboat Ditch Trail. Losing access to this trail due to apathy of government officials and lack of concern from citizenry would be a shame.

The Hunter Creek Trail is open six months out of the year, thanks to a high point below 6500 feet, providing a rare early-season opportunity to shake off the cobwebs and stretch out the legs. Spring is the best time to view the falls and enjoy the tumbling creek. Hardly the best example of trail building in the Mt. Rose Wilderness, the Hunter Creek Trail is rough, indistinct for stretches, poorly graded, rocky in parts and eroded in others. In spite of the condition of the path the trip is well worth the effort, rewarding the diligent hiker with some unexpected delights.

The efforts of an arsonist and the carelessness of teenagers have come very close to ruining the Hunter Creek area. In 1995 a campfire got out of hand, burning a small area upstream. The following year, an arsonist touched off the Belli Ranch fire. Set near Verdi, the fire quickly raged out of control consuming acres of sagebrush and light timber on a sprint toward the suburban developments of Belli and Caughlin ranches. Acres of undeveloped land were ravaged, including the area below the entrance to Hunter Creek canyon. The first mile or so of the hike now follows the old road through burned terrain. Fortunately, the fire never traveled very far up the canyon.

Trailhead: (b) Located just beyond the edge of the Caughlin Ranch subdivision, the Hunter Creek trailhead is west of Reno and south of the Truckee River. From Reno head west on Interstate 80 and take Exit #10 signed: *McCarran Boulevard West.* Head south on McCarran Blvd. across W. Fourth Street, the Truckee River and Mayberry Drive to the intersection with Caughlin Parkway and W. Plumb Lane, 1.7 miles from the freeway. Turn right (west) onto Caughlin Parkway and enter the exclusive Caughlin Ranch subdivision. Proceed 1.2 miles to a right turn at Plateau Road. Travel on Plateau Road for another 0.6 mile to Woodchuck, where you turn left. Follow Woodchuck for 75 yards until the pavement ends. Continue on a deeply rutted dirt road that climbs south up a small hill and then winds around for a half mile to a narrow turnaround, 2.4 miles from the McCarran Blvd. and Caughlin Parkway intersection The dirt road is rough in spots but should be negotiable by most sedans (as long as you stay out of the ruts). Forward progress for your auto ends at the turnaround, where there is room for about 8 cars.

Description: Begin hiking on the continuation of the rocky old road. Where the road bends south just before a diversion ditch, you have the option of proceeding south along the road and jumping the ditch or heading to the right along a faint jeep track that crosses the ditch on a bridge farther

Along the Hunter Creek Trail

downstream. The amount of water in the ditch, if any, will determine which option you select, coupled with your long-jumping ability. Beyond the ditch, proceed south along the road on the west bank toward the Forest Service trailhead through open sagebrush terrain. As you proceed, the main channel of Hunter Creek comes into view and eventually the old road crosses the creek. This crossing might be difficult. There has been an old plank one hundred feet upstream that spans the creek, but it is certainly less than a permanent structure.

A well-maintained gravel road, used to service the upstream diversion structure for the ditch, runs along the west bank of Hunter Creek. You eventually reach this diversion structure just before the road narrows to a single-track trail at the Forest Service trailhead.

The actual trail begins as a moderate climb through dry hillsides covered with sagebrush and cheat grass above the creek. The trail steepens to negotiate a rock projection and then dips and climbs, making steady upward progress through the narrow, steep, brush-filled canyon. Cottonwood, aspens, willow and elderberry are just some of the species that choke the banks of the creek. Farther up the trail, scattered ponderosa pine and jagged rock ridges add a little more character to the otherwise barren and dry terrain.

The floor of the canyon widens momentarily, allowing the trail to come alongside the stream for a stretch, but soon the trail once again climbs away from the creek

A side canyon, with two rock sentinels guarding its mouth, comes into view along the undulating trail. The canyon momentarily widens where this side canyon intersects the main channel of Hunter Creek. Just past the side canyon a short use trail leads down to a small campsite a little too close to the stream for guilt-free camping. One third mile beyond the side canyon, Hunter Creek makes a long, sweeping curve where newer trail begins a gradual climb, surmounting a rock rib jutting into the canyon. At the top of the climb a small grove of pines offers the first and only shade so far. Continuing, some mahogany trees appear in the narrow, brush-filled canyon.

As the trail nears the creek it enters a wooded grove filled with firs, pines, aspens, grasses and wildflowers. Suddenly you feel as though you had been transported to the northern California coast amid lush, water-loving plants and tall trees. The dense forest cover provides deep shade, allowing for a dramatic change in vegetation. The trail can be hard to follow in this section as the indistinct path crosses three little gurgling rivulets of clear, cool water. As you continue, the trail proceeds on a bed of pine needles and cedars make an appearance. For a brief time you experience the sensation of walking through an enchanted forest—at least within the context of Nevada. All too soon, you cross another little tributary and head up a hillside above the main branch of the creek, leaving this delightful glade behind.

Heading upstream, the trail passes an old beaver dam near a meadow where it disappears in the tall grass. Across the meadow and away from the creek the trail resumes before quickly reaching the crossing of the main channel of Hunter Creek. On the opposite side is a primitive campsite with crudely constructed lean-tos and fire pits. Just behind the campsite is another unusual feature, an actual, bona-fide waterfall. Depending on the runoff, this waterfall can be quite impressive.

Find the continuation of the trail at the south end of the camp area, where it climbs very steeply, but briefly, to surmount the falls, soon reaching a broad meadow where the creek sinuously courses through the lush grassland.

One potential disadvantage of a wilderness area so close to civilization is its accessibility to the inexperienced and the careless. In the summer of 1996 some young campers allowed a fire to get out of control, burning this area adjacent to the creek across from the meadow. Perhaps one day nature will make this location a decent place to camp—already grasses and wild-flowers have made a recovery. Scorched ponderosa pines aside, this fire may have been a good thing in a way, as this site used to hold a disgust-ingly crude log cabin as well as an assemblage of garbage left behind by sloppy campers. All that remains are the unburned tin cans.

The trail disappears for good beyond the old campsite, although one could travel a little farther upstream to check out the possibility of more beaver activity along the edge of the meadows. At the far end of the mead-ows the canyon narrows and steepens discouraging most people from con-tinuing up the gorge. Retrace your steps to the trailhead.

Trip 3 🌲
JONES CREEK–WHITES CREEK LOOP

Trip Type: Dayhike; Loop trip
Distance: 9.6 miles round trip
Season: Mid-May to mid-November
Access: Improved gravel road
Water: Available at trailhead & Jones & Whites creeks
Maps: #3
Washoe City 1994, *Mount Rose* 1992, *Mount Rose NE* 1994 & *Mt. Rose NW* 1968 (photorevised 1982) 7.5 minute quadrangles
Mount Rose Wilderness map, Toiyabe National Forest (to be released)

Introduction: A 9½ mile loop leads from low forest up to high, open terrain with grand views of the east flank of the Sierra Nevada, particularly Mt. Rose and Slide Mountain. Along the trail there are good views to the east of Washoe Valley, the Virginia Range and the South Truckee Meadows also. Along the way you can sample the surroundings of two tumbling creeks,

Jones and Whites. An abundance of quaking aspens along the creek creates a lovely display of fall color. A ½ mile side trip takes you to Church's Pond, a diminutive pool at the high point of the trip with a grand view of Mt. Rose. In spite of its proximity to Reno and a beginning in a popular county park, the Jones Creek–Whites Creek Loop sees little use. It is also open sooner than most trails in the region.

Trailhead: (c) The trailhead is southwest of Reno in Galena Creek County Park. Take U.S. 395 to the Mt. Rose Highway, State Route 431. On it go west 7 miles to the north entrance into Galena Creek Park. Past a wooden gate the gravel road wanders underneath pines and through a picnic area following road markers with arrows labeled *Trailhead*. Loop around to the parking lot 0.5 mile from the Mt. Rose Highway. Ample parking is available, and a section for horse trailers is nearby. Restrooms and water are also nearby.

Description: The route starts on a well-graded gravel road and quickly comes to a sign marked: *Jones Creek Trail* (right), *Bitterbrush Trail to Galena Creek* (straight) and *Campfire Meadow* (left). Go right, passing Campfire Meadow on the left. You hike through manzanita, sagebrush and ponderosa pine a short distance farther, to where the gravel road gives way to a jeep road bending to the right. Approximately 100 yards from the bend follow an arrowed sign with hiker and horsepacker symbols onto a narrower jeep road. As you make the turn, another sign appears, marked: *Jones Creek–Whites Creek Loop Trail.* Continuing on the narrower jeep road, you pass through an area of wildflowers and reach the boundary between the park and Forest Service land.

Beyond the boundary you begin to hear the rushing water of Jones Creek. Cross the creek on a log and you will soon reach the loop trail junction, designated by a signed 4 by 4 post, three-quarters mile from the trailhead. The trail to the right heads over a ridge to Whites Creek, and the trail straight ahead, marked *Churches Pond*, climbs up the Jones Creek drainage. Follow the latter trail as it parallels the creek for a short distance and then bends away, heading steeply up the canyon. You quickly come to the Mt. Rose Wilderness boundary, one mile from the trailhead.

The surrounding vegetation is dominated by manzanita, scattered ponderosa pine and wildflowers, including blue lupine and Indian paintbrush. The many quaking aspens that grow along the creek banks make for an excellent display of autumn color. Farther up the canyon you can see many dead ponderosa pines that succumbed to the stress of nearly a decade of drought during the late Eighties and early Nineties. As you climb steeply, views of the upper canyon open up and you get a glimpse of the ridge high above that you will eventually ascend on the Jones Creek Trail. Heading up the canyon, the trail makes a series of long, steep switchbacks that lead out of the Jones Creek drainage to the top of a ridge separating Jones Creek and Whites Creek. As you climb, views improve of the

Virginia Range over Little Washoe Lake to the east and Slide Mountain and Mt. Rose to the south.

Seven steep switchbacks finally bring you to the top of the ridge, with unobstructed views. At 2.7 miles from the parking lot, you reach a trail junction marked by another 4 by 4 post. The continuation of the loop trail over to Whites Creek heads north, while up the trail straight ahead lies Church's Pond. The half-mile trip to the pond is well worth the effort. To get there keep climbing along the ridge for 0.4 mile and then drop into the basin for another 0.1 mile to the pond. The pond is a shallow pool of water with no inlet or outlet flanked by gently sloping, sagebrush-covered slopes that sweep up nearly 2,500 feet toward the gray volcanic-rock summit of Mt. Rose. An assortment of scattered pines and aspens grow along the far shore. Church's Pond is an excellent spot for lunch or simply to enjoy the view.

Descending from the trail junction, you will soon notice a change in the vegetation from the southern exposure of Jones Creek to the northern exposure of Whites Creek. Aspens and grass-covered slopes interspersed with wildflowers near the top and white fir farther down the slope contrast with the drier terrain in the previous canyon. The trail winds down toward the bottom of the upper canyon and reaches the first crossing of Whites Creek, a mile from the trail to Church's Pond. Then the trail climbs up and away from the creek for a short distance, levels off and descends farther up the canyon above the north bank of the main channel. It follows Whites Creek on a fairly level grade for a quarter mile before reaching the next crossing, a half mile from the previous crossing and 4.2 miles from the trailhead. The creek crossing may difficult during peak runoff.

Drier vegetation on the south-facing hillside, composed of tall grass, ceanothus sagebrush and ponderosa pine, greets you along the sandy trail as it descends, with the graceful flow of the creek as your constant companion. Farther down the creek along the gentle descent, white fir, aspen and smaller, water-loving plants grow along the wet banks of the creek on the downhill side of the trail while the drier vegetation continues on the uphill side. This descent on the north side of the stream lasts for a mile and a half before coming to the last crossing of Whites Creek. During high water, this will be the most difficult of your crossings.

Across the creek the trail merges into an old road that comes up the canyon from Timberline Road off the Mt. Rose Highway. A short distance from the crossing is the signed Wilderness boundary, and 50 feet farther is a sign simply marked: *Trail.* The road descends along the south bank of the creek for another mile under light forest cover, passing a few lightly used campsites, to a junction near a large campsite marked by a small *Trail* sign, 6.8 miles from the trailhead.

From here a single-track trail climbs away from the old road on a barren hillside beneath a dense stand of mature ponderosa pines to a saddle where the pines thin and sagebrush, grasses and flowers are predominant. Once again Mt. Rose, Slide Mountain and parts of Washoe Valley pop into view. From the saddle the trail makes an angling, sidehill traverse down into the next canyon through open sagebrush. At the bottom of the drainage ponderosa pines reappear, some with scorched trunks from a recent brush fire. Climb out of this canyon and wander along the top of a minor ridge for a while before beginning the long, mild descent along the slopes above Jones Creek. After the descent a one-eighth mile climb leads to the junction with the trail up Jones Creek, 8.9 miles from your start. Turn left (east) and retrace your steps three-quarters mile to the trailhead.

Trip 4 ♣
THOMAS CREEK

Trip Type: Dayhike or overnight backpack; Out and back
Distance: 6.4 miles round trip
Season: Mid-June through October
Access: Rough dirt road
Water: Available in creek
Maps: #3
Mt. Rose NW 7.5 minute quadrangle, 1968 (photorevised 1982)
Mt. Rose Wilderness map, Toiyabe National Forest (to be released)

Introduction: A lonely and delightful canyon, minutes away from Reno, beckons the hiker to come and explore its pleasures. The trail follows a roaring stream up a broad canyon, ablaze with color in the fall, to a large verdant meadow encircled by dense stands of pines. Springtime brings a plethora of corn lilies and other wildflowers. A dramatic rock formation jutting out of the head of the canyon enhances the scenery. While hundreds of hikers may be struggling to reach the summit of nearby Mt. Rose, you may be alone or one of only a few on the Thomas Creek trail.

Trailhead: (d) Just getting to the trailhead may be the most difficult part of this trip. Take U.S. 395 to the Mt. Rose Highway, State Route 431. Go west on S.R. 431 to paved Timberline Road (2.6 miles from U.S. 395 or 1.9 miles from the U.S. 395 South offramp onto S.R. 431). Turn right (north) onto Timberline Road and head up for 0.2 mile to where the road becomes a dirt track. Continue on Timberline Road, crossing Whites Creek on a narrow wood bridge at 0.6 mile and Thomas Creek on another narrow wood bridge at 1.1 miles from the Mt. Rose Highway. Immediately after the second crossing, the road comes to a "Y", where you turn left, heading uphill on Forest Road 049, also known as the Thomas Creek Road.

As Forest Road 049 climbs up along the north bank of Thomas Creek, you will pass many turnoffs to primitive campsites scattered by the tumbling stream and nestled under aspens and pines. The road becomes rougher as it progresses up the creek, but most passenger cars should be able to carefully negotiate the lower part of the Thomas Creek Road to Thomas Meadows. Around 2 miles from the "Y" the road leaves the creek to steeply ascend a grassy hillside sparsely covered with mahogany and pines and, at 2.3 miles, it converges with two private roads at the crest of a hill. From the top of the rise the road makes a rough descent and quickly comes to a double ford of Thomas Creek. In the spring, depending on the stream and your vehicle, you may or may not want to make this crossing. The creek was a raging torrent after the winter snows and spring rains of 1995.

From the ford the road doubles back before resuming the upstream climb, reaching the upper end of Thomas Meadows and a road junction at 3.1 miles from the "Y". Without a high-clearance vehicle, most parties should be content to leave their cars at the meadows and hike the last three-quarters mile to the trailhead. In dry conditions the road straight ahead will be the best alternative. However, during wet conditions a large, spring-fed pond inundates this entire road bed for quite a distance and may appear quite capable of swallowing your vehicle. If so, you can avoid the pond by turning right into the meadows and bending around to the edge of the creek, following a narrow track 0.4 mile back to the main route above the pond. The obvious danger of this choice is the potential of becoming stuck in the boggy meadows.

If you can negotiate your way past the obstacles, Road 049 continues paralleling the creek and reaches the trailhead 3.8 miles from the "Y". Signs read: *Mt. Rose Wilderness, Thomas Creek Trail.* Parking is available for a handful of cars.

Upper Thomas Creek Canyon

Description: The trail begins by following the continuation of the old road, quickly crossing Thomas Creek, which should be an easy boulder-hop in normal conditions. A mixed forest of white pine, ponderosa pine and quaking aspen greets you as the path follows the creek. Sagebrush-covered hillsides rise away from the lushly vegetated creek to the ridges above. Continuing, your surroundings alternate between open areas permitting views toward the head of Thomas Creek Canyon and dense groves of aspen. Autumn colors, if captured at their peak here, are quite dramatic.

The road crosses two channels of the creek and then becomes a single-track trail that follows a broad curve through some tall grass where a sign with an arrow points to the creek. A new trail, constructed after the 1982 revision of the *Mt. Rose NW* quadrangle, bends north across Thomas Creek and begins to ascend the manzanita-covered hillside. About a mile from the trailhead a series of long ascending switchbacks leads to the top of the ridge through dry, open vegetation of sagebrush, rabbitbrush, mahogany and occasional ponderosa pine. From the top of this ridge, the trail makes a grand traverse that curves all the way around the head of the Thomas Creek basin. At the culmination of the traverse is a very large, green, sloping meadow surrounded by dense forest behind an angular rock outcropping dominating the upper canyon. Looking south over the wide valley below, you can see the meadow directly across from your position, one mile away. Mt. Rose, third highest point in the Tahoe Basin, is visible in the background, its dark gray slopes peering over the greener hillsides that form the rim of the Thomas Creek basin.

Beginning the ascending traverse, open terrain gives way to pine forest. After a considerable distance, the trail comes to an unsigned, inconspicuous "Y" junction with a trail that steeply switchbacks to the top of the Carson Range. From there it descends to the Mt. Rose Trail in Davis Meadows (if you choose to hike to Davis Meadows be aware that the track from the summit down to the Mt. Rose Trail has disappeared). Excellent views of Thomas Canyon occur from near the top of the ridge. From the junction continue south, back on the older section of trail shown on the topo, into a small, wildflower-laden meadow fed by springs. Proceed down the trail another quarter mile through aspens and pines to the beginning of the large meadow you saw across the canyon a mile back down the trail. Step across a narrow creek and head over to a stand of pines, where you will find some primitive campsites.

The upper meadows, a sea of green broken only by thousands of yellow corn lilies, await your exploration. Signs of any trail quickly disappear, but the area is open and easily negotiated. With the possible exception of deer hunters in the fall, few people tend to camp in these meadows in spite of their closeness to Reno. Find water back at the stream, and firewood is plentiful. The meadows provide a fine location to enjoy the sweeping views down Thomas Creek canyon. Making a loop back down the old jeep road as shown on the topo is possible, but the route is hard to locate in the meadows and is quite steep. The new trail provides an easier way up the arduous slopes at the head of the canyon. Retrace your steps back to the trailhead.

Trip 5 🌲

MT. ROSE & BRONCO CREEK
VIA MT. ROSE TRAIL

Trip Type: Dayhike to Mt. Rose; Out and back. Dayhike or overnight backpack to Bronco Creek; Out and back
Distance: 11.2 miles round trip to Mt. Rose; 11.8 miles round trip to Bronco Creek
Season: Early July to mid-October
Access: Paved highway
Water: Available in Galena and Bronco creeks
Map: #4
    Mount Rose 7.5 minute quadrangle, 1992
    Mount Rose Wilderness map, Toiyabe National Forest (to be released)

Introduction: The trail to the summit of Mt. Rose may be the most popular trail in the state of Nevada. If not, it certainly ranks near the top of the list. On a summer weekend near the trailhead you may see a string of cars lining the shoulder of the Mt. Rose Highway and a corresponding string of hikers spread out along the trail. The attractions are many, including spectacular views of Lake Tahoe from the summit, a delightful display of wildflowers in the Galena Creek drainage, and the chance to scale the third-highest peak in the Tahoe Basin.

The trail to Bronco Creek is the antithesis of the summit route. If hundreds travel up the trail to Mt. Rose on a summer weekend, you may have to wait a decade or more to see that many people on the Bronco Creek Trail. Rather than excellent views from the summit, this trail offers an excellent view of the summit from 2,000 feet below. While one can camp at spots along the trail to Mt. Rose, it remains essentially a day hike, whereas Bronco Creek lures the backpacker to stay overnight and explore the surrounding terrain.

Alpine heights or meadow lowlands, this one trip with two distinct destinations has something to offer everyone.

Trailhead: (e) Take U.S. 395 to the Mt. Rose Highway, State Route 431. Travel west on 431 to the Mt. Rose Summit, elevation 8911 feet. Descend 0.3 mile to the trailhead beside the westbound shoulder of the highway below a concrete-block telephone building. Park on the shoulder as conditions permit. Busy summer weekends may see a great number of vehicles strung out along the road for quite a distance.

Description: Pass around the closed access gate and begin hiking along the sandy road that leads to the microwave station on top of Relay Ridge. Two hundred feet past the gate the road approaches a trail register and a wilderness trailhead sign, which is something of a misnomer since the wilderness boundary is 4 miles away. Although wilderness permits are not required in Nevada, voluntary registration at the Mt. Rose trailhead allows the Forest Service to monitor use patterns on this very busy trail. Mountain bikes are permitted along the road/trail outside of the wilderness, so be on the alert for bikers speeding down the road.

As the well-graded road climbs along the hillside, scattered stands of lodgepole pine alternately block and allow increasingly spectacular views to the southwest of Lake Tahoe and the peaks of the Desolation Wilderness above the opposite shore. Below is the verdant green of Tahoe Meadows through which courses Ophir Creek down its canyon to the east and out to Washoe Lake at the base of the Virginia Range. As you continue up the road, Incline Lake, privately owned and off limits to the public, comes into view just west of the Mt. Rose Highway. The road eventually bends around to the northwest, leaving the views behind and ascending through deeper forest cover. Views ahead reveal the microwave station at the end of this service road, perched high above on Relay Ridge.

Continue to hike along the road until you reach a small pond near the head of Third Creek, beyond which the road reaches a junction with the Mt. Rose Trail on the right, 2.5 miles from the trailhead. Signs lead you to a low saddle from which a twin-tracked trail descends into meadows at the upper end of Galena Creek canyon. Cross a small tributary of Galena Creek near the far edge of the meadows where some campsites appear beneath lodgepole pines. The trail heads downhill, steeply at times, along an old jeep road that parallels a line of telephone poles servicing the microwave station. Curve around and cross another tributary of Galena Creek, at 3.2 miles from the trailhead, where the descent into the drainage ends and an uninterrupted climb to the summit begins.

Some years ago the Galena Creek area downstream from the trail was in jeopardy of being lost to the development of a destination resort. Plans for the Galena resort would have replaced the beautiful meadows and stately lodgepole pines with condominiums, golf courses, ski area and casino. Thankfully, a land exchange, worked out between the government and developers, kept this area in a pristine state.

At the peak of the season, a brilliant display of wildflowers mixes with a lush assemblage of shrubs. Varieties of flowers include lupine, paintbrush, angelica, larkspur and mule ears. Leaving the luxuriant vegetation behind, the trail makes a moderate ascent of a dry hillside until turning into a narrow, steep canyon. Climb the narrow cleft, twice crossing a seasonal creek, to the wilderness boundary 150 yards below a saddle southwest of Mt. Rose. A short climb leads up to the saddle and a trail junction amid some weather-beaten whitebark pines, 4.3 miles from the trailhead. A sign indicates: *Mt. Rose Summit* to the right (east) and *Big Meadows* straight ahead (northwest) toward Bronco Creek.

Route to Mt. Rose Summit: Although still ascending, the grade of the trail eases from the steep climb up the narrow canyon. Head slightly below a narrow ridge through scattered whitebark pines toward the gray volcanic mass of Mt. Rose. At the end of the ridge the trail steepens and begins the first of five switchbacks up the west slopes of the peak, views improving with each step. From the switchbacks, the trail makes an ascending traverse around to the northwest side of the mountain, where the stunted pines disappear and the only signs of vegetation are low-growing alpine plants. Another series of switchbacks climbs up the rocky slopes, the actual summit just out of view. As you approach what seems to be the top, one more set of three short switchbacks brings you to the summit ridge, from where it is just a short jaunt over to the top.

Below a steel pole with a sign reading: *Mt. Rose, Elevation 10,776* is a climbers' register supplied by a local snowmobiling club. Various manmade improvements at the summit consist of rock walls piled high to restrain the notorious winds that frequent the area. If you happen to arrive under calm conditions, count your blessings. Views are quite impressive in all directions. On extremely clear days you can see north all the way to the Cascade volcanoes of Lassen Peak and Mt. Shasta. On normal days the Sierra Buttes are visible in that same general direction above and beyond Prosser, Boca and Stampede reservoirs, located along the Little Truckee River north of Interstate 80. Lake Tahoe is the preeminent gem, surrounded by peaks including Pyramid Peak and Mt. Tallac in the Desolation Wilderness and Jobs Peak, Jobs Sister and Freel Peak in the Carson Range. Reno/Sparks and the Truckee Meadows are clearly visible from the summit as well.

Retrace your steps to the trailhead.

Route to Bronco Creek: From the junction in the saddle with the trail to Mt. Rose, at 4.3 miles, descend through widely scattered whitebark pines to a small meadow where the grade temporarily abates. The path grows indistinct for 100 feet at the end of the meadow before reappearing just before the descent resumes. You quickly realize the contrast between the use this trail receives compared to the more frequented Mt. Rose Trail. Signs of use are so scarce you begin to wonder if anyone ever hikes this trail. As the descent continues, the drop in elevation corresponds to an increase in the distribution of pines. Wind your way down the trail, eventually overlooking the broad, sloping meadow of the upper Bronco Creek drainage. The roar of the creek becomes louder as you descend. In shaded forest cover, the trail bends and quickly reaches an inconspicuous, unmarked trail junction 1.25 miles from the saddle. The trail to the right heads down to Bronco

Creek, crosses it and goes north out of the Wilderness along a jeep road to Davis and Big meadows. Continue heading down the trail another quarter mile to where the tread begins to disappear near Bronco Creek. At the edge of the trees are a couple of campsites close to the creek.

Bronco Creek offers solitude in the midst of a tremendous amount of activity. Less than 10 miles away gamblers are cavorting in North Shore casinos, not to mention the numerous hikers much closer, struggling along the trail to the summit of Mt. Rose. Here in the meadows, however, you have the run of the basin. The rock faces of Church Peak and Mt. Rose form a dramatic backdrop for the green meadows of Bronco Creek. Opportunities for further exploration abound, although trails shown on maps may not appear in their entirety on the ground. Campsites are primitive. There is plenty of firewood.

Retrace your steps to the trailhead.

Trip 6 ♣
OPHIR CREEK TRAIL

Trip Type: Dayhike or overnight backpack; Shuttle
Distance: 7.9 miles one way
Season: Early June to mid-October
Access: Paved road
Water: Available in creeks & lakes
Maps: #4, 5
       Washoe City 1994 & *Mount Rose* 1992 7.5 minute quadrangles
       Mt. Rose Wilderness map, Toiyabe National Forest (to be
        released)

Introduction: The only drawback to the Ophir Creek Trail is that it lies outside of the Mt. Rose Wilderness. Mountain bikes have access to the trail. However, their presence is highly unlikely on the lower half, at Rock and Upper Price lakes and in the upper parts of Tahoe Meadows. Although Ophir Creek does not enjoy wilderness protection, this trip has an abundance of positive attributes including two small but scenic lakes, a beautiful 2-mile-long meadow at 8660 feet, Ophir Creek—which tumbles down a steep canyon but glides serenely through Tahoe Meadows—and a chance to witness first-hand the results of a major geologic catastrophe.

Mark Twain, accurate observer that he was, described the east flank of the Sierra in *Roughing It,* his chronicle of life in the Far West: "The mountains are very high and steep about Carson, Eagle and Washoe Valleys— very high and very steep, and so when the snow gets to melting off fast in the spring and the warm surface earth begins to moisten and soften, the disastrous landslides commence. The reader cannot know what a landslide is unless he has lived in that country and seen the whole side of a mountain taken off some fine morning and deposited down in the valley, leaving a vast, treeless, unsightly scar upon the mountain's front to keep the circumstance fresh in his memory all the years that he may go on living within seventy miles of that place."

History repeated itself most recently in the Spring of 1983 when an entire flank of appropriately named Slide Mountain, saturated with melt water from the thawing winter snows, broke loose and plunged into Ophir Creek canyon, displacing the waters of Lower Price Lake. The massive amount of snow-soaked debris coupled with the water from the lake created a semi-liquid mass that roared down the steep Ophir Creek canyon, ripping out everything in its path and reaching Washoe Valley below in a matter of seconds. One death occurred, homes were destroyed and acres and acres of debris spread across the valley. Tons of material blocked both lanes of traffic, closing U.S. 395, the main arterial between Reno and Carson City. As a result of the slide, Lower Price Lake vanished and Upper Price Lake shrank. At several spots along the trail you can see the effects of this disaster, even though nature has done a lot of healing since 1983.

The trail, mostly on Forest Service land, begins in Davis Creek Park, administered by Washoe County. Make sure you note the closing to avoid being locked inside the park with no way to drive out until morning.

Trailhead: Bottom End: (f) From U.S. 395 (approximately 15 miles south of Reno and 10 miles north of Carson City) turn west following a sign stating: *Davis Creek Park, Bowers Mansion, ¼ mile.* Head west and then south on State Route 429, also known as Old Highway 395, 0.4 mile to the signed turnoff into Davis Creek Park. Travel into the park on paved road for 0.1 mile to a sign: *Ophir Creek Trailhead,* and turn left into the graveled parking area at the trailhead. Space is available for many cars and horse trailers.

Top End: (g) The upper trailhead at the west edge of Tahoe Meadows is 1.5 miles east of the Mt. Rose Highway summit. Take U.S. 395 to the Mt. Rose Highway, State Route 431. Head west for approximately 17 miles, over the summit to the far edge of Tahoe Meadows on the south side of the highway. A small turnout has room for only a few cars, but you can park along the shoulder of the road if those spaces are full. If coming from Lake Tahoe, the trailhead is approximately 7 miles east of the junction of State Routes 431 and 28 in Incline Village. A small wooden sign, difficult to see from the highway, reads: *Ophir Creek Trail.*

The Ophir Creek trailhead is not three-quarters mile to the east at the Tahoe Meadows trailhead, as reported elsewhere. At that location you will find restrooms, an equestrian staging area, paved parking and the Tahoe Meadows nature trail. When constructed, the Tahoe Rim Trail, beginning at the Tahoe Meadows trailhead, should provide a connection to the Ophir Creek trail, but at this time there is none.

Description: From the trailhead in Davis Creek Park, begin hiking along a split-rail fence heading west toward the heart of the park, soon coming to a large equestrian area with a faucet and horse trough, picnic tables and a barbecue pit. Proceed through widely scattered ponderosa pines, mahogany and sagebrush, following trail markers across another trail and a paved road to diminutive Davis Creek, which you cross on a small wooden bridge. Now climb away from the creek to the crest of a rise under ponderosa-pine cover. Through the trees to the east you can glimpse Davis Lake. A somewhat confusing set of signs leaves you wondering which direction to head but ignore the signs and continue straight ahead. Soon the trail bends west above a dry drainage, leaving the park behind and entering National Forest land.

The trail turns south, crossing the dry creek, and begins an ascending traverse of some hillsides. Breaking out of the pines, you have good views of Washoe Valley and Washoe Lake. Careful observation will reveal an area of light-colored debris deposited in the valley from the 1983 slide. Time has done a pretty good job of covering most of the mess, but this patch remains as a reminder of the powerful force that nature can exhibit. Bending and winding, the trail turns more westerly and climbs steeply on the northern bank of Ophir Creek to the top of the precipitous canyon, one and a half miles from the trailhead.

You can hear the roar of the churning creek well before seeing it, but once the watercourse comes into sight the deep, massively eroded, narrow, 'V'-shaped channel is impressive. On the far bank is evidence of the enormous amount of material that must have exploded down the canyon—the entire hillside is sliced away, large boulders litter the bottom and uprooted

Tahoe Meadows

trees are scattered here and there. Astute observers will soon see that the near bank, the one you are standing directly above, appears severely damaged in a similar fashion. The trail continues to climb, slightly away from the edge and just below the top of the canyon, reaching a junction 2 miles from the trailhead, right before a broad area of boulders.

Follow the trail to the right, marked by a sign reading: *Rock Lake*. Eventually, the trail disappears in a wide creek channel where tons of boulders, formerly a part of Slide Mountain, cover the drainage from one side to the other. The route across this channel can be hard to follow, as well as difficult in high water, but head for the trail that continues on the far bank, angling steeply back up the hillside and crossing the multi-channeled creek as necessary on the way. From the creek you can get a good look at Slide Mountain, the source of all this debris

Now the trail climbs away from the creek to the top of a rise and bends sharply west where white fir begins to appear amid the ponderosa pines. Make a very brief descent to a flat, which appears to be the site of an old cabin. From the flat the trail climbs more steeply through dense forest and then even more steeply up a boulder-covered hillside to the crest of a hill, where the trail mercifully levels off. Rock Lake lies just a short distance beyond, 2.8 miles from the trailhead.

Most appropriately named, Rock Lake sits in a talus-filled basin, the rocky terrain interrupted only by a grassy field along the northwest shore, where a lone campsite sits beneath tall trees. An abundance of lilypads covers the surface of the lonely lake while ponderosa pines and white firs ring the shoreline. The shallow lake depends on winter snows and perhaps a spring for its water. The lake level diminishes as summer progresses into fall, and as the park brochure warns, "don't expect the fishing to be good."

The standard route of the Ophir Creek Trail would suggest that you need to retrace your steps back to the junction and from there follow the trail to Upper Price Lake. Not only is this unnecessary, it's not the best route. You can avoid the backtracking, some extra miles and a needless loss of elevation from a descent around a ridge by hiking from Rock Lake directly southeast to the main trail. The only minor obstacle is getting around the lake to the opposite shore, easily accomplished by scrambling over some rocks at the north end of the lake. Head over to the grassy field containing the campsite and find a fairly distinct trail in the trees above as it heads on a level track southeast through the forest. About 75 yards from the lake the trail bends east, continuing on a level track through brush before climbing the hillside at the east edge of the basin. Climb amid manzanita until the trail levels out, following an old road under ponderosa pines, and then descend briefly to a trail junction at 3.5 miles from the parking area. A sign declares: *Price Lake 1.5*.

Turn uphill from the junction and climb steeply for a half mile to the crest of a broad, sandy ridge (elev. 7050 on the topo) supporting some interesting looking rock formations. You reach a well-signed junction with a dirt road used to maintain the diversion structures at Upper Price Lake.

Follow this well-used road briefly uphill and then as it traverses across the steep hillside above Rock Lake. Views of Washoe Valley, Washoe Lake and Rock Lake are quite good from the road.

At 4.9 miles from the trailhead, the road leads to a junction with a trail heading up the canyon well above Ophir Creek. A sign at the junction pointing up the trail reads: *Ophir Creek Trail No. 2007, Tahoe Meadows 2.* If Tahoe Meadows is your only goal, take the trail, but if you want to see Upper Price Lake, follow the road as it continues down toward the creek and what used to be Lower Price Lake. Just prior to reaching Ophir Creek, a nearly overgrown use trail leads to Upper Price Lake and then steeply back up to the main trail.

Side Trip to Upper Price Lake: The most difficult part of this route will be finding the trail, which is not a real trail by any stretch of the imagination. From the junction with the main trail to Tahoe Meadows continue along the road toward the creek. As you descend, watch for a faint road heading northwest approximately 50 feet north of the diversion ditch coming from Upper Price Lake. Follow this short road, and where it ends pick up the faint path that continues along the north bank of the diversion ditch. Dense vegetation has nearly overgrown parts of this path, and you may wish you had brought along some pruning shears or a machete to combat the brush. Eventually you will reach the lake—the overgrown path lasts only a little over a tenth of a mile.

Upper Price Lake is just a remnant of its former self but is still with us, unlike its neighbor Lower Price Lake, completely displaced by debris from Slide Mountain. The lower lake still appears on the USGS quadrangle in spite of the fact that the map has a publication date of 1994 and the slide occurred in 1983. One wonders about the accuracy of these new maps, especially since parts of the trail built before 1994 don't appear on the map either. Judging from the beauty of Upper Price Lake, not being able to enjoy the twin as well seems a shame. Steep slopes plunge into the icy blue waters of the lake, not as deep after the slide. The upper canyon forms a near perfect backdrop to the serene lake. If you want to camp at Upper Price Lake, you will have to carefully negotiate your way across the width of the diversion channel as well as the creek—a wrong step under the wrong conditions could lead to serious injury or death. Conventional wisdom suggests that camping at Upper Price Lake, at the base of Slide Mountain, may not be a good idea anyway. Named Slide Mountain for a reason long before the event of 1983, it definitely has a reputation. Brook trout, decimated by the slide, are making a recovery, but you probably will not find any trophy-sized fish.

From the lake the trail leads very steeply one-third mile up the south slopes of the canyon back to the main trail heading toward Tahoe Meadows. Climb up from the lake, heading west through boulders and firs to the signed junction.

From the junction with the road to Ophir Creek and the trail to Tahoe Meadows, begin climbing up the steep south slopes of the canyon, high above Ophir Creek. As you climb you can look directly across the canyon at the remains of the extensive slide that broke loose from Slide Mountain. As the trail ascends the hillside, white fir tends to dominate the north-facing slope, and higher up a mixed forest of ponderosa pine, white fir, hemlock, spruce and western white pine covers the hillside. Lining a couple of spring-fed streams, the vegetation becomes incredibly lush with wildflowers, willows and big-leaf maple mixed with moss-covered rocks. Through gaps in the forest you have excellent views of Washoe Valley and the Virginia Range—source of the Comstock Lode. Continue steadily climbing uphill until the trail momentarily descends to the junction with the trail coming up from Upper Price Lake, 5.5 miles from the trailhead.

From the junction the trail proceeds up the canyon, closer to Ophir Creek, crossing a couple of densely vegetated side streams. Leave the dense forest behind as pines and firs become widely scattered in the upper canyon. Approximately one-half mile from the trail junction to Upper Price Lake, you reach another trail junction, where a sign reads: *Ophir Creek Trail.*

A dilemma now confronts you: both trails lead to the trailhead at the end of Tahoe Meadows, but which one should you take? The trail to the left is the official route as shown on the map, leading 2 miles through dense forest and skirting the meadows to the upper trailhead; the right-hand trail climbs up the canyon directly into Tahoe Meadows and follows the delightful creek as it winds through the lush, green meadows all the way to the trailhead. The trail through the meadows is certainly more scenic but also carries with it some environmental impacts—the boggy meadows are sensitive to erosion, the trail falters in sections, and in other spots multiple parallel trails have been created. The ideal solution to this problem would be for the Forest Service to relocate the trail along the edge of the meadows near the trees. However, that would require both initiative and funding, two elements that seem to be in short supply these days. Perhaps upon completion of the Tahoe Rim Trail the connection will allow hikers to experience the meadows without trudging all the way through them. In the meantime let your conscience be your guide.

Whichever route you choose, 2 miles of hiking remain. You can follow Ophir Creek steeply up the canyon, over the lip and into the meadows and on to the car, or climb along the south side of the canyon along an old roadbed to the forested hillside above the meadows and loop around to the trailhead. Both trails end at the far edge of the meadows just west of where Ophir Creek spills out of a culvert under the Mt. Rose Highway.

OTHER TRAILS

Tahoe Meadows Nature Trail: A 1.3-mile nature trail, wheelchair-accessible, loops around the edge of the upper Tahoe Meadows from the Tahoe Rim

Trail trailhead off the Mt. Rose Highway. Lush green meadows, ponds, springs, creeks and wildflowers are the main attractions.

Tahoe Rim Trail: Presently, the TRT is nonexistent through the Mt. Rose Wilderness even though construction of a concrete block building and parking area is complete at the site of the Tahoe Meadows trailhead off the Mt. Rose Highway. Negotiations between the Forest Service and the trail builders are supposedly held up by questions regarding the alignment of the trail through the Wilderness. The TRT almost reaches the west edge of the Mt. Rose Wilderness from the trailhead along California State Route 267 one-half mile south of Brockway Summit. From the trailhead the 4 mile trail leads through forest to its end at a dirt road below Martis Peak. There is a possibility that the upcoming extension will connect the existing TRT from here to the trail to Gray Lake. The 9-mile section south from Tahoe Meadows to the existing trail at Tunnel Creek receives first priority as time and money permit.

Tail to Big Meadows: The Mt. Rose Trail continues along the top of the crest from Bronco Creek (see Hike 5) to Big Meadows and on to the Hunter Lake jeep road. The first 2 miles are in the Mt. Rose Wilderness but the rest is outside the boundary and open to off-road vehicles and mountain bikes. Slicing the Wilderness into two separate sections unfortunately deleted Davis and Big Meadows but the compromise was part of the agreement for passage of the Nevada Wilderness bill. Hiking via jeep roads all the way to the Truckee River is possible.

Gray Creek Trail: Between the tiny communities of Floriston and Hirschdale, a steep jeep road leads up into the Wilderness south from the Truckee River. The first 5 miles are outside the Wilderness. Another 3 miles inside the Wilderness bring you to Gray Lake. A junction, 2.5 miles from the start, branches off along the North Fork Gray Creek.

Kings Peak above Overland Basin

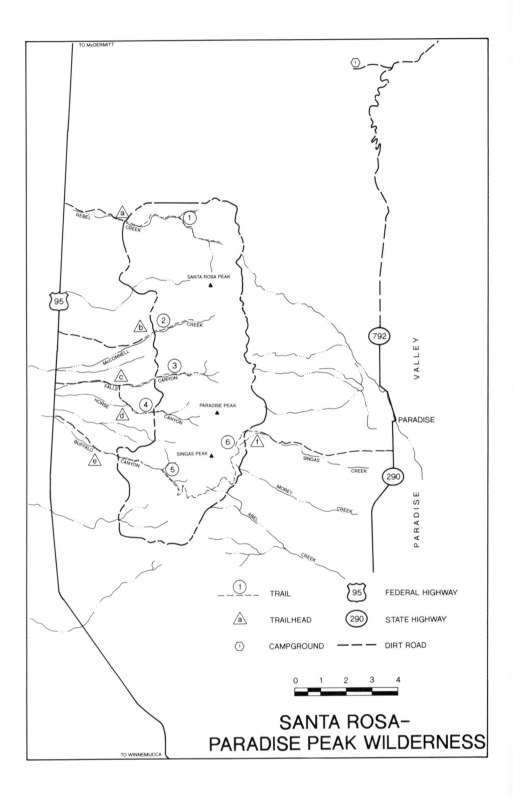

SANTA ROSA–
PARADISE PEAK WILDERNESS

Chapter 5
SANTA ROSA–PARADISE PEAK WILDERNESS

The Santa Rosa-Paradise Peak Wilderness is a 31,000-acre tract of prim-itive land straddling the Santa Rosa Range near the Oregon border. Although a federal highway parallels the range to the west and a state highway to the east, the area is a forgotten island of wilderness. Remote and seldom visited, the Wilderness is a hikers' haven, with numerous short trails penetrating the mountains from east and west.

Although the second smallest wilderness area in Nevada, the Santa Rosa-Paradise Peak Wilderness possesses many fine treasures. One of the most dramatic looking peaks in the Great Basin, Santa Rosa Peak at 9,701 feet perches majestically over an aspen-filled basin that must contain one of the largest stands of aspen anywhere in the region. A significant water-fall, at least by intermountain standards, spills over rocky cliffs a mere one-half mile from the Falls Canyon trailhead. Numerous basins beckon the recreationist and a handful of streams entice the angler.

The Santa Rosa Mountains were some of the first in the Great Basin to be visited by explorers. In 1829 Peter Skene Ogden led the fifth Snake Country Expedition, composed primarily of fur trappers, into the unknown region hoping to find a new river system rich in pelts. The excur-sion obviously led to commercial disappointment. Almost 35 years later, in 1863, a group of miners crossed the Santa Rosa Range into a lush valley at the eastern base of the range. Apparently impressed with the area, one of the prospectors, a W. B. Huff, exclaimed, "What a paradise!" and the glen became Paradise Valley. Apart from some Indian uprisings, the valley lived up to its name, becoming quite a productive agricultural region. The mountains themselves received the appellation "Santa Rosa" after Saint Rose of Lima, the first canonized saint in the New World.

Like most Nevada ranges, the Santa Rosa mountains trend along a north-south axis. In the upper part of the range are rugged granite peaks and ridges while the western base of the mountains is composed primari-ly of phyllite, a gray, metamorphic rock containing small flecks of mica. Deeply cut into the west side of the range are long, 'V'-shaped canyons that twist down from large collecting basins at the base of the 9,000 ft. crest. Ten tumbling and cascading creeks careen their way through these canyons down into the Quinn River, serenely gliding through the valley below. Typical of these western canyons are the exposed ribs of slanted phyllite rising dramatically out of the hillsides. Lush riparian vegetation thrives next to the creeks, and low sagebrush and grasses cover most of the canyons. Farther up in the basins, large stands of quaking aspen appear on the wetter slopes. Forest Service roads provide access to five west-side trails that follow the serpentine creeks up their respective canyons.

The east side of the range is much steeper, dropping from the crest 4500 feet to Paradise Valley in 3 short miles. Unlike the creeks in the long canyons of the west side, the east-side creeks quickly plummet off the precipitous slopes. Although maps indicate that the Summit Trail traverses the entire east side of the mountains, private property denies access to the north section. Much of the central section follows jeep roads outside the Wilderness. The only parts of the Summit Trail described in this chapter are the southern section from Singas Creek and Buffalo Canyon trailheads to Abel Summit, and the north section along Rebel Creek.

Most of the trails in the Santa Rosa-Paradise Peak Wilderness begin at relatively low elevation (around 5,000 feet). Summer can often be extremely hot at this altitude, making spring or fall a better time for a visit. In the springtime, green foliage carpets the basins, wildflowers are at their peak and the tumbling streams are full. In autumn the temperature has moderated and the fall colors can be breathtaking in the upper basins, particularly in Rebel Creek below Santa Rosa Peak. Short trails and few campsites make the area quite suitable for hikers, but backpackers will have to choose their routes carefully, often having to make do with extremely primitive camping spots. Much of the terrain, however, is open and lightly vegetated, just right for off-trail exploration.

Plenty of wildlife make their home in the Santa Rosa Range, including large herds of mule deer, mountain lions, bobcats, coyotes, marmots and a host of other rodents. California bighorn sheep, recently reintroduced into the mountains, may be seen clambering through the rocky terrain near the rugged parts of the upper canyons and along ridge lines. Game birds common to the area include sage grouse and chukar. Golden eagles, red-tailed hawks and goshawks are familiar raptors. A wide variety of nongame birds include mountain bluebirds, flickers, wrens and warblers. The cold streams provide perfect habitats for rainbow, brook and the threatened Lahontan cutthroat trout. Fishing can be quite good.

The Santa Rosa-Paradise Peak Wilderness is wild and rugged. Unfortunately, so are many of the roads. Access to all of the trailheads requires travel over rough dirt roads. Some are passable to the common sedan. However, most demand the use of a high-clearance vehicle.

LOCATION

Near the Oregon border about halfway across Nevada. Approximately 30 miles north of Winnemucca, the mountain range is bordered by U.S. 95 on the west and State Route 290 on the east. Forest Service dirt roads provide access to the range.

CAMPGROUNDS
No developed campgrounds exist adjacent to the Wilderness, although Lye Creek Campground is a mere 5 air miles northeast.

1. LYE CREEK CAMPGROUND $
Open June through October
Camping, Picnicking, Restrooms, Water
Located 18 miles north of Paradise Valley on State Highway 792
(just past Hinkley Summit) & 1.5 miles west on Forest Service
Road #087

RESOURCES
Limited facilities are present in the tiny communities of Orovada and Paradise Valley. Winnemucca, 30 miles south of the Wilderness, is a small town with a full range of services. Some camping gear is available from local merchants.

FOREST SERVICE

Santa Rosa Ranger District
1200 Winnemucca Blvd. East
Winnemucca, NV 89445
(702) 623-5025

Humboldt National Forest
Supervisor's Office
976 Mountain City Highway
Elko, NV 89801
(702) 738-5171

Trip 1 🌲
SUMMIT TRAIL: REBEL CREEK

Trip Type: Dayhike or overnight backpack; Out and back
Distance: 11.0 miles round trip
Season: Late May through late October
Access: Dirt road
Water: Creek
Maps: #6
    Santa Rosa Peak 7.5 minute quadrangle, 1991 (provisional)
    Humboldt National Forest map, Santa Rosa Ranger District, 1990

Introduction: In theory, the Summit Trail runs the entire length of the Santa Rosa-Paradise Peak Wilderness, but in practice much of the route is virtually nonexistent and a significant part lies outside the wilderness boundary. The section up Rebel Creek, however, is perhaps the best section of trail in the entire region.

Like all the west-side trails in the Santa Rosa Range, the Rebel Creek trail begins in a narrow, 'V'-shaped canyon beside a tumultuous creek through sagebrush-covered hills and interesting phyllite outcroppings. Unlike the other trails, however, this one does not dead-end at the head of a canyon but instead climbs to higher elevations at the crest of the range, where splendid scenery awaits. Santa Rosa Peak is a dramatic, alpine-looking, granite mountain, almost 10,000 feet high, rising a mile above the neighboring valleys. Mountaineers and technical climbers should find satisfaction with the wide distribution of potential routes on the ridges and faces of the mountain. An aspen-filled basin nestles immediately below the peak, providing shade from the hot summer sun and unbeatable autumn color. Possibilities for exploration in and around the upper basin abound and likely campsites are plentiful.

Trailhead: (a) From U.S. 95, 46.6 miles north of Winnemucca or approximately 24 miles south of McDermitt, turn east onto a gravel road (Forest Service Road #533) signed: *N. Rebel Creek Road.* Immediately cross a cattle guard and head toward the Santa Rosa Range on the well-graded road through grassy fields. At a somewhat confusing intersection, 0.8 mile from the highway, take the less traveled road toward the peaks as opposed to the better road that turns right into a ranch.

Past the intersection the road diminishes into two-track gravel, still passable to most vehicles. Follow a fence line into sagebrush passing through a closed gate, 1.4 miles from Highway 95. Make a short descent into the creek drainage, crossing the creek 4 times between 2.0 and 2.1 miles. Reach the end of the road near some groves of cottonwoods providing shade for some informal campsites.

Description: The trail begins above the north bank of the tumbling, cottonwood-lined creek on a typical canyon hillside covered with sagebrush, cheat grass and scattered wildflowers. Phyllite outcroppings add character to the narrow, 'V'-shaped canyon. Pass through an old barbed-wire gate near a rock rib that juts into the canyon and continue to the Wilderness boundary just on the other side of a dry, side drainage.

As you proceed up the canyon you cannot help but notice the steeply eroded banks of the creek and deposits of debris, evidence of a major flood some time in the recent past. Follow the winding and tumbling creek up the canyon through wild rose, elderberry, cottonwoods and occasional aspens past a side canyon and another old barbed-wire gate. Where the canyon bends, views of the upper canyon open up momentarily, and then the trail continues to climb, reaching a large side canyon. You angle into this canyon, cross a diminutive side creek and then return to the cleft of Rebel Creek. Views up the main canyon continue to improve with each step.

You skirt another side canyon and continue along a fence line above the serpentine creek where the trail becomes somewhat indistinct in a meadowy area. Climb above the creek to avoid heavy brush and steep cliffs as the canyon narrows. The vegetation thickens as the trail crosses a small stream and then heads back down toward the creek following another fence line through sagebrush. Eventually you encounter an open gate on the right where two branches of the stream merge below a large hill. Pass through the open gate and down to a crossing of the north branch of Rebel Creek, 2.9 miles from the trailhead.

From here the trail climbs above the creek into the narrow, steep canyon. Quaking aspens cover the far hillside, making for a spectacular sight in the fall. Continue on the moderate ascent until the trail seemingly dead-ends in some thick brush above the creek. Although virtually nonexistent, the path actually descends to the creek, crosses and climbs up the far side. The route becomes clear again above the creek in some aspens. The trail climbs high above the creek with the aid of two switchbacks and then bends around to the south up a steep, aspen-choked section of the upper canyon. Dramatic, gray-colored cliffs rise above the channel on the opposite side.

You continue the ascent as the trail crosses the creek in a shaded grove of aspen over moss-covered rocks where the canyon bends east again. Above the crossing some deadfalls have decimated a 100-foot-long section of trail. As the path continues to climb you ascend out of the narrow canyon into less severe topography, where the massive west face of Santa Rosa Peak comes into view. A ridge of rugged, steep granite runs along the north side of the peak toward the 9,701-foot summit, forming the east edge of a basin that rivals any mountainous area in the state for alpine beauty. Snow clings to the shaded clefts of the peak well into early summer. The basin below the peak, blanketed by what has to be one of the largest stands of aspen in the Great Basin, combines with the magnificence of the peak to create a spectacular autumn sight.

Santa Rosa Peak in late spring

Parts of the Summit Trail through the upper part of Rebel Creek canyon to the crest are difficult to follow. Red construction stakes aid in following the route until a section of already completed trail offers a more defined track. The route basically follows the creek, more or less, until reaching the slopes below the crest. One could continue on the Summit Trail over the crest into Big Cottonwood Creek on the east side of the range.

The upper basin below Santa Rosa Peak is a prime area for further explorations. Springs and creeks should supply plenty of water, and numerous potential campsites exist throughout the basin. The peak itself should supply plenty of challenges for the peak bagger, and the serious climber will find plenty of technical routes on the steep granite walls.

Retrace your steps 5 miles to the trailhead.

Trip 2 ⛰

McCONNELL CREEK

Trip Type: Dayhike or overnight backpack; Out and back
Distance: 5.0 miles round trip
Season: Mid-May through mid-November
Access: Dirt road
Water: Creek
Maps: #6
            Santa Rosa Peak 7.5 minute quadrangle, 1991 (provisional)
            Humboldt National Forest map, Santa Rosa Ranger District,
             1990

Introduction: McConnell Creek is a delightful stream with numerous cascades and swirling pools in a winding, steep-walled canyon on the west side of the Santa Rosa Range. Fishermen will find this stream to be one of the best in the area. Interesting geology adds flavor to the canyon with phyllite outcroppings in the lower section and granite composition in the upper section, culminating in the south slopes of 9,701-foot Santa Rosa Peak. Although the trail terminates a mile below the upper end of the canyon, the upper basin is open, allowing easy cross-country travel for those wishing to explore. Santa Rosa Peak is a relatively easy climb from the upper basin.

Trailhead: (b) From U.S. 95, 41.6 miles north of Winnemucca or approximately 29 miles south of McDermitt, turn east into the rest area just south of the town of Orovada. Follow the dirt road (Forest Service Road #555) that begins at the north end of the rest area and head east toward the Santa Rosa Range. Pass through a gate at 0.75 mile from the highway and over Antelope Creek at 1.6 miles. You pass through the lush grasslands of a cattle ranch before entering into typical sagebrush environment around 2½ miles up the road. At 3.0 miles reach a gate at the Humboldt National

Forest boundary and continue to the trailhead at the mouth of the steep canyon of McConnell Creek, 3.3 miles from U.S. 95. In essence, there is no parking at the trailhead as the road just dead-ends in a narrow turnaround. Parking for more than one car is available in a grassy area back down the road.

Description: The mild ascent up the McConnell Creek Trail begins just above the north bank of the creek as it heads into the steep-walled, 'V'-shaped canyon. Jagged formations of phyllite periodically jut into the canyon above the willow-lined, cascading creek. The trail passes above a number of small punch bowls and pools that will entice even the most indifferent angler. As you proceed up the trail, erosion of the creek banks and scattered debris are a testament to a major flood that roared through the canyon in the Spring of 1984. Soaring temperatures and a heavy snow-pack combined with the saturated soil to create perfect conditions for a 100-year event as mudslides and floods tore through the canyon, leaving behind the scars and debris that remain to this day.

Follow the winding creek into a grassy meadow on a bench above the creek where the trail becomes indistinct. Granite boulders scattered throughout the meadow, brought down the canyon by the flooding creek, seem out of place below the cliffs of phyllite. Discernible tread resumes past the meadow as the trail continues its serpentine nature, arriving at the signed Wilderness boundary just past a seasonal stream.

As you continue up the winding canyon, the tread becomes more distinct past the transition zone from predominantly phyllite rock to granite. The canyon widens near another grassy meadow bordered by wild rose, as

Southwest face of Santa Rosa Peak

the tumultuous creek continues to cascade and tumble down the rocky canyon. Where the canyon narrows again, the trail wanders close to the creek through sagebrush. Farther up, aspens begin to appear along the creek and in the side drainages. A brief, steep ascent surmounts a rock rib to where you gain views of the southwest slopes of Santa Rosa Peak. Then the grade steepens as the trail climbs far above the creek, passing a couple of seasonal drainages. The path all but disappears near where the creek divides into multiple branches draining the slopes of Santa Rosa Peak and the upper canyon.

The upper basin of McConnell Creek is wide open for further exploration beyond the end of the trail. The canyon extends for another mile, terminating below the crest of the range and the south slopes of Santa Rosa Peak. A climb of the peak would be an easy ascent up the moderately steep slopes. If you are planning an overnight stay, established campsites are nonexistent but you may be able to find a potential spot in the upper basin.

Retrace your steps to the trailhead.

Trip 3 🏕

HORSE CANYON

Trip Type: Dayhike or overnight backpack; Out and back
Distance: 6.2 miles round trip
Season: Mid-May through mid-November
Access: Rough dirt road, high-clearance vehicle necessary
Water: Creek
Maps: #7
     Santa Rosa Peak 7.5 minute quadrangle, 1991 (provisional)
     Humboldt National Forest map, Santa Rosa Ranger District,
       1990

Introduction: The Horse Canyon Trail is perhaps the best trail in the Santa Rosa-Paradise Peak Wilderness as far as the actual condition of the tread goes. Well-graded and distinct, the path leads along the cascading creek farther into the upper basin than other trails in the area, except for the Summit Trail. The 3-mile trail leads well up Horse Canyon to the beginning of the upper basin below a serrated, granite ridge with steep faces of rock. A fairly decent campsite is at the end of the route, providing a base camp for further explorations of the canyon.

Trailhead: (c) From U.S. 95, 39.8 miles north of Winnemucca or approximately 31 miles south of McDermitt, turn east onto a dirt road (Forest Service Road #538) signed: *Horse Canyon Road*. Immediately pass over a cattle guard and proceed up the dirt road toward the Santa Rosa Range, paralleling Horse Creek, then crossing the stream at 0.6 mile. Pass over two more cattle guards before crossing the creek again at 1.8 miles from the highway. Three-quarters of a mile farther, at 2.6 miles from U.S. 95, come to a signed intersection with Forest Service Road #539 on the right, which leads to the Falls Canyon Trail (Trip #4).

Continue on Road #538, passing over a cattle guard at 3.1 miles, and reach the trailhead at the end of the dirt track in a wide, grassy area 3.3 miles from Highway 95. At the end of the road is a primitive campsite with fire ring.

Description: The beginning of the trail follows an inconspicuous old road that heads south out of the grassy meadow, climbing steeply above the creek. Avoid the temptation to follow the more obvious route that heads down across the creek—that trail quickly evaporates in some thick brush

Horse Creek and Santa Rosa crest

farther upstream. Following the road, the route climbs above the cascading creek along the hillside on the south side of the canyon. A short, mild descent drops to a wide spot at the bottom of the canyon below some steep phyllite cliffs. Then the route becomes a bona-fide trail, staying next to the creek as it winds through the curving canyon and eventually across Horse Creek to the north bank.

The trail proceeds up the twisting canyon, above the cottonwood-lined creek, making a steady climb through sagebrush and grasses and sporadic patches of wild rose. You pass a dry side canyon and reach the Wilderness boundary. Beyond, the trail quickly surmounts a minor ridge after which the canyon widens out momentarily before making a series of 90-degree bends leading to a small meadow. From the meadow you can see the impressive granite cliffs at the head of the canyon. The topo shows the trail ending in the meadow, but a well-defined track continues upstream.

The trail follows the creek closely. Stands of aspen and cottonwoods have sprung up since the flooding in 1984 decimated the previous growth. As you head up the canyon, careful observation reveals the transition from phyllite to granite near an open area above the creek. Above the far bank a dense stand of aspen runs almost all the way up to the ridge line, interspersed with a few isolated limber pines. You pass over a small side stream and come to a rounded, boggy meadow fed by springs and ringed by young aspens. Beyond the meadow, the trail makes an exceedingly steep but short climb before mellowing out, providing good views of the serrated ridge crest above vertical granite faces at the head of the canyon.

Now you pass over a creek draining a narrow side canyon filled with quaking aspen and begin to climb a little more steeply below some granite outcroppings. Follow the canyon as it bends around, passing two more side canyons as the terrain begins to open up toward the crest and views improve correspondingly. You surmount a low rise, and continue up the trail alongside the creek to a narrow stream draining the upper slopes to the north. Cross the stream and follow the trail as it leads a short distance to trail's end near the main branch of Horse Creek. A small campsite sits above the opposite bank in a small, grassy meadow.

Retrace your steps to the trailhead.

Trip 4 🗘
FALLS CANYON

Trip Type: Dayhike; Out and back
Distance: 1.0 miles round trip to falls;
4.2 miles round trip to end of trail
Season: May through November (Trail to falls open all year if road conditions allow)
Access: Rough dirt road, high-clearance vehicle necessary
Water: Creek
Maps: #7
Santa Rosa Peak & *Five Fingers* 7.5 minute quadrangle, 1991 & 1988 (provisional)
Humboldt National Forest map, Santa Rosa Ranger District, 1990

Introduction: An easy half-mile hike leads to a rare sight in the Great Basin—a significant waterfall. To appreciate the full grandeur of the falls, one should plan a trip in spring when the creek is full of melt water. Equally as inspiring, frozen blankets of ice cling to the steep face of the falls in winter. Along with the falls, dramatic phyllite cliffs enhance the awesome character of the lower canyon.

Although the most spectacular features of this trip are in the first part of the hike, one can continue beyond the falls another mile to the upper basin, where good views of Paradise Peak abound. If isolation is your goal, you can hike up to the trail junction and over a primitive trail into the Pine Creek drainage.

Trailhead: (d) From U.S. 95, 39.8 miles north of Winnemucca or approximately 30 miles south of McDermitt, turn east onto a dirt road (Forest Service Road #538) signed: *Horse Canyon Road.* Immediately pass over a cattle guard and proceed up the dirt road toward the Santa Rosa Range, paralleling Horse Creek and crossing the stream at 0.6 mile. Pass over two more cattle guards before crossing the creek again at 1.8 miles from the highway. Three-quarters of a mile farther, at 2.6 miles from U.S. 95, come to a signed intersection with Forest Service Road #539 on the right, which leads to the Falls Canyon Trail. Straight ahead, Road #538 continues to the trailhead for Horse Canyon (Trip #3).

Turn right onto Road #539 and proceed through sagebrush terrain. Pass through a barbed-wire gate at 0.8 mile from the junction and cross Falls Canyon Creek twice before reaching the trailhead, 1.1 miles from the intersection with Road #538 and 3.7 miles from U.S. 95. If the last creek crossing seems too risky in early season, you can park in the

Falls Canyon Falls

meadow just before the stream. A number of informal campsites nestle beneath mature cottonwoods next to the creek near the trailhead.

Description: The rather primitive Falls Canyon Trail almost immediately makes a couple of tenuous traverses of the creek in the narrow canyon. From the crossings, the trail follows the densely vegetated creek into what appears to be a box canyon, but in actuality the trail follows the stream through a sharp 'S' bend below some dramatic, steep, phyllite cliffs. Where the trail curves left to climb above the rock cliffs, a use trail splits off, heading along the creek through extremely thick brush 75 yards to the base of the falls.

If you do not mind battling the brush to reach the base of the falls, the view is quite inspiring in the spring and early summer, when an abundant supply of water plunges over the lip of the rock and down into the churning pool. The wind-driven mist is definitely refreshing on a typically hot summer day.

From the use-trail junction, ascend around a rock rib of slanted phyllite pinnacles above the falls and eventually parallel the creek once more before a switchback leads down to and across the stream to the south bank. Follow the trail along a big, sweeping curve and through a narrow, rocky section of the canyon. You almost reach the level of the creek before the trail steepens and climbs well above it to the top of a ridge, where there is a good view of Paradise Peak. A little way farther, pass the signed Wilderness boundary and continue on a fairly level grade into a grassy meadow rimmed by quaking aspens.

The meadow would be a very nice place to rest or even camp if not for the trampled condition of the ground and the plethora of cow pies. The meadow would be the perfect "poster child" for a wilderness anti-grazing movement. In all fairness, however, the cows should not have to take all the blame as hunters have left a vast number of bones and other debris scattered around. In a meadow just before the trail crosses a stream draining the steep canyon to the south, you encounter an unmarked junction with a precipitous, indistinct path that climbs up the drainage to the crest and down into the Pine Creek basin.

Proceed upstream until a switchback leads down to another crossing of Falls Creek. Views of Paradise Peak are almost constant as the trail climbs above the creek into the sagebrush-covered upper basin where pockets of aspen line the drainages. Just beyond a branch of the creek draining slopes to the north, the trail ends below a large grove of aspens.

Retrace your steps to the trailhead.

Trip 5 🌲
SUMMIT TRAIL: BUFFALO CANYON

Trip Type: Dayhike or overnight backpack; Out and back
Distance: 10.4 miles round trip
Season: Mid-May through November
Access: Dirt road
Water: Creek
Maps: #7
Adorno Ranch & *Five Fingers* 7.5 minute quadrangles, 1988 (provisional)
Humboldt National Forest, Santa Rosa Ranger District, 1990

Introduction: The southern section of the Summit Trail follows a typical west-side canyon carved deeply into the Santa Rosa Mountains by a roaring, tumbling creek. The lower part of the canyon passes through phyllite cliffs below open sagebrush-covered slopes. Farther up the canyon, lush vegetation borders the creek and runs up the hillsides. Abel Summit, the pass above the head of the canyon provides excellent views to the east and west of valleys and distant ranges.

Trailhead: (e) From U.S. 95, 36.2 miles north of Winnemucca and approximately 35 miles south of McDermitt, turn east onto a gravel road signed: *Buffalo Canyon Road.* Immediately pass through a cattle guard and come to a corral where the road sweeps around to the left and then bends sharply to the right out of the corral. Head diagonally on good road toward the

Santa Rosa Range and the narrow cleft of Buffalo Canyon. As you approach the canyon, sagebrush begins to crowd the track. At 2.2 miles from the highway, the road crosses Buffalo Creek and then heads up the canyon for another 0.1 mile. You reach the end of the road and the trailhead in a wide area at 2.3 miles from U.S. 95. Parking is available for a few cars. Although parties have previously camped at the trailhead, the surroundings are not as pleasant as at some of the other west-side trailheads.

Description: The unmarked trail begins above the north bank of Buffalo Creek, climbing up to and following an old road below open hills covered with dry, sagebrush terrain. Lined with willows and cottonwoods, Buffalo

Buffalo Canyon Creek

Creek tumbles down the steep, 'V'-shaped canyon. You quickly cross over into National Forest land at a barbed-wire fence and head up the canyon to a series of narrow benches of open meadows above the creek. Beyond the third bench, the trail crosses over a phyllite ridge and comes to the signed Wilderness boundary.

The route forsakes the old road bed as it heads down to the creek and crosses over to newer trail on the south side. Continue to wander through phyllite outcroppings and ribs above the cascading creek as it winds through the serpentine canyon. A switchback leads down to another creek crossing.

Soon after, the trail passes a side canyon and then follows along a sagebrush-covered bench to additional ridges of phyllite trending perpendicular to the stream canyon. Aspens make their first appearance in a marshy area below a talus slide as the trail leads closer to the creek and its riparian vegetation. Over another phyllite outcropping the trail crosses the stream once more on moss-covered boulders.

From the crossing, the trail climbs steeply past phyllite cliffs. Where the canyon bends you get your first glimpse toward the head of the canyon, where green, carpeted slopes descend from the rocky ridge crest. Soon the canyon divides into two tributaries separated by a large phyllite outcropping. The left-hand channel drains the steep terrain to the north while the main channel lies in the canyon to the right. The trail crosses the left branch of Buffalo Creek and continues up the main branch.

While willows, wild rose and aspen line the creek, the upper slopes begin to hold mountain mahogany and an occasional limber pine. The canyon widens considerably as the trail climbs away from the creek for a stretch before returning farther upstream. You cross the stream once more in a lush area of wildflowers including lupine, columbine and monkey flower.

You reach a clearing in a meadow near an aspen grove that could be a campsite if you do not mind the numerous cow pies. The trail falters for a bit in the meadows but resumes in the sagebrush at the far side. Climb steeply above the south bank of the creek through immature aspens until the trail breaks out into the open. Where you cross a dry drainage, the ascent moderates and leads to another meadow in a flat surrounded by more aspen. One again the track becomes lost momentarily in the meadows, but it reappears just before the next crossing of Buffalo Creek.

Now the trail climbs steeply away from the creek, then moderates at a switchback. A mature grove of aspen provides welcome shade on hot days and leads to a lush side stream lined with wildflowers. You pass through another flat lined with aspens before making yet another crossing of the creek. Along the south side of the canyon, the trail climbs in and out of thick brush, aspens and cottonwoods, crossing a side stream along the way, and finally heading over the main channel of Buffalo Creek to the north bank.

Having even more creek crossings, the next section of trail wanders back and forth over the narrowing stream. Along the way the trail passes through more aspen groves, meadows, sagebrush and wildflowers to where the creek divides into two tributaries again. Follow the main channel to the right for a brief stretch to a meadow where the trail angles sharply away from the creek and begins to climb up the brush-covered slopes toward the crest. This bend in the trail, somewhat indistinct, occurs approximately 75 feet above the beginning of the meadow, where it makes a 90-degree bend to the left (about 200 yards above a light rock outcropping).

The climb to the top of the ridge begins rather mildly before steepening just below the summit. The trail is overgrown with thick brush, so hikers with anything less than rhinoceros skin will wear long pants in this section. A pair of steep switchbacks just below the top lead to a barbed wire fence running along the crest of the Santa Rosa Range. At Abel Summit fine views of the surrounding basins and ranges await you. The Summit Trail continues northeast toward the Singas Creek trailhead (see Trip 6).

Retrace your steps to the trailhead.

Trip 6 🌲

SUMMIT TRAIL: SINGAS CREEK

Trip Type: Dayhike
Distance: 11.4 miles round trip
Season: Mid-May through November
Access: Dirt road, high-clearance vehicle necessary
Water: Creeks
Maps: #8
       Five Fingers 7.5 minute quadrangle, 1988 (provisional)
       Humboldt National Forest map, Santa Rosa Ranger District

Introduction: This portion of the Summit Trail passes through some of the most luxurious vegetation found in the Santa Rosa-Paradise Peak Wilderness. The Singas Creek basin is home to a wide variety of wildflowers and shrubs as well as thick stands of quaking aspen. Farther up the trail, expansive views abound as the trail traverses around the heads of the Morey and Abel Creek basins below the steep slopes of 9415-foot Singas Peak. From the trail one could make a relatively easy ascent up steep slopes to the summit. For an easier route to better views, a side trail leads a mile up to an 8750-foot point south of Abel Summit. This trail description ends at Abel Summit, but you could continue down the Summit Trail along Buffalo Canyon (see Trip 5).

A lack of satisfactory campsites makes this a trip primarily for dayhikers, although good places to spend a night are near the trailhead along Singas Creek. The path beside Abel Creek is in desperate need of some maintenance and may be hard to follow in places.

Trailhead: (f) From U.S. 95, 22.1 miles north of Winnemucca or approximately 49 miles south of McDermitt, turn east onto State Route 290 signed: *Paradise Valley*; a Forest Service sign also reads: *Hinkley Summit 32, Lye Creek Campground 34.* Travel on Highway 290 16.8 miles to the signed turnoff for Singas Creek Road. At the junction is a sign reading: *Ranch 3C - Dave & Tom Cassinnelli* near a corral and cattle-loading facility.

Follow the wide, well-graded gravel road along fence lines and through a sample of the lush alfalfa fields of Paradise Valley toward the east front of the Santa Rosa Range. At an intersection 1.5 miles from the highway, proceed straight ahead on a narrow, two-track, dirt road where the improved gravel road bends left toward a ranch.

As the road cuts a swath through dense sagebrush, you cross a cattle guard at 2.5 miles from the highway. A lesser road branches to the left at 3.2 miles. The track is a little rougher than it has been where it heads up the right side of narrowing and deepening Singas Creek Canyon, passing over another cattle guard at 4.4 miles. The road continues to wander upstream to the trailhead, 5.6 miles from Highway 290. A wide turnaround offers park-

Lone mountain mahogany tree above Singas Basin

ing for many cars. If you desire to camp at the end of the road, there are nice campsites around the trailhead as well as a short distance up the trail.

Description: The trail begins just past the Wilderness signboard above the steep bank at the end of the road. Follow the remnants of an old, overgrown road bed, passing through alternating sagebrush and dense groves of aspen. Cross two spring-fed creeks, climbing steeply at times to the well-marked Santa Rosa-Paradise Peak Wilderness boundary. Quickly cross the main channel of Singas Creek and ascend to a junction with the Summit Trail, 0.8 mile from the trailhead, where two round poles are all that remains of the old trail sign.

From the junction, head south (left) on the more distinct path, the gently ascending grade a welcome change from the steep old road bed. You hike beneath tall aspens and amid the lush vegetation of a wide variety of wildflowers as the path makes an ascending traverse across the upper slopes of the Singas Creek basin. A pair of small, seasonal streams surrounded by moss-covered rocks and lush foliage fail to appear on the topo map. Occasionally, the trail breaks out into the open, allowing good views of Paradise Valley below, but when it reaches the top of a sagebrush-covered ridge, the views become expansive of the valley, distant ranges and the Singas Creek basin.

From the ridge crest continue to traverse drier slopes of sagebrush, scattered snowberry and sporadic clumps of lupine until you make a short descent into the Morey Creek drainage. Cross over seasonal streams flanked by groves of aspen to the willow-lined main channel of the creek, 2.0 miles from the trailhead, where wildflowers abound, including paintbrush and bluebells. Quickly climb out of the deep channel and begin a long descent around the protruding southeast ridge of Singas Peak. The trail alternates between lush foliage and open slopes of grasses and sagebrush as it declines around the nose of the ridge and into the Abel Creek basin. Commanding views to the east of Paradise Valley and distant ranges persist.

In the Abel Creek basin the Summit Trail makes a horseshoe bend below the open, sagebrush-covered south slopes of Singas Peak and then traverses across seasonal streams where aspens and willows thrive in the moist soil. Eventually, the trail makes a short descent into dense vegetation where the track becomes overgrown and hard to follow, reaching an upper tributary of Abel Creek. The trail continues over a rock-and-wire dam, constructed for no obvious reason, and then climbs up to a ridge top covered with boulders and mountain mahogany trees. From the crest, the trail becomes indistinct as it descends toward Abel Creek, and the track is easily lost in a tangle of brush and small trees before reaching the stream.

From Abel Creek, the trail ascends steeply to a ridge above, and the grade continues as the path winds toward the crest of the range. Approximately 30 yards before the actual crest, you reach a junction with a trail heading south along the top of the ridge before it descends into Andorno Creek Canyon. A wooden sign at the crest reads: *Singas Creek 5, Buffalo Creek 4, Andorno Creek 6, Abel Summit*. Views from the top of Abel Summit are impressive. The Summit Trail continues down into Buffalo Canyon and to the trailhead at the west base of the range (see Trip 5).

Retrace your steps back to the trailhead.

OTHER TRAILS

Westside Trails:

Rock Creek & Andorno Creek: Both of these trailheads are inaccessible, as the roads cross private ranch land. The trails themselves are not maintained.

Eastside Trails:

Summit Trail—Cottonwood Creek: Access is blocked by private ranch land.

Summit Trail—Little Cottonwood, Lamance & Hansen Creeks: Rough roads, requiring a high-clearance or 4-wheel-drive vehicle, lead to trailheads. Indistinct, unmaintained trails follow a somewhat confusing course through non-wilderness lands.

Summit Trail—Singas Creek (north): Trailhead directions described in Trip 6. A faint track heads north from the junction with the trail up Singas Creek, passing out of the Wilderness after 1.5 miles.

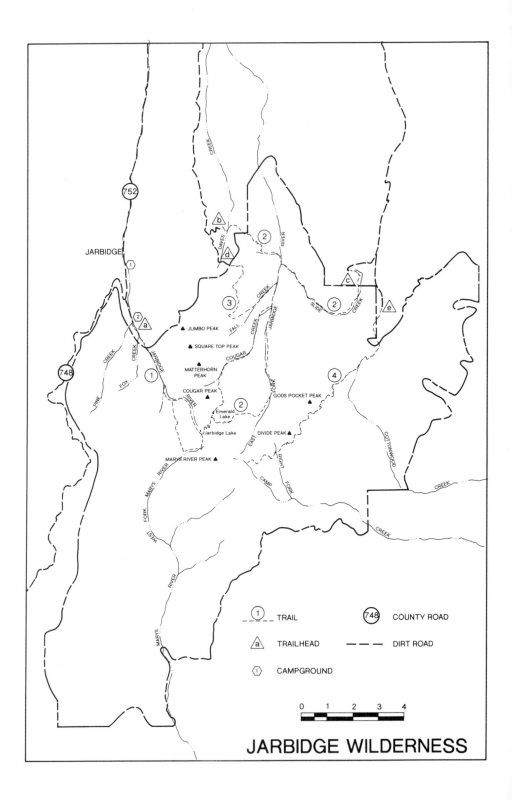

JARBIDGE WILDERNESS

Legend:
- ① TRAIL
- Ⓐ TRAILHEAD
- ① CAMPGROUND
- ⑦⁴⁸ COUNTY ROAD
- – – – DIRT ROAD

Map labels:
- 752
- 748
- JARBIDGE
- JUMBO PEAK
- SQUARE TOP PEAK
- MATTERHORN PEAK
- COUGAR PEAK
- Emerald Lake
- Jarbidge Lake
- MARYS RIVER PEAK
- GODS POCKET PEAK
- DIVIDE PEAK
- PINE CREEK
- FOX CREEK
- JARBIDGE CREEK
- JARBIDGE RIVER
- DAVES CREEK
- FALL CREEK
- COUGAR CREEK
- JARBIDGE RIVER
- SLIDE CREEK
- COTTONWOOD CREEK
- CAMP CREEK
- WEST FORK MARYS RIVER
- MARYS RIVER
- EAST FORK
- RIGHT FORK
- CREEK

Scale: 0 1 2 3 4

Trails of Northeastern Nevada

Chapter 6
JARBIDGE WILDERNESS

The only wilderness area in Nevada created by the Wilderness Act of 1964, the Jarbidge Wilderness is a perfect representation of what the authors of the bill had in mind. To the 64,830 acres in the original allotment, the Nevada Wilderness bill added 48,500 acres in 1989, for a total of 113,330. Isolated in the northeast corner of the state, Jarbidge is over one hundred road miles away from the two closest major towns, Elko, Nevada, and Twin Falls, Idaho—and a great percentage of that distance is over dirt roads. Many more hundreds of miles separate the region from the nearest major cities. Consequently the Jarbidge Wilderness is a remote, seldom-visited area.

Due to the long distances most recreationists must travel to reach the Wilderness, the few who do journey here usually spend more than just a weekend. The area, well suited to extended stays, has over 125 miles of trails. While many of the wilderness areas in Nevada are fine for dayhiking or overnight backpacks, the Jarbidge Wilderness has many long, connecting trails presenting alternatives for protracted stays in the backcountry. One could easily spend a two-week vacation within the boundaries and still not experience everything the area has to offer. Unlike trails in some of Nevada's newer wilderness areas, the trails in this one have benefited from three decades of protection—generally well built, properly maintained and appropriately signed at the major junctions.

A mostly volcanic range, the Jarbidge Mountains seem to share few of the attributes seen in the typical Nevada range. While most other ranges have a single north-south-trending crest, these mountains seem dropped in a clump by the Creator, with multiple crests and radiating canyons. Extensive stands of subalpine fir and whitebark pine add legitimacy to the National Forest appellation, which may be something of a misnomer in other similarly designated areas. Sitting just below the Idaho border, the mountains in the Jarbidge Wilderness attract a wealth of winter storms, products of the collisions of northwestern cold fronts and warm Gulf air, making it one of the wettest ranges in the state.

Tall mountains and deep canyons typify the range. Eight peaks top out at over 10,000 feet and many more almost reach that height. The canyons carry turbulent streams 3,000 to 4,000 feet below. Two subalpine lakes, Jarbidge and Emerald, nestle near the crests of their respective drainages and offer superb destinations for overnight stays. Scenic views are common from the high ridges and plateaus that abound throughout the Wilderness. Enhanced by the air quality of a Class 1 Airshed, experiencing 200-mile vistas is not uncommon. Jarbidge possesses some of the cleanest air in the nation and is one of 20 benchmark monitoring areas in the country for establishing air-quality standards.

The trails are usually snow-free beginning sometime in the middle of June, but stream flows then may be strong enough to keep hikers off trails requiring major fords. Check with the Forest Service in early season before embarking on a trip necessitating stream crossings. Early season is also the peak time for the awesome wildflower displays.

By midsummer, daytime temperatures can be quite high, especially in the lower elevations of the canyons. Ninety degrees is not unusual on a normal July or August day. At this time of year, plan for a large dose of sunshine and heat. In spite of the dying of the flowers, the drying of the grasses and the reduction of stream flows, Fall can be one of the best times to visit Jarbidge. Temperatures during the day are typically warm, and large stands of aspen in the canyons put on a spectacular show of color. Winter can offer some of the best cross-country skiing in the state, although you must avoid the steep, avalanche-prone canyons.

Any lover of flowers will be impressed by the diverse and prolific nature of the wildflowers in this Wilderness. Thanks in part to the considerable moisture, a burst of color carpets the slopes and drainages of the mountains from June to early July. Over 40 different species appear between the elevations of 6,500 and 10,838 feet. Along with the subalpine fir and whitebark pine previously mentioned, the Jarbidge Wilderness is host to other trees such as cottonwoods, aspens, mountain mahogany, juniper, and limber pine.

The Wilderness also harbors an abundance of wildlife. A trip without spotting a number of mule deer is hard to conceive. A large herd of antelope visits the area during summer and fall. An expanding herd of elk (reported to be over 100 head), reintroduced to the area a number of years ago, may be seen near the Hummingbird Spring habitat. According to the Forest Service, mountain lions and moose are in the area, but they remain unseen by the majority of hikers. More common are the smaller mammals, such as golden-mantled ground squirrels, chipmunks, rabbits and yellow-bellied marmots. Jarbidge is home to a wide variety of raptors, among which are golden eagles and red-tailed hawks. Game birds include grouse, chukar and partridge.

Fishing in the Jarbridge Wilderness is some of the best in the state. Rainbow and brook trout appear in most of the major rivers and creeks, including Jarbidge River, Canyon Creek, and Slide Creek. Redband and bull trout, sensitive species, reside in Slide, Fall and Pine creeks and the East Fork Jarbidge River. The Marys River drainages contain the threatened Lahontan cutthroat trout. Jarbidge Lake is too shallow to support any fish but Emerald Lake has a healthy population of brook trout.

The term "Jarbidge" is a corrupted form of an Shoshone Indian name, either after a word meaning "devil" or another word based on a legend about a crater-dwelling giant who wandered Jarbidge Canyon capturing Indians. The giant would carry his prey in a basket strapped to his back (perhaps the first real backpacker in Nevada) returning to his crater to devour the tasty morsels.

The region remained relatively unknown for many years. The only exception was a few sheepherders who coveted the rich grasses which covered the hillsides for their flocks. In 1908, Congress created the Humboldt National Forest and established a ranger station in Mahoney, just outside the current town of Jarbidge. Coincidentally, that same year David Bourne discovered gold in the canyon and 1500 miners poured into the region, creating the boom town of Jarbidge. In decidedly pragmatic fashion, President Taft excluded Jarbidge from the National Forest in 1911, allowing miners, or anyone else for that matter, to have private ownership of land within the town and surrounding gulches. Even to this day, the town of Jarbidge and parcels of land in Bourne, Moore and Bonanza gulches remain private land within the Humboldt National Forest.

Jarbidge was the site of one infamous bit of history: in 1916 the last stagecoach robbery in the country occurred just outside town. As in most mining towns in the West, the gold eventually ran out in the 1930's, having produced over 10 million dollars worth in a little over two decades. While the ore disappeared, the town remained, although the population never exceeded 200 once the mines closed.

Today the town of Jarbidge, Nevada, lives on, which is somewhat curious, since reaching the tiny burg requires a long drive on a gravel road that careens down a narrow canyon some 20 miles from the end of the nearest paved highway. Many structures remain from the bygone days, having been rebuilt after a fire swept through the town in 1919. Nearly 100 of them are habitable. This "in the middle of nowhere" town offers two saloons, gas station, motel, bed and breakfast and trading post. On weekends during hunting season, the town swells to a population reminiscent of the boom days.

The trails in the Wilderness offer many opportunities to witness some of the structures and artifacts left behind from more prosperous days. Remember these are cultural resources deserving of your respect and protected by Federal law. Leave any historic site or artifacts in the same condition as found.

Even by the easiest route, access to the Jarbidge Wilderness is by gravel road alone. You can access the Jarbidge River trailhead (see Trip 1) with a normal sedan but all other trailheads require a high-clearance vehicle.

LOCATION
Located near the Idaho border in the northeast corner of the state, in Elko County, the Jarbidge Wilderness is bounded by State Route 225 on the west, and U.S. 93 on the east, and is well north of Interstate 80 on the south. Providing the primary access is the Rogerson-Three Creek Highway from Rogerson, Idaho, which becomes Elko County Road 752 in Nevada. A secondary access from Elko follows rough, gravel road on the southwest side of the Wilderness on County Roads 747 &748.

CAMPGROUNDS
1. JARBIDGE
Open June through October
Camping, Picnicking, Restrooms, Water, Fishing
Just south of the town of Jarbidge on County Road 752

2. PINE CREEK
Open June through October
Camping, Restrooms, Water, Fishing
Located 0.8 mile from County Road 752 on Forest Service Road 318
Trailhead for Jarbidge River Trail (See Trip 1)

RESOURCES
The Jarbidge Wilderness is not near anything. The town of Jarbidge will supply the traveler with a limited selection of food, lodging, gas, minor automobile repairs (flats) and very basic supplies at the trading post. The closest major towns are 2 hours away—Elko, Nevada and Twin Falls, Idaho.

OUTFITTERS
FRANKLIN PRUNTY
HC 35, Box 280
Mountain City, Nevada 89831

HORACE E. or KIM SMITH
Cottonwood Ranch
Wells, NV 89835

LOWELL PRUNTY
Murphy Hot Springs
Rogerson, ID 83302

FOREST SERVICE

Jarbidge Ranger District
1008 Burley Avenue
Buhl, ID 83316-1812
(208) 543-4129

Humboldt National Forest
Supervisor's Office
976 Mountain City Highway
Elko, NV 89801
(702) 738-5171

Trip 1 🐾

JARBIDGE RIVER
TO JARBIDGE & EMERALD LAKES

Trip Type: 2 to 4 day backpack; Loop trip
Distance: 19.4 miles
Season: Late June through early October
Access: Improved dirt road
Water: Creeks & lakes
Maps: #9
    Jarbidge South & *Gods Pocket Peak* 7.5 minute quadrangles, 1986
      (provisional)
    Jarbidge Wilderness map, Humboldt National Forest, 1994
    Humboldt National Forest map, Mountain City & Jarbidge
      Ranger Districts, 1990

Introduction: A roaring river, two subalpine lakes, lofty peaks, verdant meadows and dense forests await the explorer on this loop through the northwest corner of the Jarbidge Wilderness. Although lightly used, the Jarbidge River Trail to Jarbidge and Emerald lakes is perhaps the most traveled path in the region, and with good reason. With a trailhead accessible by virtually any vehicle, the route has all the attractions the average mountain visitor would appreciate.

The beginning of the trail is testimony to the power of nature as the road once leading to the old trailhead shows evidence of destruction by slides and flooding during the Spring of 1995. High water and debris gouged out large parts of the road, resulting in the relocation of the trailhead 1.7 miles downstream to the Pine Creek Campground. Higher up the drainage, avalanche debris provides a vivid example of the occasionally powerful forces of the natural world.

The two lakes along this journey have idyllic attributes. Pleasant Jarbidge Lake is a shallow body of water tucked away into the head of Jarbidge River canyon, surrounded by green meadows and forest. The quiet and restful ambiance is the perfect setting for an afternoon nap or a long period of contemplation gazing at the lofty summits of the Jarbidge crest. Emerald Lake, a light-green tinted jewel, perched below the summit of Cougar Peak and above the deep canyon of the East Fork Jarbidge River, provides commanding views of some of the most spectacular scenery in the area. Sunrises over the eastern range of peaks are particularly spectacular from the shoreline of the serene waters.

Early summer provides a splash of color from wildflowers including arnica, columbine, crimson, fireweed, forget-me-not, geranium, Indian paintbrush, lupine, meadowrue, mint, mule ears, pale agoseris, pussytoes, scarlet gilia, sulfur buckwheat and yarrow. Add in verdant meadows and dense forests of subalpine fir, aspen, and limber and whitebark pine to create the perfect complement of flora for a fine trip into the wilderness.

Trailhead: (a) From U.S. 93, 86 miles north of Wells, Nevada, or 30 miles south of Twin Falls, Idaho, in the tiny burg of Rogerson, Idaho, turn left onto the Rogerson-Three Creek Road and proceed on the two-lane paved highway approximately 47 miles to where the surface changes to gravel. Just before the tiny community of Murphy's Hot Springs, the gravel road comes alongside the East Fork Jarbidge River and follows its course to the confluence with the main fork.

The road narrows as it winds along the serpentine course of the Jarbidge River through interesting rock formations scattered about the steepening canyon. Cross back into Nevada approximately 9 miles from the town of Jarbidge, as the road becomes Elko County Road 752. Eventually, you reach the small but thriving community of Jarbidge, Nevada, 65 miles from Rogerson, Idaho, and U.S. 93. If being on time is important, set your watch ahead an hour as the locals govern themselves by Mountain Time, since most of their trade occurs with residents of Idaho.

Drive all the way through Jarbidge and continue on the gravel road as it crosses the Jarbidge River four times before reaching the turnoff to the trailhead, 1.9 miles from town, signed: *Pine Creek C.G., Jarbidge Wilderness.* Travel down the dirt road 0.8 mile to Pine Creek Campground. The trailhead is currently on the main road at the far end of the campground, relocated downstream due to a massive slide during the Spring of 1995. Limited parking is available at the makeshift trailhead, where the only improvements consist of a gate with a *Road Closed* sign and a trail register. The adjacent campground provides a very pleasant setting next to the river, with pit toilets, campfire rings and running water.

Description: The trail starts out in the steep, 'V'-shaped canyon, following the old road above the east bank of the Jarbidge River through cottonwoods, aspens and subalpine fir. You quickly discover the reason for the relocation of the trailhead as a large chunk of the old road has vanished, gouged out of the hillside by the surging waters and debris from the slide. The temporary trail crosses the river numerous times as it alternately travels on the undamaged parts of the old road and through the remaining debris in the bottom of the drainage. Travel along this stopgap section during early-season runoff could be a highly dubious proposition. An intact wooden bridge spans the river but the road approaching the structure has washed away on both sides, a visual testament to the powerful forces that ripped through the canyon.

On a remaining section of road, 0.6 mile from the trailhead, the route encounters a signed junction with the unmaintained trail ascending Fox Creek. Cross Fox Creek on a wooden bridge and continue upstream, passing a campsite, complete with picnic table, fire pit and outhouse. A row of rocks across a remaining section of road diverts hikers to a poorly built trail that climbs up the hillside above the river, circumventing a washout upstream. This new section of trail is narrow, brushy, steep in parts and unstable in others. If you are visiting the area later in the season, finding your own way along the river will probably be easier. However, early in the summer when the water is high you will be forced to use this new path. Whether choosing the high route or the low one, eventually you arrive at the old trailhead just past Snowslide Gulch, 1.6 miles from the new trailhead. Passing over Snowslide Gulch provides a glimpse of one of the contributors to the massive slides of 1995.

The old trailhead is at the end of a wide turnaround where a pit toilet, signs and a signboard greet prospective recreationists. Continue up the canyon following the track of an old mining road as it climbs above the river, flanked by aspens, cottonwoods, subalpine firs and sporadic whitebark pines. Sagebrush, grasses, occasional junipers and mountain mahogany cover the steep hillsides above. Three-quarters mile from the old Snowslide Gulch trailhead, the path crosses the stream pouring down Dry Gulch and proceeds along the east side of the canyon until crossing the river, 2.7 miles from the end of the road.

Marys River Peak seen from the trail

Continue along the west side of the Jarbidge River on a dirt track across a dry drainage and up to Sawmill Creek. As the canyon curves east, a half mile beyond the creek and 3.9 miles from the new trailhead, in a grassy clearing you reach a junction with a trail climbing over a ridge and down into the West Marys River. Signs at the junction read: *Jarbidge Lake* (east), *W. Marys River Trail, W. Marys River 3.9, Marys River 9.7* (south). The loop trip here described will return via this trail.

The trail climbs a little more steeply above the river bank to a point where it appears that the old road continued down to the water but the newer trail bends sharply to the right. A sign reads: *Jarbidge Lake Trail, Jarbidge Lake 3.4, Emerald Lake 5.8*. The route now follows a bona-fide trail which soon begins a series of switchbacks through dense forest, climbing up the steepening canyon. The trail differs from what appears on the topo. The first group of switchbacks climb forested slopes on the southwest side of the river before crossing into open meadows on the east side. As you ascend, open slopes of wildflowers, grasses and scattered subalpine fir, downed timber and short young trees provide evidence of avalanches sweeping the slopes of the upper canyon in previous years. You cross some seasonal drainages before the next section of switchbacks meanders back into subalpine fir forest, then heads back over the creek. The last group of switchbacks climbs the steep slope below the lake through thick forest before the grade eases as it enters the upper basin. Limber pine and sub-alpine fir shelter the path as it gently ascends the last quarter mile to Jarbidge Lake (9350'), 6.7 miles from Pine Creek Campground.

The main trail passes around and above the lake—to reach the shoreline you will have to cover the short distance sans trail. Grassy meadows rim the small, deep-blue lake, which nestles in a wide-open basin below sloping hillsides covered with subalpine fir and limber pine. Wildflowers add a splash of color in early season. Mature trees shelter campsites above the south shoreline, and additional sites appear along the outlet stream. Good views of the crest of the Jarbidge Mountains, including Matterhorn Peak, are plentiful from the lake. Fish, on the other hand, are absent from the shallow waters. Since most parties tend to push on to Emerald, relative solitude at Jarbidge Lake is a justifiable expectation, whether you plan to camp or just relax for a spell near the placid waters.

The trail continues to circle above Jarbidge Lake before switchbacks lead toward the saddle directly southeast above the lake. At the saddle, 6.9 miles from the trailhead, is a three-way trail junction signed: *Cougar Mountain Trail, Emerald Lake 2.5, E. Fork Jarbidge River 5.3* (northeast, uphill) and *Camp Draw W. Marys River Trail, W. Fork Marys River 2.2, 76 Creek Divide 6.9, Marys River 8.0* (south, downhill). Views down the West Marys and Jarbidge rivers are quite impressive.

From the saddle the trail makes a moderate ascent. Five switchbacks direct you to the top of the ridge separating the Jarbidge and East Jarbidge drainages. Amid widely scattered and stunted limber pine, sweeping

Emerald Lake with Marys River Peak in background

views from impressive Marys River Peak all the way down the East Jarbidge River canyon are stunning.

A series of long switchbacks gently guides you down the steep hillside dotted with widely dispersed limber pine and subalpine fir. Once again the actual trail differs from the location shown on the topo. Below the switchbacks a long, gradually descending traverse leads above a couple of small tarns perched on an open bench to a junction amid dense timber. At the intersection, 8.5 miles from the trailhead, a trail sign states: *Cougar Creek Trail, Emerald Lake* (north), *Jarbidge Lake* (south) and *E. Fork Jarbidge River 2.5* (east). Follow the short trail up to Emerald Lake as it makes a gentle climb through moderate forest.

Emerald Lake, so named for the beautiful green complexion of the water, is a precious gem cradled beneath the red-tinged rock of 10,559-foot Cougar Peak. The serene water reflects a mirror image of the surrounding beauty. Encircled by a horseshoe basin of jagged cliffs, the lake reposes in its lofty perch above the canyon of the East Fork Jarbidge River, 1800 feet below. Scattered pines adorn the shoreline and wildflowers crown the inlet and outlet streams. A mild rise above the east shore has campsites, the nicest one above the far end of the lake. Unlike the sterile waters of Jarbidge, Emerald Lake has a healthy population of brook trout. Mornings at the 9,400-foot lake can be chilly but the sunrises are spectacular sights.

From the idyllic surroundings of Emerald Lake, retrace your steps to the saddle and the three-way trail junction directly above Jarbidge Lake. If you do not mind the associated elevation loss and gain, you can alter your return to the trailhead by descending Trail #019 to the West Marys River and climbing back over the ridge via Trail #192. If this option is unappealing, retrace your steps back down the Jarbidge River Trail to your car.

LOOP TRIP VIA TRAILS #019 AND #192

To reach the West Marys River, follow Trail #019 (Camp Draw Trail) as it descends from the saddle on a long traverse across rocky slopes dotted with limber pine and subalpine fir. Long switchbacks curve through the upper basin, the trail alternating between light forest and grassy meadows. As the descent continues subalpine fir becomes the dominant conifer, leaving the limber pines to the higher elevations. You pass through a spring-fed meadow and a seasonal drainage before sagebrush and rabbitbrush claim the lower slopes of the canyon.

Eventually, the path comes alongside the West Marys River, where the vegetation on either side stands in stark contrast to that on the other. The north-facing slopes are heavily forested, while sagebrush and grasses cover the south-facing hillsides, which are practically treeless. The trail veers away from the river near a broad meadow, and quickly a junction appears near the end of the meadow, 12.7 miles from the trailhead. A sign on a 4 x 4 post proclaims: *W. Marys River, Marys River 5.8, Jarbidge Canyon 3.9, Emerald Lake 4.7.* Just downstream from the junction, a nice campsite sits on the east bank of the seasonal stream draining the canyon.

At the junction turn north from the West Marys River Trail as the path climbs moderately, angling up the grass and sage-covered slopes. After a quarter mile the trail reaches a switchback, bending toward and then climbing parallel to the narrow canyon. A few more switchbacks lead up to an elevation where grasses replace the sagebrush and a few pines appear, and then more switchbacks lead to forested slopes in the upper canyon. You reach the crest, 14.0 miles from the trailhead, in a sandy saddle surrounded by firs. Limited views of the Jarbidge Crest appear through narrow gaps between the trees.

Small, verdant green meadows enclosed by dense, subalpine-fir forest greet you on the other side of the pass as you descend. Quickly you come to the remains of an old log cabin near a lush spring-fed rivulet flowing down a narrow canyon. The forest thins around the creek, allowing for nice views of the Jarbidge crest before the trail steeply switchbacks across sheer cliffs into dense fir and pine. The trail follows the main creek as it descends the declivitous canyon through mixed forest of subalpine fir, limber pine and aspen, crossing the creek twice before descending to the junction with the Jarbidge River Trail, 15.5 miles from the trailhead. Approximately 75 yards before the junction, a very pleasant campsite nestles below some aspens next to the creek. Now retrace your steps 3.9 miles to the trailhead.

Trip 2 🌲

EAST FORK JARBIDGE RIVER & COUGAR CREEK LOOP VIA THREE DAY CREEK & SLIDE CREEK TRAILHEADS

Trip Type: 3 to 6 day backpack; Loop trip
Length: 25.0 miles from Three Day Creek trailhead;
27.6 miles from Slide Creek trailhead
Season: Late June through mid-October
Water: Creeks & lake
Access: Dirt roads, high-clearance vehicle necessary
Maps: #10, 11, 12
Robinson Creek & *Gods Pocket Peak* 7.5 minute quadrangles,
1986 (provisional)
Jarbridge Wilderness map, Humboldt National Forest, 1994
Humboldt National Forest map, Mountain City & Jarbidge
Ranger Districts, 1990

Introduction: An extended trip into the heart of the Jarbidge Wilderness, the East Fork Jarbidge River-Cougar Creek Loop is one of the region's premier backcountry experiences. Incredible scenery is one of the many rewards of this trail, which passes through a wide variety of topography and of vegetation. Along the 20-plus mile journey, you travel past high-elevation tablelands with spectacular vistas, roaring streams coursing down precipitous canyons and even a subalpine lake beneath a towering peak.

The diverse collection of trees encountered throughout the loop includes aspen, cottonwood, mountain mahogany, juniper, subalpine fir and limber pine. Periodically, wide-open terrain of grasslands and sagebrush permits dramatic vistas in both the upper and lower parts of the canyons. Early season produces a bounty of wildflowers, among which are arnica, agoseris, balsamroot, bluebells, columbine, forget-me-not, geranium, lupine, meadowrue, monkey flower, monkshood, paintbrush, shooting star and yarrow.

Although early season is the best time to witness the incredible wildflower displays, it may also be a potentially hazardous season. Numerous fords of the East Fork Jarbidge River occur along the loop as well as crossings of Slide, Cougar and Three Day creeks, creating dangerous situations during peak snow melt. Check with the Forest Service regarding stream flows before setting out on this trip if you plan to hike during June or early July.

An unwritten rule of the backcountry seems to be that a good trail is one that starts low, climbs high and returns downhill to the car. Contrary to this rule, the East Fork Jarbidge River-Cougar Creek loop begins in the upper elevations of the respective trailheads (8020 feet at Three Day Creek and 8520 at Slide Creek) descending steep canyons to the confluence with the East Fork at 6325 feet. Heading upstream from there, the trail follows the river until it heads up Cougar Creek to Emerald Lake and back down the East Fork, closing the loop. From there one must climb up the steep canyons back to either trailhead. If you can arrange a car shuttle you can vary your return by hiking out to the opposite trailhead. In spite of this deviation, the loop is a spectacular sample of the rich wilderness of the Jarbidge Mountains.

Trailhead: SLIDE CREEK: (c) From U.S. 93, 86 miles north of Wells, Nevada, or 30 miles south of Twin Falls, Idaho, in the tiny burg of Rogerson, Idaho, turn left onto the Rogerson-Three Creek Road and proceed on the two-lane paved highway 36.5 miles to a junction, just a few hundred feet beyond the Three Creek School. A sign at the junction reads: *Jarbidge, Murphys Hot Springs* (straight) & *Pole Creek 16* (left).

Head south on graveled Pole Creek Road #074. The road crosses Pole Creek at 5.5 miles from the highway, enters Nevada at 6.4 miles and enters National Forest at 9.4 miles. Proceed on Forest Service Road #074, following the main track to a 'Y' junction, 14.7 miles from the highway. A sign at the junction reads: *Pole Creek Ranger Station 1* (right), *Canyon Creek 6, Elk Mountain 12, Oneil Basin 14* (left). Following the signed directions to Canyon Creek, bear to the left, remaining on Road #074 for 1.2 miles to another junction, 15.9 miles from the highway, where Road #074 curves east. You leave Road #074 bearing right onto the rougher surface of Road #284 for a quarter mile to a junction, 16.2 miles from the Rogerson-Three Creek Road. Road #284, signed: *Hummingbird*, proceeds straight ahead to the Hummingbird trailhead.

At the junction you turn right for 0.1 mile to a 'Y' junction where you turn left (south) following Road #285. Ignore two lesser roads and reach another 'Y' junction 1.1 miles from the junction with Road #074 marked by a sign: *Slide Creek Trailhead* (left). Follow Forest Service Road #285A a short distance to the trailhead in a grove of aspen and subalpine fir, 17.6 miles from the highway. Scattered around the trailhead, a few campsites nestle below the trees. A nearby stream supplies running water.

THREE DAY CREEK: (b) Follow the directions above to the junction with the Pole Creek Road just beyond the Three Creek School. Remain on the paved Rogerson-Three Creek Road as it continues west, eventually changing to gravel. Just before the tiny community of Murphy's Hot Springs, the gravel road comes alongside the East Fork Jarbidge River. Continue another couple of miles to Murphy's Hot Springs, about 49 miles from U.S. 93.

In the middle of the small community, turn south from the main highway near the Desert Hot Springs store at a junction signed: *Daves Creek, Wilderness.* Proceed on a dirt road (Forest Service Road #073) as it crosses the East Fork Jarbidge River and makes a steady 2-mile climb out of the canyon and up to the top of Wilkins Island. Once on the broad plateau, the dirt road heads south toward the northern mountains of the Jarbidge Wilderness. Remain on the main road as it passes underneath and then follows a powerline through grasslands. At 8.3 miles from the highway the road reaches a junction where you continue straight ahead following a sign: *Jarbidge Wilderness*.

A half mile beyond the junction the road enters National Forest at a cattle guard. Stay on the main track as the grasslands give way to sagebrush, and ignore the lesser roads branching off to the right and left. Just beyond thick forest you come to a clearing and an unsigned, hardly noticeable road on the left side, 11.7 miles from the highway. Turn down this road, which initially passes through sage and grasslands but soon enters thick, lush forest. You reach the trailhead, 0.7 miles from the turnoff and 12.0 miles from the highway. The trail begins beyond a large, open meadow near two signs. The first one reads: *Dave Creek, Jarbidge Wilderness, E. Fork Jarbidge River*. The second sign encourages hikers to register, but the trail register had disappeared in 1996.

Description: SLIDE CREEK: Begin hiking on newer trail not shown on the topo, through open vegetation of sagebrush and grasses as the trail heads east and then southeast along a small tributary. Soon the trail comes alongside the main branch of the creek as it starts to descend into the upper part of Slide Creek canyon. One mile down the trail you pass a sign indicating entrance into the Jarbidge Wilderness. Now the canyon grows deeper, the volume of the stream increases and the vegetation becomes more profuse. Subalpine fir and aspen, along with a wide variety of shrubs and flowers, crowd the stream in the narrowing canyon.

Within the next mile, the trail crosses the creek a number of times—crossings that may prove to be rather damp experiences in early season. The foliage recedes infrequently, but enough to allow for limited views of the dramatic rock cliffs that form the upper limits of the deep chasm of Slide Creek canyon. The descent continues through lush riparian vegetation until you reach a transition to the drier environment of the lower canyon. Where the canyon curves west, mountain mahogany and chokecherry begin to take over the hillsides from the aspen and subalpine fir above.

The serpentine creek bends around, heading in a northwest direction, traveling through the steep 'V'-shaped canyon. At 4.1 miles from the trailhead, Gods Pocket Creek converges with Slide Creek. This tumbling stream descends 3,000 feet in a mere 3½ miles, draining the upper slopes of Gods Pocket Peak. You continue to descend through sagebrush, grasses and mahogany toward the confluence with the East Fork Jarbidge River, and reach a trail junction at 6.0 miles, elevation 6356 feet.

THREE DAY CREEK: Follow a two-track road from the trailhead through sagebrush and grasslands until a single-track trail, perhaps marked by a duck, branches away from the road. You cross a seasonal drainage, enter into, and then skirt a dense stand of aspen and subalpine fir. Around a hillside you begin a descent into the heavily vegetated canyon of Daves Creek. As you head down, aspen, subalpine fir and whitebark pine tower over

Lush foliage surrounding Daves Creek

lush riparian vegetation. Cross the stream and begin to climb up the far bank. Immediately beyond the crossing, a gushing spring spills water over moss-covered rocks amid willows and wildflowers, including monkey flowers and bluebells.

Leave the cool shade by the creek and climb along a sagebrush-covered hillside. As you scale the slopes of Palomino Bench, impressive views open up through the clear air north into Idaho. On very clear days you can see the mountains of southern Idaho, 200 miles away. A small pocket of aspen and subalpine fir along a seasonal drainage is all that interrupts the expansive slope of sagebrush and grasses. The trail merges into an old jeep road leading to a wooden cattle trough, watered by a pipe from a spring-fed, trickling creek. Continue to gently ascend the tablelands. Just past the junction with another old road heading south, follow a single-track trail branching left. A short distance farther, you pass one more jeep road coming down the hillside to the right used by outfitters from Sawmill Ridge. After this junction your trail begins a mild descent off Palomino Bench toward the deep canyon of the East Fork Jarbidge River, passing the Wilderness boundary at 1.6 miles from the trailhead.

Beyond the boundary the trail begins to descend in earnest through thick forest of aspen, subalpine fir and limber pine. After the first of many switchbacks, the path leaves the dense forest for open slopes of sagebrush and widely scattered limber pines. The view of the massive canyons of the East Fork Jarbidge River system up to the crest of the range around Gods Pocket Peak is staggering. Follow switchbacks down grassy slopes to a bench where the grade eases somewhat before dropping steeply into the canyon of Three Day Creek. Descend steeply alongside the fir-and-aspen-lined creek for a half mile before the trail traverses away from the canyon and drops to the confluence with the East Fork, 4.4 miles from the trailhead.

Contrary to what appears on the topo, you must ford the East Fork to the trail on the east side. This crossing can be extremely hazardous during snow melt. Once on the other side, proceed south up the East Fork Jarbridge River Trail 0.3 mile to a junction with the Slide Creek Trail, 4.7 miles from the Three Day Creek trailhead.

From the junction with the Slide Creek Trail, the main trail crosses Slide Creek and climbs a low hillside above the far bank. The trail continues upstream along the East Fork Jarbridge River amid cottonwoods and subalpine firs with mountain mahogany and juniper dotting the hillsides. On the opposite bank, 0.8 mile from the junction, Fall Creek joins the East Fork. An unmaintained trail traces the canyon upstream before ascending the upper canyon to Sawmill Ridge (see Trip 3). Another 1.7 miles of gentle ascent along the river deliver you to the junction with the Cougar Creek Trail, 2.0 miles from Slide Creek. An old wooden sign at the intersection reads: *Cougar Creek*, with an arrow pointing across the river.

Now you cross over the East Fork Jarbridge River to a small campsite and begin the ascent of the Cougar Creek drainage well above the stream through juniper, aspen and mahogany. Just beyond a side stream, the trail descends to cross the creek and climb steeply above the opposite bank on slopes of sagebrush, grasses and wildflowers.

The creek remains well below the trail for a considerable distance, until the canyon begins to bend southwest as you enter a dense forest of aspen with some scattered subalpine fir. As the trail nears the roaring creek, a campsite appears next to the water amid thick fir forest. Continuing up the canyon, the trail arrives at a steep, wide-open slope sprinkled with some young firs—an environment created by an avalanche. A short distance up the trail is an even larger avalanche area. Beyond the snow-swept hillsides, three switchbacks along with some winding trail lead up to an old log cabin near a meadow-covered hillside fed by a spring.

You pass more avalanched hillsides as the trail makes a zigzag ascent up steep hillsides to another old cabin. This structure is in excellent condition, housing many artifacts which are also in good shape. If you examine the cabin, leave everything in the same condition. A short distance farther the trail passes a spring-fed meadow which probably was the water source for the cabin occupant.

Where the trail nears the head of the canyon the Forest Service has regraded the trail from the original path, which headed directly up the steepening canyon. A moderate, zigzagging ascent, incorporating six switchbacks, leads through limber pine to a pass on a ridge separating Cougar Creek from the upper East Fork Jarbridge River between Cougar and Prospect peaks. Beautiful views stretch above Cougar Creek out to the mountains of Idaho to the north and down into the deep canyon below Marys River Peak to the south.

Slide Creek and East Fork Jarbridge River canyons

A gray, gravel path leads down the back side of the ridge from the pass into limber pine and down to another series of switchbacks. As the trail descends, Emerald Lake appears below through light forest of limber pine and subalpine fir. At the bottom of the switchbacks the trail reaches the upper basin and passes a secluded campsite surrounded by stunted pines. A short, gentle stroll brings you to the northeast shore of Emerald Lake, 7.4 miles from the Slide Creek junction.

Emerald Lake, so named for the beautiful green complexion of the water, is a precious gem cradled beneath the red-tinged rock of 10,559-foot Cougar Peak. The serene water reflects a mirror image of the surrounding beauty. Encircled by a horseshoe basin of jagged cliffs, the lake reposes in its lofty perch above the canyon of the East Fork Jarbidge River, 1800 feet below. Scattered pines adorn the shoreline and wildflowers crown the inlet and outlet streams. A mild rise above the east shore has campsites, the nicest one above the far end of the lake. Emerald Lake shelters a healthy population of brook trout. Mornings at the 9,400-foot lake can be chilly but the sunrises are spectacular sights.

From the lake, make a mild descent south to a three-way junction with the trail coming over the ridge from Jarbidge Lake. A sign at the intersection reads: *Cougar Creek Trail, Emerald Lake* (back, north), *Jarbidge Lake* (ahead, south) and *E. Fork Jarbidge River* (left, east). Continue straight ahead a short distance down the trail to an inconspicuous, unmarked 'T' junction: The East Fork Trail actually bends ninety degrees to the left as the use trail, apparently more heavily used, continues straight ahead another three-quarters mile before terminating at an outfitter's camp. The junction, perhaps marked by a duck, is easily missed, so pay close attention as you hike—if you come to a tarn on a long bench you have come too far.

From the primitive intersection, the trail descends through small, widely distributed pines and firs, grasses and scattered wildflowers. A quarter mile down the trail you reach a horse camp operated by one of the local outfitters in a small, open flat surrounded by tall conifers. A somewhat obscure section of the trail bends sharply away from the flat, heading toward the canyon. The path, perhaps marked by ducks, descends across open terrain, becoming a distinct track again a short distance down the slope. Then the trail starts to descend more sharply into the deep canyon of the East Fork, crossing seasonal streams and passing through grasslands. The grasses give way to sagebrush as the trail nears the mahogany-lined creek.

Head down the trail as it parallels the East Fork Jarbidge River, passing over numerous side drainages cradled by lush foliage. Just before the canyon bends north, the trail reaches a junction with the Camp Creek Trail, 2.6 miles from Emerald Lake and 10.0 miles from Slide Creek. Two wooden signs mark the junction, the first one reading: *Slide Creek 7.0, Pole Creek Ranger Station 13.7, Camp Creek 4.5, Hummingbird Spring 12.3* and *Marys River 14.5*. The other sign states: *Emerald Lake Trail, Emerald Lake 4.5* and *Jarbidge Canyon Road 10.3*. The Camp Creek Trail crosses the cottonwood- and subalpine-fir-lined river and heads up the drainage to a pass above Camp Creek.

Continue down the East Fork over a small spring-fed creek, across dry, shrubby slopes and past a small talus slide before winding down to a crossing of the river, three-quarter mile from the Camp Creek junction. As at the other fords, crossing the East Fork Jarbidge River can be dangerous in early season.

Another quarter mile downstream, new trail differs from what appears on the topo. According to the Forest Service, avalanches decimated parts of the trail during the winter of 1986-87, resulting in the relocation of 3 miles of trail away from the bottom of the canyon. The relocated trail heads into a side canyon, crossing the diminutive side stream amid subalpine fir, cottonwood and aspen and begins a series of five switchbacks up the mahogany- and juniper-covered hillside. Once the path has gained significant elevation, a traverse leads back into the main canyon of the East Fork well above the river. Proceed across the hillside through grasses, sagebrush, wildflowers and occasional limber pine and mahogany to the next side canyon. A short descent leads to a crossing of the creek which drains this side canyon.

From the creek the trail ascends through scattered mountain mahogany up and over the next ridge, where you find excellent views down the East Fork drainage. On the crest the trail wanders through grasses, mahogany, occasional subalpine fir and limber pine. After a level section along the top of the ridge the trail descends again into the next lateral drainage. Cross the stream near a dramatic cascade surrounded by subalpine firs. Another

200 feet bring you to a crossing of a minor tributary of the main creek before the trail climbs out of this canyon via a couple of switchbacks.

The trail curves around to the crest of another short rise before a series of short switchbacks through aspens and firs lead to a long traverse into the next side canyon. You traverse the next hillside and make a quick climb to the top before a short descent curves around into yet another side canyon, this one thick with aspen, pine and fir. Two switchbacks lead across open terrain and briefly back into aspen, pine and fir before you continue amid grasses, wildflowers and mahogany. Hop over another drainage and continue downstream above the East Fork Jarbidge River before a steep descent links back with the old trail.

Now the old trail crosses a couple of side streams, alternating through sagebrush and grasses above the river and cottonwoods and subalpine fir along the bottom of the canyon. Where the trail follows an old road bed, campsites appear in a large flat next to the river. A side trail, branching toward the river, leads across the East Fork to a horse packer's camp. A short distance farther, you reach the junction with the Cougar Creek Trail, 15.4 miles from the Slide Creek junction. Follow the previously hiked trail another 2.0 miles to the junction with the Slide Creek Trail, completing the 17.4 mile loop. Retrace your steps either 6.0 miles to the Slide Creek trailhead or 4.7 miles to the Three Day Creek trailhead.

Trip 3 ⛺
FALL CREEK

Trip Type: Dayhike or overnight backpack
Distance: 3.6 miles round trip to Fall Creek
7.2 miles round trip to E. Fork Jarbidge River Trail
Season: Mid-June to early October
Water: Spring, creek (may be dry in late season)
Access: Rough dirt road, high-clearance vehicle necessary
Maps: #10
Robinson Creek & Gods Pocket Peak 7.5 minute quadrangles, 1986 (provisional)
Jarbidge Wilderness map, Humboldt National Forest, 1994
Humboldt National Forest map, Mountain City & Jarbidge Ranger Districts, 1990

Introduction: Seldom seen from this vantage, the views from the upper part of the Fall Creek Trail are some of the most spectacular in the Jarbidge Wilderness. A long traverse through open terrain allows for continuous vistas of the central Jarbidge crest, the deep canyons of the East Fork Jarbidge River system and distant points in Idaho. The trail begins near 9,000 feet on top of Sawmill Ridge, 2500 feet above the mouth of the Fall Creek canyon. Stunning views begin almost immediately and continue as the trail drops steeply and then makes a long descending traverse over to Fall Creek.

The road to the trailhead is fairly rough, particularly over the last couple of miles, making the use of a high-clearance vehicle an absolute necessity. The primitive trail is in fairly good condition in the upper section. Farther along, the path is difficult to follow as it parallels Fall Creek down to a junction with the East Fork Trail. If your plan is to hike the full length of the trail, be prepared for some bushwacking over numerous deadfalls and thick brush. In spite of these difficulties, the Fall Creek Trail is well worth the effort.

Trailhead: (d) Follow directions for Three Day Creek in Trip 2 to the unmarked junction with the road to the Three Day Creek trailhead, 11.7 miles from the Rogerson-Three Creek Road at Murphy's Hot Springs. At the junction, continue straight ahead on the main road (Forest Service Road #283) as it heads south through thick forest. The surface becomes rough, impassable to anything but a high-clearance vehicle. Reach a 'Y' junction at 12.6 miles and bear left. Cross Daves Creek 0.2 mile farther and proceed the last 0.5 mile to the end of the road at Sawmill Ridge and the unsigned trailhead, 13.3 miles from the highway. Outfitters have used the Fall Creek trailhead as a staging area, so you must park your car away from their facilities. An old road branches left from the trailhead and heads northeast from Sawmill Ridge, eventually connecting with the Three Day Creek Trail just before the Wilderness boundary.

Description: From Sawmill Ridge the unsigned trail proceeds along the continuation of the road through a wooden pole gate marked with a wilderness boundary sign. You descend through subalpine-fir and limber-pine forest, continuing on a single-track footpath where the road bends to the right. Momentarily lost in a large, grassy clearing, the trail reappears on the far side. Just beyond the clearing, you encounter a small trickle of water emanating from a spring—in late season this may be the only water along the route before the East Fork Jarbidge River. You emerge from thick forest into spectacular views of the canyon stretching into the plains of Idaho.

A series of switchbacks lead sharply downhill through sparsely distributed pine and fir to a long, gradually descending, sweeping traverse of the upper slopes above the Fall Creek basin. Across the grass- and sagebrush-covered slopes, expansive views of the canyons and the Jarbidge crest abound. Cross a couple of seasonal drainages before the long traverse arrives at the northern tributary of Fall Creek. From the creek follow the path as it descends along the drainage amid dense subalpine fir. Soon the unmaintained trail crosses the creek and disappears in a tangle of deadfalls and lush vegetation.

The seldom-traveled trail down Fall Creek receives no maintenance and consequently remains somewhat obscure. Although the actual path is hard to locate in places, the general direction of the route is easy to discern as it follows the creek down to a junction with the East Fork Jarbidge River Trail. If bushwacking down the drainage seems unappealing, the views on the way down to the creek from Sawmill Ridge are enough of a reward in themselves.

Retrace your steps back to the trailhead.

Trip 4 🌲

GOD'S POCKET PEAK TRAIL

Trip Type: 2 to 3 day backpack; Out and back
Distance: 18.8 miles round trip to Right Fork Camp Creek
Season: Late June to early October
Access: Dirt road
Water: Springs & creek
Maps: #12

Goat Creek & Gods Pocket Peak 7.5 minute quadrangles, 1986 (provisional)
Jarbidge Wilderness map, Humboldt National Forest, 1994
Humboldt National Forest map, Mountain City & Jarbidge Ranger Districts, 1990

Introduction: Solitude appears to be an accepted staple of the Jarbidge Wilderness, but even the horse packers seem to shy away from the God's Pocket Peak Trail, in spite of the fact that some of the most picturesque scenery in the wilderness occurs along this route. From the very beginning spectacular vistas reign as the chief attribute of this trip, and each step of the way seems to offer more stunning glimpses of ranges and canyons. Midway through the trip, a 3-mile traverse on narrow trail clinging to precipitous slopes (probably the reason horse packers avoid this route) offers near-constant panoramas of the vast Nevada landscape.

Campsites are few but so is the demand, and some offer excellent perches from which to drink in the views and perhaps awake to spectacular sunrises. If you're planning a trip for late season, the availability of water will be a consideration for the location of your campsites. At a junction 9.4 miles from the trailhead, the God's Pocket Peak Trail connects with three other trails, providing a nearly endless opportunity to travel through other magnificent areas of the Jarbidge Wilderness.

The one unfortunate aspect of this trip is the damage that cattle or sheep have done to the area around Hummingbird Spring. Hooves have totally ravaged the lush meadow surrounding the spring, and one can only imagine how polluted the water is from the urine and feces of that many animals.

Trailhead: (e) Follow directions to the Slide Creek trailhead in Trip 2 to the junction 16.2 miles from the Rogerson-Three Creek Road.

From the junction with the road to the Slide Creek trailhead, continue straight (south) on Road #284, following the arrow on the sign marked: *Hummingbird*. You follow a fence line, reaching a 'Y' junction at 17.3 miles where you bear left along an old pole fence for a quarter mile until the road bends and climbs toward the top of a ridge. Come to the end of the road and the trailhead on the crest of a broad ridge, 18.5 miles from Murphy's Hot Springs. Near the trailhead underneath some pines are a couple of dry campsites.

Description: The trail follows the continuation of the old road as it heads south along the crest of the broad, grassy ridge. Scattered limber pines grow sporadically along the edge of the knoll. Small chips of obsidian testify to the volcanic nature of the area as the trail continues along the crest. Some campsites appear, providing spectacular views across the East Fork Jarbidge River drainage to the Jarbidge Range, including 10,838-foot Matterhorn Peak. Continue along the ridge until the old road is briefly interrupted by a single-track trail descending from the crest through low sagebrush and grasses to a bench where the road resumes.

Momentarily enter an area of subalpine fir, limber pine and aspen before breaking out of the forest into a wide-open clearing of sagebrush and grasses. God's Pocket Peak looms large in the near distance. A moderate descent leads to Hummingbird Spring near a broad, sloping meadow. Unfortunately, grazing has decimated the area around the spring. When I was there during September of 1996, stock had completely trashed the entire meadow, and to make matters worse, a dead, fly-infested and thoroughly putrid-smelling cow was rotting a mere 15 feet from the water. If ever there was a graphic picture of the disadvantages of allowing grazing within wilderness areas, the appalling scene around Hummingbird Spring would have to be it.

Follow the trail down the hillside 200 yards from Hummingbird Spring to a trail junction near the creek originating from the spring. Two signs appear at the junction, 2.6 miles from the trailhead. The first reads: *Cottonwood Trail, Camp Creek 7.6, Marys River 21.6* and the second sign states: *Gods Pocket Peak Trail, E. Fork 11.3, Marys River 15.8*. Head across the creek, continuing on the God's Pocket Peak Trail around and over an open hillside.

A gradual descent leads through sagebrush, grasses and wildflowers into the Cottonwood Creek drainage. As you approach the first ravine, mountain mahogany, aspen, subalpine fir and limber pine begin to appear along the slopes. In an open meadow fringed with firs, the trail passes below a pipe carrying water from a spring emerging from the hillside. You cross over another seasonal stream and hike into the aspen-lined banks of the main channel of Cottonwood Creek, 4 miles from the trailhead. On the far side of the creek a faint use trail leads upstream to a pleasant campsite nestled under subalpine firs.

God's Pocket Peak

A steep climb leads away from the creek onto a hillside covered with pine and fir. The grade eases near a small knoll and the forest thins as the trail makes a curving traverse around the upper part of the hill to a saddle. From this saddle, you head south from God's Pocket Peak as the trail dips in and out of drainages on a long traverse below the crest of the range before dropping steeply down into Camp Creek.

Shortly after the trail begins traversing below the steep slopes of God's Pocket Peak, it passes a willow-lined channel where a spring sends a tiny trickle of water across the path. The track becomes a bit rocky as it passes below steep cliffs through widely scattered limber pine and subalpine fir. Fabulous views are your constant companion throughout this traverse, including the East Humboldt and Ruby Mountain ranges off in the distance to the southeast.

The traverse continues past four seasonal drainages in and out of light forest to the top of a minor ridge where a campsite sits in an open, grassy area surrounded by some firs and pines. Although you will have to travel a considerable distance back to the stream for water, the views from this grassy perch should more than make up for this minor inconvenience if you camp here.

From the ridge the trail leads back into light forest and contours around into the next canyon to a lushly vegetated spring. From the spring the trail ascends more steeply through scattered limber pines to a pass south of Divide Peak, 7.9 miles from the trailhead.

A steep, switchbacking descent awaits you on the other side of the pass as the trail drops 1,250 feet in 1.5 miles to Right Fork Camp Creek. You must leave the views behind at the pass below Divide Peak and travel through thick subalpine-fir forest. Camping is available around the creek.

One can continue another 1.9 miles to the Camp Creek junction with trails leading down Camp Creek, East Fork Jarbidge River and Marys River for longer excursions in the Jarbidge Wilderness. The trail from Right Fork to the Camp Creek junction is mostly uphill.

OTHER TRAILS

Mary's River Trail: From a remote trailhead near the southeast corner of the Wilderness, the Marys River Trail follows the Marys River up the canyon 4 miles to a junction. The trail to the right heads into Marys River Basin eventually connecting with the Camp Creek Trail. One could loop around Marys River Peak and connect back with the Marys River Trail via the route down West Marys River.

Camp Draw Trail: The Camp Draw Trail provides access into the Wilderness from the west. The trail climbs up to a pass above the Camp Draw drainage and then leads down to the West Marys River Trail.

Camp Creek Trail: From another remote eastside trailhead a trail goes steeply up Camp Creek through lush riverine vegetation and interesting rock formations to junctions with the Marys River Basin Trail and God's Pocket Peak Trail (Trip 4).

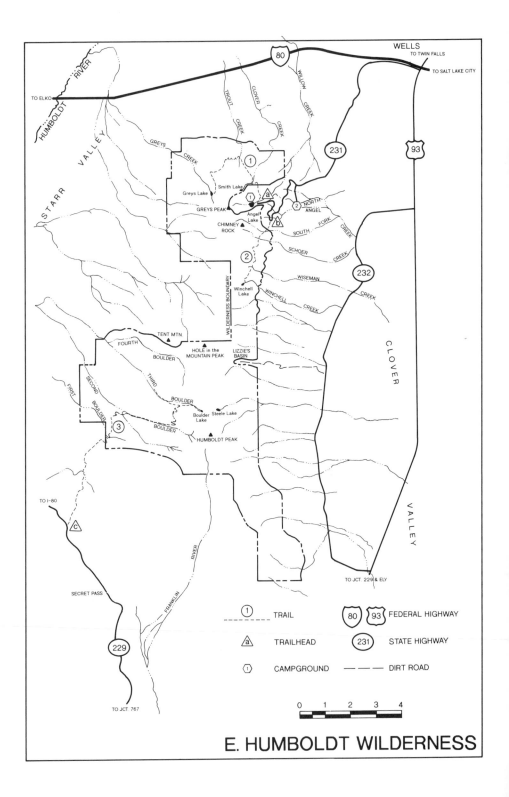

Symbol	Meaning	Symbol	Meaning
①‒‒‒‒‒ TRAIL		80 93 FEDERAL HIGHWAY	
Ⓐ TRAILHEAD		231 STATE HIGHWAY	
① CAMPGROUND		‒ ‒ ‒ DIRT ROAD	

0   1   2   3   4

E. HUMBOLDT WILDERNESS

Chapter 7
EAST HUMBOLDT WILDERNESS

The East Humboldt mountain range is a compact version of the neighboring Ruby Mountains to the southwest. Serrated peaks, glaciated basins and alpine lakes are all present in smaller numbers, as well as many rushing streams, wildflower-laden meadows and spectacular views. Just as Lamoille Canyon is a popular destination in the Rubies for recreationists and onlookers, Angel Lake also draws a good share of sightseers, picnickers, fishermen and campers. Slightly less known than its more prestigious neighbor, the East Humboldt Wilderness, comprising 36,000 acres, offers an uncrowded backcountry experience away from the Angel Lake area.

Typical of many of the Nevada mountain ranges, the East Humboldt mountains trend north and south along a spiny backbone of high peaks for 25 miles between Interstate 80 and State Route 229. The apex occurs in the middle of the range at 11,306-foot Hole in the Mountain Peak, where Lizzie's Window forms a natural break in the skyline. The next highest mountain in the chain, 3½ miles south of Hole in the Mountain Peak, is Humboldt Peak at 11,020 feet. In addition to these peaks, most of the East Humboldt crest towers over 10,000 feet, nearly 5,000 feet above the surrounding desert valleys. The rugged nature of these mountains lends a dramatic alpine flavor to the range.

An unfortunate similarity with the Ruby Mountains is the access restrictions due to private property along the western flank of the East Humboldt Wilderness. Many unmaintained trails head up canyons from the west into the heart of the mountains providing potentially superb hiking, but they remain inaccessible and untrammeled as the roads to the trailheads cross private property. As in the Rubies, the Forest Service is supposedly involved in ongoing negotiations to acquire access easements across some of the private land. The Secret-Starr trailhead into the Boulders Region at the southwest corner of the Wilderness is an example of a public-access easement through private property within National Forest land. Easements across private land outside the National Forest will be harder to obtain.

As mentioned in the chapter about the Ruby Mountains, the East Humboldts benefit from more moisture than most Nevada mountain ranges receive. The additional precipitation, combined with the impenetrable characteristic of the metamorphic rock, which keeps water near the surface, provides the basis for a very lush and damp environment, unlike the typical Nevada wilderness area. Most of the moisture falls as winter snow but be prepared for summer thunderstorms at any time.

An abundance of wildlife roams the East Humboldt mountains but do not expect to see many of the mule deer, mountain goats, bighorn sheep or mountain lions while on the trail. Animals are still timid in this range, as human contact is low. You may hear coyotes and will probably see some of the rodents that scurry around, as well as some examples of the wide variety of fowl endemic to the region. Fishing is good in the lakes and streams for brook, rainbow and cutthroat trout.

Whether you desire high alpine peaks, cirque basins with deep-blue lakes, meadows rife with wildflowers, or aspen-lined creeks, the East Humboldt Wilderness has something for just about everyone. Solitude is typically available in large doses throughout the area, with the possible exception of during hunting season, which is easily the most popular time in the East Humboldt backcountry. Off-trail exploration, extremely well suited to the region, provides opportunities for really getting away from it all. Mountaineers should find ample reasons for scaling the peaks and climbing the vertical walls. Even if you are just looking for a picturesque spot to enjoy for a few hours or a day, Angel Lake is hard to beat.

LOCATION
The East Humboldt Wilderness, located in the northeast part of the state just southwest of the town of Wells, is bordered by Interstate 80 on the north, US 93 and State Route 232 on the east, and State Route 229 on the south and west.

CAMPGROUNDS
1. ANGEL LAKE CAMPGROUND $
Open June through September
Camping, Restrooms, Picnicking, Water, Fishing, Trailhead
At the end of State Highway 231, 11.5 miles from US 93 in Wells

2. ANGEL CREEK CAMPGROUND $
Open May through October
Camping, Restrooms, Picnicking, Water
Located 1 mile off State Highway 231, 7.3 miles from US 93 in Wells

RESOURCES
Around the perimeter of the East Humboldt Wilderness, the town of Wells is the only community offering the bare necessities of gas, food and lodging. The closest town with adequate outdoor supplies is Elko, 50 miles west of Wells. See the Ruby Mountains Wilderness chapter for a list of outdoor suppliers in Elko.

OUTFITTERS/GUIDES

There are three licensed services operating in the East Humboldts providing trips into the Wilderness for recreation and hunting.

HUMBOLDT OUTFITTERS
HC 60 Box 160
Wells, NV 89835
(702) 752-3714

SECRET PASS OUTFITTERS
HC 69 Box 685
Ruby Valley, NV 89833
(702) 779-2226

NEVADA HIGH COUNTRY
OUTFITTERS & GUIDE SERVICE
PO Box 483
Carlin, NV
(702) 754-6851

FOREST SERVICE

Ruby Mountains Ranger District
428 South Humboldt
PO Box 246
Wells, NV 89825
(702) 752-3357

Humboldt National Forest
976 Mountain City Highway
Elko, NV 89801
(702) 738-5171

Trip 1 🌲

GREYS LAKE TRAIL

Trip Type: Dayhike or overnight backpack; Out and back
Distance: 10.6 miles round trip
Season: Late June through mid-October
Access: Paved road
Water: Available in creeks and lake
Map: #14
Welcome 7.5 minute quadrangle, 1967
Humboldt National Forest map, Ruby Mountains Ranger District, 1990
Ruby Mountains & East Humboldt Wildernesses, Humboldt National Forest, 1994

Introduction: This hike will take you from one spectacular subalpine lake to another in little more than 5 miles. You may start out in a mass of humanity (by Nevada standards) but in spite of the short distance you will end up with some degree of seclusion. Angel Lake, at the end of the paved highway, seems to be a satisfactory objective for the vast majority of travelers to this area, and it is a beautiful and dramatic destination offering camping, fishing, picnicking and sight-seeing. Greys Lake offers all of those activities and more. As well as the potential for solitude, bountiful displays of a wide variety of wildflowers grace the trail and particularly the lake basin. You can explore the lush basin above the lake and even climb Greys Peak. An off-trail route is also available to remote Smith Lake.

From the lake, looking down Greys Creek canyon you can get an excellent view of Starr Valley and the circular irrigation patterns of the ranches along the Humboldt River. Views of the peaks along the crest of the East Humboldts are constant companions along the trail, and the lake sits in a dramatic basin of steep rock walls and pinnacles.

Trailhead: (a) Take the *West Wells* exit #351 from Interstate 80, turning south onto U.S. 93, following a sign for *Angel Lake*. Just past the freeway turn east onto two-lane State Route 231, signed: *Angel Lake*. At 0.75 mile is another sign: *Angel Creek 8, Angel Lake 12*. Follow the paved road parallel to the freeway for 1.2 miles through sagebrush and scattered pinyon pine. The road bends and climbs a small hill beyond which the dramatic east side of the East Humboldt Range comes into view. Proceed along the hill for a couple of miles with the mountains looming above to your right before bending west and crossing the small valley drained by Willow Creek. Across the valley you enter Forest Service land at 7.0 miles from U.S. 93 and start to climb up the east side of the East Humboldt Range. At 7.3 miles is the signed turnoff on the left to Angel Creek Campground. From the turnoff the paved road narrows, steepens and winds up the foothills. Pass the Winchell Lake trailhead (see Trip 2) at 9.7 miles.

Continue to climb up hillsides covered with sagebrush and tall grass, dotted with groves of aspens and shrubs near the water. Spectacular views of Chimney Rock, Greys Peak and numerous cascades greet you as you round a curve in the highway. Turn right at 11.5 miles where a sign states: *Humboldt National Forest Campground, Angel Lake*. More signs direct you immediately to the right again to the trailhead for the Greys Lake Trail.

The trailhead has parking for 20 to 25 cars and a stock-loading area. Restrooms and running water are in the adjacent campground. At the end of the road is Angel Lake, an impressive little lake set in a dramatic basin rimmed by towering peaks, a truly heavenly site. Picnicking and fishing are two favorite activities at the lake. The area plays host to many outdoor enthusiasts and tourists during summer weekends, but leaving them all behind is a simple task involving only a few steps up the trail.

Description: The trail starts from the upper end of the parking area, climbing away from the lake up a hillside covered with young aspens and wildflowers. About 100 yards from the parking lot, a use trail from the campground meets your trail at a switchback and you continue to climb through shrubs and flowers. At the top of a short rise you reach a fence with a steel gate blocking access to grazing livestock from the Angel Lake area. Looking back you get a good look at the lake area with Greys Peak and Chimney Rock dominating the skyline. Continue the climb as the

Angel Lake area from Greys Lake Trail

vegetation shifts from lush shrubs and flowers to sagebrush. In the distance you can see the town of Wells and a piece of ribbonlike I-80. At the top of the ridge the trail reaches the Wilderness boundary.

From the boundary the trail begins a descent into the Clover Creek drainage, passing through drier and rockier terrain, where the tallest plants are scattered blue lupines. As you descend and draw closer to the creek, the vegetation begins to flourish again, until it virtually chokes the stream with aspens and brush. Clover Creek, which drains Smith Lake in the basin above, is broad but shallow and is easy to cross.

Your trail climbs up from the creek, switchbacking after 75 yards, and makes a long, ascent to the top of another ridge. From here the route traverses the northeast slopes, where you see the first lonely examples of limber pine amid the wildflowers. Views up the head of the valley are quite nice with rugged peaks rising above green-carpeted slopes. The traverse reaches the edge of a broad, sweeping canyon through which Trout Creek flows on its journey to the Humboldt River. A moderately steep descent of 700 feet leads to the bottom of the canyon, and in a dense grove of mature aspens deposits you at Trout Creek. An old sign nailed to one of the aspen trees reads: *Pole Canyon Angel Lake Trail, Trout Creek, Angel Lake 3 miles.* In actuality, the trailhead back at Angel Lake is only 2.5 miles away. Cross the creek with the aid of a couple of downed aspen snags.

For almost a mile of steep, winding ascent, the trail climbs out of Trout Creek canyon on the way to another ridge top. Head past another grove of aspens kept alive and thriving by a subterranean water supply. The long climb ends after a series of switchbacks terminate in a notch at the low point of the upper ridge below a peak sparsely forested with limber pines.

A large cairn and a long rock propped upright by previous travelers mark the windswept pass.

Continuing, a mild, rocky descent leads to a small, lush, green meadow where the previously distinct trail falters for a short stretch. A well-placed old sign, simply stating: *Trail*, points hikers in the right direction across the meadow. From the meadow the trail climbs again, wandering through limber pines up to yet another ridge top just below point 9210 on the topo.

A 1-mile descent is all that now separates you from Greys Lake. The trail switchbacks from the top of the ridge to a point where scattered limber pines allow unobstructed views of the lake and the surrounding canyon. Nestled in a basin rimmed by steep cliffs on the south and west, round Greys Lake sits below a large, sloping basin to the east that runs up toward the jagged summit of Greys Peak. Greys Creek tumbles in the canyon below, periodically cascading over low rock walls. More switchbacks beneath scattered limber pines eventually get you to the lakeshore, 5.3 miles from the trailhead.

Greys Lake is tucked into the head of a basin surrounded by high, rocky peaks on three sides. Green, sloping hillsides covered with wildflowers rise up to gray rock cliffs that pierce the clear Nevada skies. Snow fields cling to cracks and crevices on the north-facing ridge line well into summer. At the crest of the north part of the range, Greys Peak at 10,674 feet stands guard over the lake, rising nearly 2,000 feet from the water's edge. Scattered limber pines dot the gentler slopes around the shoreline. Sparkling, clear water rushes down the inlet stream into the lake from a meadow basin above the south shore. Greys Creek gently flows from the lake at the outlet before cascading out of the cirque basin in a series of short steps down the steep canyon.

Greys Lake offers limited campsites. In fact, the entire basin has a pristine, almost untouched appearance. The only truly developed site is above the lake on the west shore next to the main trail. During the height of summer, horse packers make a semi-permanent base camp out of this area, so you will probably need to camp elsewhere. Other possibilities include near the outlet of the lake and above the south shore by the inlet. Firewood is in limited supply.

Fishing at Greys Lake has the potential to be quite good for brook and cutthroat trout and you can access almost the entire shore. If further exploration sounds appealing, you can follow a faint use trail up into the upper basin to find a small pond, a marshy meadow and even more dramatic views of the cliffs and peaks above. The upper basin offers splendid scenery and spectacular views as well as the opportunity to climb Greys Peak.

Off-trail Route to Smith Lake: Return to Clover Creek, 1.2 miles from the trailhead, to begin the cross-country route to Smith Lake. A use trail heads off in the proper direction from the switchback above the north bank of the creek but quickly fades near the dense brush of the creek bottom. From this

Smith Lake

point find the least brushy way up the slopes ahead to the lake, not always an easy task. You can cross the creek where the brush is less dense or find a route away from the creek in the sagebrush. Whichever way you choose, head for three dead snags on the steep, boulder-covered hillside ahead where the brush lessens. Once above the steep slopes the grade eases and eventually you reach the northeast edge of Smith Lake 0.4 mile from the trail.

Talus slopes sprinkled with isolated limber pines lead up to rugged cliffs that envelop the clear water of the lake. Near the outlet stream, denser stands of limber pine provide some shade for two campsites. Fishing is excellent for a variety of fish including cutthroat, golden and American grayling trout. However, thick brush creates a barrier limiting access around the north lakeshore. A small, man-made dam at the outlet, built for some unknown purpose, is now of little consequence.

You can return to the trail the same way you came up or by another route that traverses east on a use trail to the shoulder of a small peak. From the lake follow cairns to a large, isolated pine tree on this shoulder. From there descend on a very faint use trail paralleling, but a good distance from, a barbed-wire fence. Pick your way through sagebrush down to the trail, and retrace your steps to the parking lot at Angel Lake.

Trip 2
WINCHELL LAKE TRAIL

Trip Type: Dayhike or overnight backpack; Out and back
Distance: 6.2 miles round trip
Season: Mid-June to late October
Access: Paved road
Water: Available in creeks and lake
Maps: #14
Welcome and *Humboldt Peak* 7.5 minute quadrangles, 1967, 69
Humboldt National Forest map, Ruby Mountains Ranger District, 1990
Ruby Mountains & East Humboldt Wildernesses, Humboldt National Forest, 1994

Introduction: The trip to Winchell Lake can be either a short day hike or an overnight backpack into the heart of the east side of the East Humboldt Wilderness. The distance is just over 3 miles and the elevation gain is a mild 1,000 feet, making for a relatively gentle hike. Because of this ease, that the trail does not receive more use is something of a wonder. Plenty of water courses through the numerous creeks en route to the lake, and a wide variety of plants and wildflowers are bountiful as well. There are excellent views of the East Humboldt peaks at numerous points along the route, and two scenic basins—one along the way and one that contains the lake. Winchell Lake offers scenery, solitude, the opportunity for further exploration and a chance to see a great sunrise.

Trailhead: (b) Follow directions in Trip 1 to the Winchell Lake Trailhead. The trailhead is on your left at 9.7 miles from U.S. 93, in the middle of a near-hairpin turn. Parking for a few cars is available up the road on the opposite shoulder.

Description: The well-graded trail to Winchell Lake, not shown on the *Welcome* topo, starts off down the road bank about 5 yards on the downhill side of the highway in lush vegetation of wildflowers and aspens. You quickly cross a small, seasonal stream under the cool shade of the aspens. Beyond the creek, vegetation thins allowing views of Chimney Rock above the green-carpeted hillsides and down into the ranches in the valley below. The trail climbs up and down through vegetation ranging from aspens, brush and wildflowers to dry, sagebrush-covered hillsides. Cross the Wilderness boundary 0.5 mile from the trailhead and shortly thereafter reach the South Fork Angel Creek. In the distance, Chimney Rock looms like a sentinel above the South Fork, which tumbles down the hillside past banks lined with a wide variety of green foliage and wildflowers.

Winchell Lake

In 0.1 mile from the first crossing, you reach another branch of the South Fork. From this area almost the entire crest of the East Humboldts is visible, from Chimney Rock in the north to Humboldt Peak in the south. You skirt a grove of mature aspens and reach the gate of a barbed-wire fence. Pass through the gate into a grassy area where the trail is in danger of being taken over by the tall grass. Then climb some more before descending to Schuer Creek, 1.1 miles from the trailhead.

You cross the brush-choked stream, wind around a hillside and descend to a dry stream. Then the trail grade moderates as it traverses for quite a distance through aspens and tobacco brush. Through the course of this traverse you realize that some four-legged beasts have been here before you: namely beavers, as evidenced by the construction of ponds on the hillside below, and cows, as evidenced by the calling cards left near your feet. The generally level grade continues for about three-quarters mile before it ends in a steeper descent toward the next creek. Just before reaching it you encounter some of the results of that beaver activity up close. The trail skirts a beaver pond, where you can get a very good look into some beaver habitat complete with dam and hut. A seep emanating from a spring a little way further down the trail has seen additional attempts to alter its flow by the big-toothed, hairy rodents. A good dirt path leads away from the construction projects to a curious trail junction where one path continues ahead and another branch climbs uphill 90 degrees to the right. The natural tendency is to go straight, but the uphill trail, marked by a cairn, is the right path.

From this unofficial junction the trail heads west and straight uphill for 75 yards before turning south again, followed by some ups and downs.

Eventually it skirts the edge of a basin on a fairly level traverse through aspens and wildflowers until reaching the edge of little hill. The route then climbs into Wiseman Creek basin, 2.3 miles from the trailhead: a spectacular, horseshoe-shaped amphitheater of dramatic cliffs with a cascade of water tumbling down the sheer rock face. As the trail wanders across the floor of the picturesque basin you expect to cross Wiseman Creek, but the water takes a subterranean path below the marshy ground before emerging in the canyon below. If you have the time, Wiseman Creek basin deserves further exploration.

From the basin the trail ascends a sagebrush-covered hillside, heads back into tobacco brush on an up-and-down course, and then climbs in earnest across a seasonal drainage. Two switchbacks lead to easier trail up into Winchell Lake.

Winchell Lake, at 8,570 feet, sits in another dramatic basin with green, sloping hillsides leading up to steep, jagged peaks. The crest of the range in this area tops out well above 10,000 feet, which is 2,000 vertical feet above the lake. Three triangular-shaped peaklets above the inlet stream form a splendid backdrop for the dark waters of the lake. Lush green meadows at the far end give way to dense green foliage around the rest of the lake. A smattering of limber pines dot the southwest slopes in the otherwise open basin that hosts a diverse range of vegetation. Sunrises are particularly nice as the sun rises directly to the east beyond the Pequop Mountains.

Camping, as in much of the East Humboldt Wilderness, is primitive, with no developed sites at the lake. If spending the night, remember to restore your camp area back to its original state. Firewood is virtually nonexistent. Fishing is good for cutthroat trout. The upper basin provides plenty of opportunities for further exploration, scrambling up the peaks, or potential wildlife viewing. In the early evening you may even hear the serenade of coyotes.

Retrace your steps to the trailhead.

Trip 3 🌲
THE BOULDERS

Trip Type: 2 to 5 day backpack; Out and back
Distance: 23.0 miles round trip
Season: Mid-June through October
Access: Paved highway
Water: Creeks
Maps: #14, 15
Secret Valley, Tent Mountain & *Humboldt Peak* 7.5 minute quadrangles, 1969
Humboldt National Forest map, Ruby Mountains Ranger District, 1990

Ruby Mountains & East Humboldt Wildernesses, Humboldt
National Forest, 1994

Introduction: The Boulders region of the East Humboldt Wilderness is perhaps one of the most superb backcountry areas in the state. The scenery is unparalleled, as are the opportunities for extended explorations into remote canyons. Some of the most luxuriant foliage and most brilliant displays of wildflowers found in the Great Basin occur in this part of the range. A very healthy supply of water, caught by the 11,000-foot crest, supports the vigorous streams, mountain lakes, ponds and vibrant meadows on the west side of the mountains.

Away from the Angel Lake area, the East Humboldts are a characteristically lonely range. Thanks to a long approach, the Boulders become a very seldom-visited part of the Wilderness. Solitude is almost guaranteed. The area, composed of four parallel canyons, is vast, presenting numerous opportunities for exploration and adventure. The ultimate experience in the region is Third Boulder, a luxuriant canyon culminating in subalpine Boulder Lake at the head of the basin. Cross-country routes lead to two additional lakes and the summit of Humboldt Peak. The route description here heads into the Boulders from Secret-Starr trailhead, ascends Second Boulder and crosses the ridge crest into Third Boulder.

The Boulders region typifies the major problem facing nearly all the Nevada wilderness areas. A lack of funding has made necessary maintenance for many of the trails virtually impossible. The Boulders have suffered from this neglect, and many of the trails, which pass through some of the most densely vegetated areas in the state, appear overgrown and have even vanished in places. If this situation persists, we will have lost access to a tremendous resource.

Trailhead: (c) From Interstate 80 east of Elko and west of Wells, take the *Halleck, Ruby Valley* exit #321. Follow State Route 229 across railroad tracks and the Humboldt River, paralleling Secret Creek along the north end of the Ruby Mountains. Continue on Route 229 for 17.4 miles to the Secret-Starr trailhead on the east side of the pavement. A wide, dirt turnaround provides parking for several cars. If coming from the south, the trailhead is 3.1 miles north of Secret Pass and 18.3 miles north of the junction between State Routes 229 and 767.

Description: The first 4 miles of the Boulders Trail passes over private land via a Forest Service easement. Please stay on the trail and respect the rights of the property owner. Oddly enough, these first 4 miles are in better shape than any of trail in the Wilderness.

From the trailhead, begin hiking up the faint old roadbed past the sign—not the well-traveled road that eventually leads to the ranch. Once on your way the path becomes more distinct as it heads through grasslands and sagebrush. The trail is very well-marked, with posts delineating the passage of every half-mile. At 0.9 mile, the trail begins to follow above a seasonal drainage for three-quarters mile, passing ponds created to supply drinking water for the range cattle. Continue to climb the moderately steep slopes beyond the drainage across a lush meadow where the trail temporarily disappears. Find the trail on the far side of the meadow where it climbs over a hill to expansive views of the west side of the East Humboldt Range.

Now climb above the upper part of Dry Creek through open sagebrush terrain and then cross over the diminutive stream before ascending steep slopes that lead to a traverse over to aspen-lined Dorsey Creek. The route crosses Dorsey Creek three times before forsaking the stream for a half-mile climb to a saddle above the Stephens Creek drainage. A quarter-mile descent deposits the hiker at the southern branch of Stephens Creek, where aspens, shrubs and wildflowers thrive in the moist soil surrounding the stream. Half way to the crossing of the northern branch of Stephens Creek, the trail leaves the private land and enters the East Humboldt Wilderness, 4.6 miles from the trailhead.

Continue through thick brush to a second crossing of Stephens Creek and begin a mile climb along brushy slopes to the ridge crest above First Boulder. From here you find good views up the drainage toward the head of the canyon below 11,306-foot Hole in the Mountain Peak. A steep, three-quarter mile descent from the crest leads through aspens down to the bottom of the canyon and the crossing of First Boulder, 6.4 miles from the trailhead.

Up to here, the trail has been in fairly good shape and easy to follow. However, the crossing of First Boulder is your introduction to the periodically dismal condition of the trails on the west side of the East Humboldt Wilderness. The path seems to disappear at the creek, but in actuality it proceeds through thick brush straight across the stream. During early season you cannot help getting wet here.

A more distinct trail awaits on the other side of First Boulder which leads 300 yards amid lush foliage of aspens, waist-high flowers and tall grasses. Continue to the crossing of Second Boulder, where campsites nestle in a grassy meadow below dense aspens on the far bank of the creek. A couple of downed aspens bridge the creek and help in crossing the flowing stream. A short distance from the creek, still in a dense stand of aspens, the trail reaches the invisible junction with the route up the Second Boulder drainage. Attached to a tree, a small metal sign with faded lettering is all that delineates the otherwise imperceptible intersection. The beginning of the trail up Second Boulder is virtually impossible to follow through waist-high flowers and grasses, but blazes on tree trunks make the impossible task merely improbable. Farther up the canyon the trail becomes slightly more distinct but not easy to track. The only solace emerges from the fact that even though the trail is easy to lose, one cannot become lost since there is just one way to travel up the narrow drainage.

You proceed up the canyon past numerous beaver ponds through dense vegetation ranging in height from knee-high to over your head. That this jungle of foliage could possibly exist within the boundaries of the Great Basin seems hard to believe. Wildflowers include blue and white lupine, daisies, corn lilies and paintbrush. Keep progressing up the canyon as best as you can, following the trail wherever possible. A mile up the drainage, the trail comes next to the creek where whitebark pine begin to appear.

Two-and-one-quarter miles up the drainage, the trail reaches a boggy area created by some springs and surrounded by dense foliage. Now an even more confusing trail situation emerges, as the main path appears to climb steeply above the springs before continuing upstream. Beyond the springs, as shown on the topo, is a junction with a trail heading north over the ridge and down into Third Boulder. However, the junction is extremely obscure. If you cannot find the actual junction, climb up the drier, lightly vegetated slope above the creek and eventually intersect the trail as it heads up the hillside toward the pass.

Ironically, the trail shown on the older topos connecting the four Boulder drainages does not appear on the newer Forest Service maps, in spite of the fact that the actual tread is in much better condition than the trails up the canyons that do appear on the newer maps. Follow the steep trail as it zigzags up the hillside through scattered wildflowers toward the crest that separates Second and Third Boulders. You reach a notch in the ridge at the top of the pass amid widely dispersed limber pine, 9.8 miles from the trailhead. Excellent views of both canyons await you at the pass. Precipitous cliffs and peaks with green rolling hillsides descending into lush green meadows grace each drainage. A large, shallow pond is directly below the pass in Third Boulder.

Now you follow switchbacks down from the crest toward the valley floor. At the beginning of the descent the trail wanders through broadly distributed limber pine and wildflowers, including asters, lupines and daisies. Farther down the slope, columbine, bluebells, forget-me-nots, potentilla, willows and grasses join the pines and other flowers. You reach a bench, 100 vertical feet above the valley, where the trail becomes faint, but it reappears with the aid of some ducks as it heads diagonally down the final slope to the creek. Cross the creek to the north bank, 10.5 miles from the trailhead.

Proceed up Third Boulder amid masses of flowers, passing a pond on your right. Climb a little more steeply toward the upper basin around rocks and through lush vegetation. Cross the creek and continue up through sagebrush intermixed with willows and wildflowers. Soon a smaller pond below Boulder Lake comes into view, quickly followed by the larger lake, at 11.5 miles.

Boulder Lake, at 9500 feet, is a rare gem, nestled into the head of Third Boulder canyon beneath sheer cliffs at the crest of the East Humboldt Range. Humboldt Peak, second highest in the range, sits majestically 1500 feet above the water level. Limber pines and green hillsides form the

Boulder Lake

perfect backdrop to the clear, blue waters of the lake. Gentle, grassy slopes above the south shore provide excellent places to camp. The cool, but not icy, waters actually provide some refreshing swimming. Brilliant sunsets create the exquisite climax to picturesque days at Boulder Lake.

Third Boulder and Boulder Lake offer some excellent opportunities for further rambles in this isolated section of the East Humboldt Wilderness. Just over the crest sits Steele Lake, the second largest in the range. It's unreachable by trail, but the cross-country jaunt over the crest provides the easiest access to this rarely seen body of water. From Boulder Lake work your way up the slopes to the saddle at the crest and carefully descend steeper slopes into the Steele Lake basin. Only those competent in off-trail travel should attempt this route. Be prepared for snow on the east-facing slopes early in the season. An ascent of Humboldt Peak is a relatively easy goal from the saddle above Boulder Lake as well. A 1-mile ascent over moderately steep terrain leads to the summit and incredible views in all directions.

Back down the valley, three-quarters mile west of the junction with the trail over the ridge from Second Boulder, a short, steep, off-trail route leads to aptly named Birdseye Lake, tucked into an airy site along the south wall of the canyon. The most notable obstacle to overcome is the thick brush near the creek that you must negotiate to reach the rocky cliffs below the lake. The reward of a birdseye view comes to the diligent. A good place to begin the ascent is where the trail crosses the creek directly below Birdseye Lake.

Additional excursions in the Boulders region are almost too numerous to count. Be forewarned, however, that trails shown on maps may not exist in the real world. If a loop trip down Third Boulder to the supposedly maintained connecting trail back to the trailhead seems like a logical plan, note that the trail at the bottom of the canyon heading back to Second Boulder appears completely overgrown and impossible to locate.

OTHER TRAILS

Lizzie's Basin: An extremely rough, 4-wheel-drive road heads west from State Highway 232 in Clover Valley on the east side of the range, to spectacular Lizzie's Basin below the rugged cliffs of Hole in the Mountain and Hole in the Mountain Peak. The basin is a worthy destination by itself but there is also an unmaintained trail heading north 3 miles to Winchell Lake. If you can negotiate the drive, Lizzie's Basin is a worthy spot and provides the least difficult approach to the highest peak in the range.

Greys Lake to the Boulders Region: An old trail from Greys Lake to the Boulders appears on the late 1960's vintage 7.5 minute quadrangles but is absent from the more current Forest Service maps. Portions of this trail still exist although much of the route has been lost over time to the forces of nature. The terrain is such that an experienced hiker with good orienteering and cross-country skills could follow this route without much difficulty, with an almost ironclad guarantee of solitude the entire distance. Crossing over the pass at the crest between Boulder and Steele lakes and then connecting with the trail at Lizzie's Basin to go north to the Winchell Lake trailhead could provide a near circumnavigation of the entire range and shorten considerably the necessary car shuttle.

Crest Route: Strong parties with good off-trail abilities have traversed the crest of the East Humboldt Mountains on a multi-day outing.

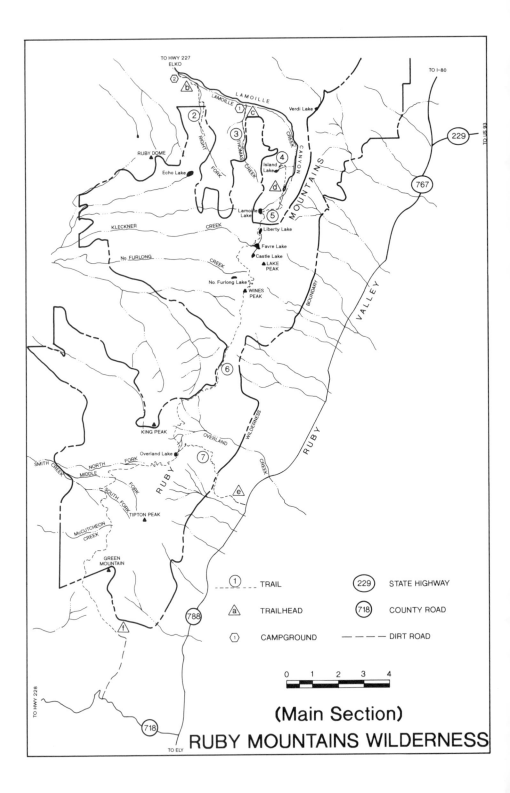

(Main Section)
RUBY MOUNTAINS WILDERNESS

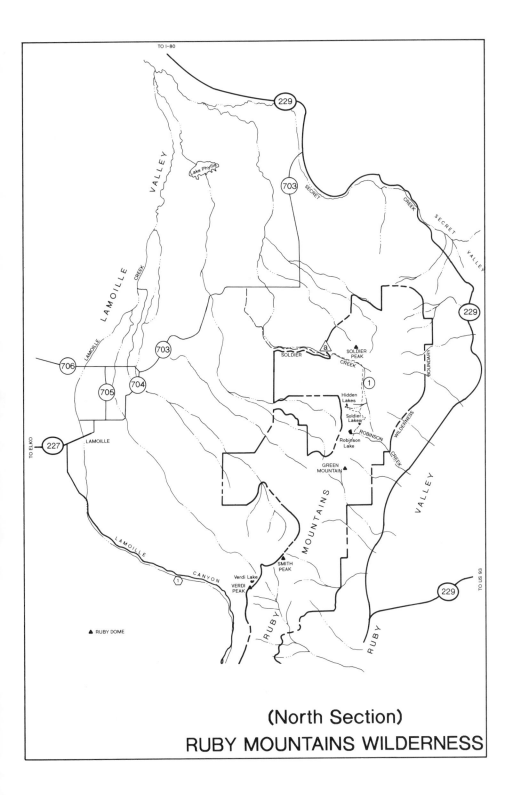

(North Section)
RUBY MOUNTAINS WILDERNESS

Chapter 8
RUBY MOUNTAINS WILDERNESS

Some consider the Ruby Mountains to be the premier range in the entire state of Nevada. Unlike most Nevada ranges, the Ruby Mountains show results of extensive glaciation in the form of deep U-shaped canyons, cirques cradling alpine lakes, hanging valleys, polished rock walls, and jagged, carved summits. Of all the wilderness areas in the state, the Rubies are definitely the most alpine-looking, and first-time visitors will be awestruck that such an environment exists in what they recognize as basically an arid, desert state. Although the Rubies are one of the best known and popular areas in the state, this is still Nevada. Overcrowding is infrequent, most people choosing to congregate around the two trailheads at the end of the Lamoille Canyon road.

The mountains received their name in the 1800's when soldiers of the U.S. Army went west to assist pioneers in their search for routes to California. Driven by a search for gold, the soldiers panned the streams flowing through the Rubies and found garnets, which they mistakenly identified as rubies. The gemstone name was applied to the mountains in which the "jewels" originated, and by the time the error was recognized, the name had stuck. Even though incorrectly applied originally, to this day the Ruby Mountains remain the "crown jewel of the Great Basin."

The Ruby Mountains have something for just about everyone. Auto-bound visitors can enjoy the scenic drive up Lamoille Canyon, dubbed "the Yosemite of Nevada." Although lacking the spectacular waterfalls and granite domes of its more famous counterpart, narrow Lamoille Canyon rewards the traveler with scenic beauty. The breathtaking scenery includes precipitous slopes leading to high, snow-clad, craggy peaks, deep-green, wildflower-covered meadows, and a rushing stream propelled by the icy runoff of countless springs and creeks flowing into the canyon. A variety of roadside turnouts help to explain the natural history of the area, and a short nature trail, the Changing Valley Trail, gives a glimpse into the forces that shaped the canyon. Campgrounds and picnic areas are plentiful along the highway. Hikers, backpackers and equestrians can experience the majesty of the canyon on their way to four of the trailheads in Lamoille Canyon (see Trips 2-5)

The Ruby Mountains have two loosely defined regions. The main part of the range, including the Ruby Crest National Recreation Trail, begins along the Lamoille Canyon road and extends south to the boundary near Harrison Pass. This part of the Rubies, beginning near Lamoille Canyon, contains the majority of dramatic peaks, alpine lakes and high meadows. Approaching Harrison Pass, the rugged topography mellows as the range forms a single, rounded backbone.

The north part of the range is a less-visited and smaller area north of Lamoille Canyon, containing the Soldier Lakes Basin. This part of the Rubies has a smattering of pinnacled rock summits but is mainly characterized by a high, open tundra that gives one the feeling of being at the top of the world. A handful of high lakes in Soldier Lakes Basin provides destinations for the relatively few hikers and anglers who journey into this area

The Ruby Mountains along with their close neighbor, the East Humboldt Mountains, receive more precipitation than most of the other Nevada ranges. Many of the Pacific storms that cross through the Northwest, missing California and Nevada, brush the northeast part of the state, bringing additional moisture to the high mountains of the Rubies and East Humboldts. Due to the impervious nature of the metamorphic rock found in the area, this excess moisture remains near the surface, replenishing lakes, ponds, marshes and meadows. Consequently, the Rubies and East Humboldts appear to be wetter than many of their Nevada counterparts, more reminiscent of other ranges in the western U.S. As one might expect, most of this precipitation falls as snow in the winter, but summer thunderstorms are frequent and notorious as well and can come at any time. Over twenty years ago, as a newcomer to Nevada, I naively journeyed into the Rubies without a tent, considering one to be unnecessary in such a dry region. Needless to say, a summer thunderstorm brewed and poured out its fury, seemingly to scold such arrogance. Fortunately, someone in our party had the foresight to bring a tarp and we became only half-soaked.

An abundance of wildlife inhabits the Ruby Mountains. However, most species are still quite timid of humans, and contact is much less common than in other, more popular, wilderness areas. Mountain goats, bighorn sheep and mule deer are plentiful, while antelope, mountain lions and bobcats are present in smaller numbers. Beavers and other rodents familiar in the mountains are the most likely mammals you will see. Raptors and game birds, such as chukar, partridge and grouse, are prevalent. In addition, the Ruby Mountains provide perhaps the best opportunity of any wilderness area in the state to fish for rainbow, brook and Lahontan cutthroat trout in the many lakes and streams.

The major drawback to the Rubies is the fact that much of the area, even though it benefits from wilderness protection, is effectively out of reach to recreationists, due to a lack of access across the private property that borders a large part of the range. Blocking the entrance to many canyons, particularly along the west side of the Wilderness, is private ranch land or the Te-Moak Indian Reservation. The Forest Service is reportedly involved in sensitive negotiations to acquire rights-of-way for some of these areas, but progress seems slow at best. If you want to reach Ruby Dome, Echo Lake or Cold Lake, for instance, you will have to travel a long distance out of the way cross-country to do so. If you have the time and energy, however, you can almost be guaranteed to experience those pristine places with an abundance of solitude. For the adventurous, much of the Ruby Mountains remain trailless and open for further exploration.

Like many of the other wilderness areas in Nevada, the Ruby Mountains area appears to be a victim of compromise, exhibiting some strange boundary deviations. Although posing little environmental damage, exclusion of an area around Lamoille Canyon allows continuation of heli-skiing operated by private vendors out of the tiny community of Lamoille. Exclusion of other areas has occurred for who knows what reason. Still allowed within the Wilderness in some areas, cattle grazing stretches one's idea of what wilderness really means—beef cows as wild animals?

LOCATION

The Ruby Mountain Wilderness is in the northeastern part of the state, 20 miles southeast of the town of Elko. From Elko, State Routes 227 and 228 provide access from the west. State Route 229 is north and east of the range and State Route 767 continues along the east edge of the mountains. The Harrison Pass Road, State Route 718, connects 228 and 767 at the south edge of the Wilderness.

CAMPGROUNDS

1. THOMAS CREEK CAMPGROUND—Forest Service $
Open June through September
Camping, Restrooms, Water, Fishing
On the Lamoille Canyon Road (Forest Road 660) 7.4 miles from
    Hwy. 227

Much of the campground was damaged or destroyed following the heavy winter of '94-'95 by flooding along Lamoille Creek. Reconstruction was not completed at the end of the following summer. Check with the Forest Service concerning current conditions. As of the summer of 1996, 17 spaces were reopened for camping.

2. LAMOILLE CREEK—Forest Service
Open as conditions allow
No facilities
Off the Lamoille Canyon road (Forest Road 660) off the dirt access
    road to the Lions Club Camp at Right Fork Lamoille Creek, 5
    miles from Hwy. 227.

Undeveloped camping has been allowed along the main branch of Lamoille Creek off a dirt access road that parallels the creek.

RESOURCES

The growing community of Elko/Spring Creek, 20 miles from the heart of the Ruby Mountains, provides all the basic services necessary for a trip into the mountains. Limited services are available in the small community of Lamoille at the west edge of the range. Do not expect to find any facilities outside of these two towns around the perimeter of the Wilderness.

OUTDOOR SUPPLIERS

CEDAR CREEK CLOTHING
453 Idaho
Elko, NV 89801
(702) 738-3950

RIMROCK MOUNTAINEERING
123 S. 10th
Elko, NV 89801
(702) 778-9339

NEVADA JIM'S OUTDOOR SPORTS
600 Commercial
Elko, NV 89801
(702) 753-5467

OUTFITTERS

Currently, the Forest Service has authorized five companies to perform guide services in the Ruby Mountains. Four of the following outfitter-guides provide pack trips in the summer and hunting trips in the fall. Services and areas differ, so contact the individual providers for further information. The Ruby Mountains Heli-Ski Guides, Inc. take individuals and groups into the area in the winter for skiing the virgin powder around Lamoille Canyon.

ELKO GUIDE SERVICE
227 Belloak Court
Elko, NV 89801
(702) 738-7539
(702) 753-6867

RUBY MOUNTAINS HELI-SKI
GUIDES, INC.
PO Box 1192
Lamoille, NV 89828

HIDDEN LAKE OUTFITTERS
HC 60 Box 515
Ruby Valley, NV 89833
(702) 779-2268

SECRET PASS OUTFITTERS
HC 60 Box 685
Ruby Valley, NV 89833
(702) 779-2226

NEVADA HIGH COUNTRY
OUTFITTERS & GUIDES SERVICE
PO Box 483
Carlin, NV 89820
(702) 754-6851

FOREST SERVICE

Ruby Mountains Ranger District   Humboldt National Forest
428 South Humboldt   976 Mountain City Highway
PO Box 246   Elko, NV 89801
Wells, NV 89825   (702) 738-5171
(702) 752-3357

Trip 1 ⛺

SOLDIER CANYON TO
SOLDIER, ROBINSON & HIDDEN LAKES

Trip Type: 2 to 4 day backpack or long dayhike; Out and back
Length: 10.6 miles round trip, plus 1.6-mile round trip to Hidden Lakes
Season: Mid-June to mid-October
Access: Dirt road
Water: Plentiful in creek and lakes
Maps: #16
Soldier Peak 7.5, 1970 & *Verdi Peak,* 1991 (provisional) 7.5
minute quadrangles Humboldt National Forest map, Ruby
Mountains Ranger District, 1990
Ruby Mountain & East Humboldt Wildernesses, Humboldt
National Forest, 1994

Introduction: Almost equal in scenic attributes, the northern section of the
Ruby Mountains nevertheless sees far fewer visitors than the more popular section surrounding Lamoille Canyon. Although there exists no guarantee that you will be completely alone while traveling in the Soldier
Lakes Basin, chances are you will see more cows than people. Plenty of
lakes, six in all and each with its own charm, provide a bounty of opportunities for exploration and enjoyment. Rugged mountain peaks stand
guard over the basin and beckon further discovery.

If you like to fish, this trip will be hard to beat. The sunrises are incom-
parable as well. The first half of the trail climbs up Soldier Creek, a bois-
terous, rowdy stream that tumbles down the narrow canyon alongside a
diverse collection of wildflowers, shrubs and trees. The upper basin is a
broad plateau carpeted with meadows and a wide variety of wildflowers.

Trailhead: (a) From Interstate 80 take Exit 321, marked *Halleck, Ruby Valley,*
and travel on two-lane paved road, State Route 229, 10.8 miles to a junction with County Road 703. A sign just before the junction reads: *Lamoille
18.* Head south (right) on County Road 703 which quickly turns from
asphalt to gravel. At 5.3 miles from the junction the road bends sharply
west and 2.0 miles farther on reaches a junction with Soldier Creek Road
#335. As signs indicate, you are passing over private land for the next 2

miles until reaching the Forest Service boundary—please respect the property rights of the owners as you pass over their land. Once on government land the two-lane gravel road becomes a one lane dirt road with few turnouts. Proceed 2.5 miles along this dirt road to the end at the trailhead. Parking is available for a half dozen cars in a grassy area adjacent to Soldier Creek.

Description: Follow the continuation of the old road, boulder-hopping Soldier Creek and climbing along the north bank. Immediately, one notices the contrast in vegetation between the road, which passes through dry, open hillsides of sagebrush, and the banks of the creek laden with lush aspens, mahogany, alders, tobacco brush and wildflowers. What a difference a little water makes. At the beginning of the trail there's a nice view up the canyon of Soldier Peak, with green meadows rolling up to a jagged rock summit. You pass through a barbed-wire gate and meet the wilderness boundary 100 yards farther. As the canyon walls narrow, the old road gives way to a steeper, single-track trail as the creek, never more than a stone's throw away, begins to tumble more precipitously down its course. Rounding a curve, the trail comes into a shady aspen grove where lush foliage thrives, including such seemingly foreign species as big-leaf maple.

You reach a side canyon where you will find physical evidence remaining from a mud flow of the severe winter of 1994-95. A devastating mud flow uprooted trees and picked up boulders, sending tons of debris roaring down the canyon. You negotiate the debris and resume the climb, eventually coming to the upper part of the canyon, where the gorge widens, the grade moderates and the open terrain allows for views once more toward the head of the range. The trail strays away from Soldier Creek for a time but then wanders back through a field of waist-high wildflowers, crossing over a spring-fed tributary. Two and a half miles from the trailhead, you gradually rise out of the steep Soldier Creek canyon and turn south, following the now tranquil stream as it etches its way through the gently ascending meadowlands of the Soldier Lakes basin.

The topography widens out dramatically, eliciting a pastoral feeling of being at the top of the world. A broad expanse of the rolling, flower-covered basin merges into jagged peaks scraping their summits in the deep blue sky. You meet a trail coming in from the northeast, accessed from the Krenka, Gardner and Ruby Guard trailheads. A sign near the junction reads: *Soldier Basin* (south), *Ross Creek, Ruby Valley* (northeast). The junction seems to be incorrect on the *Soldier Peak* topo, shown as farther south, 2.75 miles from the trailhead. Which trail gets more use is clearly seen as the other path is faint and nearly overgrown.

Your well-graded dirt trail continues on a mild ascent through sagebrush and mixed wildflowers, passing a campsite in a small grove of aspens. Cross over Soldier Creek and proceed up through an area covered with corn lilies to crossings of two creeks: one descending from the two Hidden Lakes, both concealed in their basin near the top of the ridge above, and one coming from a spring a half mile up the slope. A 0.5-mile climb from the crossing leads past wildflowers into the Soldier Lakes Basin and the first Soldier Lake.

At 4.5 miles from the trailhead, the trail passes right by the first Soldier Lake, a small, oblong, shallow lake surrounded by sage and wildflowers with a row of scattered aspens and pines along the far shore. One hundred yards downhill from the first lake is another, slightly larger lake near the headwaters of Soldier Creek. Camping is limited at both lakes.

The trail climbs a short rise and contours around to the crossing of a creek draining the largest Soldier Lake. Camping is possible at almost any spot around the lake amid the low-growing vegetation. This lake does have a rather open and exposed feel, without any trees. Nothing else grows very high for a considerable distance around the lake. Unobstructed views of the crest of the northern Ruby Mountains are abundant throughout the basin. The Forest Service reports brook trout living in the Soldier Lakes.

Wander away from the largest Soldier Lake on a level course before a mild descent leads by some small ponds and then down to Robinson Lake. Toward the bottom, the trail divides, the main path branching left and proceeding to the lake near the outlet. The right track is a use trail heading across the spring-fed channel of Robinson Creek to the east shore of the lake.

Robinson Lake is easily the largest of the lakes in the northern Ruby Mountains and certainly one of the most scenic, nestled at the base of some towering cliffs. Green sloping hillsides merge into gray slabs of angled rock beneath the jagged summits of peaks over 10,000 feet high, forming a dramatic backdrop reflected in the sky-blue water. Brook trout appear to be so numerous that you begin to hallucinate about walking across their backs to the other side of the lake. Although a path circles the entire lake, the north end is so concentrated with springs that passage there is difficult over the completely saturated ground. A spring-fed cascade of water flows down vertical cliffs at the west end of the lake, providing a potentially reliable water source. The major drawback to the whole Soldier Lakes basin are the cows allowed to graze in the area. Even if you are fortunate enough to evade these "wilderness" beasts you will not be able to avoid the cowpies they have left behind, so choose your water carefully. Limited campsites are near the outlet and at the end of the use trail on the east shore. Bring a dependable backpacking stove, since the absence of trees makes firewood completely unavailable.

Potential further wanderings abound, including exploration of the ridges along the Ruby Crest and south along the continuation of the trail into Withington Basin, a verdant, sloping valley with numerous streams below the meadow-clad and aptly named Green Mountain. The short hike up to the saddle between Withington and Soldier Lakes basins is well worth the effort for the views alone.

Side Trip to Hidden Lakes: Retrace your steps to the outlet creek of the largest of the Soldier Lakes. The lower part of the trail shown on the *Verdi Peak* topo has completely disappeared but the route is distinguishable. Climb northwest from the trail up the sagebrush-covered ridge for approximately ½ mile to a large white rock on a knoll. Near the rock you can pick up the trail as it makes a somewhat level traverse into the canyon of the Hidden Lakes outlet stream. Descend into the canyon for a short distance and then head up through the canyon, steeply at times, to the lakes. If you lose the trail watch for periodic cairns. If you cannot find the trail, do not worry, but head directly for the lakes.

Hidden Lakes, although two bodies of water, seem to be more of a single lake separated by a thin, grass-covered isthmus on which grows a row of limber pine. Nevertheless, the lakes nestle in a deep, narrow bowl virtually at the top of the ridge of the north Ruby Mountains. Steep slabs of gray rock plunge directly into the west edge of the lakes. A stand of limber pine graces the southwest edge of the water and climbs up the slopes of peak 9963. Views are magnificent of the Soldier Lakes Basin below and the East Humboldt Range to the northeast. From this lofty perch sunrises are spectacular. A use trail leads up to the top of a minor ridge at the north end of the lake for even better views and to a campsite near a dead, character-rich limber pine. Other campsites closer to the water appear along the east shore of the lakes. Some firewood is available. A very healthy population of cutthroat trout will test your fishing skills.

Retrace your steps to the trailhead.

Soldier Lake and Peak

Trip 2 🌲

RIGHT FORK LAMOILLE CREEK

Trip Type: Dayhike or overnight backpack; Out and back
Distance: 4.4 miles round trip
Season: Late June through mid-October
Access: Gravel road
Water: Available in creek
Maps: #17

> *Lamoille* 7.5 minute quadrangle, 1990 (provisional)
> Humboldt National Forest map, Ruby Mountains Ranger
>   District, 1990
> *Ruby Mountains & East Humboldt Wildernesses*, Humboldt
>   National Forest, 1994

Introduction: They call this range the Ruby Mountains for good reason, and an undiscovered jewel of a basin lies at the head of the Right Fork Lamoille Creek. Only 2 miles from the most popular campground in Lamoille Canyon lies a seldom visited, flourishing green valley rimmed by high peaks and steep canyon walls. The trail itself passes through some of the most luxuriant vegetation found in the state, alongside one of the most rambunctious creeks and into a dramatic hanging valley carved by an ancient glacier. Boundless alpine scenery and virtually unlimited opportunities for exploration await the visitor willing to invest a bit of effort to reach a truly spectacular area. Oddly enough, the upper part of the canyon does not receive wilderness protection, a concession to a local heli-skiing operation, but the area is as pristine and magnificent as any in the Ruby Mountains Wilderness.

Trailhead: (b) From Interstate 80 take the *Elko Downtown* exit #301. Head south toward town with the Ruby Mountains off in the distance. At 0.8 mile from the freeway turn left onto Business 80, following signs to downtown for another 0.8 mile to 5th Street. Turn right (south) onto State Route 228, observing signs marked: *Spring Creek, Lamoille & Jiggs* and a scenic highway emblem. Proceed out of the old downtown section of Elko, crossing the railroad tracks and the Humboldt River on an overpass. At the next signal after the overpass head left, and quickly pass the left-hand turnoff at Last Chance Road for the Humboldt National Forest Ranger Station, where you can obtain current information on the trails in the Ruby Mountains from the Forest Service personnel.

Head southeast on 4-lane Route 228, climbing out of Elko through scattered-pinyon-pine-covered hillsides, cresting Lamoille Summit at 5.3 miles from I-80. At the pass the distant range of the Rubies appears before you in all its majesty. Keep your eyes on the road and not on the mountains as you proceed 2 more miles to the traffic signal at the intersection of State

Routes 227 and 228. Following signs to *Lamoille, SR227E* you continue straight onto Route 227. The highway narrows to two lanes around 5 miles from the junction. As you draw closer to the Rubies, the more picturesque and scenic the range becomes. A half mile before you reach the small community of Lamoille, 7.5 miles from the junction with 228, you take the right-hand turnoff onto Forest Road 660, also known as the Lamoille Canyon Scenic Highway. A sign marks the junction: *Lamoille Canyon Recreation Area.*

Travel on paved road past ranch land and sagebrush toward the towering peaks of the Ruby Mountains. At 2.6 miles from Highway 227 you cross the National Forest boundary, immediately pass the Powerhouse picnic area and enter glacier-carved Lamoille Canyon. Climb up the valley and at 5 miles from Route 227 is the signed turnoff for Camp Lamoille, operated by the Elko Lions Club. Travel down the gravel road to a gate which, depending upon the administration of the camp, may be open or closed. Do not drive into the camp but park off the road in a wide parking area beside some mahogany trees just before the gate on the right.

Description: From the parking area continue on the old road as it bends into Camp Lamoille. Proceed courteously to the edge of the camp beyond some A-frame cabins where a twin-tracked jeep road eventually narrows to a single-track trail. Walk through some small aspen trees to where the trail draws near to the Right Fork Lamoille Creek before bending sharply upstream. Quickly come to a fork in the trail where the left-hand path leads across two bridges spanning the creek to the camp's archery area. Continue on the upstream path for a short distance to another informal junction, where the main trail curves down to a ford of the Right Fork Lamoille Creek. The other branch of the trail, heading straight, travels along the creek on a primitive path through a wide variety of vegetation, some of which has overgrown the trail, to a dramatic series of short cascades that tumble down rock cliffs.

Following the main trail, cross the creek over some logs if they are still there. Otherwise you will have to ford the broad, cold stream. Follow the trail along the east side of the creek through grasses, shrubs and wildflowers including monkey flowers, columbines and lupines. Soon the trail forsakes the bottom of the valley and begins to climb steeply, via periodic switchbacks, amid dense stands of aspen and lush trailside vegetation. After climbing, the grade levels and then makes a long, mild descent, passing the wilderness boundary along the way—still through lush foliage. Resuming the steep climb, the terrain opens up, revealing a series of ponds below the trail. Beyond the ponds thick brush and dense stands of aspen return, providing shaded passage across two narrow side streams.

Leaving the junglelike vegetation, the route ascends a succession of granite slabs, benches and open clearings typically rimmed by a brilliant display of seasonal wildflowers. A faded path through aspens and brush leads to an apparent dead-end near a massive rock wall that pinches off the canyon. The rock wall forces the trail to tenuously cling to a very narrow path between the base of the rock and the edge of the churning creek. Beyond this obstacle, the route becomes distinct again, climbing over more rock as it heads away from the rushing creek, forcefully cascading over the glistening granite slabs. Ducks may help guide you through this rocky area over the lip and into the upper basin.

Heading into the magnificent hanging valley of the upper canyon, the trail diminishes in the lush vegetation near a beaver dam and pond. The basin is wide open with plenty of areas for roaming despite the lack of a defined trail. If the lure of the upper part of the canyon is strong, you may extend your explorations to more than just a day, and there should be a wide variety of spots to pitch your tent. The basin is a verdant, glacier-carved valley with a clear stream coursing below serrated ridges and picturesque mountains. Mountaineers should find plenty of pitches and peaks to satiate their appetites. Truly hearty adventurers may be able to find a route over the ridge and into nearby and extremely isolated Echo Lake.

Retrace your steps to the trailhead.

Trip 3 ♧

THOMAS CANYON

Trip Type: Dayhike; Out and back
Distance: 4.0 miles round trip
Season: Late June through late October
Access: Paved road
Water: Available in creek
Maps: #17
     Lamoille & Ruby Dome 7.5 minute quadrangles, 1990 (provisional)
     Humboldt National Forest map, Ruby Mountains Ranger District, 1990
     Ruby Mountains & East Humboldt Wildernesses, Humboldt National Forest, 1994

Introduction: The Thomas Creek Trail offers one of the best views of a "mountaineer's mountain" anywhere in the Ruby Mountains. Alpine-looking Mt. Fitzgerald, at 11,215 feet, looms as a giant sentinel guarding the valley at the head of a glacier-carved canyon. A delightful stream with numerous cascades provides an added bonus. Even though this is such a short trail, you probably will not see many other people hiking up the canyon, which is something of a mystery considering the outstanding scenery. Another oddity is the strange deviation of the wilderness boundary as shown on the topographic maps. The boundary was established in this unusual manner to allow a private concessionaire access to the mountains for helicopter skiing during the winter months. In spite of the fact that this trail lies outside the Ruby Mountains Wilderness, you will not be disappointed with the surroundings or the potential for solitude.

The canyon received its name from an Elko school teacher, Raymond Thomas, who tragically died rescuing students during a surprise October blizzard in 1916.

Trailhead: (c) Follow directions in Trip 2 to the junction of State Route 227 and Forest Road 660, also known as the Lamoille Canyon Scenic Highway. Travel up Forest Road 660 7.4 miles and turn right into the Thomas Canyon campground. The signed trailhead parking area is directly ahead with room for about 9 cars. The heavy winter of 1994-95 wreaked havoc on the Thomas Canyon campground, when upstream mudslides and flooding waters completely destroyed one loop of the campground and partially damaged the other two. Repairs were ongoing at the conclusion of the summer of 1995, with much work still remaining to restore the campground. During the summer of 1996, 17 of the 42 campsites were reopened. Check with the Forest Service for current conditions if you are planning to use the campground. Drinking water and restrooms are available depending on the status of the repairs. If the campground is closed during your visit, leave your car at the campground gate and walk the short distance to the trailhead. To begin the hike, follow the paved road across Lamoille Creek to campsite number 30 (providing the Forest Service does not re-number the sites as part of their repairs). The trail starts just opposite this campsite.

Description: The trail starts as a narrow path that climbs steeply up hillsides through tall grasses not far from the creek. A short climb leads to a low overlook beneath mahoganies where you get a good look at a short, cascading waterfall. Continuing with the steep climb up the lower canyon, you quickly reach a flat where the vegetation turns drier and the grade of the trail moderates. The cool stream swirls, eddies and glides over rock shelves into small pools through this section of trail. Mt. Fitzgerald, a classic looking alpine peak with a pyramidal summit and snowfields, comes into view, dominating the head of the canyon and luring mountaineers.

The canyon widens and the grade eases momentarily as the creek takes on a gentler demeanor. Wildflowers and shrubs blanket the slopes as views open up even more toward Mt. Fitzgerald and the upper canyon. The trail comes close to the creek before resuming the steep climb near a picturesque setting of glistening cascades where the creek spills over some rock outcroppings. Continue to climb alongside the stream to a point where it would appear that the trail crosses the creek. According to the topo, the trail should continue on the right-hand (east) bank another half mile up the canyon, but the tread seems to disappear at this spot.

Travel further up the valley is possible, although you will have to contend with some brush. If you stay on the west side of the creek you will have to negotiate some boggy areas near a spring but you may find the trail again up the canyon. Travel on the east side across the creek may be easier initially. Even though the trail falters, the upper canyon is well worth the minor hassle of having to beat some brush. If you do not mind some scrambling, you can reach either a lush meadow directly below the stunning north face of Mt. Fitzgerald on the west branch of Thomas Creek or a rock basin below dramatic Snow Lake Peak above the east branch.

Retrace your steps to the trailhead.

Trip 4 🌲

ISLAND LAKE

Trip Type: Dayhike; Out and back
Distance: 3.2 miles round trip
Season: Late June through mid-October
Access: Paved road
Water: Available in creek & lake
Maps: #17
Ruby Valley School & Ruby Dome 7.5 minute quadrangles, 1990
(provisional)
Humboldt National Forest map, Ruby Mountains Ranger
District, 1990
Ruby Mountains & East Humboldt Wildernesses, Humboldt
National Forest, 1994

Introduction: The Island Lake trail offers a condensed sample of some of the best aspects of the Ruby Mountain range: a scenic mountain lake set in a steep-walled basin of rock ridges and peaks, a spectacular display of a wide variety of seasonal wildflowers, verdant mountain meadows and a cascading stream. Do not expect to be alone, as the location of the trailhead at the end of Lamoille Canyon combined with the short distance to such a beautiful area makes this a popular route for tourists and outdoor enthusiasts alike.

Trailhead: (d) Parking for the Island Lake trail is in the same area as for the north end of the Ruby Crest trail. See Trip 6 for directions to the trailhead. The signed trail starts from the north end of the loop at the end of the Lamoille Canyon road.

Description: The sign at the trailhead lists the distance to Island Lake as 2 miles but it is actually only 1.6 miles. Climb up from the parking area on well-graded trail amid lush vegetation and a fine display of wildflowers in

Island Lake

season, including paintbrush, lupine, phlox, potentilla and larkspur. The trail makes a gradual ascent along the densely foliated hillside paralleling the highway below, offering increasingly dramatic views of steep-walled Lamoille Canyon. A steady climb incorporating a few switchbacks leads into the mouth of the short canyon. You pass occasional limber pines as the trail nears the creek that drains Island Lake and the basin above.

A rock and timber bridge allows you to cross the picturesque stream as it spills out of a notch above and pours down slabs of rock toward Lamoille Creek in the valley below. Away from the stream the trail climbs sage-covered slopes in a series of switchbacks into the Island Lake basin. Above the switchbacks, after you cross the creek once more on an easy boulder-hop, the trail climbs up to the lake.

Island Lake, has a small, irregularly shaped, grassy island in the middle of the lake. The lake itself sits in a wildflower-filled basin with green sloping hillsides and gray talus slopes leading up to the nearly vertical cliffs of dark gray and reddish brown peaks. Pockets of snow cling to the upper rock faces well into the summer. Thick brush surrounds the lakeside, although it is not so dense that you cannot get to the shoreline. A few limber pines provide partial shade to a number of campsites at the east end of the lake. The upper basin is open and beckons the hiker to explore its heights.

Retrace your steps to the trailhead.

Trip 5 ♙

RUBY LAKES TRAIL: LAMOILLE CANYON TO LIBERTY, FAVRE & CASTLE LAKES

Trip Type: 2 to 4 day backpack; Out and back
Distance: 7.0 miles round trip to Liberty Lake, plus 3.1 miles round trip to Favre & Castle lakes
Season: Early July to mid-October
Access: Paved road
Water: Available in creeks and lakes
Maps: #17
Ruby Dome 7.5 minute quadrangle, 1990 (provisional)
Humboldt National Forest map, Ruby Mountains Ranger District, 1990
Ruby Mountains & East Humboldt Wildernesses, Humboldt National Forest, 1994

Introduction: The climb over Liberty Pass and into the Ruby Lakes region is by far the most popular backpack in the Ruby Mountains. If you ask someone whether they have been into the Rubies and they answer positively, invariably this is the trail they have hiked—and with good reason. In a relatively short distance (unfortunately the elevation gain is not as relative) one can enter into the high, alpine, glacier-carved basin at the head of Kleckner Creek Canyon, where three cirque-bound lakes cling to rugged, pinnacled ridges. Most hikers are content with the magnificence of Liberty Lake just over Liberty Pass, but Favre and Castle Lakes are certainly well worth the visit and provide opportunities for more solitude. In addition to these three lakes, you encounter the symmetrical Dollar Lakes and austere Lamoille Lake on the way to 10,440-foot Liberty Pass, a stark and barren environment that contrasts vividly with the lakes and meadows below. Throw in delightful Lamoille Creek, spectacular wildflower displays, great views and good fishing and you have all the elements for a wonderful trip.

Trailhead: (d) The starting point is the north end trailhead for the Ruby Crest National Recreation Trail described in Trip 6.

Description: Begin the climb on a moderate grade away from the parking area through open terrain near rushing Lamoille Creek. A bevy of wildflowers greets the hiker including corn lily, larkspur, lupine, paintbrush and yarrow. The views downstream of Lamoille Canyon grow more impressive with each step. Just after you cross the creek on a crude wooden bridge, pine trees begin to appear, continuing as your companions until the harsh conditions around Liberty Pass become unsuitable for their survival.

Lamoille Canyon

About one-third mile from the first crossing of Lamoille Creek, the trail bends east and crosses the east branch of the creek that drains the Dollar Lakes. Cross streams twice more and as you near the lakes the trail steepens until leveling out as it skirts the north edge of the two lakes. A steep ridge above the far shore adds a rugged backdrop to the pristine lakes enveloped by grassy meadows and lush willows. Both lakes are devoid of fish.

A gentle climb leads away from Dollar Lakes one-third mile to much larger Lamoille Lake, cradled in a deep gouge in the west edge of upper Lamoille Canyon. The steep walls at the head of the canyon rising up to and beyond Liberty Pass give the lake (9750') a rugged and forbidding ambiance. A few scattered campsites appear around the north edge but most visitors seem content to stay only for the day, plying the waters in search of brook trout.

Once past the placid waters of the lake, the trail steepens mercilessly for the duration of the 700-foot climb to Liberty Pass. You make a steep and winding ascent through rocky areas beneath towering peaks on a rock and dirt path. The lush vegetation below is not to be found here. Even the diminished limber pines grudgingly give in to the harsh environs of the pass. Ice and snow cling in the crevices on the north-facing walls near Liberty Pass. Patches of snow will definitely cover the trail in early summer and may even be treacherous following a heavy winter. Check with the Forest Service regarding trail conditions below the pass.

Once you reach 10,400-foot Liberty Pass, the way is all downhill to Liberty Lake. The view from the top is awesome, however, so spend enough time to soak it all in and catch your breath before rushing off to the lakes. South along the crest of the range, Lake Peak and Wines Peak grab the eye.

You cross the well-marked Wilderness boundary and begin the steep descent toward Liberty Lake, which remains temporarily out of sight, tucked well into the head of the canyon below. As you descend, the lake suddenly pops into view, creating a dramatic scene of deep-blue waters reflecting vertical rock cliffs. Travel around the west edge of the basin 0.6 mile from the pass to a lateral trail leading to the lake and to some camp-sites on the far side of the outlet.

Liberty is the quintessential mountain lake, with splendid scenery and great views. Cradled in a steep-walled rock basin, perched high above the surrounding canyon, you can appreciate the relative popularity of this lake. Travelers along Interstate 80, a mere thirty miles away, race past the range completely unaware of this tremendous beauty, assuming that Nevada is nothing more than endless sagebrush and brown mountains. Campsites are plentiful but firewood is not. Bring a stove if you expect to enjoy anything hot. Fishing is good for brook trout.

If you wish to visit Favre or Castle Lake, follow the trail as it continues down the north side of the canyon 1 mile to a lateral trail heading east. Another quarter mile leads to Favre Lake. Castle Lake lies one-quarter mile cross-country above the south shore of Favre Lake. Find detailed descriptions of both lakes in the Ruby Crest National Recreation Trail description (see Trip 6).

Retrace your steps back to the trailhead at road's end.

Trip 6 ♧
RUBY CREST NATIONAL RECREATION TRAIL

Trip Type: 4 to 7 day backpack; Shuttle
Length: 32.0 miles; plus 1.8 mile round trip to North Furlong Lake & 1.1 mile round trip to Favre & Castle Lakes
Season: Early July to mid-October
Access: Paved road
Water: Available in creeks and lakes; (a 9.5 mile waterless stretch exists between Overland Creek and North Furlong Lake)
Maps: #17-21
Harrison Pass 1985 (provisional), *Franklin Lake SW* 1968, *Green Mountain* 1985 (provisional), *Franklin Lake NW 1969, Ruby Dome* 1990 (provisional), 7.5 minute quadrangles
Humboldt National Forest map, Ruby Mountains Ranger District, 1990
Ruby Mountains & East Humboldt Wildernesses, Humboldt National Forest, 1994

Introduction: Considered by many to be the preeminent Nevada trail, the Ruby Crest National Recreation Trail offers hikers, backpackers and equestrians one of the best wilderness experiences in the state. Alpine lakes, absent from the majority of Nevada wilderness areas, are present in abundance including Overland, North Furlong, Favre, Castle, Liberty, Lamoille and the two Dollar Lakes. Even more unusual is a spectacular waterfall cascading over the lip of a vertical rock wall in Overland Creek Basin.

In the northern part of the trail lofty mountain peaks with jagged, rocky summits, many over 11,000 feet, stand guard over verdant, glacier-carved canyons with crystal-clear streams coursing through them. The southern section is characterized by grassy meadows, rolling summits and aspen-lined creeks.

Superb views are constant companions. You could easily make a scenic calendar from the photo opportunities available along this route alone. During the peak of the season, the Ruby Mountains offer one of the best wildflower displays anywhere in the state, and the Crest Trail passes through numerous wildflower-laden meadows. Mountain goats, Bighorn sheep, deer and a wide variety of fowl are abundant throughout the Crest Trail environs. Even the fishing can be outstanding!

This trip is idyllic, but, a few cautions require mentioning. First, Liberty Pass at the north end of the route is a high (10,400 ft.), north-facing pass that can harbor large, high-angle snowfields. Check with the Forest Service about conditions, especially if you plan your trip for early summer. Second, the middle of the trail contains a nearly 10-mile stretch without any water, at least without a severe detour down into one of the side canyons. Make sure you have enough containers and plan your itinerary accordingly. Last, the hike along the crest requires a long car shuttle. Allow for plenty of driving time between the two trailheads and make sure you have plenty of gas. These cautions aside, the Ruby Crest National Recreation Trail awaits you.

Most written descriptions begin in Lamoille Canyon and head south to Harrison Pass. I have chosen to reverse the direction and describe the trail from south to north for a variety of reasons. Since most people consider the Ruby Lakes to be the climax of the range, traveling from Harrison Pass to Lamoille Canyon saves the best for last. Descending from Liberty Pass to Lamoille Canyon is much less strenuous than the steep climb in the opposite direction. Finally, most hikers appreciate having the sun behind them as opposed to continually shining in their faces. Feel free to choose your own way, but traveling north from Harrison Pass to Lamoille Canyon seems preferable.

Trailhead: NORTH END: (d) Follow the trailhead directions for Trip 2 to the turnoff from the Lamoille Canyon Scenic Highway to Camp Lamoille, 5 miles from State Route 227. Continue on the highway up the U-shaped canyon to increasingly dramatic views of high peaks and meadows past the Thomas Canyon campground and trailhead at 7.4 miles. Reach the road end in a turnaround at 12.2 miles, where parking is available for a large number of vehicles. Pit toilets, water, horse unloading facilities and a picnic area are all near the parking area. The northern trailhead for the Ruby Crest Trail is at the far end of the paved loop. The Island Lake trailhead (see Trip 4) is at the opposite end of the small loop.

SOUTH END: (f) Head west from Lamoille Canyon or south from Elko to the junction of State Routes 227 and 228. Take Route 228 south, paralleling the west side of the Ruby Mountains 26.4 miles to the small town of Jiggs. On the way you can look up at the crest and see the general route of the Ruby Crest Trail as it heads toward Lamoille Canyon. Continue on paved road, passing the turnoff to Eureka 3.3 miles from Jiggs where State Route 228 inconspicuously becomes County Road 718. The road surface changes from pavement to gravel just beyond the Zaga Ranch at 32.8 miles from the junction of 227 and 228 as the route bends east and begins to climb toward Harrison Pass. Well-graded dirt road climbs and winds through sagebrush and grass-covered hillsides following the aspen- and meadow-banked course of Toyn Creek almost all of the way to the pass. Reach signed Harrison Pass at the crest of the southern Ruby Mountains 43.4 miles from the junction of 227 and 228 and 10.6 miles from the end of the pavement. Passenger cars should be able to negotiate the dirt road to the pass without any problems.

From Harrison Pass your progress to the north up Forest Road 107 depends on the type of vehicle you are driving. Sedans can park at the pass in a large grassy area or gingerly drive another half mile to a pull-out large enough for a horse trailer. High-clearance vehicles can continue along the narrow dirt track as it continues to climb north from the pass. Open a Forest Service gate at 0.9 mile from the pass, remembering to close it behind you. The roughest and steepest section of road occurs just beyond the gate, not necessarily requiring 4-wheel drive to negotiate, but some drivers may feel more comfortable having it activated. Past this minor obstacle the road climbs along a ridge paralleling a barbed-wire fence for quite a distance before bending northwest. A 4 by 4 post appears at 2.8 miles from the pass, with a sign: *Ruby Crest*. This sign seems somewhat confusing since the trailhead is another 0.4 mile up the road.

Approximately 100 yards before a large rock outcrop that towers above some aspens you reach a sign reading: *Vehicle Traffic Not Advised Beyond This Point*. Parking near this sign is available in a grassy area for a number of vehicles. Travel beyond this point is not particularly difficult and you can park another ⅓ mile up the road if you desire. But past that point, parking is hard to come by even though you might be able to negotiate the road. The trail description begins from the sign.

Description: Begin hiking from the sign that discourages vehicle traffic on the continuation of the twin-tracked jeep road. Views to the west are expansive above sagebrush-covered hillsides, although occasionally

The central Ruby Mountains from the Ruby Crest Trail

blocked by groves of quaking aspens where moist soil conditions allow the thirsty trees to flourish. You pass·a large rock outcrop beyond which the trail steepens a bit and the track turns rocky. Continue along the road to a junction in a saddle three-quarters mile from the trailhead, marked by a sign: *Ruby Crest Trail* (straight ahead) and *Green Mountain Creek* (left). The Green Mountain Creek Trail heads west down the drainage to a road that connects with the road to Harrison Pass at the base of the Ruby Mountains.

At the junction the road becomes a single-track trail and descends a couple of hundred yards to the signed Wilderness boundary before traversing a hillside above the Green Mountain Creek drainage and below the ridge leading up to Green Mountain. Aside from the drainages and areas of springs where aspens and lush shrubs and wildflowers are present, the terrain around the south end of the Ruby Crest Trail is predominantly open grasslands and scattered wildflowers. A series of interesting rock domes come into view in the valley below, perhaps providing some potential bouldering.

The dry vegetation gives way to a lush display of wildflowers and young aspen trees as the trail continues a descending traverse on the lower slopes of Green Mountain, aptly named for the green carpet of vegetation covering its flanks. You reach a three-way trail junction at 3.4 miles from the trailhead in a grove of tall aspens where a sign declares: *Harrison Lamoille Trail*. No information appears on the sign about trail #050 branching off to the left heading downhill past the domes, which actually leads to a road down Gilbert Creek and on to the town of Jiggs.

The trail begins to climb and soon comes to a shady grove of tall aspens and lush wildflowers. Just beyond this grove is a spring draining across the trail that beavers have dammed, creating a pond complete with lodge. You quickly cross another small stream and climb up around a corner where the trail begins to descend into the upper canyon of McCutcheon Creek. The good-sized creek trickles down through rocks but provides no difficulty in crossing. On the far shore is a junction with the McCutcheon Creek Trail #049 heading downstream to the northwest. Do not expect to find any developed campsites near the creek. If one desired to spend the night, however, a few level areas could potentially accommodate a small party.

From McCutcheon Creek the trail makes a mild ascending traverse before a short, steep climb leads to a saddle in the ridge separating the drainages of McCutcheon Creek and Smith Creek, 6 miles from the trailhead. From the saddle, a series of switchbacks and long, descending traverses lead 1.75 miles down into the South Fork Smith Creek drainage. As you approach the bottom of the canyon, you begin to hear the roar of the creek that helps provide much of the water used by ranchers in the verdant, green valley below. On the south bank of the creek, a sign states: *South Fork Smith Creek, Ruby Crest Trail.* In keeping with the tradition of the Ruby and East Humboldt Mountains, Smith Creek was named after an early settler, C.E. Smith.

Typical at this end of the Ruby Crest Trail, there are no developed campsites around the South Fork Smith Creek, but there are many places to camp. Aspens provide shade and windbreaks while the rushing stream serves as the perfect audio accompaniment for a restful night's sleep. To complete the setting, a dramatic view is available for your pleasure as well, toward the head of the canyon and the green carpeted hillsides that lead up to dramatic rock cliffs. South Fork Smith Creek does have one drawback. Grazing cows have left their calling cards, but more than likely you will not have to deal with the actual bovines themselves. Unless you are in a hurry to complete the Ruby Crest Trail, at 8 miles from the trailhead the creek is a fine place to spend the night.

From the creek the trail quickly ascends the dry hillside above to a knob along the ridge crest and then makes a lengthier descent into the lush, north-facing hillside on the south side of Middle Fork Smith Creek. The descent continues into the narrow canyon, crosses the cramped creek and then steeply climbs the far bank. Due to the steep nature of the drainage, do not expect any places to camp at Middle Fork.

As you climb the hillside away from Middle Fork you can look downstream and see more results of beaver activity in the canyon below. Over hillsides of bitterbrush, good views of the distant mountain ranges to the west occur near the top of the next ridge, which divides the Middle Fork and North Fork basins. Once again, the trail descends from the top of the ridge on a dry, sage-covered slope. However, unlike in the previous two basins, the path does not drop to the creek, but makes a mild ascent up the

canyon along the southern hillside. Small aspens and an abundant display of wildflowers grace
the path as it heads up the
drainage. As you climb gently
east up the valley, the destination
of this section of trail looms
before you at the ridge crest, two
and a half miles away and 2,000
feet higher.

The trail heads quickly downhill into a grove of mature aspens,
soon arriving at a "Y" intersection, 9.75 miles from the trailhead, where a trail sign reads:
Smith Creek Trail (straight) and
Ruby Crest Trail (uphill, east).
Smith Creek Trail #109 does not
appear on the *Franklin Lake NW*
topo but in actuality it descends
northward a quarter mile to the
creek, crosses the North Fork and
follows the north bank of the
creek downstream, where it

The climb to the pass above Overland Lake

appears on the *Green Mountain* topo. While there are no decent campsites
along the creek near the Ruby Crest Trail, you can hike down the Smith
Creek trail a short distance to the water's edge where there are some undeveloped places to camp.

From the junction, the trail begins to make a more serious ascent, coming into open vegetation of sage, grasses and flowers. You cross a dry
drainage and approximately 50 feet farther is a willow-lined, small creek—
the last water before Overland Lake basin. On the far bank of the small
stream is a use trail, an extension of the Smith Creek Trail. From here your
trail steepens even more and begins a series of switchbacks that will not
end until you have conquered the pass above Overland Lake. A long,
uphill grind usually is the time for repetitive, mind-numbing songs or for
deep, meaningful questions like, "Why am I doing this?" One thought you
may be prone to contemplate is, "Why do they call this the Ruby <u>Crest</u>
Trail?" The last time you were actually near the Ruby Crest was in the car
on the approach. Eventually, above the Overland Lake drainage, you will
actually be astride the spine of the Rubies for quite a while. Comfort yourself with the notion that if you had been on the crest all this time you
would be mighty thirsty by now, since water is almost nonexistent along
the crest.

The long, dry ascent through grasses and sage finally concludes at the
ridge crest near a rock outcropping. An old sign, letters worn away by the

elements, testifies to the harsh conditions on the apex of the range. Views open up to the east of Ruby Valley, Franklin Lake and the Pequop Mountains.

Now the route winds up and away to the east from the ridge crest through austere surroundings of sparse vegetation, scattered limber pines and bare rock. Just before reaching the rocky crest above Overland Lake, the trail switchbacks and then climbs quickly to the top. The lake basin immediately comes into view, a classic glacier-carved canyon with a sub-alpine lake and a smaller tarn nestled in a steep-walled, rocky depression. Descending switchbacks wind through the barren, rocky upper basin down to the oblong tarn just above the lake. Light-gray cliffs and talus rim the tarn, with green meadows around the outlet. A clear, cold stream gushes from the tarn, passes a lush stand of willows and plunges steeply over rocky slopes to the lake below. You might think you were in the High Sierra rather than in a Nevada mountain range.

From the tarn above Overland Lake, follow the waist-high willows along the outlet stream, and then bend away from the creek, crisscrossing a flower-strewn hillside of buttercups, asters, paintbrush, lupines and shooting stars. Contour around the lake above the east shore, passing a campsite amid some limber pines to reach an old cabin at the far end of the lake near a sign declaring: *Overland Lake.*

Overland Lake was not named for a specific settler but for the Overland Farm that supplied feed for the horses of the Overland Mail Company, which served the residents of the Ruby Valley during the 1860's. The old cabin at the north end of the lake almost looks as if it belonged to the same era. Aside from providing shelter during extreme weather, the old structure appears unappealing for human habitation. However, the metal roof should discourage use during lightning storms. Horse packers appear to use the cabin for storing some of their gear during the outfitting season.

You can camp in some of the flat areas around the cabin, but the best site is across the outlet creek beneath some tall limber pines. So far, packers have tethered their horses on the east side of the creek and set up camp a good distance downstream. Hopefully, this practice will continue since manure, flies and trampled, muddy ground can detract from even the most oblivious camper's experience. Firewood is extremely scarce.

The lake itself is an oval shape with green-tinted, clear water, occupying a rugged notch near the crest of the range, thousands of feet above the Overland Creek basin below. Talus slopes and rock slabs lead up to steep gray and tan peaks that ring the basin on three sides. Limber pines gracefully add character to the shoreline. Swimming is chilly but under the right circumstances can be refreshing. Fishing is fair for brook trout. Although not heavily used, Overland Lake is a prescribed stop for parties hiking the entire Ruby Crest Trail. Few backpackers come in on the 5.2-mile Overland Lake Trail from the east (see Trip 7), but many of the horse parties originate there.

The Ruby Crest Trail heads downhill from the cabin, initially through a patch of alders and flowers and then through a boulder field dotted with scattered pines. Continue from the lake 0.4 mile to an intersection with the Overland Lake Trail, climbing up from State Route 267 in Ruby Valley to the east. Ten feet beyond the actual junction is a sign proclaiming: *Ruby Crest Trail.* An additional sign, faded over time by the elements, lists the mileage to Favre Lake as 18—but the actual mileage is closer to 14.

On the next leg of the journey, over 4 miles of trail are required to traverse the vast Overland Creek basin, where you encounter green hillsides, clear, cold streams and towering gray-rock peaks. The scenic basin is so expansive that perspective becomes difficult to maintain. From the junction the trail descends, steeply at times, occasionally switchbacking through meadows filled with wildflowers and scattered limber pines. As the trail winds downhill it eventually reaches the first of the many tributaries of Overland Creek cascading down rock slabs. The trail cuts below the slabs as it begins the long traverse around the head of the Overland Creek basin. Placement of some 2 by 4 wooden bridges allows for easier travel through the lush and boggy areas near the creeks. You soon cross another series of streams surrounded by willows and tall wildflowers fed by springs and a small pond sitting on a bench 150 feet above the trail. The traverse continues amid drier vegetation to where the trail divides into an upper and a lower route. Although the lower route is shorter, I recommend the upper option as it leads around the canyon over rocky terrain to a spectacular waterfall amid an impressive display of wildflowers.

By Yosemite standards this waterfall would not garner much attention, but it's classified as a real gem in the Ruby Mountains. Thin ribbons of water glide over vertical rock slabs before collecting into a narrow channel where the water tumbles and frolics over steps of boulders through a garden of deep-green grass, vivid wildflowers and willows. Add a stone pagoda and a few bonsai plants and you would have the ideal Japanese garden. If your sense of smell detects the aroma of onion, you have not been away from real food for too long—wild onion flourishes along the edge of the creek. Overland Creek falls deserves a long visit, but the need to move on propels you forward as the next decent campsite with water is still 11 miles ahead.

As the trail continues a general traverse around the basin, the massive bulk of austere 11,031 foot Kings Peak dominates the skyline above. If you can afford the hours necessary to reach the summit, the peak can be ascended rather easily. You reach a branch of the creek at the end of an uphill stretch of trail. Farther on a spring emerges from the ground 10 feet below the trail and heads down a willow-choked channel. Above the spring is an abundant display of wildflowers. A short distance from the spring you pass yet another branch of Overland Creek. A spectacular meadow is just beyond the creek, carpeted with wildflowers including paintbrush, lupine and yellow daisies. A short, uphill climb leads to yet another branch of Overland Creek. The trail continues the traverse through much drier areas below rock cliffs over to a grassy hillside. You ascend more steeply in tall grass to a small rock knob where a couple of switchbacks lead up to the crest of a minor ridge. From this vantage you have a good view of the Overland Creek basin, including now tiny-appearing Overland Lake, barely visible in its own basin above.

A steeper climb of the next hillside awaits as the trail heads up through limber pines. The grade eventually moderates as you break out of the pines and into grassy slopes with intermittent wildflowers, after which the trail winds up and down through some steep, rocky cliffs. Meadows resume just before the last branch of Overland Creek in a field of flowers. Late in the season or following a dry winter, this stream may not have an adequate flow, so fill up at the previous creek.

Now you climb up and away from the creek to a sub-ridge, traverse over to another sub-ridge, and climb through some rock cliffs and through some more meadows before reaching the first in a series of switchbacks leading out of the Overland Creek basin. You begin to ascend a boulder-covered hillside as the trail zigzags up to a notch, offering fine views of the basin. From the notch the trail makes an ascending traverse for one third mile before the switchbacks resume. As the trail steepens the vegetation changes to sagebrush, wildflowers and a smattering of stunted pines. Near the top, the foliage diminishes to low-growing sage and widely scattered flowers.

Approaching the summit of peak 10,207 the grade abates and the trail reaches the top, 5.3 miles from Overland Lake and 18.7 miles from the trail-head. A low sign attached to a 4 by 4 post reads: *Ruby Crest Trail*. Views are quite dramatic of the Overland Creek basin, dominated by the massive summit of multi-spired Kings Peak. Overland Lake is 2½ air miles away (5 miles by trail) and looks extremely small at the other end of the basin beneath a triangular-shaped peak. Ruby Valley with Franklin Lake below and the Ruby Marshes in the distance appear clearly in the east. To the north the craggy, central Ruby peaks come into full view, including Ruby Dome, at 11,387 feet, the highest mountain in the range. More immediate is the dry ridge that the trail will follow for the next 6 miles, culminating at Wines Peak, a romantic-sounding appellation but from this vantage point a rather undistinguished looking hummock. The outstanding views, just like the waterfall, must remain behind as water still lies out of reach, 7.5 miles away.

Descending, the trail heads around a hillside and into a saddle. Just past the saddle the trail gently ascends below peak 10,394 through very sparse, low-growing vegetation where the highest object around is an occasional lupine. Where the trail levels, nearly reaching the crest, a sign marked: *Long Canyon* appears with an arrow pointing down the canyon. However, no trail is evident here although the way would be clear in spite of the lack of a defined track. Those in desperate need of water can descend into Long Canyon approximately 1 mile to the creek.

The trail proceeds to ascend the hillside toward the summit of the next peaklet, reaching a saddle at the crest of the ridge with the aid of six switchbacks. Views open up to the east and you may get your first glimpse of the lightning-caused Ruby Valley fire of 1995 that charred many acres of sagebrush-covered terrain at the eastern base of the Ruby Mountains.

A welcome downhill stretch comes to a sudden end as the trail climbs to a minor point along the ridge before descending again to a narrow saddle. From the edge of this saddle you can get a much better look at the devastation left by the '95 fire. From the saddle the trail climbs moderately steeply and reaches the next point along the ridge with the assistance of four switchbacks. Wines Peak, the last of these rollercoaster ascents, looms closer but is still out of reach 2 miles away. More switchbacks lead down from this high point into yet another saddle, this one very broad with even better views to the east of the fire, Ruby Valley, Franklin Lake and the distant Ruby Marshes to the south.

A gentle, upward ascent traverses below peak 10,679 and as you round a corner, the much steeper trail up Wines Peak comes into view. A more level traverse leads into the final saddle below the peak, where out in the middle of nowhere, a low sign attached to a 4 by 4 post reminds you that you are still on the Ruby Crest Trail. The low-growing, sparse vegetation has remained constant since the Overland basin. The climb to the top of Wines Peak begins as a long, angling ascent up to a series of four short switchbacks that lead steeply to the pass, 10.6 miles from Overland Lake. The trail does not reach the actual summit of broad Wines Peak, and distant views are somewhat occluded by its mass. Find better vistas by wandering over to the true summit, where views of the central Ruby Mountains are spectacular. The peak, named after early rancher Ira D. Wines, seems to be a rather unimpressive looking peak, but derives some stature from being the southern guardian of the Ruby Lakes and the highest point along the Ruby Crest Trail.

Descending steeply from the pass, the trail makes a series of seven switchbacks before easing along the gently declining, lower slopes on the north side of Wines Peak. From the bottom of the switchbacks, the trail continues down into the upper North Furlong Creek drainage. At the bottom of the basin you reach a sign: *Ruby Crest Trail, Favre Lake* (straight), and *Overland Lake* (back)—though the trail junction to North Furlong Lake is farther ahead. Cross a small stream, the first water in 9½ miles, and proceed a short distance to a campsite in a grove of limber pines where a sign reads: *Furlong Creek Trail*, 12.2 miles from Overland Lake.

Side Trip to North Furlong Lake: Head southwest down the sloping canyon across a lush, open basin dotted with wildflowers. The closer you get to North Furlong Creek, named after another early settler N. Lawrence Furlong, the denser the vegetation becomes. The trail is indistinct in places but the way is clear and the location of North Furlong Lake in a large basin rimmed by steep cliffs to the south is easy to determine. Occasional cairns will help you stay on track. The trail comes close to the inviting creek for a while as it meanders through green-carpeted meadows before heading away from the stream to avoid the dense willows. Eventually the trail bears south, crossing the clear, cold stream, and heads across a large flat above the north side of the lake, where the trail all but disappears. However, the route is obvious from here over to North Furlong Lake, 0.9 mile from the junction with the Ruby Crest Trail.

Kidney-shaped, shallow North Furlong Lake lies at the base of the steep, gray cliffs of Wines Peak—a much more impressive landmark from this vantage than from the crest trail. A dense stand of limber pines rises up from the south lake shore to the slopes above. A large green meadow at the west end adds a pastoral feel to views down the mouth of the canyon, especially pleasant at sunset. There is no permanent outlet for the lake, which depends on snow melt and a high water table for its depth. A delightful little stream cascades out of the upper basin and gurgles down a narrow channel that cuts through lush, green meadows to the lake.

Find campsites among the pines on the south shore and in the meadows on the west. A flat to the north above the lake will accommodate large parties. Firewood is relatively plentiful. The shallow lake offers relatively warm water for swimming but the bottom is so muddy that the lake can easily become a giant mudpuddle. Fishing can be even less productive for the brook trout that inhabit the lake. Despite these drawbacks, North Furlong Lake, with excellent scenery and good potential for solitude, is an excellent stop for hikers weary of the long hike from Overland Lake.

From the junction with the North Furlong Creek Trail, the Ruby Crest Trail proceeds up to the pass that separates North Furlong Creek from Kleckner Creek to the north. As you near the pass, the trail unexplainably descends before resuming the steep climb through widely scattered limber pines to the top, 0.5 mile from the junction. An excellent view of the next basin occurs at the pass, but the lakes lie out of sight behind the massive slopes of peak 10,468. One can see the deep U-shaped canyon of Kleckner Creek below the towering, rocky summits of the central Rubies.

The trail zigzags steeply down the austere, boulder-strewn upper basin before stands of limber pine and wildflowers soften the surroundings. As the circuitous descent continues into lower elevations and less extreme conditions, limber pines are taller, wildflowers more prolific, and green meadows softly caress large boulders beneath the low, rocky cliffs. In the height of the season, wildflowers cover the slopes above the basin, including paintbrush, asters, bluebells, buttercups, lupine, yarrow and wild onion.

After a mile descent, the grade eases and a curiously placed 4 by 4 post with sign confirms that you are on the Ruby Crest Trail. As the trail rounds a hillside and comes into a large, open basin near the head of Kleckner Creek, another 4 by 4 post says the same. From this post an old trail, shown on the *Ruby Dome* topo, used to head east to Favre Lake, but it has since been blocked by the Forest Service. The Ruby Crest Trail continues a very short distance north to Kleckner Creek, where another 4 by 4 post appears, not surprisingly marked: *Ruby Crest Trail.* An old use trail bearing east along the south bank of the creek toward Favre Lake has been blocked to foot travel as well. You boulder-hop across Kleckner Creek and begin to climb the hillside above the north bank, reaching another of those 4 by 4 posts seemingly in the middle of nowhere, 0.2 miles from the creek. This point, 1.5 miles from the pass, is the junction with the official trail to Favre Lake.

Side Trip to Favre & Castle Lakes: Favre Lake is absent from the 4 by 4 post at the junction but it does come into view about 10 feet down the trail. Most parties come in from the north, and the location of the lake will have been obvious to them from Liberty Pass onward. As you head downhill, a lone limber pine next to the trail offers a small campsite well above the lake. Just before the trail bends sharply southwest, a sign reads: *Favre Lake, Elevation 9500 feet.* The trail proceeds down to the outlet stream, which is crossed with the aid of a combination of rocks and logs, into an area of campsites amid some low pines. You reach the lake one-quarter mile from the junction.

Favre Lake, at 9500 feet, sits in a broad, open bowl at the head of Kleckner Creek canyon, surrounded by green sloping hillsides gently dipping into the lake. The rugged, gray cliffs of the north ridge of Lake Peak highlight the limber-pine-covered hillside above the southeast shore. A wonderful wildflower meadow lines the outlet creek, and several agreeable campsites nestle amongst limber pines and shrubs along the south shore. Much of the remaining willow-lined shoreline may hinder anglers from capturing the brook trout inhabiting the lake, although access is good on the east side. Firewood is somewhat scarce.

Although a defined trail does not exist up to Castle Lake, the route is evident and brief, lasting only a quarter mile. A use trail begins where a dead tree is leaning against a group of limber pines above the south shore. If you cannot follow the use trail all the way to the lake, make your own way up the steep slope to the lip of the basin, where the grade eases considerably. Another 0.1 mile of easy walking delivers you at the north shore of Castle Lake.

Do not look too long at the rugged cliffs of Lake Peak above Castle Lake searching for the namesake of the lake—it does not exist. Both Favre and Castle lakes were named after Forest Service employees. Do not bring your rod either. According to the Forest Service, there are no fish in this lake. In spite of the lack of a castle or a fish, Castle Lake is a delightful place to spend a couple of hours or a couple of days. Carved out of a steep, horseshoe-shaped basin and flanked by the steep, craggy cliffs of Lake Peak, Castle Lake has much more of an alpine character than Favre Lake. Patches of snow cling to crevices in the gray rock walls well into the summer, adding to the alpine flavor. The shoreline is embraced by meadows and

Liberty Lake from below Liberty Pass

willows, with occasional stands of limber pine inching their way up the lower slopes of the basin. Campsites are in the pines at the north end of the lake close to the outlet stream and, unlike at Favre Lake, firewood is readily available. The extra effort involved in reaching Castle Lake should reap big dividends in solitude.

From the junction with the lateral to Favre and Castle lakes, the Ruby Crest Trail begins the long climb toward Liberty Lake and Liberty Pass. You can see the outlet stream cascading down the steep slope from Liberty Lake, but the lake itself remains out of view behind a large rock dike. The trail surmounts the dike by way of a long, angling switchback. As you climb, beautiful views of Favre Lake, Castle Lake and Lake Peak get better with each step. Another 4 by 4 post is at a junction with a short lateral trail wandering over toward the outlet of Liberty Lake, 1.0 mile from the junction to Favre and Castle lakes.

Liberty Lake is the undisputed crown jewel of the Ruby Mountains. Hundreds of hikers cast ballots with their feet every season, making Liberty Lake the preeminent destination for the overwhelming majority of recreationists trudging over Liberty Pass from Lamoille Canyon. The 1,600-foot climb helps keep the lake in a pristine condition. Everything one expects in a classic mountain lake can be found at Liberty Lake: a glacier-carved, steep-walled cirque basin perched high above the surrounding terrain, deep-blue waters reflecting precipitous rock peaks, incredible views across the deep canyon to Favre and Castle lakes below Lake Peak, cascading outlet stream bordered by flower-strewn meadows, excellent campsites near scattered limber pines, and a good supply of large trout.

Resuming the climb toward Liberty Pass from the lake junction, the trail climbs steeply, avoiding cliffs, winding up to a point high above the western edge of Liberty Lake. A profusion of wildflowers grow in the nooks and crannies between large boulders along the steep hillsides. A short, fairly level traverse rounds the head of the basin before the trail resumes a steep climb of the south slopes below the pass. In a series of switchbacks, leading to the pass, a large rock shelf provides the last good look at Liberty Lake.

Continue up the switchbacks until a tall steel pole with a sign high above the ground greets you, proclaiming: *Liberty Pass, 10,400 feet* at the signed Ruby Mountains Wilderness boundary. The pass is a cold, wind-swept, austere, rocky aerie. Stunted limber pines, grasses and wildflowers cling to life at what seems to be the top of the world. None of the lakes behind or ahead are visible. However, you can gaze southward upon Wines Peak, Lake Peak and the mountains beyond. To the north your vision extends all the way down to the parking lot at road's end in Lamoille Canyon, where tiny people scurry around like ants. Three miles of trail are all that separate the pass from those tiny figures.

The trail winds down from Liberty Pass through a barren area of rock, boulders and slabs. Very few plants can grow in this harsh environment, and quite often snowfields blanket the north-facing slopes well into the summer months. Check with the Forest Service about the snow conditions at the pass before you begin your journey, especially after heavy winters like the one of 1994-95 when the trail did not open until the end of July. Mountaineering gear may be necessary to get down the pass early in the season if heavy snows remain on the upper slopes.

As the trail switchbacks steeply down through the desolate terrain, you eventually reach an overlook of Lamoille Lake still a long way below you. After nearly a mile of steep decline, the trail levels out just before a junction with a lateral trail to Lamoille Lake, marked by another of those familiar 4 by 4 posts.

The short lateral trail quickly leads to the south end of the green-hued waters of Lamoille Lake. At 9750 feet, the lake has an alpine feel, occupying the head of a basin formed by steep rock walls and slopes that rise from the lakeshore over a thousand feet to the peaks above. Sparsely placed, weather-beaten limber pines add to the alpine aspect. A green hillside sweeps up to a low pass above the western shore providing cross-country access into Box Canyon and to some of the central Ruby Mountain peaks. A couple of campsites are available around the shore but most of the activity at the lake consists of fishermen up for the day, pursuing the elusive brook trout that glide through the chilly waters.

Resuming the descent, the trail heads gently down past the two Dollar Lakes, so named for their symmetrical resemblance to the silver dollar. The shallow lakes have an impressive backdrop of rugged peaks typical of upper Lamoille Canyon. Willows and meadows surround the shorelines of both lakes. Between the two lakes is a marsh with deep green, grassy hummocks. Fisherman pass right by Dollar Lakes on their way to the upper lakes since there are no fish in either lake.

You cross the outlet of the Dollar Lakes on a crude wooden bridge, gain a hillside and then resume the steep descent, passing lush slopes covered with willows and wildflowers. A series of four switchbacks lead downhill to a long descending traverse through a dense stand of limber pines. Two more switchbacks take you into more open terrain and alongside Lamoille Creek, which you follow for a while and then cross, either on another crude wooden bridge during high water or by a boulder hop in low water conditions. The trail wanders away from the creek as the descent continues under pines. Eventually the trail will cross Lamoille Creek twice more before breaking out of the trees and into the lushly vegetated slopes above the parking area. Finally, you reach the Lamoille Canyon parking lot 3 miles from the pass and 32 miles from the Green Mountain trailhead.

Trip 7 🦌
OVERLAND LAKE TRAIL

Trip Type: Overnight backpack or dayhike; Out and back
Distance: 10.4 miles round trip
Season: Mid-June to mid-October
Access: Gravel and dirt roads
Water: Available at lake only
Maps: #19
Franklin Lake NW 7.5 minute quadrangle, 1969
Humboldt National Forest map, Ruby Mountains Ranger District, 1990
Ruby Mountains & East Humboldt Wildernesses, Humboldt National Forest, 1994

Introduction: If you don't object to the long drive to the trailhead, the Overland Lake trail offers one of the few opportunities to reach the heart of the Ruby Mountains from the east side of the range. A continuous climb of 5.2 miles begins virtually at the base of the mountains at the edge of Ruby Valley and ascends nearly 3,000 feet through high desert terrain to the alpine setting of the lake. Due to the remoteness of the trail, solitude may be your only companion, although horse parties do use this route.

Overland Lake offers a spectacularly beautiful setting perched high above the Overland Creek basin and below towering rock cliffs. The picturesque lakeshore offers some of the best camping in the Ruby Mountains Wilderness. The area around the lake is ripe for further exploration, either scrambling up the peaks or strolling along the Ruby Crest National Recreation Trail (see Trip 6).

Trailhead: (e) The Overland Lake trailhead is off of State Route 767 on the east side of the Ruby Mountains toward the south end of the Wilderness Area. Follow State Route 229, either 36 miles southeast from I-80 at Exit 321, *Halleck, Ruby Valley*, or 14 miles west from U.S. 93, to the junction with State Route 767. Proceed south on asphalt Highway 767 for 2 miles, until the surface turns to well-graded gravel. Continue on the gravel road paralleling the mountain range, crossing Overland Creek at 14.5 miles from the junction. Another 1.4 miles lead to a dirt road heading west into the mountains near a sign marked: *Humboldt National Forest Access*. A sign along a barbed-wire fence paralleling the dirt road reads: *Overland Lake Trail*. If you miss the turnoff and travel to Rock House you've gone 0.8 mile too far.

If you are concerned about driving your passenger car up the dirt road, park your car in the grassy area to the left and hike the extra half mile. Those with more durable, high-clearance vehicles can continue on the dirt road 0.5 mile up the grassy hillside and park near the closed Forest Service gate. If you have a 4-wheel drive you can pass through the gate and travel even further up the steep, rocky road to a small knoll where the earth has been bermed to prevent further progress. Parking is available here for 3 or 4 cars. The route description, however, begins back down the road at the gate.

Description: From the Forest Service gate, begin hiking along the dirt road over dry, grassy hillsides to the knoll where an earth berm blocks vehicles from proceeding any farther. Soon the road dwindles to a single-track trail and you quickly come to the Wilderness boundary and a sign: *Overland*

Old cabin at Overland Lake

Lake Trail, Humboldt National Forest. From the boundary the trail continues to climb and wind through sagebrush and grasslands typical of the lower foothills, presenting a stark contrast to the terrain that awaits you in the heart of the mountains. Views upward of verdant, green slopes leading up to rugged peaks with snow clinging to cracks and crevices seem to exacerbate the hot, dry conditions typically present at these lower elevations.

Eventually the trail winds to a small saddle and passes some interesting rock outcrops. Above the outcrops the vegetation begins to shift to sage, shrubs and wildflowers interspersed with groves of aspens. A series of switchbacks leads to a long traverse that rounds a corner at 2.75 miles from the trailhead and enters the Overland Creek basin. The Ruby crest, seen across the deep, wide chasm of the basin, exhibits scenery more reminiscent of what one expects in the mountains—steep, green canyons with rushing streams and jagged, rocky summits.

The trail continues the unrelenting climb over open slopes, broken occasionally by groves of aspens and dotted with wildflowers. Cross a dry drainage, shown as a seasonal stream on the topo, after which you encounter another series of switchbacks. The long zigzagging climb up the steep hillside ultimately reaches a junction with the Ruby Crest Trail 4.8 miles from the trailhead.

From the junction you turn left heading up another set of eight short switchbacks through scattered limber pines on a boulder-strewn slope. The trail moderates at the lip of the lake's basin and you reach Overland Lake 0.4 miles from the trail junction. Nearby is an old log cabin with a metal roof.

Thousands of feet above the valley, at the lip of the basin, Overland Lake occupies a rugged notch perched near the crest of the range, the green-tinted water reflecting the rugged peaks that encircle the lake. Talus slopes and rock slabs lead up to steep gray and tan peaks that ring the basin on three sides. Limber pines gracefully dot the edge of the lake and add character to the shoreline. Swimming is chilly but under the right circumstances can be quite refreshing. Fishing is fair for brook trout and most of the lakeshore is accessible.

Overland Lake is not heavily used, but it is a prescribed stop for parties hiking the entire Ruby Crest Trail. You may not see many backpackers along the Overland Lake Trail, but horse packers use it with some frequency

The old cabin at the north end of the lake has little appeal for habitation except during extreme weather. However, common sense dictates that the metal roof should discourage use during lightning storms. Horse packers appear to use the cabin for storing some of their gear during the outfitting season.

You can camp in some of the flat areas around the cabin, but the best site for camping is across the outlet creek beneath some tall limber pines. So far, horses have been confined to the east side of the creek and horse outfitters have been setting up camp a good distance downstream. Hopefully, this practice will continue, since manure, flies and trampled, muddy ground can detract from even the most oblivious camper's experience. Firewood is extremely scarce.

Retrace your steps to the trailhead.

OTHER TRAILS

Changing Valley Nature Trail: Eight miles up the Lamoille Canyon Road is the turn-out for this third-mile-long trail. A display at the edge of the pavement explains the glacial formation of the main and side canyons. Numbered posts, corresponding to entries in a free brochure, provide information about the natural history of the area along the trail. The trail is aptly named as it is the best spot to view the devastation around Lamoille Creek caused by melting snows and heavy rains during the spring of 1995 that resulted in large deposits of mud and debris throughout the creek basin.

Gardner Creek, Krenka Creek & Ruby Guard Trailheads: These three trailheads provide alternate ways into the north section of the Rubies and the Soldier Lakes Basin. All three are located close to one another near the Secret Pass area off of State Route 229. Seldom used, these trails offer remoteness and solitude, culminating in the beauty of Soldier, Robinson and Hidden lakes (see Trip 1).

Colonel Moore: A short, steep trail heads west from the east side of the Ruby Mountains into a basin below the summit of the range. Adventurous types can continue on an arduous cross-country route over the crest into the Ruby Lakes area. The rough road, requiring a 4-wheel-drive, turns west from State Route 767 one-quarter mile north of Ruby Valley School.

Long Canyon: The Long Canyon Trail is the only canyon route into the Rubies from the west. Access is supposedly provided from County Road 714 through portions of the Te-Moak Indian Reservation, although directions are difficult and signs posted in the reservation send dubious signals about just how welcome you are. The trail divides 1.6 miles from the trailhead, the northern branch heading along North Furlong Creek to North Furlong Lake and the Ruby Crest Trail. Reaching the Ruby Crest Trail cross-country at the end of the southern branch up Long Canyon is possible, but the entire route to the crest lies outside of the Wilderness on Forest Service land. ·

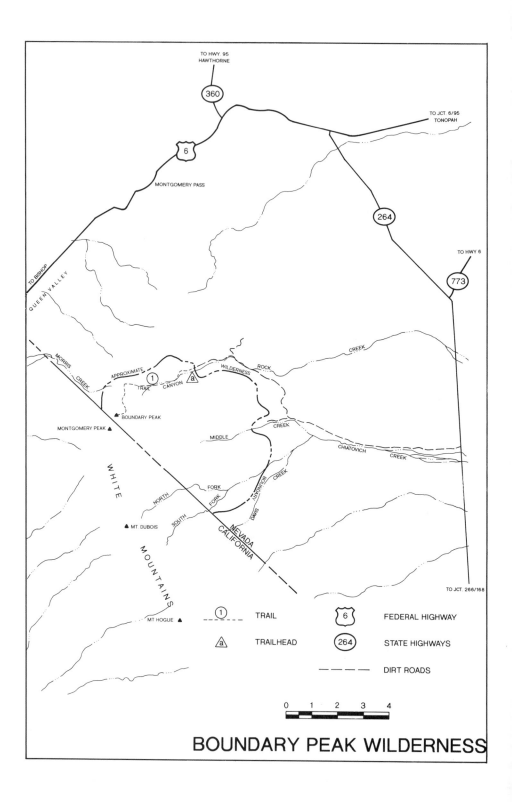

BOUNDARY PEAK WILDERNESS

Trails of Western & Central Nevada

Chapter 9
BOUNDARY PEAK WILDERNESS

Boundary Peak, striking the dramatic profile of a rugged mountain, sits prominently at the north end of the White Mountains along the western edge of the state, its lofty, pinnacled mass visible for many miles in virtually every direction. The peak stands out like a constant beacon for travelers along the state and federal highways that circumnavigate the range.

Most of the White Mountains lie within California. Some argue that the peak itself is not really a mountain at all but a mere subsidiary point on the north ridge of nearby Montgomery Peak. If the Von Schmidt Line of 1873 were still recognized as the boundary between Nevada and California, the issue would be moot, since the summit would lie wholly within California. The current recognized boundary between the two states places Boundary Peak squarely in Nevada. The origin of the name is certainly no mystery. Whether you consider Boundary Peak a mountain unto itself or a point on a ridge, it is still the highest piece of terra firma in Nevada and worthy of your efforts.

The Boundary Peak Wilderness lies completely within Nevada and is a relatively small region at approximately 10,000 acres. The White Mountain range extends into California for another 25 miles, providing an abundance of other hikes and climbs. If you desire to see the extensive groves of ancient bristlecone pines for which the range is famous, you will definitely have to include an excursion into the California section. In addition to the many other trails, adventurous types can do a multi-day, cross-country backpack along the top of the range, all the way from Boundary Peak south to the access road heading north from State Highway 168. Obtain information about routes in the California portion of the White Mountains from the Inyo National Forest in Bishop.

As with many high points, Boundary Peak offers a superb view from the summit. Nearly 10,000 feet of elevation in a mere seven miles separate the summit of the White Mountains from the bottom of Owens Valley, allowing for unimpeded vistas of the majestic Sierra Nevada to the west as well as a portion of unique Mono Lake. Sunrise from the top of the range is an extremely rewarding and awe-inspiring experience. Countless other ranges march in succession across the Nevada desert to the east, interrupting the Great Basin with linear rows of mountain ridges. A superb view of the rest of the White Mountains is another reward of the arduous climb to the apex of Nevada.

Sitting in the rain shadow of the slightly higher Sierra Nevada, the White Mountains receive a fraction of the precipitation of their western neighbor. As with most Nevada mountain ranges, most of the moisture that does reach these mountains falls as winter snow, a smaller percentage occurring as summer thunderstorms. Another dramatic variance between the two ranges is the dissimilar geology. Although scientists speculate that both ranges uplifted about the same time, the composition of the Sierra Nevada is heavily glaciated granite while the gracefully rounded White Mountains contain primarily older, sedimentary rock.

LOCATION

Boundary Peak, at the north end of the White Mountains, is at the western border of Nevada approximately 35 miles due north of the town of Bishop, California. The area is bounded on the north and west by U.S. 6 and on the east by State Route 264.

CAMPGROUNDS

No developed campgrounds are close to Boundary Peak. The closest Forest Service campground is near the Schulman Grove at the south end of the White Mountains, accessed from California State Highway 168. Although there are no official campsites near the peak, you can camp in undeveloped sites in Trail Canyon along the creek near meadows, toward the end of the access road.

RESOURCES

Limited services are available in the small communities of Benton, California, on U.S. 6 and Dyer, Nevada, on State Route 264. The nearest source of backpacking supplies is in Bishop, California.

FOREST SERVICE

White Mountain Ranger Station
798 North Main Street
Bishop, CA 93514
(619) 873-2500

Trip 1 ♣

BOUNDARY PEAK

Trip Type: Dayhike; Out and back
Distance: 7.8 miles round trip
Season: Summer through fall
Access: Dirt road
Water: Available in creek
Maps: #21
Boundary Peak 7.5 minute quadrangle, 1987 (provisional)
Benton Range BLM 30 X 60 minute quadrangle, 1988

Introduction: The Boundary Peak Wilderness is the smallest wilderness area in Nevada and contains the highest peak. Some argue that Boundary Peak is not a mountain by itself but just a bump on the ridge of 13,441-foot Montgomery Peak to the south. Disregarding Boundary Peak as the highest "mountain" in Nevada would make Wheeler Peak in Great Basin National Park at 13,063 the highest summit in the state, no doubt pleasing fans of the park. The argument is moot anyway, since Boundary Peak, whether you consider it a real mountain or not, is still worth the trip and remains the highest "point" in Nevada. The best answer to the argument is to climb both peaks!

Who can pass up the opportunity to stand upon the highest point in the most mountainous state in the lower 48? Impressive vistas of distant ranges and dramatic views of closer peaks reward the diligent hiker at the summit. For those desiring an early morning start, there are campsites available in meadows adjacent to the creek near the trailhead. Even though Boundary Peak is the high spot of Nevada, because of its remoteness you should have the place to yourself. You won't have to battle the crowds standing in line to get a permit to reach the summit as you would for Mt. Whitney, the highest point in California, 90 miles to the south. Allow 8 to 12 hours for the trip.

Trailhead: (a) Access the Boundary Peak trailhead off State Route 264 either by U.S. 6/95 from the north, U.S. 95 from the east, or U.S. 395 from the west. The peak itself is a prominent landmark, dominating much of the surrounding country and is a virtual beacon for the hiker. If traveling from the south or southwest, you can get to State Route 264 from State Route 266; from the northwest directly from U.S. 6; and from the northeast via State Route 773.

Turn west onto dirt road from Route 264 in Fish Lake Valley 5.8 miles south of the junction of State Routes 264 and 773, or about 10.5 miles north of the community of Dyer. The junction is approximately 200 yards north of a ranch house adjacent to Chiatovich Creek. Drive on the main road through sagebrush for 7.1 miles to a prominent intersection where a sign points straight ahead to *Middle Canyon* and to the right to *Trail Canyon*. Turn right and follow the main road as it heads north and then northwest into Trail Canyon. Pass a man-made pond on the left and reach lush meadows next to the creek, where campsites should be available, 12.2 miles from the highway. At 13.2 miles you come to a grassy parking area on the right with room for half a dozen vehicles. Find additional campsites just up the trail in another, smaller meadow not far from the creek.

Description: The route to the summit of Boundary Peak begins on the continuation of the old road as it heads upstream adjacent to Trail Canyon Creek, quickly passing the trailhead register. Follow the road through a meadow, where you can camp if you do not mind carrying your gear for a short distance, and past the lush creekside vegetation of willows and wildflowers. About one-eighth mile from the trailhead, the road narrows to a single-track trail. At 0.4 mile from the trailhead, you cross to the south bank of the creek and proceed on a distinct path just above dense foliage. Unfortunately, as you head up the canyon, a distinct trail becomes hard to follow in places. If you are lucky you just might be able to proceed on a bona-fide trail all the way to Trail Canyon Saddle, but most likely you will lose the trail in sections. Your destination of the saddle at the head of the canyon is obvious, although the easiest route is not always discernible. In general, travel up the south side of the canyon while avoiding the temptation to hike too close to the creek and the dense brush surrounding it. Try not to stray too far from the creek either, or you may end up battling thickets of sagebrush and snowberry. In addition, during wet years you may end up having to dodge boggy patches near some of the springs as well.

Toward the head of Trail Canyon beyond the last spring, the creek dries up (with the obvious exception during snowmelt in the spring). Farther up the canyon a stand of limber pine breaks up the sagebrush-covered hillsides on the south side of the drainage. Somewhere on the last hillside below the saddle, the route crosses the dry drainage and ascends to Trail Canyon Saddle, 2.2 miles from the trailhead. Scattered pockets of grasses and ground-hugging plants are all the vegetation that survives in the harsh environment of the saddle. Portions of the High Sierra come into view, but are just a precursor of more spectacular views awaiting you on the summit.

From Trail Canyon Saddle, a number of use trails head up the steep, rocky slopes to the south. Try to pick the trail that will keep you directly on, or close to, the top of the ridge and you will be able to follow it almost to the summit. There are just a couple of exceptions, where you have to scramble over some rocks for short sections. A steep climb of 1200 feet in one-half mile brings you to the top of a pass where views open up of the north side of Boundary Peak. The surrounding terrain up to the pass would suggest that Boundary Peak would be nothing more than a big talus pile, but the peak has a dramatic appearance, with jagged spires and slanting rock faces of gray granitic rock. Snow patches hang in the clefts and gullies late into the season.

You continue from the pass as the trail makes a gentle, short traverse beneath a peaklet to another saddle above the side canyon, heading into Trail Canyon from the southwest. Avoid the tendency to take the "shortcut" down this canyon on your return from the summit, as it is a tedious descent of a seemingly endless slope of loose talus. As below, remain on the trail closest to the actual ridge top as you resume the climb away from the saddle. The climb curves around to the west as you follow the ridge below the summit. Turn the final pinnacle on the right and ascend large talus blocks to the summit, 0.9 mile and 1050 feet from the last saddle.

From the top of Boundary Peak, you have a commanding view to distant horizons in nearly all directions. To the south vistas are blocked by Montgomery Peak and the rest of the White Mountains, including Mt. Dubois, the immense plateau of the Pellisier Flats, and White Mountain Peak, at 14,245 feet the highest summit in the range. The man-made boundary between California and Nevada runs right through the bottom of the deep cleft that separates the massive hulks of Boundary and Montgomery peaks. The spectacular and popular Sierra Nevada looms large in the west. To the northwest you can even see a bit of Mono Lake. Toward the east, distant, remote, and certainly less well known ranges parade in seemingly endless succession. Perhaps the most awesome picture is that of the rugged west faces of Boundary and Montgomery peaks, dropping dramatically 6500 feet to Queen and Benton valleys.

During certain weather patterns in the height of summer, thunderstorms can be a concern. Then, the best plan is to start early and be off the summit before mid afternoon. Afternoon winds can also create a wind-chill factor on the summit that is dramatically different than temperatures below. Be sure to carry appropriate clothing. If those are not enough cautions, altitude can be an objective hazard also. Make sure that you acclimate for a climb up to 13,140 feet above sea level, following the most current recommendations for avoiding altitude sickness. Allow plenty of time to adjust and drink plenty of fluids. Water is not available beyond the creek in Trail Canyon, so carry plenty of liquids for the long, arduous climb.

If you wish to traverse the ridge and climb Montgomery Peak, plan on a couple of hours for the ascent and the return to Boundary Peak. Like its smaller neighbor, Montgomery Peak is not technically difficult, but a rope may be helpful for some less experienced parties.

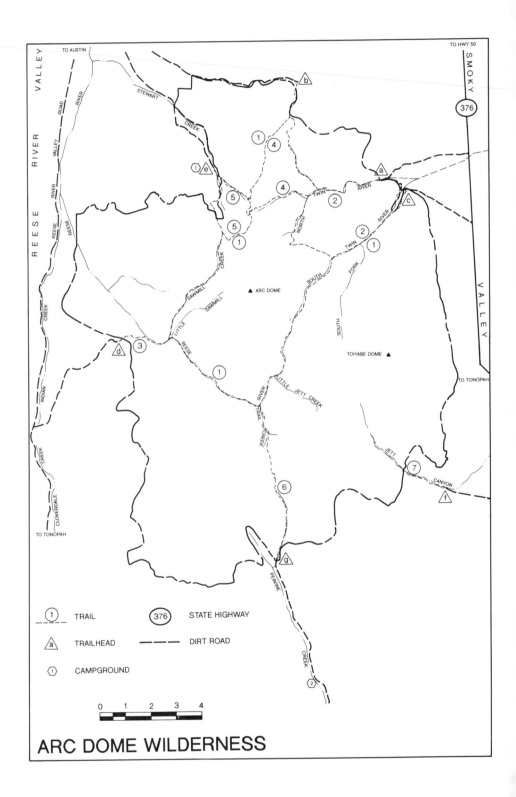

TO AUSTIN

TO HWY 50

376

REESE RIVER VALLEY

SMOKY VALLEY

STEWART CREEK

b

1 4

e 1

4

5

5 2

5 1

1

2

2 1

a

c

ARC DOME

NORTH

TWIN RIVER

SOUTH FORK

TWIN RIVER

SOUTH

TOIYABE DOME

SAWMILL CREEK

LITTLE SAWMILL CREEK

LITTLE REESE RIVER

3

d

1

LITTLE JETT CREEK

REESE RIVER TRAIL

CREEK

INDIAN CREEK

6

JETT

7

CANYON

f

TO TONOPAH

CLOVERDALE CREEK

TO CLOVERDALE

TO TONOPAH

g

PEAVINE

CREEK

2

| 1 | TRAIL | 376 | STATE HIGHWAY |

| a | TRAILHEAD | | DIRT ROAD |

| 1 | CAMPGROUND |

0 1 2 3 4

ARC DOME WILDERNESS

Chapter 10
ARC DOME WILDERNESS

Arc Dome, at 115,000 acres, is the largest wilderness area in the state. Comprising the southern third of the Toiyabe Mountains, it holds a convoluted grouping of ridges and canyons, unlike the linear nature of most Nevada mountain ranges. At the north end of the Wilderness, the 125-mile-long range does narrow to a single spine that continues north past the town of Austin. For 50 miles of that run, the crest never dips below 10,000 feet, presenting a massive wall of mountains rising over 4,000 feet above the surrounding valleys. Ruling majestically over this mountainous domain, Arc Dome crowns the range at 11,788 feet, tenth highest summit in the Silver State.

In the arid center of the Great Basin, the Toiyabe Range benefits greatly from its lofty height, soaking up a relative abundance of moisture from the weather systems that cross the state. Consequently, a myriad of waterways course through the area, including three named rivers: the Reese, South Twin and North Twin. Mark Twain, writing in *Roughing It*, had this to say about rivers in Nevada: "People accustomed to the monster mile-wide Mississippi grow accustomed to associating the term "river" with a high degree of watery grandeur. Consequently, such people feel rather disappointed when they stand on the shores of the Humboldt or the Carson and find that a "river" in Nevada is a sickly rivulet which is just the counterpart of the Erie Canal in all respects save that the canal is twice as long and four times as deep. One of the pleasantest and most invigorating exercises one can contrive is to run and jump across the Humboldt River till he is overheated, and then drink it dry." The deceptive titles of these streams were creations of the Reese River Navigation Company, a scam designed to bilk Easterners out of investment dollars. The company purportedly needed funds to develop a system of ships used to transport ore from nearby mines along these rivers to processing plants. Despite Mr. Twain's disdain for the misleading appellation of the term "river" in Nevada, the water courses in the Arc Dome Wilderness are a welcome delight and support a diverse ecosystem of flora and fauna.

One of the blessings of this Wilderness is the extensive network of trails. Truly a backpacker's paradise, numerous trail connections allow for the possibility of many extended trips. A variety of trails lead along canyons providing routes through rich, riparian environments. From the apex of the range, the 65-mile Toiyabe Crest National Recreation Trail offers magnificent vistas through the clear, rarefied air of central Nevada. From high points throughout the Wilderness, to make out the Sierra Nevada on the western horizon, over 100 miles away is not unusual. Victims of the all-too-common dilemma facing Nevada wilderness areas of a lack of maintenance, some of the less popular trails within the Arc Dome Wilderness are on the verge of being lost. Fortunately, the topography is generally open, allowing hikers with modest off-trail skills to travel in the Wilderness with relative ease.

The Toiyabe Crest Trail, longest maintained trail in Nevada, is the centerpiece of the Arc Dome Wilderness. Beginning at the northeast corner of the Wilderness, the trail leads along the South Twin River, the Reese River and Big Sawmill Creek before gaining the crest of the range 7 miles south of Ophir Summit at the north boundary. Our trail description ends here but the north half of the trail continues along the spine of the range, finishing the 65-mile route in Kingston Canyon. If you plan to complete the entire route, be aware that the section outside the Wilderness Area is dry, requiring backpackers to descend into the side canyons to find springs and creeks. Early in the season is an optimum time for the trip when lingering snow banks provide additional sources of water. Within the Wilderness, water is readily accessible along the Crest Trail, except for the last 7 miles along the ridge. Even though the northern section of trail lies outside the protection of the Wilderness, the Forest Service manages the narrow corridor of trail as de facto wilderness, closed year long to mechanized travel. The one-way trip on the Toiyabe Crest Trail requires a car shuttle or pickup, necessitating a long drive between trailheads, particularly if you're walking just the Wilderness section.

The large acreage of backcountry within the Arc Dome Wilderness is a benefit to wildlife as well as to recreationists. The range supports large herds of deer, and the Forest Service reports sightings of migrating elk in the Toiyabes. Mountain lions, bobcats, coyotes and beaver also make their homes here, along with the usual conglomeration of smaller rodents. Bighorn sheep were once common, but competition from domestic sheep have reduced herds to isolated corners of the Wilderness near the steep, craggy ridges of the Twin Rivers and Jett canyons. Chukar and sage and blue grouse are common game birds sharing the skies with a variety of raptors such as golden eagle, northern goshawk and prairie falcon. The extensive waters of the area provide some of the best stream fishing for trout in Nevada, including the threatened native Lahontan cutthroat species. Non-native species of eastern brook, rainbow and German brown trout are also present.

In spite of the diversity of the wildlife within the Arc Dome Wilderness, the most often seen animal, as in most Nevada mountain areas, is the range cow. Even if you miss the beasts themselves, the evidence of their roamings will be impossible to escape. Unfortunately, cows and people find some of the same areas appealing for similar reasons. Trampled meadows and an abundant supply of cow pies represent the visible damage that dampens enthusiasm for camping in certain areas. Who knows what might remain unseen in the water supplies. At least the four-legged brutes avoid most of the crest.

The Toiyabe Range is somewhat geologically diverse. Plutonic, volcanic and sedimentary rocks are all present in substantial amounts throughout the mountains. Most of the rock found within the Arc Dome Wilderness has reddish tones and is of a volcanic nature. The steep spires and serrated crests found in some of the canyons are leftover portions of an old crater. The highest portions of the crest surrounding Arc Dome are victims of the forces of glaciation, most evident in the deep cirques carved into the edges of the broad crest directly north of Arc Dome's summit.

LOCATION

Located in Nye County, approximately 50 miles north of Tonopah and 50 miles south of Austin, the Arc Dome Wilderness encompasses the southern third of the Toiyabe Range. U.S. 6/95 is south and U.S. 50 is north of the Toiyabe Mountains. Provided by Forest Service roads, access to the Wilderness branches from State Route 376 on the east side of the range and from the Reese River Valley Road on the west.

CAMPGROUNDS

1. COLUMBINE—Forest Service
    Open May 15 through October
    Camping, Picnicking, Restrooms, Trailer Sites, Stock Loading
       Facilities, Fishing
    Trailhead for Stewart Creek Trail (see Trip 5)
    At the northwest edge of the Wilderness, 9 miles east from the
       Reese River Valley Road up Forest Service Road 119

2. PEAVINE—Forest Service
    Open May through October
    Camping, Picnicking, Restrooms, Trailer Sites, Fishing
    South of the Wilderness, 9.3 miles from State Route 376 off Forest
       Service Road 020

3. KINGSTON CANYON—Forest Service
    Open May 15 through October
    Camping, Picnicking, Restrooms, Trailer Sites, Fishing
    Near northern trailhead for Toiyabe Crest Trail (see Trip 1)
    North of the Wilderness, 5.5 miles west of State Route 376 on
       Forest Service Road 002

4. BOB SCOTT—Forest Service
Open May 15 through October
Camping, Picnicking, Restrooms, Trailer Sites, Water, Litter pick-up
Approximately 6 miles east of Austin on U.S. 50

5. BIG CREEK—Forest Service
Open May 15 through October
Camping, Picnicking, Restrooms, Trailer Sites, Fishing
North of the Wilderness, on Forest Service Road 002 approximately
17 miles west of State Route 376 and 12 miles south of U.S. 50

RESOURCES

Two old mining towns on opposite ends of the Toiyabe Range provide
the nearest services for travelers entering the Arc Dome Wilderness.
Tonopah, at the junctions of U.S. 6 and 95, is 50 miles south of the Arc
Dome Wilderness, offering food, lodging, service stations, entertainment
and limited shopping. Some camping equipment is available for purchase.
Austin, to the north on U.S. 50, is the only other major town in the vicinity and offers the same services as Tonopah on a smaller scale. The small
community of Carvers on the east side of the range on State Route 376
offers gasoline, food, lodging and a convenience store. Another convenience store with gas is along Route 376 near the turnoff to Kingston. No
services are available on the west side of the range.

FOREST SERVICE

Tonopah Ranger District
PO Box 3940
Tonopah, NV 89049-3940
(702) 482-6286

Austin Ranger District
100 Midas Canyon Road
PO Box 130
Austin, NV 89310-0130
(702) 964-2671

Toiyabe National Forest
Supervisor's Office
1200 Franklin Way
Sparks, NV 89431
(702) 331-6444

Trip 1 ♔
TOIYABE CREST NATIONAL RECREATION TRAIL

Trip Type: 3 to 5 day backpack; Shuttle
Distance: 30.2 miles
Season: Mid-June through October
Access: Dirt roads (high-clearance vehicle recommended for Ophir
Summit trailhead)
Water: Rivers, creeks, springs (the final 7 miles are dry)

Maps: #22, 23, 24, 25,
> *Carvers NW, South Toiyabe Peak, Arc Dome, Bakeoven Creek* 7.5
> minute quadrangles, 1971, 1979, 1980, 1980
> Toiyabe National Forest map, Austin Ranger District, 1968
> (revised 1990, 91)

Introduction: Just as the Ruby Crest Trail is the premier trip in the Ruby Mountains, the Toiyabe Crest Trail in the Toiyabe Range is the highlight of any venture into the Arc Dome Wilderness. The total trail is 66 miles long, but this description covers only the first 30 miles through the Wilderness Area. Outside the Wilderness, the trail is truly a "crest" trail as it goes along the spine of the Toiyabe Crest for 36 miles to the north end of the route in Kingston Canyon. Within the Arc Dome Wilderness, the trail avoids the top of the range as it curves around the south end of the Wilderness, until the final 7 miles run along the crest to the Ophir Summit trailhead.

Beginning on the South Twin River, the Crest Trail follows the drainage nearly 8 miles up to a low pass separating it from the upper Reese River. The trail leads alongside the Reese River for another 8 miles until a long climb of 7 miles up Big Sawmill Creek finally leads to the true crest just north of Arc Dome. The next 7 miles of trail stays on or close to the actual crest for the duration of the trip through the Wilderness.

Between the elevations of 6,200 and 11,100 feet the Toiyabe Crest Trail passes through a wide range of environments. Sampling lush, riparian foliage along three major drainages, the trail exposes the traveler to a diverse mixture of trees, shrubs and wildflowers. Along these streams the relatively small amount of water amazingly transforms the high desert into a luxuriant display of vegetation. Significant stands of aspen carpeting some of the high drainages put on a dramatic display during the autumn season. Above the rivers and creeks, juniper, pinyon pine and mountain mahogany adorn the lower, sagebrush-covered slopes, while limber pine graces the higher slopes of the ridges and upper canyons. On the 11,000-foot rocky plateau north of Arc Dome, dwarf sagebrush and tiny alpine wildflowers soften the austere surroundings.

The trail, built during the 1930's, was a work project of the Civilian Conservation Corps. Unfortunately, over the subsequent years, due to its obscurity and a lack of proper funding, the trail has not received the care and attention that the original craftsmen gave to their project. Although rarely maintained, the path remains in fair condition and is easy to follow for the most of the route through the Wilderness. A couple of trail junctions are a bit confusing but easily negotiated by alert hikers possessed of rudimentary map-reading skills. Other sections of trail are faint and hard to follow, but for only short distances and present no major routefinding problems.

While the first few miles of trail are moderately steep and brushy and require numerous fords of the South Twin River, the middle section of the trail along the wide open, rolling terrain of the Reese River is ideal for horse packing. Anyone vaguely familiar with old western movies may envision a posse of white hats chasing a band of cattle rustlers through the open country along the river. Anglers will enjoy the opportunity to experience some of the best fishing in the state in the South Twin and Reese rivers and the lower reaches of Big Sawmill Creek. Peak baggers will enjoy the chance to reach the summit of Arc Dome via the 3-mile summit trail. Vistas from the top of Arc Dome, along with those from the crest, are spectacular in beauty and scope.

One major advantage that the Wilderness section of the Crest Trail has over the portion outside the Wilderness is the availability of water. Following major rivers and creeks, the trail is never far from water until the last section along the crest. If planning to complete the entire 66-mile trail, consider an early-season trip when water is more abundant and lingering snow banks along the crest provide additional water sources. Otherwise you will have to descend down into side canyons to retrieve it.

Trailheads: SOUTH TWIN TRAILHEAD: (c) The turnoff from State Route 376 for South Twin River trailhead, signed as such, is 40 miles south of U.S. 50 and 60.5 miles north of U.S. 6. Travel northwest on single-lane gravel road 3.0 miles to the trailhead. A wide turnout on the south side of the road is available for parking.

OPHIR SUMMIT TRAILHEAD: (b) The Ophir Creek road traverses the Toiyabe Range at the north end of the Arc Dome Wilderness. From the east the road is passable only to durable, 4-wheel-drive, high-clearance vehicles, and is blocked by an impasse approximately 4 miles from State Route 376. Without a viable access to the trailhead from the east side, a long drive around the range is necessary to complete the car shuttle. A high-clearance vehicle is necessary to negotiate the road west from the Reese River Valley as described below.

FROM TONOPAH: From the junction of U.S. 6 and 95 in Tonopah, head west on 6/95 approximately 5 miles and turn north onto Gabbs Poleline Road. About 31 miles from the junction, turn northeast onto Cloverdale Road and follow it for 5.5 miles to Forest Service Road #018. Head north on #018 for another 30 miles to the junction with Forest Service Road #017 to Ophir Summit, just south of the Reese River Guard Station and the school. Continue as described below "All Routes."

FROM HIGHWAY 50 HEADING EAST: If traveling east along U.S. 50, head south on State Route 361 toward Gabbs. Just before the town of Gabbs, turn east on a paved road, State Route 844, following signs to Ione and Berlin-Ichthyosaur State Park. Follow this road 18 miles to a junction and head northeast another 6 miles to Ione. From Ione follow well-graded gravel Forest Service Road #027 over the Shoshone Mountains 8 miles down into the Reese River Valley. The junction with Forest Service Road #017 to Ophir Summit is just north of this intersection of #027 and the Reese River Valley Road. Continue as described below "All Routes."

FROM AUSTIN/U.S. 50 HEADING WEST: Head west on U.S. 50, turning south onto paved road approximately 0.75 mile west of the junction with State Route 305 to Battle Mountain. Head southwest on State Route 722 about 7 miles to the junction with the Reese River Valley Road. Travel south, initially on pavement which eventually turns to gravel, for approximately 25 miles to the Reese River Guard Station. The junction with Forest Service Road # 017 to Ophir Summit is just south of the school. Continue as described below "All Routes."

ALL ROUTES: (b) A Forest Service sign at the intersection of the Reese River Valley Road and Forest Service Road #017 reads: *Stewart Creek 10, Clear Creek 1, Ophir Wash 7, Crane Creek 5, Mohawk Canyon 6.* Travel east on Road #017 toward the Toiyabe Range on gravel surface, crossing the Reese River 0.1 mile from the junction. At 0.4 mile reach a 'Y' junction where Road #119 branches southeast to Stewart Creek. Remain on Road #017 following a sign: *Ophir Wash, Mohawk Canyon, Crane Canyon.* Road #118 heads to the left at 0.7 mile as you continue on the more heavily traveled track.

Proceed through typical sagebrush terrain, passing a couple of side roads at 3.2 and 5.1 miles. Briefly enter a grove of pinyon pine before returning to sagebrush. A pair of signs warn: *Narrow Steep Road* and *Travel Not Advised for Less than All Wheel Drive Vehicles.* The road does narrow and the track becomes rougher as the grade begins to increase. As you climb, extraordinary views open up of the north portion of the Arc Dome Wilderness. Continue the steep ascent, passing the remains of an old mine next to the road at 10.2 miles. A half-mile farther, at 10.7 miles from the Reese River Valley Road, you crest the range at Ophir Summit and reach the undistinguished trailhead. Trail signs were missing in 1996. The trail begins where a two-track road heads south along the ridge. Limited parking for a couple of vehicles is all you will find at the trailhead.

Description: The trail does not start by heading up the South Twin River on the continuation of the road but follows a trail that cuts diagonally in the opposite direction up the steep hillside above the trailhead. The road, built unfortunately in 1980 to service a small mining claim on the South Fork, makes a seemingly endless number of fords across the South Twin River within the first three quarters mile. In spring the crossings can be hazardous, and in early to mid-summer a foot-soaking pain. Unless you are blisteringly hot and clad with an old pair of tennis shoes, avoid the road.

From the trailhead, follow the trail across the hillside to a switchback. After the switchback, the trail climbs steeply through pinyon pine, sagebrush and ephedra toward a cluster of sharp cliffs. Crest the first rise, make a gentle descent and then join the mining road from below, climbing sharply to another knoll, 0.85 mile from the trailhead. A remarkable vista unfolds as you gaze down into the deep cleft of the canyon, which is enclosed by steep, dramatic and jagged cliffs. While staring at the majestic view, you can not help wondering how the South Twin River managed to cut such a circuitous path through the maze of cliffs near the entrance to the canyon.

Descend via the road through pinyon pine-juniper woodlands down into the South Twin River drainage. Once you reach the roaring river, the path takes on a gentler aspect as it wanders along the east bank of the river through willows, alders and cottonwoods. As the rocky road continues upstream, wild rose, currant, chokecherry and desert peach appear in the lush, riparian vegetation of the creek bed, as well as a variety of wildflowers, including columbine, paintbrush, lupine, bluebells and penstemon.

Having avoided the lower fords along the mining road, the route crosses the river eight times below serrated cliffs before arriving at a mining relic—an old mill wheel that utilized water power to process ore from a nearby mine. Past the mill, the road crosses the South Twin River, encounters a campsite, fords the river a second time and reaches a junction with the trail from the South Fork, 3.3 miles from the trailhead. A decent campsite is just 50 feet up the South Fork.

Leave the mining road, as a single-track trail continues through lush, riparian foliage, including cottonwoods, wild rose and grasses. More fords await you as the trail climbs along the river to the next trail junction, 1.3 miles from the South Fork Trail. At 4.6 miles a sign nailed to an old tree limb reads: *Trail 2027, N. Twin River Trail, N. Twin River 4, N. Twin River Road 7* (see Trip 2). A primitive campsite is next to the river a short distance from the junction.

From just below the North Twin River Trail junction, the canyon has widened, and the steep, impressive rock walls are replaced with sloping, sagebrush-covered hillsides. A gentle, three-quarters mile walk leads to the broad, moist meadow called South Twin Pasture on the USGS and Forest Service maps. Pleasant campsites are amid the meadow as long as you do not have to share your spot with the cattle that sometimes graze the canyon.

Beyond the half-mile meadow of South Twin Pasture, the grade increases as the trail climbs along the east bank of the diminishing river. A quarter mile from the meadow, the trail passes a side canyon on the opposite side of the river which holds a delightful campsite near a creek. A well-defined use trail heads up the twisting side canyon toward Arc Dome.

The trail follows the course of the narrow river through the upper canyon, characterized by open sagebrush slopes, pockets of aspen-lined river banks and dense stream-side vegetation. Crossings of the stream become easier as the reduced flow allows for easy hops from one bank to the other. Scattered limber pines begin to show themselves above the sea of sagebrush in the upper canyon. Continue to ascend the wide-open canyon alongside the river to a broad side canyon on the west, where through the gorge the summit of Arc Dome appears. You reach a crudely signed junction with the summit trail to the peak at 6.9 miles from the trailhead. The sign gives the distance to the top of Arc Dome as 2½ miles.

Proceed from the junction on soft dirt tread through meadow grass and sagebrush. Limber pine and quaking aspen cover the slopes of the upper canyon, and lupines add a touch of blue to the hillsides. The grade becomes steeper as the trail heads toward the end of the canyon and you near a pass on the divide separating the South Twin River and Reese River drainages. At 7.7 miles, you arrive at the grassy pass in a grove of mountain mahogany and widely distributed limber pine. The broad basin of the upper Reese River spreads out before you—the rolling hills, endless skies and hue of sagebrush green create the perfect image of cowboy country—the only missing piece is the Marlboro man astride his horse.

From the pass, the Toiyabe Crest Trail makes a gradual, continuous 9-mile descent to the confluence with Big Sawmill Creek. Head down through dwarfed limber pine to the bottom of the wide-open canyon filled with sagebrush, grasses and wildflowers. Cross the tiny headwaters of the Reese River and follow the narrow trickle until a side stream emanating from a spring adds its flow to the main channel. The path, easily lost in grassy sections in the upper canyon, is found again downstream with relative ease.

The trail crosses a tributary stream near a small canyon where Arc Dome briefly returns to view. Just beyond the stream, you ascend a low hill before the trail returns to the river and makes a couple of crossings. Continue heading downstream gently along a soft dirt tread through sagebrush, lupine and paintbrush. Cross the river once and proceed to Little Jett Canyon, 10.3 miles from the trailhead.

Just below some beaver ponds, you can cross the Reese River to a camping area beneath a grove of tall aspens alongside Little Jett Creek. A number of campsites are in this area and even if you do not plan to spend the night, the relaxing spot makes a great place to stop for lunch or a snack. A fairly well defined trail, marked by an old metal sign reading: *Jett Canyon*, runs by the creek and heads up the canyon toward the ridge separating Little Jett and Jett canyons. The beaver ponds create the perfect opportunity for dangling a line.

For the next 1.2 miles, the trail wanders between grassy meadows and more sagebrush, crossing the river once and arriving at a junction with a trail up Trail Creek to Tom's Canyon (see Trip 6). At the junction, 11.5 miles from the trailhead, signs read: *S. Twin River, Cow Canyon* and 200 yards up Trail Creek a crude wooden sign simply notes: *TH 6*. Translation: Trailhead 6 miles. By midsummer Trail Creek is typically dry.

From the junction cross the drainage of Trail Canyon into thick brush as the trail bends around to the west following the course of Reese River. Asters and daisies have joined the retinue of wildflowers growing amid the stream-side vegetation. Soon the trail crosses to the north bank and passes through sagebrush and rabbitbrush away from the water on a dirt and gravel tread. Beavers have lived up to their reputation of being busy by creating a number of dams and ponds along this stretch of the river. The trail cuts across a gravel bar, fords the river and heads over more gravel to a meadow at the base of a hillside. Tucked into alders, a large campsite appears next to the meadow. From the meadow the trail continues its descent along the Reese River. Dense vegetation remains constant along the river banks, while sagebrush interspersed with rabbitbrush and grasses dominates the terrain away from the water. The trail makes numerous river crossings in the next 3 miles, most of which present little problems. However, the fifth crossing after the meadow occurs in the backwaters of a beaver dam, requiring wading through the pond even in late summer when the waters are relatively shallow.

The trail climbs onto cliffs above the steep declivity of Wrango Canyon before descending back alongside the Reese River. Numerous additional fords occur over the next 1.25 miles until the trail comes next to a fence line, leading to a large camp area nestled beneath some widely spaced, mature aspen trees above the north bank of the river. Fire pits, logs and a grassy floor create an inviting atmosphere for an overnight visit. A private corral used by horse packers is across the river.

From the camp, the trail passes another, smaller campsite with outhouse before encountering two more fords of the Reese River. Climb steeply up a rise and come to the opening of Battero Canyon, 15.0 miles from the trailhead, where for the first time in a long while you get an unobstructed view of Arc Dome. Continue another 1.2 miles through sagebrush terrain to Little Sawmill Creek. Make the easy crossing and walk another 0.1 mile to an obscure trail junction immediately before the crossing of Big Sawmill Creek, 16.2 miles from the trailhead. A sign at the junction reads: *Big Sawmill Creek, 7 Stewart Creek* (arrow pointing straight ahead, west). The most distinct path does indeed continue straight ahead across the creek but is the Reese River Trail (see Trip 3). The Toiyabe Crest Trail turns 90 degrees north, passes through an opening in a barbed-wire fence, and leads up the east side of Big Sawmill Creek. The faint path becomes well defined as it parallels the stream.

Immediately struck by the lush vegetation of the slender canyon, you begin the climb up Sawmill Creek. Sagebrush, rabbitbrush, and wild rose cover the ground below quaking aspen, while wildflowers, including columbine, primrose and lupine, add a splash of color. Quickly the trail crosses Big Sawmill Creek to ascend the west bank between low cliffs and through dense riparian foliage to a small grassy clearing, formerly used as a campsite. The rocky cliffs force the trail back over the creek to the east side as willows and alders begin to appear along the creek bed. After approximately one-third mile, the trail returns to the west side where the canyon widens, and leads away from the dense growth surrounding the creek to a more open hillside. Arc Dome, hidden for miles,

Arc Dome from the Upper Reese River

now becomes an intermittent companion looming high above the neighboring terrain.

As the trail approaches a pyramidal cliff, it bends down to Big Sawmill Creek again to avoid steep rocks on the west side of the canyon. Under the shade of mature aspens, a wide clearing offers a nice campsite along the stream. A short distance farther up the trail is an even better campsite in a glade of aspens containing fire pits, logs to sit on and a small gated corral.

Once again the trail leads away from the creek, passing through typical sagebrush terrain. Soon the canyon narrows and the hillsides grow taller and steeper. Entering the upper canyon, the trail alternates between the lush, riparian foliage by the creek and the drier sagebrush vegetation along the hillsides above the stream. You pass a narrow side canyon where a small, seasonal stream joins the main channel, and crosses the creek below steep canyon walls lightly covered with mountain mahogany and limber pine. From the crossing the trail climbs sharply up the drainage until a short descent leads to a crossing of a side stream labeled on the *Arc Dome* topo as the main branch of Big Sawmill Creek.

After the crossing you climb well above the level of the tributary stream on a sagebrush-covered hillside. A moderately steep ascent leads to a small gorge where an aspen-lined, spring-fed rivulet provides a brief respite from the laborious climb. Cross the pleasant little brook and follow the trail back into the main canyon, remaining quite a distance above the stream bed. The trail and the creek briefly converge farther up before the path forsakes the stream again, climbing up the hillside and curving toward the head of the canyon.

Now you climb above a grassy, spring-fed meadow and crest the top of a rise to a large, wide-open grassland where the trail disappears. Follow cairns across the grassy meadow to the far edge and find distinct trail again. Impressive views appear to the west of the Shoshone Mountains and distant ranges. Step over a dry drainage as the trail climbs gently upward over the hillside to an unmarked junction, 21.5 miles from the trailhead, between the Toiyabe Crest Trail and the trail down Stewart Creek (see Trip 5) to Columbine Campground. The trail to Columbine continues straight ahead while the Crest Trail angles back sharply, following an old jeep road toward the hillsides above.

Turn southeast from the junction and climb across the hillside through low-growing sagebrush and grasses to the edge of the plateau at the crest of the Toiyabe Mountains. Follow the gently rising tableland to the junction with the summit trail to Arc Dome, 22.8 miles from the trailhead. The Arc Dome trail heads south 3 miles to the 11,773-foot summit, gaining and losing nearly 2,000 feet of elevation along the way to the top of the peak. Views from the summit are quite rewarding. The whole of the Arc Dome Wilderness with its peaks and deep canyons lies at your feet, while the nearby ranges of the Toquima, Monitor and Shoshone mountains appear close enough to reach out and touch. On clear days the outline of the Sierra Nevada is visible to the west, over 100 miles distant.

From the Arc Dome junction, the trail bends northeast, eventually leaving the crest to descend into the upper canyon of a tributary of the North Twin River. A three-quarter mile descent leads to another trail junction, at 23.9 miles, with the trail heading down that tributary to the North Twin River Trail (see Trip 4). Turn north from the junction, following three short switchbacks up to a high, windswept saddle along the crest. A half-mile descent from the saddle leads through limber pine and shrubs to the unmarked junction with the Stewart Creek Trail (see Hike 5), 24.5 miles from the trailhead. As the trail ascends from the junction, the foliage thriving vigorously in the Stewart Creek drainage is a vivid contrast to the struggling vegetation along the exposed, unprotected crest.

Now the trail makes a moderate climb back to the crest, to the top of a minor peak providing a commanding view of the northern Arc Dome Wilderness. A more gradual climb awaits along the crest as the trail gradually ascends over the shoulder of the next peak. Large cairns appear periodically, in spite of the excellent condition of the trail. They would have been much more valuable in the trail-less sections of the previous canyons. A high traverse around the shoulder of a ridge leads to a gradual descent to a notch in the crest. From the notch you have excellent views of the canyon you just ascended, as well as the impressive cliffs of the North Twin River canyon.

From the notch, a descent wraps around a shoulder of the mountain and back to the crest where low-growing sagebrush, scattered wildflowers and occasional limber pines grow below outcroppings of volcanic rock. Traverse around the back side of a ridge in a northwesterly direction until a moderately steep climb takes you up to a minor crest. A mild descent then leads to a descending traverse of another hillside through a grove of mature limber pines over to another saddle on the ridge crest.

From the saddle, the trail ascends mildly until the grade increases near a grove of mountain mahogany as the trail curves around, beginning a steep, winding ascent. You crest a sub-ridge and descend briefly to begin a long traverse around the west side of the crest, continuing through low-growing sagebrush and isolated limber pines. At the end of the traverse, an exceedingly steep but short climb leads across the crest and back to the saddle and to a junction, 28.8 miles from the trailhead, with a trail leading down another tributary of the North Twin River (see Trip 4).

From the saddle, the trail makes an ascending traverse above the canyon of Last Chance Creek and then climbs steeply to another saddle on the crest of the range. Another traverse along the western slopes of a minor peak provides unobstructed views across the Reese River Valley to the Shoshone Mountains and distant ranges. When you climb over a short rise, you can see the Ophir Summit Road. From the rise, the route follows a two-track jeep road to the trailhead, 30.2 miles from the South Twin River trailhead.

The Toiyabe Crest National Recreation Trail continues outside the Arc Dome Wilderness another 35.5 miles to the north terminus in Kingston Canyon.

Trip 2 ⌂

NORTH TWIN-SOUTH TWIN RIVERS LOOP

Trip Type: Overnight backpack; Loop or loop-shuttle
Distance: 13.4 miles (0.9-mile hike of road between North and South Twin trailheads)
13.0 miles (car shuttle between North and South Twin trailheads)
Season: Mid-June through late October
Access: Dirt road
Water: Plentiful in rivers and creeks
Maps: #22
Arc Dome, Carvers NW, & South Toiyabe Peak 7.5 minute quadrangles, 1980, 1971 & 1979
Toiyabe National Forest map, Austin Ranger District, 1968 (revised 1991, 92)

Introduction: Only by Nevada standards is referral to these two streams as rivers possible, but what the North and South Twin rivers lack in volume they make up for in vibrancy, drama and scenic wonder. These twins share a family resemblance of winding down narrow gorges and cutting through towering cliffs that rise abruptly from the valley floor, sharply piercing the deep blue sky with pinnacles and serrations. Both streams roar down their lower canyons in resounding cacophony through numerous cascades, swirling pools and churning cataracts.

Subtle differences between the two canyons reveal themselves as you hike along the trails. North Twin is a slightly narrower canyon, while taller and more exciting cliffs appear in South Twin. While both rivers support healthy riparian foliage, particularly in the lower reaches of their canyons, North Twin appears to possess the more lush environment. With their respective similarities and minor differences, the North and South Twin rivers are two precious siblings, highlights of the Arc Dome Wilderness.

Early in the season, especially after a winter of heavy snowfall, the route can be potentially hazardous as it crosses both rivers numerous times in the first 2 miles. Consult the Forest Service for current conditions. Even in low-water periods, packing a pair of old tennis shoes or sandals for the various fords is a wise idea. With so many opportunities for slipping off a wet rock into the roaring stream, even the most adroit hiker can not avoid the operation of the law of averages. Beyond the first 2 miles of trail, the problem resolves, each canyon being wide enough to allow the trail to remain on the same side of the stream for lengthier distances. The volume of water in the upper rivers is less, so the infrequent fords are much easier to negotiate.

Although more or less limited to the specific locations noted in the description below, campsites occur at strategic locations along the route and generally are quite nice. Opportunities for further explorations abound, including off-trail routes as well as a climb to the summit of 11,788-foot Arc Dome.

Trailhead: NORTH TWIN: (a) Following a sign reading: *North Twin River,* turn west from State Route 376 in Big Smoky Valley, 37.5 miles south of U.S. 50 and 63 miles north of U.S. 6. Drive west on Forest Service Road #080, on a single-lane gravel road. Enter Toiyabe National Forest 2.3 miles from Route 376. At 3.5 miles, reach an intersection with a road that heads over to the South Twin River trailhead. Continue straight ahead 0.3 mile to a large parking area near a pile of boulders. The actual trailhead is 50 yards up the road but a limited parking area handles no more than two or three vehicles. A nice campsite is next to the creek.

SOUTH TWIN: (c) Only 0.9 mile of road separates the two trailheads. Most small parties are satisfied to walk the short distance rather than encumber themselves with two vehicles. If traveling with a larger group, you can leave a car at each trailhead and save the third of a mile walk along the dirt road. You must cross S. Twin River, however, which can be a foreboding experience early in the season during high water. If concerned about the crossing, travel back to the highway and up the road to the other trailhead.

The turnoff from State Route 376 for South Twin River trailhead, signed as such, is 2.6 miles south of the turnoff for North Twin River, 40 miles south of U.S. 50 and 60.5 miles north of U.S. 6. Travel on a single-lane grav-el road 3.0 miles to the trailhead. A wide turnout on the south side of the road is available for parking.

Description: The trail from the North Twin River trailhead begins at the Wilderness boundary, following the river as it winds among cottonwoods, junipers and pinyon pines. Quickly the path makes the first of many river crossings, a process repeated around 15 times during the first 2 miles as the trail weaves back and forth through the narrow, twisting canyon. The river tumbles and churns on a steep course toward the mellow slopes of Big Smoky Valley, cascading beneath the steep, rugged cliffs of the lower canyon.

After the first 2 miles of trail, the canyon widens and the grade eases as the river glides along through pinyon pine, willows and wild rose. Briefly, the canyon narrows again amid scattered, mature aspens but it quickly opens up into an area of meadows. Beyond the meadows, the vegetation becomes quite lush. For a moment, the reality of being in the middle of Nevada is easily forgotten.

You cross the creek one more time to an extensive, aspen-covered mead-ow near the trail junction with the Ophir Summit Trail (see Trip 4), 3.0 miles from the trailhead. Crude signs mark the junction: *2028, Toiyabe Trail, Bingham Pasture, Dewey Creek Trail, Toiyabe Summit Trail, N. Twin Summit 2½* (arrows pointing southwest), *Ophir 3½* (arrow pointing northwest). Under the shade of mature quaking aspens, the meadow is a lovely place to camp (unless cattle have beaten you to the spot).

From the junction, the path wanders through dense cover of aspens and thick brush, crossing the narrowing stream five more times to an unsigned junction with a trail up a tributary of the North Twin River (see Trip 4), 3.6 miles from the trailhead.

Now you cross the main river and a small side stream into open slopes of sagebrush and shrubs. Scattered Indian paintbrush and lupine add a splash of color to the open terrain. After a stretch along the drier hillside, the trail descends back into the lush riparian vegetation near a flat, where a couple of small campsites lie next to the creek. After another crossing of the North Twin and a small tributary, the trail begins to climb away from the river, initially through aspens and then on exposed, sagebrush-covered hillsides.

The trail steeply ascends the open slopes toward the ridge that divides the South and North Twin River drainages. Acres of sagebrush cover the slopes, interrupted briefly by a grove of aspens. Lupine, paintbrush, blue-bells and other wildflowers complement the gray-green hue of the sage. Higher up the slopes, scattered groves of mahogany offer small amounts of shade as the trail climbs to the top of a ridge. A short descent leads to a small stream coursing through a gully, which actually turns out to be the upper North Twin River. Away from the stream, the ascent continues as the trail passes through a significant stand of aspen and limber pine on the

South Twin River Canyon

way to the pass on the divide. At 5.4 miles, the trail arrives at the grassy pass near a grove of mountain mahogany trees, providing just enough shade for a relaxing break to enjoy the excellent views of the surrounding canyons and peaks.

From the pass you descend somewhat steeply through a moderately dense grove of mahogany and widely scattered limber pines into the canyon of a seasonal stream that drains into the South Twin River. Follow the stream downhill as it cuts a channel into the sagebrush-covered hillside. Farther down the canyon, the trail alternates between the lush, riparian vegetation of the creek and the drier slopes above until it traverses a long talus slope. After the talus, the trail keeps up the tradition of the Arc Dome Wilderness by crossing the creek a few times. Toward the bottom of the canyon, cottonwoods, willows and wild rose begin to reappear along the banks of the stream, while sagebrush and mahogany dominate the hillsides. Just before the confluence with the South Twin River, the trail passes through a grassy meadow, crosses the seasonal creek for the last time and reaches an intersection with the South Twin River Trail.

You reach a junction with the South Twin River Trail 7.9 miles from the trailhead. A sign nailed to an old log reads: *Trail 2027, N. Twin River Trail, N. Twin River 4, Twin River Road 7*. The canyon of the South Twin River seems to be drier than the North Twin River canyon. Pinyon pine covers most of the hillsides, along with some juniper and even less limber pine.

From the junction, head northeast, following the river downstream and making numerous crossings of the river as the canyon deepens. The lower canyon of the South Twin River is wider than that of its counterpart, with steep dramatic cliffs towering above the agitated water. Follow the trail as it bends around a massive, rugged hillside 1.3 miles to a junction with the South Fork Trail, 9.2 miles from the trailhead. A fairly decent campsite rests above the South Fork about 200 feet up the trail.

Beyond the junction, the trail follows an old mining road, extremely rocky in some areas. The road wanders across the creek, above the creek and along the banks in a seemingly arbitrary fashion. Impressive rock cliffs thrust themselves out and pierce the sky as the river forces its way through the rugged terrain. Where it appears impossible for the river to burst out from the seemingly enclosed canyon, the trail begins a steep climb to the top of a ridge overlooking the canyon. A dramatic picture of the South Twin River canyon awaits you at the crest.

From the top of the ridge, the old road makes a curving descent into the canyon and alongside the river. Avoid the urge to travel this way as the route along the river is difficult, requiring numerous, almost continuous crossings that even the most sure-footed individual will not be able to negotiate without becoming soaked at least once. During the peak of snowmelt this route can be extremely hazardous. Rather than following the road from the ridge top, head along the hillside on the single-track trail to the next rise of cliffs. Climb up through pinyon pine, sagebrush and ephedra to the top and then descend a half mile to the South Twin trailhead, 12.5 miles from the North Twin trailhead.

If you are not completing a shuttle trip, you must follow the road from South Twin over to the North Twin trailhead. Cross the South Twin River, which under most circumstances will be a wide but shallow crossing, and continue on the road as it wraps around the base of the hills to the North Twin River. The road avoids the direct crossing of North Twin, thanks to a diversion which pipes the water from the river to a ranch in Big Smoky Valley. The trailheads are 0.9 mile apart, completing the 13.4-mile loop.

Trip 3 🏕

COW CANYON TRAIL

Trip Type: Dayhike or overnight backpack; Out and back
Distance: 5.0 miles round trip
Season: June through October
Access: Dirt road
Water: Reese River
Maps: #24
Bakeoven Creek 7.5 minute quadrangle, 1980
Toiyabe National Forest map, Austin Ranger District, 1968
(revised 1990, 91)

Introduction: A short hike through some big country leads to the Reese River and the Toiyabe Crest Trail. The terrain on this trip is wide open and the skies as big as Montana. Impressive views of 11,775-foot Arc Dome and the Reese River drainage occur almost constantly along the first mile of trail. Anglers will enjoy the easy access to the best fishery in the Arc Dome Wilderness. Horse packers will find the open terrain and gentle grades of the trail appealing as well. Interesting rock formations near the trailhead complete the captivating environment.

Trailhead: FROM TONOPAH: From the junction of U.S. 6 and 95 in Tonopah, head west on 6/95 approximately 5 miles and turn north onto the Gabbs Poleline Road. About 31 miles from the junction, turn northeast onto Cloverdale Road and follow it 5.5 miles to Forest Service Road #018. Head north on #018 for another 13 miles to a junction with Forest Service Road #121, just past Clover Summit at the end of Indian Valley. Continue as described below "All Routes."

FROM HIGHWAY 50 HEADING EAST: Along U.S. 50, head south on State Route 361 toward Gabbs. Just before the town of Gabbs, turn east on a paved road, State Route 844, following signs to Ione and Berlin-Ichthyosaur State Park. Follow this road 18 miles to a junction and head northeast another 6 miles to Ione. From Ione follow well-graded gravel Forest Service Road #027 over the Shoshone Mountains 8 miles down into the Reese River Valley. Turn south onto the Reese River Road and proceed nearly 17 miles to an intersection with Forest Service Road #121. Continue as described below "All Routes."

FROM AUSTIN/U.S. 50 HEADING WEST: Head west on U.S. 50, turning south onto paved State Route 722 approximately 0.75 mile west of the junction with State Route 305 to Battle Mountain. Head southwest on Route 722 about 7 miles to the junction with the Reese River Valley Road. Travel south, initially on pavement which eventually turns to gravel, for approximately 25 miles to the Reese River Guard Station. Continue almost 17 miles to an intersection with Forest Service Road #121. Continue as described below "All Routes."

ALL ROUTES: (d) From the junction of the Reese River Valley Road and Forest Service Road #121 head east toward Arc Dome and the Toiyabe Mountains. Reach a junction at 0.6 mile where a sign reads: *Cow Canyon 121* (left) and *Ledbetter Canyon 122* (right). Bear left and continue on Road #121. Just beyond the 3-mile mark, pinyon pines and junipers begin to appear. At 5.6 miles a sign reads: *Cow Canyon Trailhead.* A short distance farther up the road are a horse tie-bar, pit toilet and primitive campsites. Plenty of parking is available. The trail begins off to the left near a wilderness sign.

Description: The well-defined path immediately enters the Arc Dome Wilderness, climbing up a low formation of volcanic rock. Mountain mahogany, juniper and pinyon pine grow here and there amid the sagebrush. The path is fairly level as it rounds a corner where Arc Dome comes into view, dominating the surrounding landscape. A vertical distance of 4500 feet extends from the Reese River to the top of the peak. The wide-open expanse of terrain makes the countryside appear grand in scale.

The Cow Canyon Trail begins a steady descent across the sagebrush-covered hillside down to the bottom of a wide canyon where the Reese River glides serenely northwest toward the Reese River Valley. You reach a 'T' junction with the Reese River Trail at the base of the canyon near a barbed-wire fence line in a meadow area above the west bank of the river, 1.4 miles from the trailhead. To the north, the indistinct trail passes through a gate in the fence and heads downstream along the Reese River 4.5 miles to the edge of the Wilderness and the boundary of the Yomba Indian Reservation. Access beyond the boundary is by permission only.

Turning upstream heading south, the Reese River Trail stays west of the fence, paralleling the alder- and willow-lined river. Pleasant, almost level walking through open sagebrush leads along the west bank. You pass a large meadow before coming to a crossing of the wide river. Just before the crossing is a campsite, nestled into tall willows and alders in a sandy area not far from the water. Early in the summer a ford of the river may be impossible without getting wet.

Beyond the crossing, the trail climbs above the east bank and continues upstream. Where the path wanders from the edge of the river it passes through sagebrush and widely scattered junipers. Ponds behind beaver dams provide the perfect habitat for trout in the Reese River and consequently for anglers as well.

As the canyon continues around a big sweeping bend, the trail comes to and crosses Big Sawmill Creek. On the opposite side in a grassy clearing near a fence line, you reach an indistinct junction with the Toiyabe Crest Trail (see Trip 1), 2.5 miles from the trailhead. A sign to the right reads: *Big Sawmill Creek, 7 Stewart Creek*. Continuing straight ahead, the Crest Trail follows the Reese River for many miles as it curves around to the north. To follow the Crest Trail north along Big Sawmill Creek, pass through an opening in the fence line opposite the sign, heading along the east bank of the creek.

Retrace your steps back to the Cow Canyon trailhead.

Trip 4 🏕

OPHIR SUMMIT–NORTH TWIN RIVER LOOP

Trip Type: 2 to 3 day backpack; Loop
Distance: 14.7 miles
Season: Mid-June to late October
Access: Dirt road, high-clearance vehicle necessary
Water: Creeks, no water along crest
Maps: #25

South Toiyabe Peak 7.5 minute quadrangle, 1979
Toiyabe National Forest map, Austin Ranger District, 1968
(revised 1990, 1991)

Introduction: Sample the highs and lows along this 15-mile route—the wide range of elevations between the deep canyons of two tributaries of North Twin River and the actual crest of the Toiyabe Range. A sum of 2,700 feet separates the high point along the Toiyabe Crest Trail and the low point on the North Twin River Trail. The difference in altitude and terrain allows the backpacker a chance to experience the best of both worlds. The trail along the crest has a continuous stream of outstanding vistas of far-off ranges and valleys as well as striking views of the peaks and canyons of the Arc Dome Wilderness. Down in the drainages, the trail passes through lush riparian vegetation next to the creeks, and meadows and open basins in the upper canyons.

One striking contrast of this trip is the difference in the condition of the trails. Along the ridge, the Toiyabe Crest National Recreation Trail cuts a well-defined track, while some portions of the trail down in the canyons have totally disappeared. However, with modest navigational skills and a little extra time, traveling through the canyons is not difficult in spite of the absence of a defined trail. The additional effort is rewarded by an almost guaranteed promise of solitude and the opportunity to view some of the wildlife that roams the countryside.

Begin the trip with an ample supply of water. There is no water at any point along the crest, and the upper canyons can be dry as well, unless your visit occurs in early season. North Twin River and its tributaries will provide plenty of water through the middle portion of the trip. Since this route is so little used, developed campsites are rare, but you should be able to find a number of potential spots for a camp along streams in the lower canyons.

Trailhead: (b) Follow directions to the Ophir Summit trailhead as described in Trip 1.

Description: The Toiyabe Crest Trail heads south, rather inauspiciously, along the crest of the range, high on top of the windswept ridge. You quickly climb to the top of a low knoll through open terrain of low-growing sage, wildflowers and tiny plants where views are spectacular. To the east above Big Smoky Valley are the Toquima and Monitor ranges and to the west you gaze across Reese River Valley to the Shoshone Mountains. After a gentle climb to a low saddle the trail traverses the western slopes of a hillside, curving around to another saddle where magnificent views continue of the Reese River Valley and the Shoshone Mountains.

Through the saddle, the trail begins a slightly descending traverse of the east slopes of the next peak. On the more protected hillside, limber pines grow amid wildflowers, including lupine, paintbrush and bluebells. Along the route, excellent views of Toiyabe Peak open up across the canyon. The path curves around into the next saddle near an outcrop of quartzite, 1.4 miles from Ophir Summit, where an old post signifies the junction between the Toiyabe Crest Trail and the trail down the canyon of a tributary of the North Fork Twin River.

The Toiyabe Crest Trail has been in relatively good condition and easily discernible, but that advantage quickly changes as you leave the Crest Trail to descend into the drainage. Faint remnants of a path exist in places in the upper canyon but are extremely hard to follow for the duration of the descent. The alignment shown on the topo is consistent with the route on the ground. However, heading east from the junction, following the ridge to the stream, and moving directly down the stream channel may be easier than the map route. Whichever choice you make, a more defined path awaits you alongside the creek farther down the canyon.

Once you reach the creek, a distinct path leads past lush, riparian vegetation along the creek and past sagebrush-covered hillsides above. Near the point where the trail terminates on the topo, remains of a prospector's stone cabin and mining tunnels repose next to a rounded butte where two stream channels converge with the main canyon. The path, momentarily lost in some small meadow areas, is easily found again on the opposite side of the meadows. As you descend the canyon, the trail makes a number of crossings over the creek and back. Near the confluence with North Twin River, tall aspens fill the bottom of the drainage.

You reach the junction with the North Twin River Trail (see Trip 2) 4.8 miles from the trailhead, in an extensive, aspen-covered meadow. Crude signs mark the junction: *2028, Toiyabe Trail, Bingham Pasture, Dewey Creek Trail, Toiyabe Summit Trail, N. Twin Summit 2½* (arrows pointing southwest), *Ophir 3½* (arrow pointing northwest). Under the shade of mature quaking aspens, the meadow is a lovely place to camp (unless cattle have beaten you to the spot).

From the junction, the path wanders through dense cover of aspens and thick brush, crossing the narrowing stream five more times to the unsigned junction with the trail up another tributary of North Twin River, 5.5 miles from Ophir Summit.

A somewhat confusing system of trails ascends the canyon away from the North Twin River Trail. You should work up through the dense forest cover alongside the main branch of the tributary for a short stretch before crossing the creek and ascending drier slopes away from and south of the main channel. Approximately a mile up the canyon the trail crosses back to the north side of the creek just below two rounded hills. The trail traverses slopes below the pair of hills before a switchback leads above them and around to the creek. Follow the trail alongside the willow- and aspen-lined creek, passing through a couple of delightful patches of green meadows. Due to the light use that this canyon receives, established campsites are few and far between, but you should be able to find adequate spots scattered throughout the drainage.

Continue the ascent next to the creek until the trail veers away, surmounting a low ridge into an expansive stand of quaking aspen. Once under cover of the aspens, the trail begins a series of switchbacks leading up the steep hillside. After the steep climb, the trail moderates as it heads through a small gap into the upper basin of the canyon. You pass through a nice sloping meadow, an excellent place to camp—although you might have to descend quite a way down the canyon for an adequate water supply. Another series of switchbacks takes you steeply out of the upper canyon through widely dispersed limber pine to the crest below some steep volcanic cliffs. At 8.4 miles from Ophir Summit, you meet the Toiyabe Crest Trail near some signs that read: *Arc Dome 4* and *Ophir 5.*

Turn north from the junction, following three short switchbacks to a high, windswept saddle along the crest. A half-mile descent from the saddle leads to the unmarked junction with the Stewart Creek Trail (see Hike 5), 9 miles from the trailhead. As the trail ascends from the junction the foliage thriving vigorously in the Stewart Creek drainage is a vivid contrast to the struggling vegetation along the exposed, unprotected crest.

The trail makes a moderate climb back to the crest and to the top of a minor peak, providing a commanding view of the northern Arc Dome Wilderness. A more gradual climb awaits along the crest as the trail ascends over the shoulder of the next peak. Large cairns mark the trail periodically, in spite of the excellent condition of the trail. They would have been much more valuable in the trail-less sections of the previous canyons. A high traverse around the shoulder of a ridge leads to a gradual descent to a notch in the crest where you gain excellent views of the canyon you just ascended, as well as views of the impressive cliffs of the North Twin River canyon.

From the notch, a descent wraps around a shoulder of the mountain and back to the crest where low-growing sagebrush, scattered wildflowers and occasional limber pine grow below atypical outcroppings of exposed volcanic rock. Traverse around the back side of a ridge in a northwesterly direction until a moderately steep climb rises up to a minor crest. A mild descent then leads to a descending traverse of another hillside through a grove of mature limber pines to another saddle along the ridge crest.

From the saddle, the trail mildly ascends until the grade increases near a grove of mountain mahogany, curving around and beginning a steep, winding ascent along a hillside. You crest a sub-ridge and descend briefly to a long traverse around the west side of the crest, continuing through low-growing sagebrush and isolated limber pines. At the end of the traverse, an exceedingly steep but short climb leads across the crest and back to the saddle and a trail junction, 13.3 miles from the trailhead. Now retrace your steps 1.4 miles back to the trailhead at Ophir Summit.

Trip 5 ♣
STEWART CREEK LOOP

Trip Type: Dayhike or overnight backpack; Loop
Distance: 7.7 miles
Season: Mid-June through late October
Access: Dirt road
Water: Creeks (none along crest)
Maps: #25
  Arc Dome, Bakeoven Creek, Corral Wash and *South Toiyabe Peak*
   7.5 minute quadrangles, 1980, 1980, 1979, 1979
  Toiyabe National Forest map, Austin Ranger District, 1968
   (Revised 1991, 92)

Introduction: Columbine is one of the nicest Forest Service campgrounds in the Nevada system, a wonderful setting for a night's rest before hitting the trail. Two different trails branch from a junction a quarter mile above the campground, creating an opportunity for a loop trip that passes through a multiplicity of environments. Add in the possibility of a climb to the summit of 11,773-foot Arc Dome and you complete the scenario.

The first part of the loop climbs steeply through one of the most vegetatively luxuriant drainages in central Nevada. Thick stands of quaking aspen fill the canyon from one side to the other and create a blaze of color in autumn. An abundance of wildflowers grace the hillsides, and a profusion of riparian foliage crowds the banks of Stewart Creek. Just below the Toiyabe crest, limber pines majestically cover the slopes of the upper canyon.

Two miles above the trailhead, the route joins the Toiyabe Crest Trail and climbs to the top of the world on an 11,000-foot plateau, providing spectacular views in every direction. A 3-mile trail, an offshoot of the Crest Trail, branches from the plateau and leads to the summit of Arc Dome, gaining and losing nearly 2,000 vertical feet along the way.

Dropping off the crest, the trail heads across barren sagebrush slopes with more incredible views into another branch of the Stewart Creek drainage. You pass an expansive green meadow before heading back into the dense vegetation of the lower canyon above the campground.

Although this is as an overnight backpack, campsites are hard to come by away from the lower canyons. If you desire a higher camp near the crest, you will have to bring quite a lot of water or else travel a long distance to get an adequate supply.

Trailhead: (e) Follow the directions under Ophir Summit Trailhead in Trip 1 to the Reese River Valley Road junction with Forest Service Road #017 just south of the Reese River Guard Station and the Reese River Valley School. The junction is marked by a Forest Service sign which reads:

Stewart Creek 10, Clear Creek 1, Ophir Wash 7, Crane Creek 5 and *Mohawk Canyon 6.*

Head east toward the Toiyabe Mountains on Road #017, crossing the Reese River at 0.1 mile and proceeding to a 'Y' junction with Forest Service Road #119 at 0.4 mile. Bear right on Road #119, following directions on a sign marked: *Stewart Creek, Clear Creek.* Reach another 'Y' junction at 1.0 miles signed: *Stewart Creek 4, Clear Creek 5,* where you bear right. The road crosses a creek and immediately arrives at another 'Y' junction, where you bear left past a sign reading: *Stewart Creek 4, Clear Creek 5, Road 119.* Yet another 'Y' junction greets you at 1.6 miles. Bend to the right, following a sign for *Stewart Creek, Clear Creek* and *Columbine Campground.*

Near a fence line, 2.7 miles from the Reese River Road, bear to the right at this 'Y' junction where a sign reads: *Clear Creek 3* (left) and *Stewart Creek 5* (right). Farther on, near a *Toiyabe National Forest* sign, follow the main road to the right. The road heads down to a crossing of Stewart Creek at 5.7 miles, climbs out of the drainage and bends east.

Continue east on Road #119 for 3 miles into the narrowing, aspen-lined canyon of Stewart Creek, passing a horse loading area at 8.7 miles. Then immediately pass a sign at the base of a steep hillside which reads: *Toiyabe Crest Trail.* This is a lateral trail for horse packers. Remain on the road heading up the canyon a short distance over a cattle guard and into the Columbine Campground, 9.0 miles from the Reese River Road.

A *Crest Trail* sign on the right side of the road marks the Stewart Creek Trailhead near a pole gate. Parking is available around the campground loop for about a half dozen cars.

Description: Follow the track of an old jeep road away from the campground through aspens, brush and wildflowers. Soon the trail breaks into the open, allowing views of the upper canyon and the mountains above. After about 150 yards, the trail re-enters aspen cover and quickly arrives at a trail junction, 0.25 mile from the trailhead. The old jeep road, the return route of your loop, continues to the right, heading south, to connect with the Toiyabe Crest Trail near the head of Sawmill Creek. The trail to the left heads directly east, climbing steeply up to reach the Crest Trail 1.6 miles north of the jeep road route. A sign at the junction, with arrows pointing away from the road and down the trail, states: *Stewart Creek Trail, Toiyabe Crest Trail ½* (the ½ mile distance is wildly inaccurate—2 miles is correct).

Bear left at the junction and follow the single-track trail as it heads through thick brush and aspen cover to a crossing of Stewart Creek. Wind your way uphill amid lush vegetation, wildflowers and aspen to the top of a minor ridge where the trail momentarily breaks out into the open. Follow the crest of the ridge separating two branches of Stewart Creek as you climb back under the filtered shade of light aspen cover. Briefly back out into the open again, dramatic views of the Reese River Valley and the Shoshone Mountains stretch out behind you to the west.

You crest a small knoll in a sea of sagebrush and wildflowers where the grade of the trail eases for a short time. Across a small meadow of grasses and wildflowers fringed by aspens, a curiously placed sign, denoting a junction, reads: *Toiyabe Crest Trail* (arrow to the left) and *N. Twin River 5, Big Sawmill Creek 4* (arrow to the right). Vegetation has overgrown the traces of any trail in the meadow, offering little help in discerning the pattern of this junction, which does not appear on the topo or Forest Service maps. To the right a use trail heads southwest around the hillside 0.4 mile connecting with the return part of your loop trail, which follows a jeep road to the junction 0.25 mile out of Columbine Campground.

Your trail continues heading east up the drainage, a more defined track resuming past the meadow. The grassy flat could provide a pleasant place to camp. Continue to climb through lush foliage of grasses, wildflowers, and shrubs with occasional patches of aspen. Cross the creek to the north side of the narrowing canyon as limber pine and mountain mahogany begin to appear. Then the grade of the trail increases, eventually switch-backing up the steep hillside. Above the switchbacks, the grade eases until you resume the steep climb via another set of switchbacks in the upper canyon. Some weather equipment with transmitter sits just off the trail. Keep climbing steeply until you reach the unsigned junction with the Toiyabe Crest Trail (see Trips 1 and 4), 300 feet below the actual crest of the Toiyabe Range and 2.0 miles from the trailhead.

Continue to climb from the unsigned junction through low-growing shrubs and scattered limber pines a half mile to a pass on the crest. From the pass, three short switchbacks lead to the junction with the trail coming up from North Twin River (see Trip 2). Signs mark the junction reading: *Crest Trail, Arc Dome 4* (south), *Ophir 5* (north).

A short traverse leads over to a seasonal drainage which the trail follows, climbing steeply at first and then easing before heading through a low gap onto the broad plateau at 11,000 feet. Arc Dome dominates the skyline, a mere 2 air miles away. You reach the junction with the summit trail 1.6 miles from the Stewart Creek Trail junction and 3.6 miles from the Columbine trailhead. The 3-mile hike to the top of Arc Dome gains 250 feet before it drops 600 feet to a saddle and then steeply ascends 1,025 feet in the last mile to the summit.

From the Arc Dome junction, the trail gently descends west across the mildly sloping plateau before descending steeply via an old jeep road across a sagebrush-covered hillside to an unmarked trail junction, 1.3 miles from the Arc Dome junction and 4.8 miles from the trailhead. The Toiyabe Crest Trail makes a radical bend 300 degrees south into the Big Sawmill Creek drainage a half mile away. Continue on the road straight ahead, which returns to Columbine Campground.

The twin-tracked jeep road winds down from the junction, heading directly northwest toward the Shoshone Mountains across the Reese River Valley. As the trail cuts across the side of the hill, a large green meadow comes into view below. The path narrows into a single track momentarily, circling around behind some cliffs and running into another jeep trail coming up from the valley to the west. The trail winds down into the Stewart Creek drainage and over to a crossing of the creek. After the dry, barren slopes above, the riparian vegetation around the stream is almost overwhelming.

Proceed along the east bank of Stewart Creek until it bends into a lush, verdant meadow. If the meadow did not have a fence around the perimeter, containing a herd of grazing cattle, it would be a picturesque wilderness setting. The trail passes above the meadow along a hillside and leads to a gate at the far end. From the meadow, descend moderately steeply through sagebrush, grasses and wildflowers into dense stands of aspen in the Stewart Creek drainage. Soon you reach the junction with the use trail connecting to the other branch of the Stewart Creek Trail. A sign at the junction reads: *Stewart Creek Trail, Columbine Campground 1, Reese River Ranger Station 12.*

Continue on the defined track as it heads into lush vegetation beneath mature aspens, quickly coming to a branch of the creek. Reach a sloping meadow where some old campsites appear just before the trail junction with the other branch of the Stewart Creek Trail. Retrace your steps 0.25 mile to the Columbine trailhead.

Trip 6 ♈

TOM'S CANYON TO TRAIL CREEK

Trip Type: Dayhike or overnight backpack; Out and back
Distance: 12.8 miles round trip
Season: June through October
Access: Dirt road
Water: Creek (seasonal) and springs
Maps: #26
          Arc Dome, Toms Canyon 7.5 minute quadrangles, 1980
          Toiyabe National Forest map, Austin Ranger District, 1968
          (revised 1990, 91)

Introduction: The trail up Tom's Canyon and down into Trail Creek, provides the hiker with a quick entrance into the upper Reese River and the Toiyabe Crest Trail. Along with this easy access, the 9,350-foot pass on the ridge separating these two drainages offers some fine views of the south end of the Arc Dome Wilderness, including a dramatic glimpse of Arc Dome itself. A 1.5-mile side trip from the pass presents an additional opportunity of reaching even better views from the summit of 10,050-foot Peavine Mountain. From the Toiyabe Crest Trail junction at the Reese River, the options for additional wanderings are numerous.

Ample water should be available along the trail, but after midsummer both creeks will have dry stretches. Fortunately, springs will keep the creeks from going completely dry. However, you should stay alert to take advantage of the perennial sources. If backpacking, be apprised that campsites are limited until you reach the Reese River country, although a reasonable spot occurs near an aspen-lined side stream in Trail Creek canyon, approximately 5.5 miles from the trailhead.

Trailhead: (f) Travel on State Route 376, 34 miles north of U.S. 95 or 61 miles south of U.S. 50, to the turnoff for Forest Service Road #020, signed: *Peavine Campground 9, San Antone Ranch 9, Ione 56, Gabbs 63*. Immediately cross a cattle guard and proceed along well-graded, wide gravel road 1.75 miles to a junction where a sign reads: *Peavine Campground 7* (straight ahead), *Ione, Gabbs* (left).

Old shed along Toms Canyon Trail

As you continue up the gravel road, pass the Peavine Ranch and enter Toiyabe National Forest land at 5.2 miles. Beyond the ranch, the road has narrowed to a single track as it climbs into the mountains, passing numerous ranches. The road is badly washboarded in places but should be passable to the average sedan. Stay on the main road, ignoring turns at 7.9, 8.0 and 8.4 miles. Signs to Peavine Campground will keep you on track. Cross Peavine Creek at 9.3 miles and instantly come to a 'Y' junction with the entrance road on the left to Peavine Campground. Head to the right at this junction following a sign reading: *Upper Peavine Canyon*.

Cross the creek again at 10.4 and 12.0 miles as the road continues through sagebrush and occasional pinyon pine and juniper. A major junction occurs at 14.3 miles where the left hand road heads up Peavine Canyon while your road to the right proceeds up Tom's Canyon. Beyond a primitive camping area the road reaches the trailhead at 15.0 miles. Plenty of parking is available beneath the shade of pinyon pine and juniper. The trail begins about 50 yards from the parking area where boulders block the old road.

Description: Follow the old road past Forest Service signs across the creek and up the canyon through pinyon pine and juniper forest. Typical riparian vegetation runs along the creek bed, with cottonwood the dominant tree. Quickly pass back over the creek near a crude wooden sign nailed to a tree: *Reese River 6*. Follow alongside the stream as the trail continues up the canyon on an old jeep road. Three more fords of the narrowing creek lead to the end of the road near an old cabin that appears to have been a storage shed of some type.

Single-track trail continues past the cabin, making more crossings of the creek before veering away from the main canyon up a side drainage, 1.6 miles from the trailhead. The well-graded dirt trail climbs moderately through the narrower drainage amid pinyon pine-juniper forest. Two crossings of the diminutive stream lead 0.9 mile to a spring just above a wooden trough, where even in late summer you should be able to get water.

Nearing the head of the canyon, the trail grade increases as it begins a series of switchbacks to the top of a hill. After surmounting the hill, the trail winds more gently along the ridge crest to a high saddle above the drainage of Trail Creek, 4.7 miles from the trailhead. At the saddle a fainter trail branches northwest from the main path 1.5 miles to the top of Peavine Mountain. Views from the 9300-foot saddle of the surrounding terrain are awe-inspiring. The summit mass of Arc Dome dominates the horizon, rising up out of a broad base of green-carpeted hillsides. In the foreground, the beginnings of Trail Creek canyon curves gracefully down sagebrush-covered slopes dotted with occasional limber pines toward the confluence with the Reese River.

The trail, which has been in good condition and very discernible up to this point, becomes lost in a sea of low-growing sagebrush on the northern flank of the saddle. To make matters more confusing, the route through the basin below has been re-aligned since the publication of the *Arc Dome* topo. Newer trail contours around the east slopes at the head of the upper basin of Trail Creek, rather than alongside the stream as shown on the map.

The easiest way to proceed from the saddle involves walking through the opening in the barbed-wire fence, heading straight down the steep slope, and finding the more distinct trail as it curves east below the saddle. Once back on the main trail, the track remains distinct as it descends above the stream on the east slopes of the canyon. You descend through the widely distributed limber pine of the upper drainage across a seasonal rivulet supplying just a trickle of water from a small spring. Continue down the canyon well above the creek to a large stand of quaking aspen near a side ravine containing a vigorous, spring-fed stream. A small campsite is on a sloping meadow of grass beneath some aspens just a short way upstream.

The trail continues to wind down through aspens until sagebrush covers the lower slopes of the canyon, eventually reaching the banks of Trail Creek. Follow along the creek until you reach the junction with the Toiyabe Crest Trail (see Trip 1) at the Reese River, 6.4 miles from the trailhead. From here retrace your steps.

Trip 7 ♣
JETT CANYON

Trip Type: Dayhike; Out and back
Distance: 9.2 miles round trip
Season: June through October
Access: Dirt road
Water: Creek (seasonal)
Maps: #27
    Arc Dome, Pablo Canyon & *Toms Canyon* 7.5 minute quadrangles 1980, 1971, 1980
    Toiyabe National Forest map, Austin Ranger District, 1968 (revised 1990, 91)

Introduction: An unmaintained trail heads up an old road through a long canyon in the southeast quadrant of the Arc Dome Wilderness. The first couple of miles follow a jeep road outside the Wilderness boundary amid dramatic, vertical cliffs before a single-track trail leads along a creek into wild and untrammeled backcountry. If solitude is what you seek, the trail up Jett Canyon will not disappoint you. About 4.6 miles from the trailhead, the trail disappears and further progress relies on off-trail travel. A potential cross-country route heads over the crest and down Little Jett Canyon to the Toiyabe Crest Trail at the Reese River (see Trip 1). Keep a keen eye out for bighorn sheep. They seem to prefer the craggy terrain along the upper slopes of the canyon.

Trailhead: (g) Turn east from State Route 376 onto Jett Canyon Road 1.2 miles south of State Route 378 to Round Mountain, approximately 48 miles south of U.S. 50 or 47 miles north of U.S. 95. The turnoff, signed: *Jett Canyon,* is directly opposite the Smoky Valley Road.

    Head east on Forest Service Road 090 as it makes a steady ascent toward the Toiyabe Mountains. Continue straight, ignoring side roads at 2.3, 2.7 and 3.2 miles. Cross a cattle guard at 4.9 miles—just beyond is a small campsite on the right. The road is washboarded in sections and gets rougher the closer you get to the canyon. Five miles from Route 376 is a sign: *Road Closed Ahead* and at 5.2 miles is a Forest Service gate. Parking for a couple of cars is available just before the gate. Otherwise you will have to park back at the campsite near the cattle guard.

Description: Follow the old road as it wanders below the jagged, serrated cliffs of Jett Canyon to a crossing of the creek. Cottonwoods and large shrubs grow alongside the creek in a narrow, deep canyon with towering, vertical cliffs.

    Along the route through the lower portion of the canyon, pieces of an old pipe used to divert water for some unknown purpose are visible along the roadside. Numerous improvements to the road, creek and water system appear randomly throughout the lower canyon until the old road splits, 1.6 miles from the trailhead. The right branch leads to a dam near a concrete-block building containing a valve for the water diversion. The structures appear to have seen recent use, but were inoperative in 1996. A small fire ran through the area just below the dam but seems to have been contained to a fairly small acreage.

Follow the road to the left as it heads above the south side of the creek. A little way farther, another road bends up a side canyon to some old cabins on the left. Continue up the main canyon, having left the dramatic cliffs behind, following the main road as it crosses the creek a number of times. Cottonwoods, willows, wild rose and other shrubs grow profusely along the creek, with wildflowers occasionally adding a splash of color in early season. On the hillsides, pinyon pine, juniper, mountain mahogany and sagebrush cover the slopes in varying degrees.

Where the canyon bends north on the *Arc Dome* topo, 4.6 miles from the trailhead, the unmaintained trail crosses the stream, heads onto an open, sagebrush-covered slope and disappears. The terrain above is open and the route-finding fairly easy, but farther progress up the canyon requires a certain amount of bushwacking.

Retrace your steps back to the trailhead.

Lexington Arch from the trail

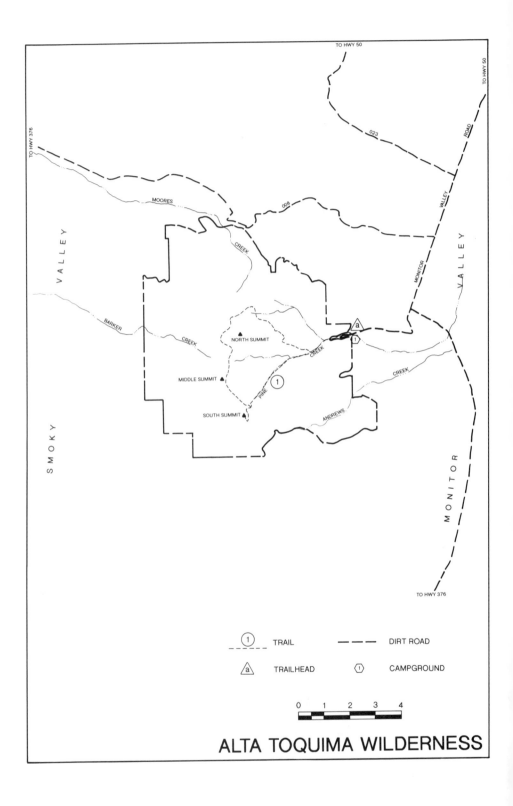

ALTA TOQUIMA WILDERNESS

Chapter 11
ALTA TOQUIMA WILDERNESS

Soaring above the surrounding valleys, Mt. Jefferson, in the central part of the Toquima Range, creates an imposing figure on the skyline of central Nevada. Wild, remote and seldom visited, the Alta Toquima Wilderness beckons the adventurous hiker and backpacker to partake of the unique wonders of this mountainous terrain. Situated in the middle of three wild ranges, the wilderness area boasts dramatic, glacier-carved canyons filled with tumbling creeks and high alpine tablelands with views spanning across the state from the mountains of California to the peaks of Utah.

Located near the geographic center of Nevada, the Alta Toquima Wilderness comprises 38,000 acres of untrammeled backcountry. The Wilderness straddles a linear range of mountains trending north-south above two low basins, the Monitor Valley to the east and Big Smoky Valley to the west. Triple-peaked Mt. Jefferson is the centerpiece, with South Summit claiming the title of highest mountain in central Nevada at 11,941 feet. The three summits rise up from a ridge eight miles long and up to two miles wide. A high plateau in the center of the range has some unique tablelands above rugged, glaciated canyons. Deep canyons on the north and south separate the Mt. Jefferson crest from the remainder of the Toquima Range, creating the appearance of a massive bulk of a mountain standing isolated above the surrounding landscape.

The vegetation of the Wilderness is typical of most central Nevada ranges also. Sagebrush and grasses carpet the lower slopes, pinyon-juniper woodlands cloak the middle elevations and scattered limber pine appear in the upper canyons and hillsides. The tableland along the top of Mt. Jefferson contains a variety of unique desert-alpine plant species. Pine Creek, a hearty, vibrant stream draining the steep canyons below the summits of Mt. Jefferson, offers a profuse covering of riparian vegetation, particularly in the lower reaches of the Pine Creek Trail. Cottonwood and aspen crowd the stream, producing a splash of yellow-orange in autumn.

Although the maps of the area indicate a 50-mile system of networking trails covering the Wilderness, many of the trails have become little more than routes, thanks primarily to inadequate funding for trail maintenance, combined with a basic lack of use. A well-known maxim of the governance of backcountry trails is that the most used trails get the lion's share of maintenance funding, leaving the little traveled trails of the Alta Toquima with few resources. The Pine Creek Trail, the most used trail in this lightly visited Wilderness, is a delightful exception. The track is excellent, providing a direct approach to the South Summit and the Mt. Jefferson plateau. But once out of the canyon, the tread disappears. If you wish to complete the loop via Bucks Canyon, be prepared to do some off-trail hiking and route finding—although, by cross-country standards, the terrain is easy and the route readily determined. The trails in the Alta Toquima Wilderness are primitive, but offer spectacular scenery and guaranteed solitude.

The Toquima Range is an interesting area rich in human as well as natural history. The name "Toquima" literally means black backs, and refers to a band of Mono Indians who once roamed the nearby lower Reese River Valley. In 1978, archeologists discovered remains of an Indian village on top of Mt. Jefferson which has turned out to be the highest known Indian settlement in North America. According to the scientists' theories, males used the site 7,000 years ago as a hunting camp. Much later, around 1300 A.D., entire families inhabited the area, but no specific reason for their habitation has come to light. Subsequently, due to the scientific and cultural importance of the region, the Mt. Jefferson Research Natural Area became established, encompassing the higher elevations around the summits of the mountain. In more recent times, John Muir explored the upper slopes of the Toquima Range, concluding from the geologic evidence that glaciers played an important part in the sculpting of the Great Basin mountains.

The ancient Indians may have hunted bighorn sheep that roamed the higher elevations, but earlier in the 20th century the animals disappeared from the range. Recently, biologists reintroduced a small band of desert bighorns into the Mt. Jefferson region, and they are carefully monitoring their comeback. Along with the sheep, the Toquima Range supports significant populations of deer, mountain lions, coyotes and small rodents. Game birds include grouse and chukar. The plateau offers excellent opportunities to gaze upon raptors rising on thermals above the precipitous canyons. Pine Creek, a perennial stream, has a good supply of rainbow and brook trout.

LOCATION

Located in Nye County, approximately 60 miles north of Tonopah and 50 miles south of Austin, the Alta Toquima Wilderness is east of State Route 376 and west of the Monitor Valley Road to the east. U.S. 50 is the nearest major highway to the north and U.S. 6 to the south. Forest Service roads access the five trailheads in the Wilderness.

CAMPGROUNDS

1. PINE CREEK

Open May through Mid-October
Camping, Picnicking, Restrooms, Trailer Sites, Stock Loading, Fishing
Trailhead for Pine Creek Trail (see Trip 1)
At the end of Forest Service Road #009 (see Trip 1 for description)

Primitive camping is available at or near the other trailheads.

RESOURCES

The nearest major towns are Tonopah and Austin, providing basic services including gasoline, auto repairs, food and lodging. Obtain gas and snacks along State Highway 376 in Carvers and find a convenience store near Kingston. No services are available in Monitor Valley.

FOREST SERVICE

Tonopah Ranger District
PO Box 3940
Tonopah, NV 89049-3940
(702) 482-6286

Toiyabe National Forest
Supervisor's Office
1200 Franklin Way
Sparks, NV 89431
(702) 331-6444

Trip 1

PINE CREEK TO MT. JEFFERSON

Trip Type: Dayhike or overnight backpack; Out and back to Mt. Jefferson plateau and South Summit, Loop via Bucks Canyon
Distance: 11.2 miles round trip to Mt. Jefferson plateau
13.6 miles round trip to South Summit
15.9 miles via off-trail route through Bucks Canyon
Season: Mid-June through mid-October
Access: Dirt road
Water: Creeks
Maps: #28, 29
Pine Creek Ranch & *Mount Jefferson* 7.5 minute quadrangles, 1971 (photorevised 1982) & 1971
Toiyabe National Forest map, Tonopah Ranger District, 1968 (revised '91 &'92)

Introduction: Pine Creek and Mt. Jefferson have much to offer the visitor to this seldom seen land. Beginning in juniper-pinyon pine woodland, the trail quickly encounters lush riparian vegetation along the creek as you ascend toward the Toquima Crest. The tumbling creek presents the best

fishing in the Toquima Range. As the trail gains elevation, aspen and limber pine dominate the upper canyon before desert-alpine vegetation takes
over at the crest.

Near the head of the basin, the Pine Creek Trail intersects the Mt.
Jefferson Trail, heading north-south along the crest of the Mt. Jefferson
massif. The southern route to South Summit, the highest of the three summits of Mt. Jefferson at 11,941 feet, is a short, technically easy climb from
the trail to the sixth tallest peak in Nevada. South Summit provides the
ultimate vantage point for surveying the vast countryside. The trail north
of South Summit climbs onto the Mt. Jefferson plateau, a long, narrow
tableland above glaciated canyons. The path fades after leaving the Pine
Creek drainage, but the open, alpine vegetation along the summit plateau
allows for easy travel in places where the old trail has disappeared. Views
from the Mt. Jefferson plateau stretch from one horizon to the other, offering long-range vistas that span the state.

A 15.6-mile loop trip wanders across Mt. Jefferson and descends into the
remote upper reaches of Bucks Canyon before cresting a saddle and
returning to Pine Creek. Although the trail has vanished from much of the
route, the travel is not exceedingly difficult, and it offers a rare opportunity for the off-trail hiker to experience pristine backcountry that few will
ever witness.

Trailhead: FROM TONOPAH: head east on U.S. 6 for 5.4 miles to the junction
with State Route 376. Head north on 376 approximately 13 miles to the
junction with the Monitor Valley Road, shown as State Route 82 on the
Forest Service map. Travel on the Monitor Valley Road, initially asphalt
and then gravel, for 46.5 miles to the junction with the Pine Creek Road.
Continue as described below "All Routes."

FROM AUSTIN: Go east on U.S. 50 about 12 miles to the junction with State
Route 376. Turn south onto 376, immediately turn again to the southeast
on the gravel road to Toquima Cave, and go 28 miles to the Monitor Valley
Road. Follow this road south 33 miles to the junction with the Pine Creek
Road. Continue as described below "All Routes."

FROM EUREKA: Head west on U.S. 50 for 30 miles to the junction with the
Monitor Valley Road. Travel south on the Monitor Valley Road 57 miles to
the junction with Pine Creek Road. Continue as described below "All
Routes."

ALL ROUTES: (a) At the junction with the road to Pine Creek is a BLM sign
which reads: *Pine Creek* (straight), *Belmont* (southeast) and *Moores Creek,
Northumberland* (north). Head south on the gravel road for 0.95 mile to a
junction where you bear right. The road straight ahead goes to a ranch.
Your road curves west, heading directly toward Mt. Jefferson. At 2.9 miles
from the junction with the Monitor Valley Road, enter signed Toiyabe

National Forest on Forest Service Road #009. Travel through pinyon-pine forest to the Pine Creek Campground, 3.4 miles from the Monitor Valley Road. The campsites are straight ahead while the unsigned trailhead is just up a road to the right. Park in a wide clearing immediately north of the campground.

Description: Follow the continuation of the old road a short distance until a trail heads away to the left as the road bends uphill. A short distance farther, a side trail from the Pine Creek Campground joins the main trail above Pine Creek. Dense groves of quaking aspen crowd the creek, while pinyon pine sparsely covers the hillsides. You cross a seasonal drainage and immediately reach the Wilderness boundary. A crude wooden sign attached to a cottonwood tree reads: *Jefferson 6.*

In the next half mile, the trail crosses the densely vegetated creek three times before reaching a junction with the Pasco Canyon Trail, 1.2 miles from the trailhead. Another crude wooden sign nailed to a tree marks the junction stating: *Pasco Canyon 4½* (right, north), *Pine Creek* (straight).

Continue up the trail through lush riparian vegetation as the path crosses Pine Creek four more times. At what appears to be a fifth crossing since the junction to Pasco Canyon, newer trail remains on the north side of the creek, climbing steeply up the hillside away from the creek and over some cliffs. Return to the creek and make additional crossings as the trail continues up Pine Creek. At 1.9 miles from the trailhead, you pass the completely obscure junction with the trail heading northwest into the head of Bucks Canyon and up to the Mt. Jefferson Crest. A loop trip returning via this trail is possible. Be forewarned, the route from the crest down Bucks Canyon and over to Pine Creek is accomplished without the aid of a defined trail for the most of the route.

Continue up the creek as the trail wanders up the stream from one side to the other. Near a crossing from the north bank to the south, the trail passes a campsite nestled beneath some mature aspens approximately 3.8 miles from the trailhead. You wind up through lush grasslands, decorated with the blue and red of lupines and paintbrush, under a grove of small-to-medium aspens. After a considerable distance, you leave the aspens behind as the trail enters an open area of grasses and sagebrush, allowing good views ahead toward the sweeping upper canyon of Pine Creek. Four miles from the Pine Creek Campground, the trail veers over and crosses the narrowing creek to a spring-fed meadow where the trail disappears in the verdant grass. Watch for ducks to guide you across the meadow to more-distinct trail.

The grade of the trail increases as it climbs through lush underbrush and beneath the filtered shade of aspens and limber pine on rocky tread. In and out of forest cover, the path continues to ascend toward the upper basin. By midsummer, stretches of the upper reaches of Pine Creek may be dry but a spring will provide an abundant supply of water, 4.5 miles from the trailhead. Leave the limber pine behind just beyond the spring and ascend steeply across grassy slopes. Around 0.3 mile above the spring, cross the creek bed just below a couple of small springs sending a trickle of water into the creek.

Now you ascend into a wide-open, sloping basin just below the crest of the range, where grassy slopes merge into austere, rocky hillsides. The trail, in remarkably good condition up to this point, disappears in the meadow grass; ducks and cairns will guide you to a more distinct junction near a large pile of rocks where a weathered tree limb supports a crude wooden sign reading: *S. Summit, North Summit.*

The South Summit of Mt. Jefferson, at 11,941 feet, is the highest of the three summits. To reach the top, follow the summit trail southeast as it ascends across a talus slope out of the basin to the top of a ridge at 5.8 miles, where you encounter the faint junction with the trail from Windy Pass. Bear west from the ridge, climb steeply below the east face of the peak to the south ridge, and ascend easy slopes to the summit.

To reach the broad plateau of Mt. Jefferson, including Middle and North summits, bear northwest from the junction and continue up the canyon to crest the low point in the ridge above. As you climb out of the basin, the trail grows faint again, but ducks lead past rock cliffs just below the ridge line and then the path becomes distinct once more. After a switchback, the trail curves around to the crest and disappears.

The long plateau of Mt. Jefferson stretches out before you. The alpine vegetation struggles to reach three or four inches—diminutive wildflowers live out a brief existence in the early summer. Awe-inspiring, 360-degree views are commonplace from the Mt. Jefferson crest. Mountains all the way from California to Utah are visible on clear days. Across Big Smoky Valley to the west, Arc Dome, 11,788 feet high, presides over the Toiyabe Range and the Arc Dome Wilderness. Across Monitor Valley to the east, the vast mesa-like plateau of Table Mountain, the centerpiece of the 100-mile-long Monitor Range, rises across the horizon. Within the Toquima Range, South Summit, Spanish and Shoshone peaks dominate the foreground. Much less spectacularly, the massive scars of the Round Mountain Mine mar the lower slopes on the western flank of the Toquima Mountains.

Although maps indicate a trail along the length of the tablelands, in actuality only short sections of the path are the least bit discernible. However, rudimentary skills are all that is necessary to negotiate the open topography across the sloping tableland of Mt. Jefferson.

Once on the crest, the route proceeds a mile gradually up to the rocks just below Middle Summit, by far the easiest of the three summits to reach. From Middle Summit the pseudo-trail leads along the crest for 1.25 miles before a mild descent leads to a large open meadow. The topo map indicates a creek running through this meadow. However, the water is more bog than stream and a herd of cattle frequent the area.

From the meadow, ascend east of a hill to a saddle. From the saddle the more pronounced track appears to descend into the Barker Creek drainage—a good option if you're searching for a nice place to camp. The main trail, however, bears to the right on faint track, climbing steeply up a rocky hillside to milder slopes above. Once back on the plateau, the path heads north to what at one time may have been an actual junction with the trail into Bucks Canyon. Shown as the Mt. Jefferson Trail on the Forest Service map, the route continues, heading north, and descending steeply down the Moores Creek drainage to a trailhead just off Forest Service Road #008.

To make the off-trail loop back to Pine Creek by way of Bucks Canyon, work your way over to the high point marked on the topo as *11,691 x.* Head northeast along the rocky ridge and look for the most reasonable route down the precipitous slopes above Bucks Canyon. Once the hardest part of the trip is behind, you may find a faint path that leads across the creek and along the slopes below North Summit to a saddle. From the saddle descend into the tributary of Pine Creek and follow it down to the Pine Creek Trail. Now retrace your steps 1.9 miles to the trailhead.

OTHER TRAILS

The trails within the Alta Toquima Wilderness are primitive and receive only sporadic maintenance, if any. Be prepared to find complete sections of trails appearing only on maps. Adequate skills in route finding and cross-country travel may be necessary for successful travel in the area.

Moores Creek: The northern terminus of the Mt. Jefferson Trail is just off Forest Service Road #008, approximately 2.5 miles west of Moores Creek Summit. The trail initially follows Moores Creek before steeply ascending a hillside to the top of a long, flat ridge. Rejoin the creek and climb to the head of the canyon. A very steep ascent leads to the north edge of the Mt. Jefferson plateau.

Red Rock: About 0.8 mile east of Moores Creek Summit, Forest Service Road #52 turns south from Road #008. An unmaintained trail follows the continuation of an old jeep road south through Red Rock Canyon and on toward Pasco Canyon. The old road terminates before Pasco Canyon but one could continue through open terrain down into the canyon and to the trail connecting the Pasco Canyon and Pine Creek trailheads.

Pasco Canyon: Approximately 0.4 mile from the Monitor Valley Road, Forest Service Road #420 leaves Pine Creek Road and heads northwest and then west to the Pasco Canyon trailhead. The trail drops into Pasco Canyon and follows the canyon floor before climbing a side drainage to a saddle separating Pasco and Bucks canyons. Descend the northern tributary of the Bucks Canyon creek to the Pine Creek Trail. Another 1.25 mile leads to the Pine Creek trailhead.

Jefferson Summit: Access to the south end of the Alta Toquima Wilderness and the Mt. Jefferson Trail is by a road along Meadow Creek. This road turns east from the Monitor Valley Road about 32 miles north of that road's junction with State Highway 376. The road initially follows the narrow canyon until reaching a series of meadows. Turn west onto Forest Service Road #010 and follow this road to the trailhead at Jefferson Summit. The trail begins at 8,770 feet and ascends along the ridge toward the South Summit of Mt. Jefferson. The 4-mile climb is the most direct route to South Summit but is completely dry.

Windy Pass: If you have an extremely durable, 4-wheel-drive vehicle you can drive within 2 miles of South Summit. Follow the directions to Jefferson Summit continuing straight at the junction with Road #010, up the deteriorating Meadow Canyon Road all the way to the end at Windy Pass. The trail climbs toward the head of Andrews Creek, to the junction with the Mt. Jefferson Trail in a saddle below the northeast slopes of South Summit. Turn west here for the last mile to South Summit or head northwest to the Mt. Jefferson plateau.

Spring near Big Sawmill Creek in Arc Dome Wilderness

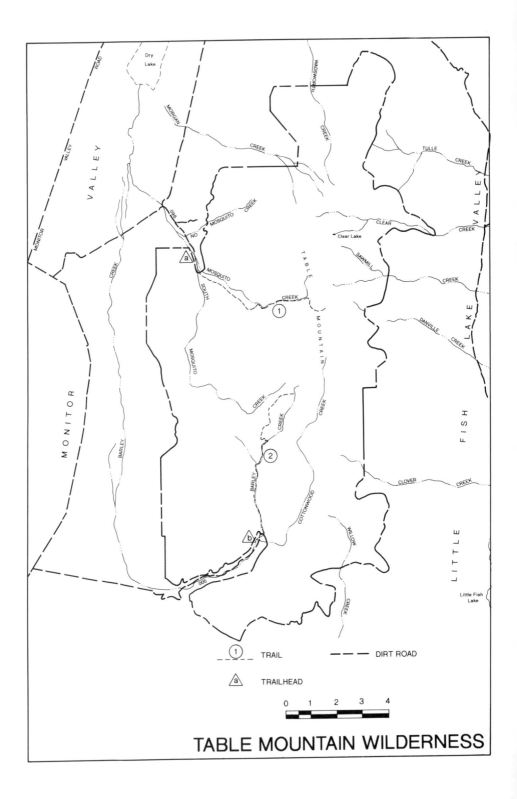

TABLE MOUNTAIN WILDERNESS

Chapter 12
TABLE MOUNTAIN WILDERNESS

In the heart of central Nevada, separated by Big Smoky and Monitor valleys, three parallel mountain ranges contain three designated wilderness areas. From west to east, Arc Dome Wilderness covers the south end of the Toiyabe Range, the Alta Toquima Wilderness embraces the highest section of the Toquima Mountains, and the Table Mountain Wilderness straddles the mesa-like high country of the Monitor Range. Behind the Arc Dome and Jarbidge Wilderness areas, Table Mountain, at 98,000 acres, is the third largest wilderness area in the state, and contains a corresponding number of hiking trails.

Similar to many Great Basin mountains, the Monitors are a classic example of the long and narrow range. Nearly 115 miles long, they never seem to attain any greater width than about 10 miles. In contrast, the Table Mountain Wilderness possesses some unique characteristics that set it apart from the others. At a lofty height above 10,000 feet, a 12-square-mile tableland is the crowning landmark and namesake of the Wilderness. Blessed with a relative abundance of moisture, the upper slopes of the mountains contain some of the most massive stands of quaking aspen anywhere in the Great Basin, producing a spectacular display of golden yellow during the fall. Another uncommon attribute of the range is the herd of Rocky Mountain elk that thrive in the particular environment created by the Monitors. Introduced to the area in 1979, the herd has grown to over 300 individuals, presenting opportunities for wildlife observers and sportsmen.

Five perennial streams course down the Monitors, providing fishermen with the opportunity to test their skills on the rainbow, brook, brown and Lahontan cutthroat trout inhabiting the waters. Besides the elk, the Monitor Range supports one of the largest mule deer herds in the entire state. Other large mammals living in the Wilderness include mountain lion, bobcat and coyote. The engineering feats of the beaver appear along many of the perennial creeks. Important game birds are the chukar, blue grouse and sage grouse. Birds of prey, such as golden eagles, northern goshawks and prairie falcons, patrol the skies above the grasslands and meadows found throughout the Wilderness.

While the prolific stands of aspen create dramatic focal points within the Table Mountain Wilderness, other species of deciduous trees and conifers appear in a variety of locales. Small pockets of limber pine cover slopes near the crest, typically the only species of pine growing in the upper elevations of the central ranges between the Sierra Nevada and the mountains at the eastern edge of Nevada. Charlet reports in *Atlas of Nevada Conifers* that bristlecone pines show up in the range—although north of the Wilderness, near Antelope Peak. At the lower elevations, typical juniper-pinyon pine woodlands cover much of the range. In the juniper-pinyon zone, groves of mountain mahogany occasionally appear on the drier, sagebrush-covered slopes, while cottonwoods thrive along the banks of the creeks at the lower elevations. Wherever a significant amount of water occurs in stream beds, lush riparian foliage carpets the banks, providing a stark contrast to the drier slopes, usually filled with sagebrush and grasses.

The Monitor Range is a remote and seldom-visited region. Located far away from a town of any size, access to the area requires long drives on gravel or dirt roads. In spite of the road conditions, many of the trailheads are accessible to passenger cars with care. The vehicle of choice, however, is a durable truck or utility vehicle.

Due to the tableland topography at the crest and the mildly graded trails, the Table Mountain Wilderness appeals to horse packers and equestrians as well as hikers and backpackers. Over 100 miles of trail form a network covering the crest and connecting with access trails, providing myriad possibilities for extended trips and loops of varying length. Trails are usually snow free and passable by early summer when meadows are green and wildflowers in bloom. In many ways, fall is the best time for a visit, when acres of turning aspens and the occasional bugle of a bull elk create a fine backcountry experience in the unique Table Mountain Wilderness.

LOCATION

In Nye County, 65 miles northeast of Tonopah and 55 miles southeast of Austin, the Table Mountain Wilderness is bounded by the Monitor Valley Road on the west, U.S. 50 on the north and U.S. 6 on the south. Surrounding Forest Service roads provide access into the Wilderness.

CAMPGROUNDS

No developed campgrounds are in the immediate vicinity of the Wilderness, but along the access roads and at the trailheads are many primitive campsites. The nearest Forest Service campground is on Pine Creek directly west of Table Mountain at the base of the Toquima Range (see Chapter 11).

RESOURCES

There are no services in either Monitor Valley on the west side of the mountains or Little Fish Lake Valley on the east. Tonopah, Austin and Eureka are the nearest towns with the basics of food, lodging, gasoline and car repair services. A few merchants in Tonopah carry a limited selection of camping gear.

FOREST SERVICE

Austin Ranger District
100 Midas Canyon Road
PO Box 130
Austin, NV 89310-0130
(702) 964-2671

Toiyabe National Forest
Supervisor's Office
1200 Franklin Way
Sparks, NV 89431
(702) 331-6444

Tonopah Ranger District
PO Box 3940
Tonopah, NV 89049-3940
(702) 482-6286

Trip 1 ⚐
MOSQUITO CREEK

Trip Type: Dayhike or overnight backpack; Out and back
Distance: 15.0 miles round trip
Season: June through October
Access: Dirt road—high-clearance vehicle necessary
Water: Creek
Maps: #30, 31
Mosquito Creek, Danville 7.5 minute quadrangles, 1971
Toiyabe National Forest map, Tonopah Ranger District, 1968 (revised 1991, 92)

Introduction: A moderate trail into the heart of the Table Mountain Wilderness, the Mosquito Creek Trail provides entrance to hillsides and tablelands covered with the trademark stands of quaking aspen endemic to the Wilderness. The first 3.5 miles of the route evade the creek as you pass through dry slopes of sagebrush, dotted with pinyon pine, juniper and mountain mahogany. Once the path returns to the Mosquito Creek environs, large groves of aspen line the creek and fill the basin. Above the origin of the stream, the trail ascends the steep slopes below the summit plateau to the Table Mountain crest.

A base camp situated toward the upstream end of Mosquito Creek provides almost unlimited opportunities for further explorations across Table Mountain. The extensive stands of aspen and the chance to view bugling elk make autumn an ideal time to enjoy the wonders of this trail.

Trailhead: FROM TONOPAH: Head east on U.S. 6 for 5.4 miles to the junction with State Route 376. Head north on 376 approximately 13 miles to the junction with the Monitor Valley Road, shown as State Route 82 on the Forest Service map. Travel on the Monitor Valley Road, initially asphalt and then gravel, for 45.3 miles to the intersection with the road to the Mosquito Creek trailhead, signed: *Morgan Creek-Mosquito Creek.* Continue as described below "All Routes."

FROM AUSTIN: Go east on U.S. 50 about 12 miles to the junction with State Route 376. Turn south onto 376 and immediately turn again to the southeast on the gravel road to Toquima Cave, and go 28 miles to the Monitor Valley Road. Follow this road south 34 miles to the junction with the road to the Mosquito Creek trailhead, signed: *Morgan Creek-Mosquito Creek.* Continue as described below "All Routes."

FROM EUREKA: Head west on U.S. 50 for 30 miles to the junction with the Monitor Valley Road. Travel south on this road for 58 miles to the junction with the road to the Mosquito Creek trailhead, signed: *Morgan Creek-Mosquito Creek.* Continue as described below "All Routes."

ALL ROUTES: (a) From the intersection with the Monitor Valley Road, travel northeast on the Morgan Creek-Mosquito Creek road 5.7 miles to the junction with Forest Service Road #096. Turn east, following a sign reading: *Mosquito Creek.* Continue 2.0 miles to the trailhead next to Mosquito Creek. Two nice campsites are at the trailhead near some cottonwoods and pinyon pines. A large stock loading area is available as well.

Description: The trail begins by crossing Mosquito Creek and bending upstream through widely spaced sagebrush, ephedra, juniper and pinyon pine to the signed Wilderness boundary. Soon the dirt track passes a crude sign nailed to a pinyon pine which simply reads: *Table Mtn 7.* The trail climbs well above and away from the creek, avoiding the stream for the first 3.75 miles. Steeply ascend a hill as the trail switchbacks up the slope, winding through rocks to the top. Excellent views unfold to the west of the Toquima Range and Mt. Jefferson.

At the top of the hill the vegetation has diminished except for pinyon pine. Continue up the trail on a more moderate grade for a considerable distance until you ascend another hill, where the sandy trail breaks out into open sagebrush amid a few scattered pines. Follow the trail along a seasonal drainage to the top of the crest, approximately 3 miles from the trailhead, where mountain mahogany begins to appear and views return of Mt. Jefferson across the Monitor Valley.

Descend briefly into a shallow canyon, cross the seasonal stream in the gently sloping floor of the canyon and bend left, climbing out of the canyon through tall sagebrush. Crest a short rise near some mahogany trees and head into the Mosquito Creek drainage for the first time. The main trail actually avoids the creek, but you can easily wander over to the aspen-lined stream for a refreshing break. Small campsites nestle beneath the aspens alongside the creek.

Bend up a small valley to the left away from Mosquito Creek. Amid a sea of sagebrush, crest another rise to a grand view of some large stands of aspen, one of the most impressive features of Table Mountain. Circle down into the next canyon, pass a large stand of aspen and climb out to an unmarked junction with a trail heading south. The main trail continues east. Your trail assumes a level course as it passes through a field of sagebrush, fringed by pockets of aspen running up the hillside.

Continue through sagebrush as the trail descends toward aspen-lined Mosquito Creek, about 4.75 miles from the trailhead. The trail, not shown on the 1971 *Mosquito Creek* and *Danville* topos, heads upstream close to the water's edge for the next 1.25 mile. Plenty of nice campsites are in the grass beneath the mature trees. Apparently perfectly balanced, the soil and water conditions in this drainage grow aspens with some of the thickest trunks imaginable. Continue to ascend alongside the creek until breaking out into the open, where nailed to one of the last trees before the clearing, a crude wooden sign reads: *Mosquito Cr TH 7*. Follow the creek through a small meadow where the trail grows indistinct. Find it again at the far edge and continue to an area of confusion where it appears that the main trail bends north to follow the creek as it wraps around a low hill. This trail eventually connects with the Morgan Creek Trail, part of a possible shuttle trip with the Morgan Creek trailhead.

However, if you want to reach the crest of Table Mountain and Danville Pass from here, follow as best as you can an indistinct path directly east up the hillside. To make matters worse, there are two different routes just above that ascend to Table Mountain. One follows an old jeep road diagonally southeast on a mildly ascending path through open terrain to the crest. The other route is a single-track trail that climbs more steeply up the drainage of a seasonal stream directly to Danville Pass. You can reach both trails by continuing to climb the hillside eastward on an extremely obscure path until it becomes more distinct farther up. Follow the path as it bends around a grove of aspens and heads south. A crude 2 x 6 sign nailed to an aspen reads: *4½ Morgan Cr. TH, Danville Pass 1/*. Continue along a more distinct path as it follows the drainage to the junction of the trail and the road, 6.6 miles from the trailhead. Proceed on the path of your choice onto the crest of Table Mountain. Danville Pass is almost another mile up the trail, 7.5 miles from the trailhead.

At the conclusion of your journey retrace your steps to the trailhead.

Trip 2 🌲
BARLEY CREEK

Trip Type: Dayhike or overnight backpack; Out and back
Distance: 14.4 miles round trip
Season: June through October
Access: Dirt road
Water: Creek and springs
Maps: #32
  Barley Creek, Green Monster Canyon 7.5 minute quadrangles,
    1971
  Toiyabe National Forest map, Tonopah Ranger District, 1968
    (revised '91 &'92)

Introduction: A mellow 3.5-mile hike begins the Barley Creek Trail as it gently ascends the mildly sloping drainage through typical medium-elevation vegetation. Beyond this stretch of trail, the grade increases as you ascend steeper terrain toward the crest of Table Mountain. Most of the route passes through open slopes of predominantly sagebrush-covered hillsides—7 miles lead to the prolific stands of aspen that bring notice to the Table Mountain Wilderness. Near the top of the range, impressive views open up to the west of the Toquima and Toiyabe ranges.

Horse packers and equestrians find the mildly graded trail appealing and seem to account for the majority of travel along the trail. Like many of the trails in the Wilderness, the Barley Creek Trail connects with other trails near the crest of Table Mountain for extended trips into the backcountry. A campsite along upper Barley Creek is an excellent base camp for further explorations.

Trailhead: FROM TONOPAH: Head east on U.S. 6 for 5.4 miles to the junction with State Route 376. Head north on 376 approximately 13 miles to the junction with the Monitor Valley Road, shown as State Route 82 on the Forest Service map. Travel on the Monitor Valley Road, initially asphalt then gravel, for 33.3 miles to the intersection with the road to the Barley Creek trailhead, signed: *Barley Creek 8.* Continue as described below "All Routes."

FROM AUSTIN: Go east on U.S. 50 about 12 miles to the junction with State Route 376. Turn south onto 376 and immediately turn again to the southeast on the gravel road to Toquima Cave and go 28 miles to the Monitor Valley Road. Follow the Monitor Valley Road south 46 miles to the junction with the road to the Barley Creek trailhead, signed: *Barley Creek 8.* Continue as described below "All Routes."

FROM EUREKA: Head west on U.S. 50 for 30 miles to the junction with the Monitor Valley Road. Travel south on the Monitor Valley Road 70 miles to the junction with the road to the Barley Creek trailhead, signed: *Barley Creek 8.* Continue as described below "All Routes."

ALL ROUTES: (b) From the intersection with the Monitor Valley Road, head east on the well-graded road to Barley Creek. Immediately another sign appears stating: *Barley Creek, Cottonwood Creek, House Canyon.* Cross over a cattle guard and reach a major 'Y' junction at 4.3 miles from where the left-hand road goes to the Barley Creek Ranch. A sign at the junction reads: *Barley Creek Ranch* (left), *S. Fork Barley Creek 1, Barley Creek 2, Cottonwood Creek 5* (right).

Bear right at the junction onto rougher and narrower road, entering Toiyabe National Forest land at 5.5 miles from the Monitor Valley Road. Reach a 'T' junction at 5.8 miles signed: *S. Fork Barley Creek, Willow Creek AS 12* (right) and *Barley Creek ½, Cottonwood Creek 4* (left).

Turn left onto Forest Service Road #005 and enter a shallow canyon filled with sagebrush and lightly scattered juniper and pinyon pine. At 6.2 miles from the Monitor Valley Road, come to another 'T' junction marked: *Barley Creek Ranch ½* (left) and *Cottonwood Creek 4* (right). Basically, the route has made a detour around the private property of the Barley Creek Ranch. Turn right at the intersection and proceed on single-lane, dirt road passable to most sedans. The canyon is broad beneath the slopes of rolling hillsides covered with pinyon pine and juniper. Willows choke the creek channel.

The canyon narrows as we travel upstream, crossing Barley Creek four times before reaching the trailhead at a broad turnaround, 10 miles from the Monitor Valley Road. Along the way up the canyon, the road passes numerous primitive campsites and a pit toilet. The trailhead has many new improvements, including a stock loading area, pit toilet, picnic tables, campsites and a small corral.

Description: The well-marked trail begins by following a new section of single-track path as it climbs along a low hillside above the road to a gate signed: *Barley Creek Trail.* An interesting rock-walled corral is near the gate, evidently used by horse packers during hunting season. The number and quality of improvements near the trailhead seem out of character for the National Forest lands within central Nevada.

Follow the gently ascending path of the old road as it winds along the drainage below steep, rocky cliffs, crossing back and forth over the small, willow-lined creek. Throughout the initial miles of the trip, the trail crosses the creek numerous times, which should not present any problems with the possible exception of early in the spring during peak flows. Reach the signed Wilderness boundary where the foliage diminishes, allowing excellent views up the canyon.

The canyon divides and the old road follows the main branch to the left. The mild grade of the old road continues as the trail heads upstream through tall sagebrush. Widely distributed pinyon and juniper rise above

Crude trail sign nailed to a mountain mahogany

the sage on the canyon slopes, while the creek remains choked with water-loving willows. Draining a significant side canyon to the west, the trail crosses a seasonal stream near a small grove of mountain mahogany. A crude sign attached to one of the trees reads: *Table Mtn. 9.* Continue to follow the path of the old road for another 1.75 miles as it proceeds on a gentle grade up the canyon.

At 3.1 miles, the trail bends northeast following Barley Creek, contrary to the topo, which shows the trail heading towards Big Meadow. Follow along the east bank of the creek by head-high willows into the narrow, steep canyon. Near a substantial side canyon, 3.5 miles from the trailhead, reach the junction with the connecting trail heading east to the Cottonwood Creek Trail. The trail junction is somewhat indistinct but a 2 x 6 sign 25 feet up the path reads: *Cottonwood Cr 3.*

Continue up the Barley Creek Trail past a tiny spring to some campsites in a grove of quaking aspens. The area appears big enough to accommodate three or four tents. Beyond the camp the trail climbs steeply up the canyon to an area of extensive beaver activity. Numerous beaver dams and ponds have radically altered the terrain in the narrow gorge, and many aspens toppled in the process. The flurry of construction lends credence to the phrase "busy as a beaver."

Past the last beaver dam, the trail crosses Barley Creek and begins a steep climb up the far hillside to a gap in the ridge above. As you climb out of the canyon, the lush foliage along the creek stays behind as the vegetation returns to sagebrush slopes dotted with widely scattered mahogany, juniper and pinyon pine. From the top of the rise, views open up to the west of Mt. Jefferson and the Toquima Range. You curve around a minor drainage and then traverse west across slopes into the next minor drainage. Along the eastern slopes, the trail climbs through open sagebrush toward the lower slopes of Table Mountain. Now pass through the opening in a barbed-wire fence to an unmarked trail junction, approximately 5.5 miles from the trailhead.

From the junction, take the right-hand path, which follows an old jeep road as it gently climbs to the top of a rise and then descends into the upper portions of Barley Creek. From the rise, you have an excellent view of the upper part of Table Mountain. Substantial stands of aspen cover the slopes from the creek up to the top of the tablelands. Follow the old road as it leads through an open fence down to the banks of Barley Creek, 7.2 miles from the trailhead. Cross the meadow-lined creek to the far bank, where a use trail heads upstream to some idyllic campsites near a grove of aspen. The main trail continues, climbing steeply away from the creek a mile to the Table Mountain crest.

Retrace your steps back to the trailhead.

OTHER TRAILS

Morgan Creek: At the northwest end of the Wilderness, a short trail leads through an immense stand of aspen up to the northern end of Table Mountain.

Clear Creek, Danville Canyon, Green Monster Canyon & Clover Creek: These are east side trails that head up the steeper side of the range to connect with trails on Table Mountain.

Willow Creek: From the southeast edge of the Wilderness, a three mile trail leads to the Cottonwood Creek Trail from the Barley Creek trailhead.

South Mosquito Creek: From the Mosquito Creek trailhead a trail heads south along the South Fork Mosquito Creek through lower country on the west side of the range until connecting with the Barley Creek Trail below Table Mountain.

North Mosquito Creek: Access is by 4-wheel-drive only. A rough trail travels 4 miles to a junction with the Morgan Creek Trail.

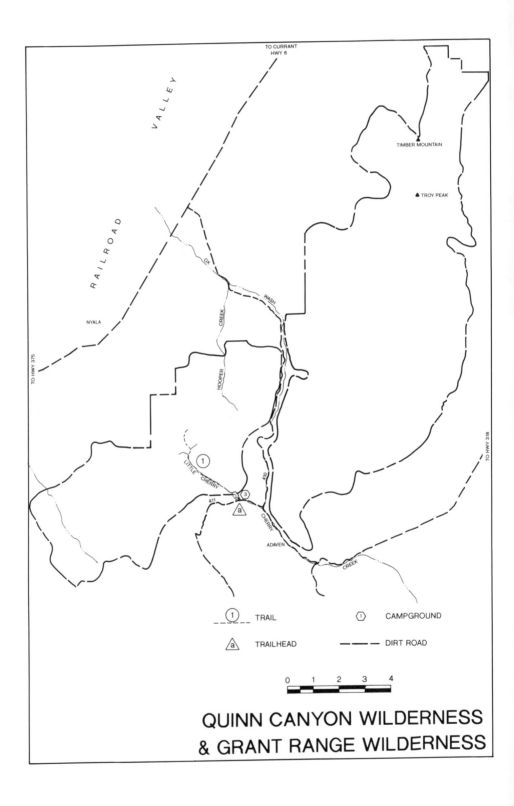

TO CURRANT
HWY 6

VALLEY

RAILROAD

TIMBER MOUNTAIN

▲ TROY PEAK

OX

NYALA

WASH

CREEK

HOOPER

TO HWY 375

TO HWY 318

LITTLE CHERRY

①

430

411

③

ⓐ

CHERRY

ADAVEN

CREEK

①   TRAIL   ①   CAMPGROUND

ⓐ   TRAILHEAD   — — —   DIRT ROAD

0   1   2   3   4

QUINN CANYON WILDERNESS
& GRANT RANGE WILDERNESS

Chapter 13

CURRANT MOUNTAIN, GRANT RANGE & QUINN CANYON WILDERNESSES

Three small, forgotten and isolated wilderness areas lie in the east-central part of the state. To refer to an area in Nevada as remote begins to become a cliché, but no truer designation applies to this group of island mountains. Far from the crowd, these three wilderness areas offer solitude in diverse and unique settings. Trail users will be a bit dismayed by the lack of maintained trails in this region. Only one exists, the Little Cherry Creek Trail in the Quinn Canyon Wilderness. The terrain, however, is open and well suited to cross-country travel, beckoning the adventurous to roam the undefiled backcountry.

Currant Mountain Wilderness is an area of 36,000 acres in the White Pine Range approximately 50 miles west of Ely. The area, characterized by rugged limestone formations, has two peaks, Currant Mountain and Duckwater Peak, with elevations over 11,000 feet. Desert Bighorn sheep inhabit the range along with antelope and mule deer. More biologically diverse than many Nevada mountains, the White Pine Range is home to a wide variety of conifers including white fir, juniper, pinyon, limber and ponderosa pine, as well as extensive stands of bristlecone pine at the higher elevations. Water is somewhat scarce, thanks primarily to the limestone composition of the range that soaks up the moisture. Currant Mountain Wilderness offers many fine opportunities for primitive wilderness experiences.

The Grant Range Wilderness, 120 miles southwest of Ely and 120 miles north of Las Vegas, comprises 50,000 acres along the crest of the Grant Range. Thanks to a composition of predominantly limestone, surface water is hard to come by in this mountain range as well. The highest summit, Troy Peak at 11,298 feet, lies in the north part of the Wilderness along a north-south trending crest, rising nearly one mile above the basin of Railroad Valley to the west. Desert Bighorn sheep, mule deer and mountain lions are the chief mammals. The Grant Range is also complex biologically, with the same species of conifer as Currant Mountain, including significant stands of bristlecone pine.

Located directly west of the Grant Range, the Quinn Canyon Wilderness has 27,000 acres of pristine land straddling a ridge of high, unnamed peaks extending for approximately 10 miles, cresting at 10,229 feet. Unlike her two sister ranges, the composition of Quinn Canyon is primarily volcanic rock. Consequently, more surface water is available for recreationists and wildlife, including desert bighorn sheep, mule deer and mountain lions. Just like Currant Mountain and the Grant Range, a diverse assortment of conifers calls this range home. A Federally listed sensitive plant species, *Primula nevadensis*, with purple blossoms around 1" across, is found only in this area and the Snake Range.

Quinn Canyon Wilderness is the home to the only designated, maintained trail in the three wilderness areas—Little Cherry Creek Trail, which ascends a delightful canyon on the east side of the range. Cherry Creek Campground is a primitive site at the trailhead and offers a fine base camp for explorations into the backcountry of the Quinn Canyon Range.

These three wilderness areas offer prime opportunities for backcountry travel and exploration. Almost the entire region is inaccessible by trail, but for the hearty adventurer willing to leave the beaten path, these mountain ranges have much to offer.

LOCATION

Currant Mountain Wilderness is 50 miles west of Ely, Nevada. U.S. 6 provides access from the south, State Route 379 from the west. A network of County and Forest Service roads surrounds the Wilderness.

The Grant Range Wilderness and Quinn Canyon Wilderness are southwest of Ely and north of Las Vegas. U.S. 6 bounds the areas to the north and State Routes 375 and 318 to the southwest and east respectively. Well-graded gravel roads connect these major highways to Forest Service roads to the wilderness areas.

CAMPGROUNDS

1. CHERRY CREEK—Forest Service
   Open April through October
   Camping, Picnicking, Toilets
   Between the Quinn Canyon Wilderness and the Grant Range
      Wilderness, one mile on
   Forest Service Road #411 from Forest Service Road #410
   Trailhead for Little Cherry Creek Trail

2. CURRANT CREEK—Forest Service
   Open May through September
   Camping, Toilets
   At the southeast end of Currant Mountain Wilderness on U.S. 6

3. WHITE RIVER—Forest Service
   Open June through September
   Camping, Toilets
   Near the east edge of Currant Mountain Wilderness approximately
       10 miles from U.S. 6 up County Road 1163

RESOURCES

There are no services of any substance close to any of these wilderness areas. Ely is the closest major town to the Currant Mountain Wilderness (approximately 50 miles).

FOREST SERVICE

Ely Ranger District
350 8th Street
PO Box 539
Ely, NV 89301
(702) 289-3031

Humboldt National Forest
Supervisor's Office
976 Mountain City Highway
Elko, NV 89801
(702) 738-5171

Trip 1 ⚴
LITTLE CHERRY CREEK

Trip Type: Dayhike or overnight backpack; Out and back
Distance: 8.0 miles round trip
Season: May through mid-November
Access: Dirt road
Water: Creek
Maps: #33
     Nyala 7.5 minute quadrangle, 1985 (provisional)
     Humboldt National Forest map, Ely Ranger District, West
          Half, 1990

Introduction: To be the only maintained trail in three wilderness areas alone makes the Little Cherry Creek Trail special and unique. The 4-mile hike passes through riparian, pinyon-juniper and fir-forest zones before reaching the end of the trail in a saddle separating the Little Cherry Creek and Hooper Creek drainages. Rugged cliffs and unique rock formations add character to the canyon as the trail climbs from 6800 feet to 8200 feet. Little Cherry Creek maintains a healthy flow of water throughout the season, even in the fall, when the bottom half of the spring-fed stream is still running.

Trailhead: (a) One must travel a great distance on some forlorn roads in order to reach the Cherry Creek trailhead. A wide, well-graded gravel road connects the town of Currant on U.S. 6 with State Route 375, passing through the tiny community of Nyala on the way. From the junction of

Highways 6 and 375 at the abandoned town of Warm Springs, travel east on 375 for 15.9 miles to a signed turnoff: *Nyala, Adaven*.

Turn onto the gravel road and travel 20.8 miles to a 'Y' intersection, where you should bear right. The left-hand road proceeds into a ranch near the site of Nyala. A mere 1.2 miles farther is the northern junction with the previous road from Nyala where a sign reads: *Cherry Creek C.G. 17, Currant 51* (ahead); *State Highway 25 22, Warm Springs 38* (behind). Continue on the gravel road northward another 2.6 miles, 24.6 miles from Highway 375, to an unmarked junction with a narrow gravel road heading east near a large mailbox marked: *Meadow Mountain Ranch*.

The two-track, narrow gravel road heads up toward the mountains through grasslands, across an open wash and up the other side. At 5.4 miles a side road heads over to the Meadow Mountain Ranch, and the main road continues straight ahead in juniper and pinyon pine with sagebrush and rabbitbrush. Your road eventually reaches Cherry Creek Summit at 10.8 miles from the junction and heads downhill into narrow Cherry Creek Canyon. At 14.1 miles, reach the unsigned turnoff of Forest Service Road #411 and turn west up Sawmill Canyon.

Follow Road #411 0.1 mile to an informal 'Y' junction near a signboard at the entrance to Cherry Creek Campground. Bear left, remaining on Road #411 for another 0.1 mile, to where a short dirt road heads to the right past a campsite and to the trailhead. Posted just above the south bank of Little Cherry Creek, a trail register seems out of place in this lonely and isolated environment.

Description: The trail begins at the edge of a campsite equipped with picnic table and fire pit. Cottonwood, pinyon pine and juniper, along with the thick brush common to riparian zones, shelter the small creek. Immediately cross the small stream on two small logs. Numerous crossings of the stream make up the first portion of the trail as the path attempts to find the least resistance up the narrow, overgrown canyon. The lower portion of Cherry Creek maintains a good flow of water and, combined with the vegetation, produces a moist, cool environment for the appreciative hiker.

Eventually, where the canyon widens, the trail heads for drier, mahogany-covered slopes, passing a Quinn Canyon Wilderness sign. Continue on pleasantly graded trail as it follows an old roadbed into the widening canyon. Away from the dense foliage of the first part of the trail, some fine views open up above the sagebrush toward the head of the canyon. The tread, momentarily lost in some lush grass, quickly resumes along a straight path through medium-dense sagebrush. Many paths wind through the brush, making remaining on the designated path difficult, thanks primarily to the wandering hooves of cows allowed to graze in the canyon. All routes seem to lead in the same direction, however. Even if you do not choose the right path initially, any path should eventually get you on the right track.

Close to an old fence line, a side canyon to the north enters the main canyon near a meadow, which would provide a pleasant campsite if the numerous cow pies scattered around the grass were not there. Unfortunately, cows, just like humans, seem to prefer the nicer areas. Continue through sagebrush upstream toward an area of pinyon pine-juniper forest, pass through another old fence line and cross over the creek. The trail proceeds up the wide canyon below low cliffs into an old burn area, where the new trees have reached the same height and stature of the burned trees. Beyond the burn, a two-story rock projection juts out of the ground near the creek.

The mild grade continues as the canyon narrows once again. Pass the remains of an old water trough, where pipes used to bring water from a small spring on the far side of the creek. By midseason this spring typically provides the last running water in the drainage. A little way up from the spring, the trail passes a hunters' campsite, complete with fire pit and places to hang meat.

The trail curves around, crossing the creek again, as the steep canyon forces the trail to the opposite bank. Follow the drainage as it makes a reverse 'S' bend and the trail crosses back and forth over the creek. Pinyon pine and sagebrush remain the dominant vegetation, but as you climb white fir appears on the north-facing slopes.

The grade increases in the upper canyon as you reach a grove of mahogany trees. Wind around more steeply to the crest of a low divide separating the Little Cherry Creek and Hooper Creek drainages. Despite indications on the Forest Service map that the trail continues down into Hooper Canyon, it seems to terminate in the saddle. The terrain, although rugged, is generally open and would provide relatively easy travel if one desired to descend Hooper Creek. You could easily reach the crest of the Quinn Canyon Range from the saddle by ascending moderately steep slopes to the west.

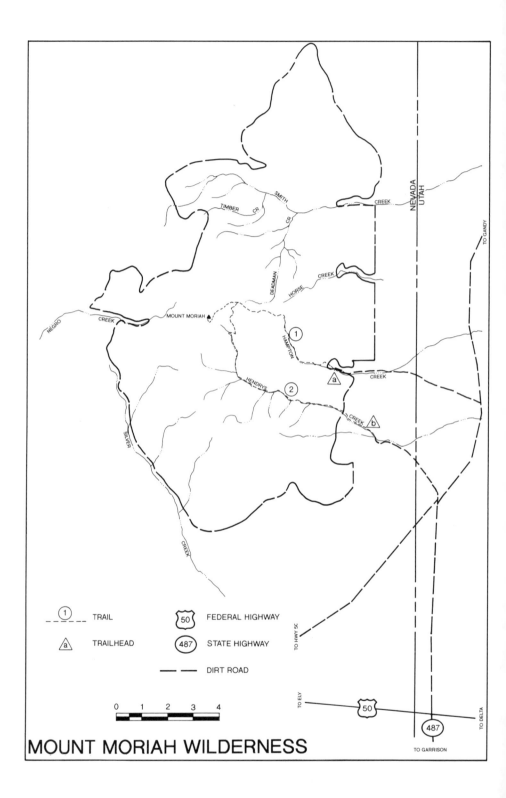

TIMBER CR
SMITH
CR
CREEK
NEVADA
UTAH
TO GANDY
DEADMAN
HORSE
CREEK
NEGRO
CREEK
MOUNT MORIAH ▲
HAMPTON
①
CREEK
ⓐ
HENDRYS
②
CREEK
ⓑ
SILVER
CREEK

① ----- TRAIL

ⓐ TRAILHEAD

🛡50 FEDERAL HIGHWAY

⟨487⟩ STATE HIGHWAY

— — — DIRT ROAD

TO HWY 5C

0 1 2 3 4

TO ELY

🛡50

TO DELTA

⟨487⟩

TO GARRISON

MOUNT MORIAH WILDERNESS

Trails of Eastern Nevada

Chapter 14
MT. MORIAH WILDERNESS

A nearly forgotten neighbor to the north of more renowned Great Basin National Park, the Mt. Moriah Wilderness straddles the north end of the Snake Range in the remote east edge of Nevada. Piercing the clear, pure air and deep blue skies of this distant region, Mt. Moriah, at 12,067 feet, thrusts its summit above the surrounding basins as the fifth highest peak in the state. Just a thousand feet below the peak, a broad, slightly sloping tableland, The Table, is another unique feature of the Wilderness. Bordered by some of the most interesting examples of bristlecone pine in the Nevada mountains, sparse vegetation otherwise covers the one-square-mile plateau. Easy travel makes The Table a perfect spot for rambling, off-trail explorations.

Composed primarily of two types of sedimentary rock, quartzite and limestone, the range centers around the apex of Mt. Moriah, with steep, rugged canyons spiraling away from the towering crest toward Spring Valley to the west and Snake Valley to the east. The summit of Mt. Moriah stands regally above the surrounding peaks and canyons and truly is the centerpiece of the Wilderness. Reminiscent of the popular phrase, "all roads lead to Rome," practically all the trails in the Mt. Moriah Wilderness lead to the top of the peak, no matter how far away the trailhead. Although a few more trails appear on the maps of the area, only two route descriptions occur in this chapter, as most of the other trails do not seem to exist in their entirety on the ground. Affirming the remoteness of the terrain, most of the backcountry remains trailless, inaccessible to all but the hearty cross-country enthusiast.

The top of Mt. Moriah holds only the smallest of alpine plants, but the trails used to reach the peak pass through one of the most diverse series of ecosystems in the Great Basin mountains. Found within the Wilderness are conifer species ranging from pinyon pine, juniper, white, Douglas and subalpine fir to ponderosa and limber pine, and the most revered tree of all:

the bristlecone pine. Cottonwoods in the lower elevations and quaking aspens higher up are present in large numbers as well. Autumn colors can be quite spectacular in certain drainages, such as the upper part of Hendry's Creek, when most of the hillside appears carpeted with the shimmering yellow leaves of the prolific aspen.

Rocky Mountain bighorn sheep inhabit the steep upper slopes of the Wilderness. Other mammals that reside in the northern Snake Range include deer, mountain lions, bobcats, coyotes and a wide variety of rodents. The most frequently seen inhabitants will most likely be some of the many species of birds that find their homes in the rich and diverse forests that cover the slopes of the hills and canyons. Raptors such as golden eagles, hawks and falcons spiral upward in the thermals above the steep canyons.

If one of the major concerns about the viability of Great Basin National Park is the location, with tourists having to travel tremendous distances from major population centers, this concern certainly may also apply to the Mt. Moriah Wilderness. A little more remote and without the luxury of a paved road, the northern Snake Range offers a great deal of solitude. If "getting away from it all" is your goal, this area will rarely disappoint.

If the Mt. Moriah Wilderness seems isolated and remote in the summer months, imagine what a trip into this area might be like in the winter. Although information is lacking about winter recreational activities, the cross-country skiing in and around The Table would have to be superb.

LOCATION

Located in the extreme eastern part of the state, the Mt. Moriah Wilderness' eastern edge is a mere 2 miles from the Utah border. Principal access is from the south by U.S. 50 to an improved gravel road that travels along the range on the east. Forest Service roads lead west into the Wilderness from this road. Another improved dirt road heads along the west side of the range, providing access to 4-wheel-drive roads into the mountains. The closest major towns are Ely, Nevada, and Delta, Utah.

CAMPGROUNDS

Currently, no developed campsites exist near the Mt. Moriah Wilderness. Great Basin National Park offers the closest campgrounds in the south part of the Snake Range. The Hampton Creek trailhead does have a pleasant undeveloped campsite near the creek at the end of the road (see Trip 1).

RESOURCES

Services around the Wilderness are severely limited. The Border Inn, on U.S.50 at the Nevada-Utah border, is the closest facility offering gas, a restaurant-bar, a motel and showers. Baker, Nevada, a small community at the gateway to Great Basin National Park, offers a limited selection of groceries, two restaurant-bars, a gas station handling minor repairs and a small motel. The nearest town of any substance is Ely, Nevada, 60 miles west of the turnoff from Highway 50.

FOREST SERVICE

Ely Ranger District
350 8th Street
P.O. Box 539
Ely, NV 89301
(702) 289-3031

Humboldt National Forest
Supervisor's Office
976 Mountain City Highway
Elko, NV 89801
(702) 738-5171

Trip 1
HAMPTON CREEK

Trip Type: Dayhike; Out and back
Distance: 15.2 miles round trip
Season: Mid-June to mid-October
Access: Dirt road, high-clearance vehicle necessary
Water: Creek
Maps: #34, 35
The Cove, Old Mans Canyon & *Mount Moriah* 7.5 minute quadrangles 1986 (provisional)
Humboldt National Forest map, Ely Ranger District, East Half

Introduction: If such a thing exists as the short way to the summit of Mt. Moriah, it would have to be the trail up Hampton Creek. Unfortunately, shorter often means steeper, and such is the case with this trail. Gaining almost 5,000 feet in nearly 8 miles does not sound terribly rigorous, but it is a good day's work.

The trail climbs up through a steep canyon, with dense, mixed forest obstructing views of the higher elevations for the first 4.5 miles of the hike. Once on The Table, a broad, sloping tableland at 11,000 feet, spectacular vistas abound of Mt. Moriah, the surrounding wilderness and Wheeler Peak to the south.

Camping is extremely limited in the canyon and water is unavailable at the higher elevations. If you desire to backpack in the Mt. Moriah Wilderness, try the hike up Hendrys Creek (see Trip 2).

Trailhead: (a) Along U.S. 50, approximately 58 miles east of Ely, Nevada and 90 miles west of Delta, Utah, is the signed turnoff to Great Basin National Park and the small town of Baker. Directly opposite this turn to the south leading to the park is an unmarked paved road heading north. Turn onto this road, passing an electrical substation approximately 200 yards down the asphalt. At 0.5 mile from U.S. 50 a sign reads: *Hendry's Creek 15, Hampton Creek 21, Horse Creek 24* and *Smith Creek 28*. Cross over a cattle guard and at 2.0 miles the road switches to gravel passing through the Silver Creek Ranch.

Continue on the gravel road as it narrows around 3 miles from the highway. At 9.3 miles, the road crosses the border into Utah and immediately after the junction with the road to Hendrys Creek reaches a 'Y' intersection with another gravel road from the south. A sign nearby states: *Hampton Creek 11, Horse Creek 14, Smith Creek 17*. Remain heading north on the gravel road until encountering the unsigned junction near a ranch at 14.8 miles from U.S. 50.

Head west toward the mountains on a narrow dirt road that is quite a bit rougher than the gravel one. At 3.9 miles is a one-man mining operation practically right on the road. A mile-and-one-half farther, the route crosses into National Forest land as it climbs alongside the heavily vegetated creek. Six miles from the gravel road you pass some old mining structures from an abandoned garnet mine. The road divides at 6.2 miles, where the left branch heads down toward a small campsite near the creek and the right hand track climbs quickly up to the trailhead.

Parking is available for about a half dozen vehicles. A trail register and a *Closed to Motor Vehicles* sign mark the beginning of the path. For those desiring to camp, the site down by the water has a picnic table and a fire ring. A short way down the road is a pit toilet.

Description: The trail, perhaps marked by ducks, begins a moderate climb through pinyon-juniper forest following the track of the old road as it continues up the canyon. A piece of newer trail heads away from the road, switchbacking up the hillside before rejoining the old road higher up the hillside. You reach a 'Y' junction and head up the more traveled road, perhaps marked by ducks, to the right. Soon you encounter another road where the route bends to the left and, after a mere 50 feet, reaches the Wilderness boundary.

After the moderate climb, the grade abates for a while as the road winds around a hillside well above Hampton Creek, still through pinyon-juniper forest. You come alongside a seasonal creek where aspen, ponderosa pine and white fir make their first appearances. Under mixed forest, the path soon encounters an abandoned ditch, probably used to divert water for the garnet mine. Beyond the ditch, the grade steepens again and the trail crosses two more seasonal streams. The road changes into an actual single-track trail as it continues to climb through mixed forest of aspen, pine and fir.

The path veers into drier vegetation of mountain mahogany before winding back into mixed forest and across Hampton Creek. You cross a couple of side streams before ascending a series of 6 switchbacks through predominantly Douglas-fir forest with some scattered white fir and ponderosa pine. The dense forest cover shades the trail as it keeps on climbing up the canyon, crossing the creek many times. As the elevation increases, limber pine and then bristlecone pine begin to join the mixed forest.

Climb up the steep canyon through an extensive grove of aspens until reaching a grassy meadow where the trail becomes lost in the grass and cairns lead across the meadow to mixed forest. Near the meadow is the unmarked junction with the primitive trail ascending Horse Creek.

Follow cairns and ducks through an area of light subalpine fir until the trail becomes distinct again. Where the grade eases, bristlecone pine becomes the dominant species of conifer, intermixed with subalpine fir. A clearing allows the first views of Mt. Moriah as you continue to climb toward a ridge top at the edge of The Table, a broad, sloping, rocky plateau, where even better views of Moriah and the Snake Range await you.

Weather-beaten bristlecone pine

Cairns mark the route of the trail across The Table, where contorted trunks and limbs of widely dispersed bristlecone pines add character to the picturesque views. Pieces of the trail appear, disappear and reappear along the route across The Table, but the terrain is open and the way is obvious. Reach the junction with the trail up Hendrys Creek at a low sign propped up by a pile of rocks, 5.9 miles from the trailhead.

The Hampton Creek trail proceeds across The Table and down into Big Canyon on the east side of the range. Although, to reach the summit of Mt. Moriah you continue on the trail only another one-quarter mile before leaving it and ascending the northeast ridge. Cairns and ducks lead you up the steep slope to the crest of a ridge and across the back side over to a saddle where you pick up a distinct trail again.

The trail traverses across the slope below the satellite peak just northeast of the true summit. Continue to make a general traverse below the saddle between the two peaks and across the east face of Mt. Moriah. Unexplainedly, the trail stops cold at the southern edge of the peak, as if the trail crew took a break for lunch and never returned. However disconcerting the end of the trail appears, the route from here to the top is easy and uneventful. Views from the summit, as expected, are incredible.

Retrace your steps to the trailhead.

Trip 2 ♠
HENDRYS CREEK

Trip Type: Long dayhike or overnight backpack; Out and back
Distance: 23.0 miles round trip
Season: Mid-June through mid-October
Access: Dirt road
Water: Creek
Maps: #34, 35
   The Cove, Old Mans Canyon & Mount Moriah 7.5 minute quad-
      rangles 1986 (provisional)
   Humboldt National Forest map, Ely Ranger District, East Half

Introduction: The Hendrys Creek Trail is almost a full 4 miles longer than
the Hampton Creek Trail, but if you desire a backpack, this is the trail for
you. Plenty of nice campsites appear along the way, offering pleasant
places to lay one's head next to the soothing babble of Hendrys Creek.

Hendrys Creek offers a wide variety of terrain along the length of its
canyon. Initially the vegetation is open, allowing for fine views of the dramatic rock cliffs that form the steep sides of the canyon. Farther up, the
trail passes through dense forest cover and views become limited until you
reach the higher elevations.

A wide variety of plant zones occur along the trail as well, from pinyon-juniper to bristlecone pine forest. In-between you will encounter
conifers such as ponderosa pine, limber pine, white fir, Douglas fir and
subalpine fir; deciduous trees include cottonwoods in the lower canyon
and large stands of quaking aspen farther up the drainage. The slopes in
the upper part of Hendrys Creek are so extensively covered with aspens
that the autumn color is quite spectacular.

The highlight of any trip to the Mt. Moriah Wilderness, however, has to
be Mt. Moriah itself and the broad plateau near the base named The Table.
After a lengthy hike up the heavily forested Hendrys Creek drainage, the
terrain opens up dramatically on a broad, sloping plateau covered with
small alpine plants and rimmed by weather-beaten bristlecone pines. From
here, a trail leads almost to the top of 12,067-foot Mt. Moriah, where views
of the distant basins and ranges are superb.

Trailhead: (b) Follow directions in Trip 1 to the junction with the road to
Hendrys Creek, 10.7 miles from U.S. 50, immediately before a 'Y' intersection with a gravel road from the south. The narrow dirt road heading
northwest to Hendrys Creek is marked by a sign: *Hendrys Creek 4*, and by
a concrete headstone with a mailbox reading: *Hatchrock, Mt. Moriah Stone,
Inc.*

You turn northwest onto the narrow, two-track, dirt road as it heads
toward the mountains, crossing back into Nevada at 1.6 miles from the

turnoff from the gravel road. Pass over a cattle guard at 2.8 miles, where old signs for the Hatchrock operation warn against the illegal removal of stones. Continue straight ahead another 0.1 mile, to where a lesser road bends to the right. After an additional 0.1 mile, stay to the right on the main road where an old mining road comes in from the left. At 3.2 miles from the gravel road, bear to the left at a 'Y' junction, following a sign marked: *Trailhead*. The road to the right heads into the defunct Hatchrock operation.

Proceed through an open fence and cross into National Forest land at 3.9 miles, quickly reaching the trailhead a short distance farther at a wide, gravel turnaround where parking is available for quite a few cars. There is evidence of previous visitors camping at the trailhead, but the surroundings are not nearly as nice as those at the Hampton Creek trailhead. A trail register and signs mark the trail.

Description: The trail begins as it follows the continuation of the old road on the right side of Hendrys Creek, alongside riparian foliage next to the creek and sagebrush covering the drier slopes. Where the canyon makes a sweeping bend, good, open views of the topography reveal rugged cliffs at the rim of the basin above steep, dry hillsides. After approximately 200 yards, the path veers down and across the creek, and then quickly over a spring-fed side stream through shrub oak, cottonwoods, juniper and pinyon pine. The gently graded tread passes beneath some bronze-colored cliffs through open terrain until the trail is forced into dense cottonwoods where the canyon narrows.

Ponderosa pine begins to appear with the cottonwood, juniper and pinyon pine as wild rose and alders join the oak shrubs. You cross over the main creek two more times and cross some side streams before reaching the marked Wilderness boundary. The trail continues through and around the light forest beneath dramatic, rust-red cliffs. As you proceed up the canyon, quaking aspen and white, subalpine and Douglas fir begin to appear, eventually achieving a density blocking the views of the canyon. An old stone chimney is all that remains of the cabin near the site of the old Hendrys sawmill, and even it seems destined to be nothing more than rubble in the near future. You could camp here.

Beyond the cabin site, the trail comes alongside a lovely, flower-lined stream, crosses it twice and reaches the origin of the flow where a spring emerges from a low hillside bursting with wildflowers. Varieties include columbine, Indian paintbrush, daisies, asters and shooting star. Where the canyon narrows considerably, you pass through an old log fence and cross Hendrys Creek in mixed forest interspersed with thick groves of quaking aspen. One of those aspen stands contains a small campsite near an unusual piece of iron machinery.

Continue up the drainage to where the canyon bends north under mixed forest cover. The grade becomes steeper as the trail ascends the narrow, 'V'-shaped canyon toward The Table. Farther up the slender gorge,

Meadow along upper Hendrys Creek

three aspen-covered meadows, each with its own comfortable campsite, interrupt the predominantly fir forest, composed of Douglas, white and some subalpine fir in the higher elevations. The trail makes numerous crossings of the diminishing creek and of smaller tributaries on the way to a long, thin meadow. The meadow is fed by a spring and is full of wildflowers, and limited views of Mt. Moriah appear for the first time. Climb up through the meadow along the west side of the canyon before heading east across the upper edge of the meadow to a hillside.

Steeply ascend the hillside through limber pine as the trail winds its way to a ridge top. Follow the path along the crest, where bristlecone pine becomes the dominant species of conifer. Leave the ridge behind where the trail starts a traverse across a hillside to a seasonal drainage and over to the crest of another ridge. Then drop down from the ridge, crossing one more seasonal drainage, before a brief climb leads to the junction with the Hampton Creek Trail (see Trip 1) on the southeast edge of The Table, 9.8 miles from the trailhead. Nestled into a pile of rocks is a low sign at the junction which reads: *Hendrys Cr.*

From the junction, the Hampton Creek trail proceeds west across The Table and down into Big Canyon. To reach the summit of Mt. Moriah, turn west at the junction and proceed on the faint track of the Hampton Creek Trail just one-quarter mile before leaving it and ascending a route up the northeast ridge. Cairns and ducks lead you up the steep slope to a ridge crest and across the back side over to a saddle where you pick up distinct trail again.

The trail traverses across the slope below the satellite peak just northeast of the true summit. Continue to make a general traverse below the saddle between the two peaks and across the east face of Mt. Moriah. Unexplainedly, the trail stops cold below the south edge of the peak, as if the trail crew took a break for lunch and never returned. However disconcerting the situation appears, the route from the end of the trail to the top is easy and uneventful. Views from the summit, as expected, are incredible.

Retrace your steps to the trailhead.

OTHER TRAILS

Horse Canyon: 20.2 miles from the asphalt and gravel road's junction with U.S. 50, a dirt road turns west from the gravel road along the east side of the Wilderness. The road leads to the Horse Canyon trailhead at around 7,000 feet. The trail is the shortest way into the Mt. Moriah area but is also one of the steepest, gaining 5,000 feet of elevation in about 5 miles. The route is indistinct in parts and nonexistent in others, but follows the Horse Creek drainage as it bends around to the south, joining the more defined tread of the Hampton Creek Trail.

Smith Creek: Just north of the Horse Canyon road is the dirt road leading to the Smith Creek trailhead. If the trail is hard to find in Horse Canyon, it will be even more difficult up this drainage. The terrain, however, is awesome with steep, rugged cliffs forming the walls of the canyon and becoming more dramatic with each step. At the junction of Smith and Deadman creeks you have the option of traveling up either canyon, without the aid of a defined trail. You may get a glimpse of the band of bighorn sheep that inhabit the Mt. Moriah Wilderness in one of these drainages. If ever there was a trip that deserved to see some trail improvements, the route up Smith and Deadman creeks would be a worthy candidate.

Four Mile Spring & Negro Creek: Two routes on the west side of the range leave the Eightmile Ranch Road in Spring Valley. Most of the trail up Negro Creek lies outside the Mt. Moriah Wilderness, and the route up from Four Mile Spring into the northwest corner of the Wilderness is mainly on a closed 4-wheel-drive road.

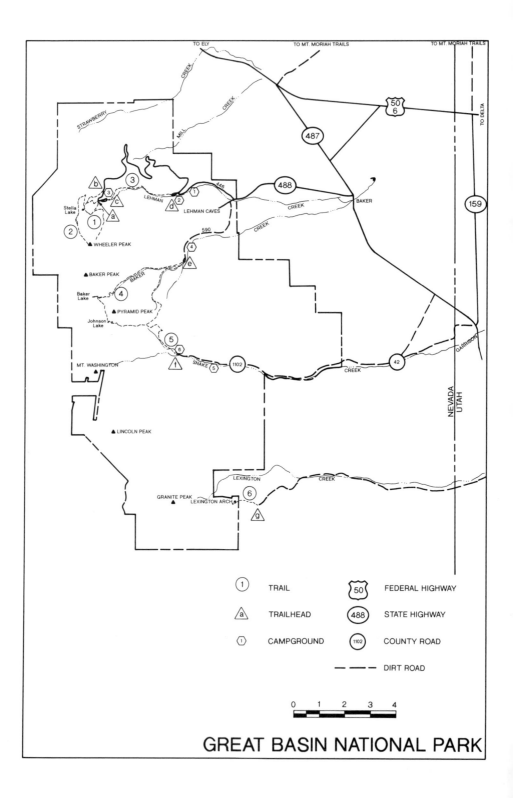

GREAT BASIN NATIONAL PARK

Chapter 15
GREAT BASIN NATIONAL PARK

After a long history of struggle, defeat and compromise, Great Basin National Park finally became a reality in 1986. The idea of setting aside the lands around Wheeler Peak as a park was first introduced in the 1920's, during the establishment of Lehman Caves National Monument. Although some interested parties pushed for a much larger area for the monument, it included only a small acreage immediately adjacent to the caves.

Over the years, the concept of a national park resurfaced a few times, always with the same result. Many different groups were in strong opposition to any park designation that might interrupt or prevent any of their activities. Ranchers, having used the seasonal range lands in the mountains for grazing cattle and sheep since the 1800's, expressed vehement opposition to the possible removal of their grazing rights. Miners were equally determined to hold onto their operations, particularly a beryllium strike on the west side of Mt. Washington. Although there was never a tremendous amount of wood harvested from the Snake Range, the active timber interests in the area had obvious misgivings about the creation of a park that would end their livelihoods. Hunters understood that national-park status would permanently ban their traditional hunting activities. Anglers showed concern about what a change in policy might do to their recreational habits and the fisheries. If this was not enough opposition, the Forest Service had little interest in turning over their jurisdiction of any part of the Humboldt National Forest to anyone, favoring their mission of multiple use over the more preservation-oriented policy of the National Park Service.

As time wore on, new developments added for setting aside the lands around Wheeler Peak as a national park. Both the discovery of a nearly 5,000-year-old bristlecone pine and the rediscovery of a bona-fide glacier within the Great Basin inspired scientists to join the chorus of those already committed to the idea of a park for scenic and recreational purposes. The Forest Service agreed to an intermediate step of creating a much smaller Wheeler Peak Scenic Area, which included construction of a scenic highway. Management of the region would be similar to that of a wilderness area, but with a continuing emphasis on multiple use. Oddly enough, however, economics eventually cast the deciding vote for the creation of Great Basin National Park.

Ely, Nevada, was a town of almost 10,000 residents, forty air miles west of the Wheeler Peak area. It was a thriving community, with an economy based almost exclusively on mining, until the bottom fell out when two major operations pulled out of the area in the late Seventies and early Eighties. The resulting loss in population and high unemployment of those left behind inspired some people to consider new sources of revenue to bolster their decimated wallets. The creation of a new national park around Wheeler Peak suddenly gained a slew of new supporters, who viewed it as a godsend stimulating their economy by creating new jobs via increased tourism.

With this new assistance, the proposal gained momentum, and became a reality in October of 1986—though only after numerous compromises with those still in strong opposition. The most significant of these deals had to do with mining and ranching. Miners influenced the choice of the final boundaries of the park, excluding some of their mines, which may see renewed activity if the price of minerals increases. Ranchers could contin-ue their grazing privileges forever—although, ten years after the inception of the park, an environmental organization is establishing a fund to buy back the grazing rights from the local ranchers, thereby closing the grass-lands to cows and sheep. The creation of the park left the Forest Service "out in the cold," along with the hunters; fishermen decried the policies of the Park Service, which canceled the stocking practices of the Forest Service in favor of returning the streams to their native species.

Unfortunately, the cash cow that Ely desired has failed to deliver all the anticipated bounty, even though thousands of visitors enjoy the park each year. Nevertheless, the creation of Great Basin National Park has improved many of the facilities and has made the region more accessible to individ-uals and families. Despite the recent ramblings of a short-sighted, budget-conscious congressman, declaring the area unworthy of park status and suggesting its closure as a cost-saving measure, Great Basin National Park remains, possessing many unique features and a little of something for just about everyone.

Despite the name, Great Basin is a park of mountains and mountainous terrain, with alpine lakes, meadows, a glacier and numerous ice-carved canyons; the basins at the foot of the range lie outside the Park boundaries. Comprising 77,100 acres, the park straddles the crest of the southern Snake Range and includes seven named peaks over 11,500 feet in elevation, including the 13,063-foot crown jewel, Wheeler Peak (second highest in the state). Mountaineers have many opportunities to test their skills, from easy scrambles to technically challenging routes.

Possessing many unique features, Great Basin National Park offers a variety of trails into some of the most interesting terrain in the entire state. Short hikes lead to one rarity after another. The Alpine Lakes Loop leads to alpine lakes, seemingly more reminiscent of the Rocky Mountains than a range in Nevada. They nestle in cirque basins beneath the steeply erod-ed cliffs at the crest of the Snake Range. The Bristlecone-Glacier Trail leads up past an awe-inspiring grove of bristlecone pines to a dramatic, glacier-carved cleft where you will find a geologic wonder—a glacier, the only one in the entire Great Basin. In the southeast corner of the park, a six-story limestone arch rests boldly in a narrow canyon. The summit of Wheeler Peak, offering extraordinary views spanning across Utah and Nevada, perched majestically at the end of the Summit Trail, is a mere 3 miles and 3,000 feet above the trailhead at the end of the Wheeler Peak Scenic Drive. If biodiversity excites you, the Lehman Creek Trail goes through a wide variety of vegetation zones, exposing the hiker to a veritable plethora of different species of plants and trees, providing a rich example of the varied Great Basin mountain environment.

One would have to travel all the way across the state to the east edge of the Sierra Nevada to find an area that is as biologically diverse as the Snake Range. Eleven different species of conifer inhabit these mountains, including three of juniper, white fir, subalpine fir, Englemann spruce, limber pine, pinyon pine, ponderosa pine and Douglas fir, as well as the grand patriarch of them all—the bristlecone pine. A mere 1-mile hike from the end of the Wheeler Peak Scenic Drive leads to classic examples of this oldest living organism.

If backpacking is your desire, trails to Baker and Johnson lakes will satisfy even the most demanding recreationist. Relative solitude is a reasonable expectation at these seldom-visited tarns, located only a half day's journey from their trailheads. The majority of the southern Snake Range is trailess, but access is easy through the open terrain. If you want cross-country travel, numerous routes lead to spectacular, untouched regions of the park—the only limits are time and your imagination.

Countless other diversions lure hikers and backpackers away from the trails in Great Basin National Park. Sightseers can enjoy the trip up the paved Wheeler Peak Scenic Drive, stopping to relish the views and peruse the informative displays. No trip to this area is complete without the guided tour of the Park's premier attraction, Lehman Caves, discovered by Absalom Lehman, a rancher and miner, in 1885. Rangers colorfully expound on the different speculations concerning how Mr. Lehman originally found the caves, along with other equally entertaining and interesting facts about the caves, on the 1½ hour tours provided by the Park Service (cost in 1996: $4). The ¼ mile limestone cave has many rooms, blessed with numerous examples of a wide range of interesting cave formations and is well worth the time and money.

Some of the best campgrounds in the state are within the park. Wheeler Peak Campground is especially nice and well suited to the typical hiker/backpacker. Nearly 10,000 feet above sea level, the campground is at the end of the Wheeler Peak Scenic Highway, which has too many curves for the average motor home or trailer, leaving the 37 sites primarily for those willing to sleep in a tent. During the summer months, Park rangers participate in informative campfire talks about a wide range of outdoor-related topics each evening at the group campfire area. The Forest Service

Bristlecone pine

offers similar programs at Upper and Lower Lehman Creek Campgrounds. The proximity to short day hikes along with the comfortable surroundings makes Wheeler Peak Campground especially nice for family vacations.

Winter activities are available in the park, including cross-country skiing, snowshoeing and mountaineering. The visitor center and Lower Lehman Creek Campground remain open year-round.

LOCATION

Great Basin National Park lies at the east edge of the state, the east edge of the park being a mere 5 miles from the Utah border. The closest town of any substance is Ely, approximately 70 road miles away. The park is bounded by U.S. 50 on the north, U.S. 93 on the west, and State Route 487 on the east. The primary access to the park is on State Route 488 from the junction with S.R. 487 in the town of Baker, Nevada.

CAMPGROUNDS

1. LOWER LEHMAN CREEK $
   Open all year
   Camping, Picnicking, Water, Pit toilets
   Located 1.8 miles up the Wheeler Peak Scenic Road

2. UPPER LEHMAN CREEK $
   Open May 15 - October 15
   Camping, Picnicking, Water, Pit toilets, Group Area, 1 Wheelchair
      accessible site
   Lower Trailhead for Lehman Creek Trail (See Trip 3)
   Located 2.4 miles up the Wheeler Peak Scenic Drive

3. WHEELER PEAK CAMPGROUND $
   Open June 15 - September 15
   Camping, Picnicking, Water, Pit toilets, 1 Wheelchair accessible site
   Upper Trailhead for Lehman Creek Trail (See Trip 3); Near Trailhead
      for Alpine Lakes Loop & Bristlecone-Glacier trail (See Trip 1)

Located 11.7 miles up the Wheeler Peak Scenic Drive at the end of the road

4. BAKER CREEK CAMPGROUND $
Open May 15 - September 15
Camping, Picnicking, Water, Pit toilets, 2 Wheelchair accessible sites
Located 2.9 miles up the Baker Creek Road

5. SNAKE CREEK CAMPGROUND
Primitive Sites
Camping, Picnicking
Approximately 11/2 miles from the end of the Snake Creek Road

6. SHOSHONE CAMPGROUND
Primitive Sites
Camping, Picnicking
At the end of the Snake Creek Road
Trailhead for Snake Creek Trail (Trip 5)

RESOURCES
Limited facilities are located around the Park. The tiny community of Baker, Nevada, offers a limited selection of groceries, two restaurant-bars, gas station handling minor repairs and a small motel. Garrison, a small town across the Utah border, offers similar services. The nearest large towns are Ely, Nevada, and Delta, Utah.

NATIONAL PARK SERVICE
Great Basin National Park
Baker, NV 89311
(702) 234-7331

Trip 1 🌲
ALPINE LAKES LOOP & BRISTLECONE–GLACIER TRAIL

Trip Type: Dayhike or overnight backpack; Loop
Distance: 5.6 miles
2.4 miles to Alpine Lakes
3.2 miles to Bristlecone grove and glacier
Season: Mid-June through October
Access: Paved road
Water: Lakes, creeks
Maps: #36
Wheeler Peak & *Windy Peak* 7.5 minute quadrangles, 1987 (provisional)

Humboldt National Forest map, Ely Ranger District East Half,
   1990
Hiking Map & Guide Great Basin National Park, Earthwalk Press
   1993

Introduction: One of the most popular trails in Great Basin National Park is
the hike to Stella and Teresa Lakes. The other most popular is the trail up to
the Bristlecone Interpretive Trail and on to the glacier below Wheeler Peak.
Part of this popularity is due to the shortness of both trails, but a larger part
must be due to the magnificent features these two routes have to offer.

In early season, the Alpine Lakes Loop offers two beautiful alpine lakes
reflecting precipitous canyon walls and fields of wildflowers. Later in the
season, the water level of both lakes drops considerably, but the scenery is
still quite pleasant. Gouged out by glaciers long ago, the basins of these
two tarns near the heads of the canyons offer serene settings perfect for
contemplation, a leisurely lunch or an afternoon nap. Stands of limber pine
and Englemann spruce grace the shoreline and provide fragrance and
shade. For those desiring an easy backpack, there are campsites along the
inlet stream at Teresa Lake.

The Bristlecone–Glacier Trail honors its name by including a grove of
mature, character-rich bristlecone pines as well as a trip to the only glacier
anywhere in the Great Basin, set in the dramatic cirque beneath 13,063-foot
Wheeler Peak. The Bristlecone Trail provides the easiest way in the entire
state for the average person to experience the magnificence of these extraordinary trees. Oddly enough, the bristlecone thrives in the worst of situations, surviving thousands of years in harsh environments while dying
out in milder conditions at a relatively young age of a couple of hundred
years. Many unique representatives appear along the interpretive trail.

Beyond the bristlecones lies an unmatched Great Basin experience: a
glacier. Almost incomprehensibly, a body of ice lies beneath the steep north
face of Wheeler Peak, parts of it buried beneath tons of debris and the
whole technically called a rock glacier. Noted by the U.S. Geological
Survey in the 1800's, then forgotten until 1955, the glacier remains
unknown to this day by the vast majority of people unfamiliar with the
Park. The glacier is a unique feature set in one of the most strikingly dramatic canyons in the state.

Although the season for these two trails is said to begin in June, the
glacier may be under snow for quite some time longer than the trail to
Stella and Teresa lakes. Check with the Park Service regarding conditions
before setting out on your hike.

Trailhead: (a) Along U.S. 50, approximately 58 miles east of Ely, Nevada,
and 90 miles west of Delta, Utah, is the signed turnoff to Great Basin
National Park and the small town of Baker. From there go 5 miles southeast on State Route 487 to Baker, a tiny community where merchants have
benefited from the park designation and where travelers can find gas, a

Wheeler Peak from the Bristlecone Trail

small garage, food, drink, lodging, trinkets and limited groceries. From Baker turn west onto State Route 488 and climb through sagebrush and then juniper-pinyon forest to the Park entrance (no entrance fee as of 1996). Continue into the Park, quickly arriving at the signed junction with the Wheeler Peak Scenic Drive, 4.8 miles from Baker.

Turn right onto the Wheeler Peak Scenic Drive, and begin climbing up Lehman Creek canyon on the steep highway, passing Lower Lehman Creek Campground at 1.8 miles and Upper Lehman Creek Campground at 2.4 miles from the junction with Route 488. Signs mark the change of elevation every 500 feet as you climb out of the canyon, initially through juniper-pinyon forest and then into firs around 4 miles up the road. Pass the Osceola Ditch exhibit at 4.7 miles and the Mather Overlook at 6.7 miles as the road maintains the precipitous ascent, now through spruce and Douglas fir. Soon you encounter the Wheeler Peak Overlook, 9.6 miles from the junction, providing dramatic views of the peak and the glacier-carved cirque.

At 11.0 miles drive by the Summit Trailhead parking area and continue up the road to the entrance to Wheeler Peak Campground and the Bristlecone Trailhead at 11.7 miles, elevation 9885 feet. The trailhead has a large paved parking lot ringed with aspens, picnic tables, group campfire area and toilets.

Description: Across the paved road heading into the campground, the well-marked, well-graded and well-used trail begins through mixed forest of Douglas fir, limber pine and Englemann spruce. Cross a wooden bridge over the north branch of Lehman Creek and head up into the forest, quickly reaching a trail junction. A metal sign reads: *Bristlecone-Glacier Trail 1.3*

Miles Elevation Gain 1200' One Way, Alpine Lakes Loop Trail 1.3 Miles Elevation Gain 450.'

Head to the right, following the sign for the Alpine Lakes Loop Trail, which winds through dense forest before crossing a small, gurgling stream on another wooden bridge. In a clearing, there is a good view of Wheeler and Jefferson Davis peaks. Briefly head back into a mixed forest of limber pine, Englemann Spruce and quaking aspen before reaching a large, open meadow and a signed trail junction with the trail from the Summit Trailhead. The Alpine Lakes Loop Trail and the Summit Trail share the tread for 0.1 mile before the route to Wheeler Peak turns north and your trail continues through widely scattered spruce and pine another 0.1 mile to Stella Lake.

Shallow Stella Lake is a beautiful gem nestled beneath steep walls of rock and rimmed by spruce and pine. Early in the season, the lake is full and the wildflowers are in bloom, creating a picturesque setting unequaled in beauty except for her exquisite neighbor, Teresa Lake. A rock dam, constructed in a previous era, seems to be ineffective in holding the waters of the lake, allowing the level to diminish into a large pond late in the summer.

The trail passes Stella Lake above the east shore and continues through predominantly Englemann spruce with occasional limber pine. A descent of 0.75 mile leads to a small spring-fed creek lined with lush grass and plants that empties into lovely Teresa Lake, 1.7 miles from the trailhead.

Symmetrical Teresa Lake, encircled by rocky slopes, is dotted with trees except for the grassy area surrounded by Englemann spruce alongside the inlet creek. Find a couple of shaded campsites nestled beneath the spruce. The same misfortune befalling Stella Lake seems to affect this lake as well, since later in the season the water level declines significantly. Early in the summer, however, Teresa Lake is a spectacular setting and very photogenic.

The trail traverses above the west shore of Teresa Lake before descending away amid rocky terrain and scattered spruce and pine. A tenth of a mile north of the lake is the signed junction with the Bristlecone-Glacier Trail heading east, 1.9 miles from the trailhead.

From the junction, the Alpine Lakes Loop Trail continues to descend through scattered spruce into denser stands of spruce and limber pine. You arrive back at the intersection with the path to Stella Lake and retrace your steps down to the trailhead near the parking lot.

Bristlecone–Glacier Trail: From the junction with the Alpine Lakes Loop Trail, climb over a short hump and down into a dry, rocky drainage where the trail bends away, crossing a talus slope. Now climb up along a forested hillside covered with Englemann spruce, bending around into the canyon originating in the cirque below the summit of Wheeler Peak. Nestled among trees, you can see Brown Lake to the east, and although it is bypassed by the trail, a short 0.1-mile cross-country jaunt leads to the lake. The trail makes a brief descent across the drainage and then resumes the climb up the far side of the rocky canyon among spruce and then bristlecone pine.

Eventually the trail arrives at the junction with the Bristlecone Interpretive Trail, from where a short path leads among older examples of the majestic trees. A series of informative signs provides the reader with interesting facts about the oldest living species on earth, including details on growth habits, cross-dating and growth rings. One of the old monarchs has been dated at 3200 years of age. Included along this trail are some of the most dramatic-looking trees, providing excellent photo opportunities.

Back on the main trail, you soon encounter a switchback and then a 4 by 4 post with a sign: *Glacier Trail*. Leave the bristlecones behind and as you climb up into the cirque basin, all that remains, other than some plants and some small tufts of grass, is rock and more rock. After an interpretive sign discussing the formation and effects of the glacier in the canyon, the trail becomes steeper as it winds up the canyon into an amphitheater of tall pinnacled ridges and the strikingly vertical face of Wheeler Peak. A Park Service sign at the base of the moraine advises hikers not to proceed any further due to unstable rock and the possibility of injury from the falling debris. A terminal moraine comes into existence at the bottom end of a glacier when the glacier—or at least it's end—melts, and rock debris, carried in the ice, is deposited at the terminus of the glacier to form a hummock or berm of rock. A nonmaintained trail, distinct and easy to follow, proceeds up along the side of the moraine and then on top of the rock for quite a distance before ending at a 4 by 4 post near the glacier.

A mild controversy, begun in the mid-Fifties, continues to this day as to whether this body of ice is technically a glacier or really just an icefield. To further complicate the controversy, if it is a glacier, is the lower portion a rock glacier? A glacier forms when snow accumulates in an area and does not all melt during the summer. The unmelted snow is covered by additional snowfall the following winter and the underlying layers are compressed and transformed into a body of granular ice. As the ice thickens, the whole mass, an advancing glacier, moves down the valley, plucking out underlying material as it goes. If snow accumulation does not exceed or equal the amount of melting, then the glacier retreats back up the valley, a retreating glacier. Most of the glaciers in the continental United States are classified as retreating glaciers. A rock glacier forms when an active glacier is covered over by a exterior layer of rock debris but otherwise continues to evidence the normal characteristics of a glacier. The controversy basically boils down to whether or not the glacier is moving, or active.

Whatever the scientists ultimately conclude, whether considered a glacier or just an icefield, the body of ice in the Wheeler Peak cirque is the only one of its kind in the entire Great Basin: a rarity formed by the accumulation of snow in a north-facing, steep-walled canyon where a combination of elevation, temperature, shade and snowfall creates a truly unique environment.

Beyond the nonmaintained trail, proceed cross country into the basin at your own risk, carefully observing the slopes above for possible rockfall. Towers, jagged peaklets and widely eroded features abound on the rim of the quartzite cirque, made potentially unstable by the constant freezing and thawing of the rock that occurs at this elevation during the summer. If you are bold enough to climb all the way to the head of the basin, you could observe the bergshrund, a large chasm at the head of the canyon where the ice of the glacier separates from the rock wall above. Compared to the austere beauty and the overwhelming stature of the vertical bulwark of the basin, one can only develop a sense of one's own insignificance.

Retrace your steps back to the trail junction with the Alpine Lakes Loop Trail and down to the trailhead.

Trip 2 ♧

SUMMIT TRAIL TO WHEELER PEAK

Trip Type: Dayhike; Out and back
Distance: 8.2 miles round trip
Season: Late June through mid-October
Access: Paved highway
Water: None
Maps: #36

Wheeler Peak & Windy Peak 7.5 minute quadrangles, 1987 (provisional)

Humboldt National Forest map, Ely Ranger District East Half, 1990

Hiking Map & Guide Great Basin National Park, Earthwalk Press 1993

Introduction: The climax to any hiker's trip to Great Basin National Park is the climb to the summit of Wheeler Peak along the aptly named Summit Trail. Thanks to a start at nearly 10,000 feet, the climb to the top of the 13,063-foot peak is not an overwhelmingly laborious task, although it is definitely not a stroll in the park either.

The first half of the trip climbs easily through lush vegetation before wandering among widely distributed Englemann spruce and limber and bristlecone pine. Views of the peak are quite majestic along this part of the hike. At the crest of the ridge, you near the midpoint of the trip, where the elements combine to create a harsh environment for the remaining conifers. *Krummholz*, a German word meaning crooked wood, refers to the windswept, twisted condition of the limbs and trunks, common at this elevation. The trail's second half is steep, rocky and virtually devoid of vegetation as it climbs up rugged, boulder-strewn slopes to the summit. On top of the peak, views are incredible in every direction.

The peak itself is one of the most dramatic-appearing mountains in the entire state. The vertical northeast face plummets 1500 feet to the only glacier in the Great Basin, which is cradled in a deep, glacier-carved cirque as magnificent as any to be found in the western U.S (see Trip 1). The rugged quartzite rock walls of the cirque are testament to the power of the glacial forces that carved the canyon. Towering above the surrounding valleys by nearly 8,000 feet, Wheeler Peak dominates the skyline from the west and east.

Once considered to be the highest point between the Rocky Mountains and the Sierra Nevada, Wheeler Peak is below 13,140-foot Boundary Peak, on the opposite side of the state in the White Mountains. A minor controversy continues as to whether Boundary is a real mountain or just a satellite peak along a ridge of Montgomery Peak, originating in California (see Chapter 9). To consider Boundary Peak as part of Montgomery Peak would make Wheeler the highest summit in Nevada.

The mountain was named after Lieutenant George M. Wheeler, leader of the U.S. Army's Geographic Survey West of the 100th Meridian. He actually made two explorations into the Wheeler Peak area, climbing the peak and establishing a preliminary summit elevation of 13,000 feet on his first visit. The next day he climbed the peak again and, using more sophisticated instrumentation, calculated an accurate elevation of 13,063 feet. Wheeler's first expedition is considered to be one of the most important surveys of the Great Basin in the 19th century.

Although the trail is easy by technical standards, there are a few noteworthy concerns to take into account. Always carry plenty of water. There is none along the route except for a spring 0.1 mile from the trailhead. Also, keep an eye on the weather. Since you are the tallest object around for 2 miles along the upper part of the climb, developing thunderstorms require a rapid descent. Keeping in mind that temperatures can vary significantly from the warm trailhead to the windy summit, pack the appropriate clothing.

Trailhead: (b) Follow the directions in Trip 1 on the Wheeler Peak Scenic Drive to the Summit Trailhead, 11.0 miles from the junction with State Route 488. Make a left turn into the Summit Trailhead parking area. The asphalt lot has parking for about 20 cars. The trail begins at the southeast edge of the lot.

Description: Passing through sage, shrubs and wildflowers, the trail quickly enters mature aspen forest amid lush ground foliage. You come alongside a small creek through a lush stretch of beautiful wildflowers and plants, and then veer away into shrubby aspens. More lush vegetation is fed by springs. The trail heads down into an open area to the junction with the Alpine Lakes Loop Trail. Two metal signs read: *Summit Trail Parking 1.0 mile, Wheeler Peak Campground 0.7* and *Stella Lake 0.2*.

These two trails share a path for almost 0.2 mile before the Summit Trail bends uphill to the right (northwest) at another signed junction, 1.1 miles from the trailhead. A gradual climb winds around the head of the basin through open terrain of widely scattered limber pine toward the crest of the ridge above. Excellent views of Wheeler Peak and the surrounding

Wheeler Peak

countryside abound along this section of trail. As you curve around to the crest, Stella Lake comes into view directly below. Approximately half way along the route and 900 feet above the trailhead, you gain the top of the ridge in a broad saddle. From here the trail steepens considerably, gaining another 2200 feet in 2 miles.

From the saddle, the trail initially climbs steeply through widely scattered, stunted limber pine before reaching timberline. Ascend along the path through rocky terrain toward the summit of Wheeler Peak. The trail may be hard to follow in some areas but ducks may help to guide you to a more distinct path farther up. An upward traverse of the east side of the mountain leads to a final switchback and to the long, rocky summit ridge.

Constructed over the years, a plethora of rock towers and windbreaks dot the summit of Wheeler Peak. The summit register is in an old mailbox stuck into the walls of a windbreak at the high point of the ridge. Spectacular views occur in all directions: to the south a cavalcade of summits parade across the southern part of the park, to the north lies Mt. Moriah, to the east is the broad expanse of Utah, and to the west across Spring Valley are the Schell Creek Mountains followed by rows of other ranges. Those without an overwhelming fear of heights could walk over to the edge and peer into the impressive glacial cirque below. All of the immediate surroundings of the park are visible from the summit, including Stella, Teresa, Brown, Baker and Johnson lakes.

Follow the trail back to the trailhead, but be extra careful as you descend over the ankle-twisting rock on the upper section.

Trip 3 🌲

LEHMAN CREEK

Trip Type: Dayhike, Shuttle
Distance: 3.5 miles
Season: June through late October
Access: Paved road
Water: Lehman Creek
Maps: #36

> *Windy Peak* 7.5 minute quadrangle, 1987 (provisional)
> Humboldt National Forest map, Ely Ranger District East Half, 1990
> *Hiking Map & Guide Great Basin National Park*, Earthwalk Press 1993

Introduction: The vegetation along the Lehman Creek Trail is as diverse as a sampler box of chocolates. A steady climb between the elevations of 7750 and 9800 feet leads through a wide variety of plant zones. On the way, you will encounter such trees as pinyon pine, juniper, mahogany, aspen, Douglas fir, white fir, limber pine and Englemann spruce. A wide variety of shrubs occur as well, including sagebrush, barberry, wild rose and even some examples of prickly-pear cactus. The trail follows close to the creek for only a short distance, but the stay in the shade of the riparian zone is quite pleasant. The Lehman Creek Trail provides a perfect classroom for the study of diversity in the Great Basin environment.

While the Alpine Lakes Loop and the Bristlecone-Glacier trails are teeming with tourists, the trip along Lehman Creek attracts far fewer visitors, virtually assuring a level of solitude for those looking to "get away from it all." The description of the hike leads from the bottom to the top. Reverse the direction if you prefer the downhill trip.

Trailhead: LOWER TRAILHEAD: (d) Follow the directions in Trip 1 on the Wheeler Peak Scenic Drive to the turnoff into Upper Lehman Creek Campground, 2.4 miles from the junction with State Route 488. Follow the road in the campground to the upper campsites and find the small parking area off a short turnoff to the right. A sign at the trailhead reads: *Lehman Creek Trail, Wheeler Peak Campground 4*.

UPPER TRAILHEAD: (a) Follow the directions in Trip 1 on the Wheeler Peak Scenic Drive to the Wheeler Peak Campground at the end of the road, 11.7 miles from the junction with State Route 488. Continue into the campground, finding the trailhead at the end of the main loop. Parking is available for a few cars. Near the trailhead is a white sign with green letters: *Lehman Creek C.G. 4*.

Description: The trail begins in a mixed forest of mahogany, pinyon pine, juniper and aspen following an old roadbed. Sporadically spaced sagebrush and prickly-pear cactus make up the initial groundcover. You pass through a gate designed to let hikers in and keep cows out. During certain parts of the season, campers in the Lehman Creek Campgrounds may have to share their sites with a herd of grazing cows (see Introduction). Continue the mild climb as the trail nears the aspen-lined creek and then quickly veers away. Shortly the trail reaches the remnants of an abandoned ditch.

Ten miles away, gold was discovered in 1872 at Dry Gulch, and the town of Osceola sprung into existence, reaching a population of 1500 residents. The lack of water nearby made large-scale mining impossible without a source. Construction of the Osceola Ditch, begun in 1889 and completed the following year, diverted water 18 miles from Lehman Creek to the Osceola mines. The diversion continued until abandoned in 1901 due to periods of drought and a less-than-expected yield. In the end, the area produced nearly 2 million dollars in gold.

As the path continues to climb, other species of trees and shrubs begin to appear, including Douglas fir, white fir and wild rose. You hike along Lehman Creek for a stretch, enjoying the forest cover of aspens, white fir and Douglas fir, and the profusion of wildflowers adjacent to the water's edge. Leave the tranquillity of the creek behind as a switchback leads away from the creek and into a dry drainage.

The dry terrain at this elevation creates the perfect environment for manzanita to flourish. As the trail makes a steady climb away from the roaring creek, scattered limber pine starts to appear in the mix of white and Douglas fir. Ascend into a broad, level, open area where you have your first glimpse of Wheeler Peak at the head of the canyon. Level walking leads across the clearing, interrupted only by the occasional sagebrush or mahogany tree. Once across, the trail returns to forest cover with the sound of running water in the distance.

Now come to a wide, shallow stream coursing over moss-covered rocks, which you can cross on some sawed log rounds. Away from the stream, the trail steepens again and climbs along the hillside on periodic switchbacks. The grade eases again near some young aspens and another cow-people gate, where the foliage parts enough to allow another look at Wheeler Peak. Now follow the easy path to the Wheeler Peak Campground, 3.5 miles from the trailhead in Upper Lehman Campground.

Trip 4 ♣

BAKER CREEK LOOP
TO BAKER & JOHNSON LAKES

Trip Type: Long dayhike or 2 to 3 day backpack; Loop
Length: 12.4 miles
Season: Late June through late October
Access: Gravel road
Water: Lakes and creeks
Maps: #36
Wheeler Peak & Kious Spring 7.5 minute quadrangles, 1987 (provisional)
Humboldt National Forest map, Ely Ranger District East Half, 1990
Hiking Map & Guide Great Basin National Park, Earthwalk Press 1993

Introduction: Two scenic alpine lakes are just part of the many attractions of this trip into the heart of Great Basin National Park. Baker and Johnson lakes sit majestically at the heads of their respective canyons, beneath the rugged walls of glacial cirques, near the crest of the Snake Range. Baker Creek and South Fork Baker Creek are delightful streams that tumble down forested canyons as diverse as any in the Great Basin. At the head of the South Fork is a verdant, pastoral, park-like meadow.

For the peak-baggers, this trip offers easy routes to the top of Baker and Pyramid peaks, the third and fourth highest summits in the Park. Plenty of historical interest provides opportunities for further exploration, particularly around Johnson Lake, where a high-quality tungsten mine led to the construction of a tramway, a stamp mill and numerous log cabins. If you decide to poke around these sites, please leave everything just as you found it.

Although it is possible for moderately strong hikers to complete this loop in a long day, the rich attractions that abound along the route are better appreciated over a two-to-three day backpack. While many of the other trails in the Park see quite a few visitors, this trip can promise a relatively large amount of solitude and plenty of campsites away from the crowd.

Trailhead: (e) Follow directions in Trip 1 to the junction of State Route 488 and the Wheeler Peak Scenic Drive. Continue on 488, following signs to Lehman Caves, another 0.15 mile to the left-hand turn for the Baker Creek Road signed: *Baker Creek Road, Trailhead, Campground.*

Head south along the well-graded, two-lane gravel road through pinyon-juniper forest. At 2.9 miles from the junction pass the entrance into Baker Creek Campground and continue another 0.5 mile to the trailhead at the end of the road where it narrows and forms a loop. There is room for a half dozen cars in the wide shoulder of the loop. Across the road near the trailhead are green outhouses.

Description: Signs at the trailhead read: *Baker Trail, Baker Lake 6* and *Johnson Lake 7.5, No Camping.* Begin hiking to the north of Baker Creek in the transition between thick forest on your left of aspen, white fir and Douglas fir, and sagebrush to your right. On a wooden rail bridge, cross a rivulet running through meadow grass. Reach a large open area of grass where you pass through a cattle-people gate at the far end before entering back into dense forest.

A series of metal signs on steel poles grab your attention as you walk up the trail, markers for a cooperative government snow survey. Continue through cool white-fir forest until the path wanders away from the creek into drier vegetation of pinyon pine, mountain mahogany, sagebrush and widely scattered fir. The detour away from Baker Creek is short-lived, however, as the trail soon comes directly alongside the roaring creek.

Follow the trail next to the creek under cool forest cover for a considerable distance, until a steep switchback leads away from the creek and then the trail bends around, continuing upstream through mahogany and manzanita. An open, mixed forest of mahogany, white fir, limber pine and aspen above slopes covered with manzanita allows partial views up the canyon. Triangular-shaped Baker Peak comes into full view as you climb up the trail.

Now cross a strong-flowing side stream near a lovely pool surrounded by lush vegetation of moss, grasses, columbine and other wildflowers. This serene grotto provides an ideal setting for a relaxing break. As the trail reenters mixed forest, which now includes some ponderosa pine, you cross another side stream of water trickling down narrow, twin channels of rock. Farther on, a wooden walkway bridges some boggy meadows where the steep slopes on the south side of the canyon come into view across the drainage.

Briefly leave the mixed forest as the trail passes through a small meadow of grasses, wildflowers and widely dispersed white fir, where another side stream meanders down toward the main creek channel. As the trail heads back into mixed forest cover, it reaches a switchback, crosses a drainage on a four-log bridge and contours back into the main canyon of Baker Creek. The trail follows the creek, passing some campsites nestled below the trees, before crossing above a profuse spring. Here, gallons of water burst forth from the slope, tumbling over boulders and through a beautiful array of monkey flowers and deep, green grasses.

From the spring, the canyon widens and a large meadow appears on the opposite side of the creek. Continue up the canyon, soon coming to a series of switchbacks that climb up the steep hillside amid predominantly Douglas-fir forest with some limber pine and white fir. In the midst of the switchbacks is a small campsite next to the creek. Above the last switchback, the trail crosses the branch of the creek that seasonally acts as the out-

Spring and wildflowers near Baker Creek

let for Baker Lake. The crossing is made on a four-log bridge before you head over to the main branch of Baker Creek. Follow the creek up to Dieshman Cabin, a fairly intact remnant of a bygone era.

At the cabin, the trail makes a 110-degree bend to the right through a mixed forest of Douglas fir, limber pine and Englemann spruce. Another series of switchbacks leads up to a trail junction, 4.4 miles from the trailhead. A duck on a tree stump and a sign nailed to a spruce tree reading: *Baker Lake .6, Johnson Lake 1.1,* mark the intersection. Continue straight ahead, following the sign to Baker Lake.

Now gently meander through Englemann spruce forest until the trail becomes significantly steeper near a switchback. The trail curves around and wanders over to the end of the canyon where Baker Lake lies at the head of the cirque, 5.3 miles from the trailhead.

Baker Lake, named after an early rancher of Snake Valley, is another of the shallow tarns left over from the last active period of glaciation. Early in the season, the icy blue waters of the full-bodied lake reflect the rugged cliffs that rim the upper walls of the cirque. By midsummer the lakeshore recedes considerably, exposing a wide band of rock around the basin. Talus slopes rise up from the water's edge to dark, steep cliffs enclosing the lake on three sides. On the northern bank, a grassy meadow surrounded by a dense stand of Englemann spruce provides excellent campsites. The shallow lake holds a reasonably healthy population of trout and the entire shoreline is accessible to fishermen.

One mile north of the lake, Baker Peak, at 12,298 feet, is the third highest peak in the park behind Wheeler and Jeff Davis Peaks and is a technically easy climb. To reach the summit, ascend the steep slopes above the east side of the lake, heading northwest until you reach the ridge crest. Turn north following the south ridge of Baker Peak to the top of the peak. Across the deep chasm of the North Fork of Baker Creek are excellent views of the south faces of Wheeler and Jeff Davis peaks.

From Baker Lake, you need not return via the same trail. Rather, head southeast along a faint trail marked by a sign nailed to a spruce tree reading: *Johnson Lake 1.4*. Find this path at the southeast end of the lake just up the canyon from the other trail. Although indistinct, the trail, marked by ducks and cairns, crosses green, sloping meadows just below the talus slides at the base of the cliffs. Complete the traverse by crossing a boulder field, entering a broad meadow, and intersecting the trail from Baker Creek, where a sign attached to an old tree states: *Baker Lake .3, Baker Lake Trailhead 3.7*.

The trail coming up Baker Creek is very faint and continues to be so as it heads up the canyon and over a saddle to Johnson Lake. However, the route up to the saddle is obvious. Portions of the old trail remain but the easiest way is to climb the open slopes directly to the saddle. From the saddle, the surrounding countryside is laid out before you, including the south sides of Wheeler and Jeff Davis peaks, the continuation of the Snake Range to the south and Johnson Lake immediately below. The summit of Pyramid Peak, fourth highest in the Park at 11,926 feet, is an easy 600 vertical feet from the pass, offering even better views.

A distinct trail from the saddle heads downhill across the steep slope above Johnson Lake. At a switchback, a side trail heads up to the remains of the Johnson Mine, which include the remnants of an old log cabin, as well as numerous entrances to abandoned mines. The tungsten ore extracted from these mines traveled down to the rock outcropping above the west shore of the lake, via the cable that still remains perched above the slopes. From the lake mules took the ore down the canyon for processing at a mill. The tungsten operation began just after the turn of the 20th century and continued until a massive snowslide destroyed the structure on the rock outcropping during the 1930's. Much of the wreckage ended up in the lake itself and is still visible near the outlet. The trail passes directly by the remaining debris on the outcropping before reaching the lake above the south shore, 7.0 miles from the trailhead.

Johnson Lake is certainly the most interesting and, in some respects, perhaps the nicest lake in Great Basin National Park. Numerous artifacts of historical interest fill the basin and the water level does not suffer the same shortage later in the summer that affects the other lakes in the Park. Miners attempted to increase the level of the lake even higher by constructing a rock dam at the outlet, but the project was less than successful.

Steep, dramatic cliffs that are part of the crest of the Snake Range ring the symmetrical lake. Rock outcroppings add character above the west shore. A small spring above the south side sends a clear, cold stream of water into the lake. Limber pines climb up the hillside above the spring and a verdant meadow caresses the meandering outlet stream as it heads

Johnson Lake

down the canyon. Campsites abound on the south shore and amid the trees above the outlet. A number of old cabins, downstream from the lake, testify to the potential for seasonal habitation. Full of history and scenic beauty, Johnson Lake is a great place to spend a day or two.

Follow the old, rocky road east from the lake along the outlet through spruce forest. If you have the time, the exploration of the various cabins in a flat just south of the creek is quite interesting. Remember, this is a historic site—leave everything as you found it.

Continue down the road, following the refreshing-looking outlet stream until it bends across the road and proceeds down the drainage. Soon the trail brings you to another set of cabins, among which is a large, split-level structure that housed the stamp mill which concentrated the tungsten ore before it was hauled by wagon to Frisco, Utah, and then shipped by rail to a smelter in Salt Lake City. Gone are the wagon wheels, but the boots of hikers and backpackers still travel down the old road.

The grade of the road improves east of the cabins, making for much more pleasant walking on a dirt track. You leave the Englemann spruce behind as a mixed forest of white fir, limber pine and aspen provides cool shade. Where the trail bends sharply north, a dry campsite occupies a flat. Shortly after, you reach a closed Forest Service gate. That any vehicles have come up this road in the last ten years appears doubtful.

In dense forest 8.5 miles from the trailhead and 1.5 miles from Johnson Lake, you come to the trail junction where a small metal sign reads: *Baker Creek Trailhead 4.4* (left), *Shoshone Campground 1.5* (straight ahead), and *Johnson Lake 1.7* (back). From the junction, your trail climbs steeply northeast up the side of a ridge separating Snake and Baker creeks, initially through dense stands of aspen and then through open sagebrush with very widely scattered limber pines. An ascent of 0.6 mile leads to a saddle on the ridge. At the top a 4 by 4 post set in a pile of rocks holds a sign which reads: *Snake Creek Divide, Johnson Lake 1.5*. Head directly west on the crest for a very short distance until another sign reading: *Baker Creek Trailhead 3.4* leads you down off the ridge along a faint trail through limber pine and Douglas fir.

A half-mile descent crosses a couple of small drainages and heads into a broad meadow where the trail disappears. A sign, seemingly in the middle of nowhere, marks an unseen trail junction: *Baker Creek Trailhead via S. Fork 3.1, via Timber Creek 2.8*. To make matters more confusing, the topo places this intersection 0.4 mile south of the actual location. The route down Timber Creek is 0.3 mile shorter than the South Fork Baker Creek route, but it is not a maintained trail. Turn west at the junction, following the arrow on the sign, and find a distinct trail again across the meadow at the edge of some trees.

The upper part of the South Fork canyon is a beautiful, park-like basin with green, sloping hillsides and a thin ribbon of sparkling water bordered by mounds of lush grass. The only aspect that detracts from the idyllic setting is the periodic presence of grazing cows. As you descend down the canyon, the stream develops a stronger flow. Soon you cross over to the west side and proceed on distinct, well-graded trail through aspen, white fir and Douglas fir. Continue in mixed forest for a mile to a large meadow.

Beyond the meadow, the trail steepens considerably as the creek plummets down the precipitous lower canyon. A half mile from the meadow, the trail catches up with the rapidly descending creek and crosses to the south side. Eventually the forest becomes mixed as the trail wanders to the junction with the trail coming down Timber Creek. Now a northerly track leads across a couple of minor drainages and then over two bridges across Baker Creek to the trailhead.

Trip 5 ♣

SNAKE CREEK TRAIL TO JOHNSON LAKE

Trip Type: Dayhike or overnight backpack; Out and back
Distance: 7.2 miles round trip
Season: June through October
Access: Gravel road
Water: Creek and lake
Maps: #36
   Wheeler Peak 7.5 minute quadrangle, 1987 (provisional)
   Humboldt National Forest map, Ely Ranger District East Half, 1990
   Hiking Map & Guide Great Basin National Park, Earthwalk Press 1993

Introduction: This is the short way to Johnson Lake, up the old road that wagons used earlier in the 20th century to haul tungsten ore from the mine above the lake. It is shorter, but unlike Trip 4, you must return via the same trail. Johnson Lake is a beautiful tarn set in a bowl beneath steep, rugged cliffs near the crest of the Snake Range. Artifacts left over from the mining days provide plenty of opportunities for exploring the rich history of a bygone era.

Trailhead: (f) From State Route 487, 5 miles south of the town of Baker, turn west near a sign marked: *Snake Creek Canyon*. Immediately after the turn, another sign reads: *Johnson Lake Trailhead 13*. Proceed up the wide, well-graded gravel road, passing the Spring Creek Rearing Station at 3.7 miles from the highway. Beyond the rearing station, the road narrows and deteriorates somewhat. Enter National Forest land at 4.1 miles and Great Basin National Park at 5.2 miles.

The road comes alongside Snake Creek and leads past some interesting cliffs on the north side of the road, including Standing Snake Pinnacle. As you drive up the road, you pass numerous campsites with picnic tables and fire pits next to the creek. For approximately 4 miles the creek bed is dry thanks to a diversion structure 10.7 miles from the highway. The purpose of the diversion seems a mystery.

Above the diversion, aspens and firs line the stream banks beyond the end of the road, which terminates in a wide clearing at 12.6 miles. Primitive Shoshone Campground provides pit toilets, picnic tables and fire pits. A large wooden sign at the trailhead reads: *Johnson Lake 3.2, Baker Lake via Johnson Lake 4.7, Baker Trailhead via Baker Lake 10.7,* and *Baker Trailhead via Baker Meadows 5.9*.

Description: Begin hiking up the continuation of the old road on rocky tread in the transition zone between aspen, white fir and occasional ponderosa pine and sagebrush on the opposite side. Follow the bend of the trail into mixed forest and cross Snake Creek on a wooden plank-and-log bridge. Beyond the crossing, the trail bends away from the creek and enters a large clearing, offering a good view up the canyon of the hillsides above. A minor descent leads across a seasonal drainage and into an open area of sagebrush.

In the sage, the trail begins a steep climb up the hillside, circling around toward the head of the basin through mixed forest and up to the junction with the trail heading northeast to Timber and South Fork Baker creeks. A metal sign reads: *Baker Creek Trailhead 4.4* (right), *Shoshone Campground 1.5* (back) and *Johnson Lake 1.2* (ahead).

From the junction, reverse the description in Trip 4 for 1.5 miles to Johnson Lake.

Trip 6 ♤
LEXINGTON ARCH

Trip Type: Dayhike; Out and back
Distance: 2.8 miles round trip
Season: May through early November
Access: Dirt road
Water: None (except early in season)
Maps: #37
 Arch Canyon 7.5 minute quadrangle, 1987 (provisional)
 Humboldt National Forest map, Ely Ranger District East Half,
 1990
 Hiking Map & Guide Great Basin National Park, Earthwalk Press
 1993

Introduction: Tucked away into an obscure corner of Great Basin National Park is another unique feature peculiar to the Great Basin: a limestone arch. The scenery is truly awe-inspiring and well worth your consideration. Reaching the six-story structure involves a relatively easy hike up a narrow, picturesque canyon, but one must drive a considerable distance from the center of the Park's activity to get to the trailhead. Part of the journey is nearly 12 miles over gravel and dirt roads, but they should be passable to most cars under normal conditions.

Some geologists hypothesize that creation of Lexington Arch occurred in the traditional way, by erosional agents such as ice, wind and chemical weathering, although composition of most arches in the West is sandstone, not limestone. A second theory is that the arch is actually all that remains of a large cave system that has since crumbled. Another idea is that perhaps Lexington Arch is not an arch at all but a natural bridge, created not by the forces of wind, ice or chemicals but by the carving effects of an ancient stream. Whatever formed the structure, Lexington Arch is a scenic wonder.

Trailhead: (g) From the junction with State Route 488 in the town of Baker, continue south on State Route 487, 6.1 miles to the Utah border, where the road number changes to Utah State Highway 21. Beyond the border, enter the small community of Garrison, Utah, and reach the junction with Highway 159 at 7.1 miles from Route 488. Remaining on Highway 21, you travel another 3.4 miles to Pruess Lake before reaching the Lexington Arch turnoff, 12.1 miles from the junction with Route 488. A large Great Basin National Park sign designates the turn to the west.

Travel up the well-graded, wide gravel road, heading directly toward the dramatic mountains of the Snake Range. At 0.4 mile from the highway is a sign reading: *Lexington Arch Trailhead 11, Lexington Arch 12.5.* Initially, the road leads through sagebrush, saltbush and grasses before encountering pinyon-juniper forest farther up the sloping terrain. At 9.4 miles, the road reaches a gate, which you must open and close behind you.

Immediately after the gate is a pronounced 'Y' intersection where a sign marked: *Lexington Arch* directs you to the left.

Another road bears left at 10.3 miles, but you continue straight ahead, following another sign to the Arch. The last mile-and-one-half are the roughest of the journey, but should be easily passable to most vehicles. Reach the trailhead signed: *Lexington Arch Parking Area* 11.5 miles from Highway 21. Parking is available for about a half dozen vehicles.

Description: Begin hiking up an old road through juniper and pinyon-pine forest intermixed with occasional mountain mahogany. Wild rose, chokecherry and currant are the predominant shrubs. A dilapidated old cabin and a pile of tailings pre-

Lexington Arch

sent clear evidence of previous mining activity in the canyon. Where the road narrows to a single track, you pass a trail register and immediately cross the usually bone-dry creek. At this elevation, temperatures can be quite hot during the summer months, so little, if any, water is available from the stream except during snowmelt. Make sure you have plenty of water before starting this hike.

The trail winds up through the narrow canyon, steeply at times. Thick brush nearly overgrows the trail in places but the vegetation seems to thin as you proceed up the canyon. Just beyond a grove of white fir, the arch momentarily comes into view, only to disappear again. Continue to climb up the canyon, following the main trail as it ascends steeply to the left of the arch. Do not take the use trail that climbs up to the front of the arch. Rather, follow ducks leading across the creek and up the other side. Proceed quite a distance past the arch before doubling back on switchbacks that climb up the hill on the back side through mahogany, ephedra and currant.

Lexington Arch, 75 feet above the base and 120 feet across, seems much larger when you're standing at its base than you expected when viewing it from the canyon below. The arch classically frames the extraordinary views east into Utah and west toward the Snake Range. The limestone opening seems to act as a funnel for the wind as it roars down the canyon. Reddish-brown lichen adds a splash of color to the grayish rock.

Retrace your steps to the trailhead.

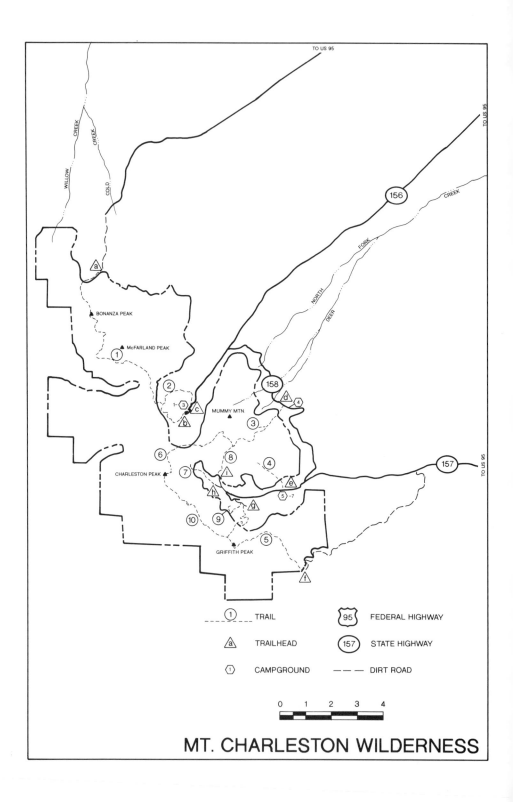

TO US 95

WILLOW CREEK

COLD CREEK

156

CREEK

NORTH

DEER

FORK

TO US 95

a

BONANZA PEAK

McFARLAND PEAK

1

2

158

d

4

1-3

c

b

MUMMY MTN.

3

6

8

4

7

i

157

TO US 95

CHARLESTON PEAK

e

h

5-7

g

10

9

5

GRIFFITH PEAK

i

| 1 | TRAIL | 95 | FEDERAL HIGHWAY |

| a | TRAILHEAD | 157 | STATE HIGHWAY |

| 1 | CAMPGROUND | - - - | DIRT ROAD |

0   1   2   3   4

MT. CHARLESTON WILDERNESS

Trails of Southern Nevada

Chapter 16
MT. CHARLESTON WILDERNESS

Imagining a more extreme contrast than the one between the glitzy glamour and excesses of the man-made Las Vegas strip and the natural beauty of the Spring Mountains would be difficult. Although separated by a mere 30 miles, the two are worlds apart. As the tentacles of tract-home developments, built at an alarming rate to house the burgeoning population of Las Vegas, stretch out toward the base of the mountains, let us hope that future expansion will spare the pristine qualities of the terrain around the Mt. Charleston Wilderness Area. Currently, a small ski area, a hotel and a lodge, along with a small community of private homes are all that interrupt the native surroundings.

Charleston Peak, nearly 12,000 feet high, was inauspiciously named after the town of Charleston, South Carolina, while the Spring Mountains received their appellation from the many springs that bubble up out of the predominantly limestone rock that composes most of the range. Geologists speculate that these limestone deposits, initially under sea water, thrust-faulted upward thousands of feet to form the Spring Mountains. Careful observation will yield many examples of small marine fossils preserved in the limestone rocks.

The Mt. Charleston Wilderness, at 43,000 acres, is a hikers' paradise. Backpackers must choose from limited campsites along the lengthier routes, but day hikers have an abundance of trails from which to choose. Whether you want short hikes up canyons to waterfalls, caves or vistas, full-blown assaults on Charleston or Griffith Peak, or a hike into a steep canyon so narrow that you can touch both walls with your hands, the region has something for everyone. In addition, the Spring Mountains contain the largest collection of bristlecone pines in the intermountain region and many of the trails in the Wilderness pass among these trees, the oldest living things on earth.

All of the trails in the Mt. Charleston Wilderness are in very good condition, having been well maintained, thanks primarily to the work of the Spring Mountain Youth Camp. You will not have to spend extra time hunting for trails that have disappeared or find yourself staring in bewilderment at a topo map attempting to determine the location of an unmarked trail junction. Mt. Charleston probably is the most civilized of all the Nevada wilderness areas.

Some of the shorter trails are quite popular in the summer when 100-degree temperatures send many Las Vegas residents up into the Spring Mountains to escape the heat. Other trails, even during peak season, offer a reasonable opportunity to leave the crowds behind. Summer is the most popular season with hikers and backpackers in the Mt. Charleston Wilderness, when temperatures can range from the 80's into the 90's during midday but nights are usually cool. As well as being hot, summers are usually dry, interrupted only by the occasional thunderstorm. Most of the precipitation that falls and replenishes all those springs for which the mountains received their name comes as winter snows, a much smaller amount coming as spring rain. Although summers are the busiest time of year for the trails, each season has its appeal in the Mt. Charleston Wilderness: Spring is the time for viewing the waterfalls and the wildflowers, fall is often very pleasant with mild temperatures, changing colors and fewer people, and traditionally mild winters offer all of the delights of ski season and the opportunity for some valley dwellers just to see what snow is actually like.

State highways lead up the two canyons on the east side of the Spring Mountains that provide the main focal points in the Mt. Charleston Wilderness. State Route 156 up Lee Canyon, the northern route into the range, accesses the Lee Canyon Ski Area, picnic areas, campgrounds and the trailhead for the Bristlecone Trail. State Route 157 up Kyle Canyon, the southern access, leads to many of the backcountry trailheads along with the Mt. Charleston Hotel, campgrounds, picnic areas, a restaurant/bar and vacation homes. Another road, State Route 158, running north-south, connects the two highways and accesses picnic areas, campgrounds and the North Loop trailhead.

So far there are no gas stations or stores in either Lee or Kyle canyons, meaning that travelers to the Spring Mountains may be able to procure a meal and a bed, but should arrive with all necessary supplies and enough gas to get them home.

LOCATION
The Mt. Charleston Wilderness is approximately 30 miles northwest of Las Vegas and 15 miles east of Pahrump. U.S. 93 is adjacent to the region along the east and north and State Route 160 along the south and west. Access into the range is primarily on State Routes 156, 157 and 158.

CAMPGROUNDS

1. DOLOMITE CAMPGROUND $
Open May through October
Camping, Picnicking, Restrooms, Water
In Lee Canyon off State Route 156

2. McWILLIAMS CAMPGROUND $
Open May through October
Camping, Picnicking, Restrooms, Water
In Lee Canyon off State Route 156

3. LEE CANYON RV CAMP $
Open May through October
Trailer parking, Picnicking
In Lee Canyon off State Route 156
* Reservations required

4. HILLTOP CAMPGROUND $
Open May through October
Camping, Picnicking, Restrooms, Water
Near the summit of State Route 158

5. FLETCHER VIEW CAMPGROUND $
Open May through October
Camping, Picnicking, Restrooms, Water
In Kyle Canyon off State Route 157

6. KYLE CANYON RV CAMP $
Open May through October
Trailer Parking, Picnicking
In Kyle Canyon off State Route 157
* Reservations Required

7. KYLE CANYON CAMPGROUND $
Open May through October
Camping, Picnicking, Restrooms, Water, Handicapped Access
In Kyle Canyon off State Route 157

RESOURCES
The greater metropolitan area of Las Vegas offers more of everything than anyone could possibly want . . . and then some. Indian Springs on U.S. 93 at the north end of the range offers limited services including gas and food.

OUTDOOR SUPPLIERS

ADVENTURE OUTFITTING
2550 S. Rainbow Blvd.
Las Vegas, NV 89102
(702) 252-7114

DESERT ROCK SPORTS
7034 W. Charleston Blvd.
Las Vegas, NV 89117
(702) 254-1143

CLIMBING SUTRA
(custom packs, harnesses & repairs)
(702) 255-2222

OUTFITTERS/GUIDES

LEE CANYON SKI AREA
PO Box 26207
Las Vegas, NV 89126

FOREST SERVICE

Las Vegas Ranger District
2881 S. Valley View Blvd., Suite 16
Las Vegas, NV 89102-0152
(702) 873-8800
(702) 222-1597 (24 hr. recorder info)

Kyle Canyon Guard Station
Kyle Canyon—Highway 157
(702) 872-5486

Trip 1 ♧
BONANZA TRAIL

Trip Type: Dayhike or overnight backpack, Shuttle
Distance: 16.8 miles
Season: Late May through October
Access: Gravel road
Water: Wood Spring only
Maps: #38
      Cold Creek, Willow Peak, Wheeler Well & Charleston Peak 7.5
         minute quadrangles, 1984 (provisional)
      Toiyabe National Forest map, Las Vegas Ranger District, 1991

Introduction: Perhaps the most remote trail in the Mt. Charleston Wilderness, the Bonanza Trail passes through abundant stands of bristlecone pine and offers fantastic views of Charleston and McFarland peaks. The opening section of trail climbs steeply from the toe of the range almost to the summit of Bonanza Peak, passing a variety of flora including mahogany, pinyon pine, juniper, white fir, and ponderosa, limber and bristlecone pine. Water is scarce, but you can replenish your supply 5.8 miles into the hike at Wood Spring. If you choose to backpack this trail rather than complete the hike in one day, you will have to create your own campsite. The best potential spots are in the canyon below Wood Spring.

This trail receives little use, due to the length of the hike and the relative remoteness of the trailhead at the northeast end of the range. If you desire solitude, this is definitely the best bet in the Mt. Charleston Wilderness. Excellent scenery abounds all along the route, including the rugged, seldom-seen south face of McFarland Peak.

Trailhead: NORTH END: (a) The trail begins at the site of Bonanza Camp, an old mining camp, along the northeast edge of the wilderness. To reach the trailhead, drive north from Las Vegas on U.S. 95 5.5 miles past the road to Lee Canyon to the turnoff signed: *Cold Creek.* Heading west you immediately pass another sign: *Cold Creek Picnic Area 12, Cold Creek Campground 15, Lower Creek Campground 19, Wheeler Pass 23.* Continue along a paved road north of the prison and begin a long, steady climb through Joshua trees out of the desert floor. Cross into National Forest land at 12.0 miles from the highway and enter a residential area. At 13.1 miles, continue straight ahead where you reach a gravel road heading off to the right signed: *Willow Creek 3, Wheeler Pass 7.* Proceed another 0.9 mile as the road surface turns to gravel. Follow the rougher, gravel road another 2.2 miles to the large graveled trailhead, 16.2 miles from U.S. 95. The area around the trailhead is large enough to provide primitive campsites.

SOUTH END: (b) From downtown Las Vegas, drive north on U.S. 95 approximately 29 miles to the junction with State Highway 156, also known as Lee Canyon Road. Head west toward the eastern foothills of the Spring Mountain range. At 14 miles you reach the junction with State Route 158, also known as Deer Creek Highway, which heads south to the Kyle Canyon area. Continue straight on Lee Canyon Road 2.5 miles to the unsigned right turn to the trailhead, 100 feet before the entrance to McWilliams Campground. Head into the large gravel parking area. The trailhead has a signboard that reads in part: *Welcome, Bristlecone Trail #148.*

Description: Start the hike near a large trailhead sign which reads: *Bonanza Trail No. 151, Bonanza Peak 4, Lee Canyon 14.* The trail wanders briefly through an open area before ascending through mixed forest of mahogany, white fir, ponderosa pine and pinyon pine. Soon you begin a long, winding, steep ascent incorporating a series of over 50 switchbacks that climbs 2300 feet in 3 miles. As you travel up the east flank of the range, the forest changes into predominantly fir, then limber pine, and ultimately bristlecone pine. Views of the desert floor improve until you finally reach the top of the ridge, 3.1 miles from the trailhead. The effort to reach the ridge top at 9850 feet is rewarded by a view of your progress all the way down to the trailhead and out to the desert floor 7,000 feet below.

Once on the ridge, with the most difficult portion of the trail behind you, the grade eases, although you continue to ascend toward Bonanza Peak through exposed limestone and bristlecone pine. For the next mile, the trail repeats a pattern of mildly ascending along the west side of the

McFarland Peak above the Bonanza Trail

ridge and then switchbacking toward the crest until reaching the slopes below 10,397' Bonanza Peak, 4.2 miles from the trailhead. Two hundred feet of easy scrambling lead to the summit.

From the peak, the route begins a long descent into an unnamed canyon on a dirt track, still through bristlecone-pine forest. As you descend and the trees periodically part, Charleston Peak comes into view. Soon limber pines reappear mixed in with the bristlecones, and farther down the canyon ponderosa pine enters the mix. After a series of switchbacks, the trail reaches Wood Spring where a small-diameter pipe brings water straight out of a rock. Fill your bottles at the spring, since it is the only reliable water along the 16-mile route.

From the spring, the trail continues the winding descent across drainages to the bottom of the canyon at 6.5 miles from the trailhead, where white fir and ponderosa pine fill the basin and impressive limestone cliffs form the walls of the upper canyon. Early in the season you may find water in the creek.

Now the hiker is faced with the task of regaining most of the elevation that was lost descending from the ridge below Bonanza Peak to the bottom of the canyon. Another series of switchbacks awaits you as the climb out of the canyon heads through mixed forest toward the top of the southwest ridge of McFarland Peak. A 1.25-mile climb to the crest culminates in dramatic views of Charleston Peak and the steep limestone cliffs on the south face of McFarland Peak. Bristlecone pines once again dominate the immediate surroundings.

From the crest, the trail begins a gentle traverse past limestone cliffs and bristlecone pines across the head of the canyon, below the precipitous slopes of McFarland Peak. Short, steep switchbacks end the traverse as the trail climbs out of the canyon to a low, flat saddle, 10.8 miles from the trailhead, offering excellent views of McFarland and Charleston peaks.

With the last of the steep ascents behind, the trail assumes a gentler grade for the next 2 miles as it makes a mildly undulating traverse on or near the ridge crest. Bristlecone pine comprises a light forest with lesser amounts of limber pine and white fir. Across the steep canyon to the south, Charleston Peak is almost a constant companion perched high above the surrounding terrain.

You reach a trail junction 13.1 miles from the Camp Bonanza trailhead, marked only by a Mt. Charleston Wilderness sign. The trail heading south continues along the ridge another half-mile before ending. Bend around the main trail as it heads down from the ridge through dense forest of pine and fir. After three long switchbacks and 0.6 mile, the trail intersects the Bristlecone Trail (Trip 2) in a wide, gravel clearing, 13.7 miles from the trailhead. A sign at the junction reads: *Bonanza Trail No. 131, Trailhead 13 miles.* Another sign reads: *Bristlecone Loop Trail No. 148, Upper Bristlecone Trailhead 2, Lower Bristlecone Trailhead 3.* From the flat a panorama of expansive views greets you including Mt. Charleston, Mummy Mountain, and the Lee Canyon Ski Area.

Turn left (east) onto the Scout Canyon Road, which descends from the flat on gravel roadbed. Follow the road as it loops around and descends into Scout Canyon. Near a large grove of quaking aspens, the road makes a sharp bend to the east again, and off to the left near a barricade of rocks and timbers is a trail with a sign: *please stay on the trail.* This path leads down to the Old Mill Picnic Area.

Stay on the road as it continues to descend and curve around toward Lee Canyon Road and McWilliams Campground. The route passes through a mixed forest of fir, pine and aspen until reaching the closed gate above the trailhead near the highway, 3.1 miles from the Bristlecone-Bonanza junction.

Trip 2 🌲
BRISTLECONE TRAIL

Trip Type: Dayhike; Loop or shuttle
Distance: 5.8 miles loop, 5.0 miles shuttle
Season: Spring through Fall
Access: Paved road
Water: None
Maps: #38
Charleston Peak 7.5' quadrangle, 1984 (provisional)
Toiyabe National Forest map, Las Vegas Ranger District, 1991

Introduction: The Bristlecone Trail lies wholly outside of the Mt. Charleston Wilderness, allowing mountain bikers access to the trail. You may have to yield the right-of-way on occasion, but the only developed trail in the Lee Canyon area is certainly worth the minor inconvenience. The center portion of the aptly named Bristlecone Trail travels through a vast stand of bristlecone pines, although there are relatively few examples of the popular images of the gnarled and twisted bristlecones of antiquity. Isolated stands of aspen along the lower portions of the trail provide a nice touch of color in the fall.

Majestic views of the Lee Canyon area, including Mt. Charleston and Mummy Mountain, abound from the upper part of the trail. Make sure that you take enough water as there is none available along the route. If you want to avoid the 0.8-mile hike up along the Lee Canyon Road at the end of the trip, you will need two vehicles for the shuttle.

Trailhead: (b) From downtown Las Vegas, drive north on U.S. 93 approximately 29 miles to the junction with State Route 156, also known as Lee Canyon Road. Head west toward the eastern foothills of the Spring Mountain range. At 14 miles, you reach the junction with State Route 158, also known as Deer Creek Highway, which heads south to the Kyle Canyon area. Continue straight on Lee Canyon Road 4 miles to the end of the highway in the parking lot for the Lee Canyon Ski Area. Find the trailhead at the end of the road near the turnaround/helipad.

For a car shuttle to avoid the hike back up the road, park a car in the gravel parking lot 100 feet north of the McWilliams Campground entrance, 0.8 mile back down the Lee Canyon Road.

Description: From the northwest edge of the turnaround/helipad head up the unmarked trail on a well used, gravel and dirt path along the ridge above the parking lot. As you begin the climb, the Lee Canyon Ski Area comes into view until you leave it behind, hiking along a dry stream under a mixed, dense forest of aspen, pine and fir. Continue to climb up the drainage to an unsigned junction with a trail heading to the right to Gary Abbot Campground. Stay left at this junction.

The route leaves the drainage and the aspens behind as it contours around a hillside before resuming the ascent beneath forest of limber pine, ponderosa pine and white fir. Isolated specimens of bristlecone begin to appear throughout this section of trail. Where you reach the top of a minor ridge, the forest cover abates enough to grant a partial view of the canyon. Leaving the ridge, you travel just below it on well-maintained dirt path and then contour around the slope.

At 2.1 miles the route bends northward and suddenly changes from dirt trail to the old roadbed of Scout Canyon Road as it changes from a moderate ascent through dense, mixed forest to a mostly level traverse amid open stands of bristlecone pines. Excellent views open up of the massive limestone cliffs on the opposite side of Lee Canyon. Maintaining a mostly level traverse for a third of a mile, the trail reaches a sweeping turn, climaxing in a large flat where it reaches a junction with the Bonanza Trail (see Trip 1) signed: *Bonanza Trail No. 131, Trailhead 13 miles.* Another sign states: *Bristlecone Loop Trail No. 148, Upper Bristlecone Trailhead 2, Lower Bristlecone Trailhead 3.* From the flat a panorama of expansive views greets you, including Mt. Charleston, Mummy Mountain, and the Lee Canyon Ski Area.

Bear right, still on Scout Canyon Road. Good views across the canyon remain as the gravel road heads east and descends from the flat. Follow the road as it loops around to the west and descends into Scout Canyon. Near a large grove of quaking aspens, the road makes a sharp bend to the east again, and off to the left, near a barricade of rocks and timbers, 4.2 miles from the trailhead, is a trail with a sign: *please stay on the trail.* This path leads down to the Old Mill Picnic Area.

Stay on the road as it continues to descend and curve around to Lee Canyon Road and McWilliams Campground. The route passes through a mixed forest of fir, pine and aspen until reaching the closed gate above the McWilliams trailhead near the highway, 5.0 miles from the Bristlecone trailhead. Unless you arranged a car shuttle, you will have to hike the remaining 0.8 mile back to the upper trailhead at the end of the highway. For the avid wilderness hiker, having to hike along a paved highway is bad enough, but the ultimate discouragement is to have to go uphill while doing so.

Trip 3 ♧
MUMMY SPRING TRAIL

Trip Type: Dayhike; Out and back
Distance: 6.2 miles round trip
Season: Spring through fall
Access: Paved highway
Water: Spring
Maps: #39
    Angel Peak and *Charleston Peak* 7.5 minute quadrangles, 1984 (provisional)
    Toiyabe National Forest map, Las Vegas Ranger District, 1991

Introduction: A short but moderately strenuous climb leads to a unique spring nestled into a cool canyon with lush vegetation. Quite a few people use the North Loop Trail on their way to lofty Mt. Charleston, but few take the side trip down to Mummy Springs, where a somewhat secluded oasis awaits those interested in escaping the crowds. If you want a glimpse of the oldest living species on the planet, an added bonus is the prolific stands of bristlecone pines on the upper sections of the trail. Some even have the characteristic twisted appearance for which older bristlecones are famous.

Trailhead: (d) Drive approximately 15 miles north from downtown Las Vegas on U.S. 95 to the junction with State Route 157, also known as Kyle Canyon Road. Proceed west up 157, climbing from high desert floor to the foothills of the Spring Mountains. In about 17 miles, you reach the junction with State Route 158, also known as Deer Creek Highway. Turn right onto Highway 158 and head up the road as it climbs on the east slopes of the mountains. At 4.4 miles from the junction with Highway 157 you pass Hilltop Campground on your right. The trailhead is 0.2 mile farther on the west side of the road at the edge of a wide turnout with parking for about a dozen cars.

Description: For the first 2.75 miles the Mummy Spring trail coincides with the North Loop Trail to Mt. Charleston (see Trip 6). Leave the parking area on a wide dirt-and gravel track that climbs above the highway before turning west. The trail initially climbs through mahogany and occasional ponderosa pines, reaching the Wilderness boundary just after the first of many switchbacks. As you continue up the switchbacks, white fir and then bristlecone pine become the dominant trees. Steeply ascending the forested slopes, at 1.3 miles you reach a knob amid old, gnarled and twisted bristlecone pines that are reminiscent of the images that scenic photography has made popular.

The grade moderates briefly, passes a dry campsite with excellent views of Mummy Mountain, and then resumes its climb through mixed forest of ponderosa pine, limber pine, white fir and bristlecone pine. A series of 12 switchbacks lead you up to exclusively bristlecone-pine forest and to the top of the ridge that separates the drainages of Kyle Canyon and Deer Creek. From here, you continue to climb along the ridge to a saddle where you get a commanding view of the massive limestone face at the southern extension of the Mummy Mountain massif, having a shape suggestive of the profile of a 1950's-vintage streamlined diesel train engine. The grade of the trail mercifully eases and it even makes a mild descent, still through mature bristlecone forest, to a level spot and another dry campsite. Along the back side of the ridge, your route levels and reaches a trail junction in another saddle just below the huge limestone face, 2.75 miles from the highway. A sign nailed to a large bristlecone says: *Charleston Peak 8, Kyle Canyon 4, Deer Creek Road 3* and *Mummy Spring ½*. Turn right (northwest) and make the descent 0.35 mile to Mummy Spring.

Mummy Spring lies in a lush canyon with aspens, gooseberries, wildflowers, ferns, grasses and other thirsty plants. The northeast-facing ravine tucked back into the densely forested slope of Mummy Mountain produces somewhat cooler temperatures, creating a microclimate in which the lush vegetation seems to thrive. A rock wall lies just below the springs, allowing the water to run over the limestone face and leave behind some travertine deposits. Mummy Spring is particularly scenic in the fall when the aspens are turning and colder temperatures freeze the water draping over the rock wall. The sloping canyon above provides limited opportunities for further exploration.

Retrace your steps to the trailhead.

Trip 4
FLETCHER CANYON TRAIL

Trip Type: Dayhike; Out and back
Distance: 3.8 miles round trip
Season: Spring through Fall
Access: Paved highway
Water: Intermittently available in creek
Maps: #39
Angel Peak and *Charleston Peak* 7.5 minute quadrangles, 1984 (provisional)
Toiyabe National Forest map, Las Vegas Ranger District, 1991

Introduction: The Fletcher Canyon trail is a short, easy hike into one of the most unusual environments in the Mt. Charleston Wilderness. Diverse varieties of vegetation border the trail for the entire length. Steep, narrow limestone walls toward the end of the route form a canyon reminiscent of a slot canyon in Zion or Grand Canyon National Park. This little-used trail will provide plenty of discoveries for the ardent hiker. If photography is your passion, bring a tripod and speedy film for the low light conditions in the canyon.

Trailhead: (e) Drive approximately 15 miles north from downtown Las Vegas on U.S. 95 to the junction with State Route 157, also known as Kyle Canyon Road. Proceed west up 157 about 17 miles to the junction with State Route 158, also known as Deer Creek Highway. Continue past the junction 0.5 mile to the trailhead on the north side of Kyle Canyon Road. Keep a careful watch for the trailhead, since driving past the narrow gap of Fletcher Canyon is easy. Parking is available for only two cars at the trailhead, but additional parking is available on the opposite highway shoulder.

Description: The signed trail begins just up from the road on gravel tread, sometimes in the actual wash of the canyon. Follow a bona-fide trail that gently leads out of the stream channel on the north side, crossing twice more before reaching the wilderness boundary 0.5 mile from the highway. The diverse nature of the surroundings is striking, with many more species of plants and trees than you typically see on the other trails in the wilderness. Some of the varieties include shrub oak, mahogany, manzanita, pinyon pine, ponderosa pine and Utah juniper.

Spout and pool, Fletcher Canyon

As the trail continues up the canyon, water may appear in the creek channel and then quickly disappear again almost as often as your trail crosses the drainage. Where the canyon begins to narrow, the grade of the trail increases. Vertical limestone walls grow taller and narrower the further up the canyon you go. Vegetation changes as well in response to shade, cooler temperatures, and the availability of moisture. About 1.5 miles from the trailhead the canyon begins a sweeping bend northward as it continues to narrow, to where you can almost touch the rock walls with your hands.

Eventually the trail all but disappears, forcing you to use the bottom of the slim canyon as your path. Reaching a point where the grade increases, the canyon suddenly splits in two, 1.9 miles from the trailhead. In the left canyon, a spring cascades down the steep, narrow cleft, climaxing in a chute that the forces of erosion have carved in a limestone boulder, spilling into a gravel basin. Travel beyond this point up the steep left branch is difficult, but you can proceed approximately 50 yards up the right branch before rock climbing skills become necessary. Retrace your steps to the trailhead.

Trip 5 🌲
GRIFFITH PEAK TRAIL

Trip Type: Dayhike or overnight backpack; Out and back
Distance: 11.2 miles round trip
Season: Spring through Fall
Access: Gravel & dirt road, high-clearance vehicle necessary
Water: None
Maps: #39

      Griffith Peak & *La Madre Spring* 7.5 minute quadrangles, 1984 (provisional); Toiyabe National Forest map, Las Vegas Ranger District, 1991

Introduction: Griffith Peak may be 856 feet lower than Mt. Charleston but it's also 3½ to 5 miles closer to a trailhead than its taller neighbor. Named for Senator E. W. Griffith, who developed the Charleston Park resort in Kyle Canyon, Griffith Peak offers a relatively short route to the top of one of the highest peaks in the Spring Mountains and one of the best 360-degree views in the range. Vistas include Las Vegas, Lake Mead and the heart of the Spring Mountains, including Charleston Peak, as well as numerous desert mountain ranges and basins. If you might feel slighted because on Griffith Peak you are not standing on the highest point in the Mt. Charleston Wilderness, a strong party can double-summit both Griffith Peak and Charleston Peak from this trailhead in a long and strenuous round-trip hike of 19 miles. For the less driven, this trip offers solitude along a little used trail, mountain meadows filled with wildflowers in season, and pleasant scenery along with the incredible views from the top.

The trail is somewhat strenuous, gaining 3,350 feet in 5 miles after limiting access to those with a durable, adequate clearance vehicle—the price of solitude this close to a major metropolitan area. Oddly enough, in spite of all the attributes of the summit of Griffith Peak, no developed trail exists all the way to the top, but the final 0.1 mile from the trail to the summit is easily done on a use trail beaten into the earth over time by hundreds of devoted hikers. Griffith is a peak well worth bagging!

Trailhead: (f) From Las Vegas, drive north on U.S. 95 approximately 15 miles from downtown to the junction with State Route 157, also known as Kyle Canyon Road. Proceed west on paved Kyle Canyon Road approximately 8fl miles to signed Harris Springs Road and turn left onto graveled road. Initially Harris Springs Road climbs uphill out of Kyle Canyon through sagebrush and cactus. Pinyon pines start appearing on a long descent and at 3.25 miles from Route 157, you reach a 3-way junction where a wooden sign declares: *Harris Springs Ranch ½ mile, Private Property* to the left and *Harris Peak 6 miles* to the right. Turn right onto rougher road and climb through denser stands of pinyon pine. As you gain elevation, note the different species of pines and firs mixed in with the pinyons, signaling a gradual change in vegetation corresponding to the change in altitude and in proximity to the mountains. After a long ascent you reach the trailhead at Harris Saddle on top of a ridge with sweeping views at 8.9 miles from Route 157 (5.65 miles from the junction with the road to Harris Springs Ranch). Parking is available for about a dozen cars. A high-clearance vehicle is recommended for the road beyond the junction to Harris Springs Ranch, but most durable vehicles with adequate clearance should be able to make the trip under normal conditions.

Description: The trail begins near a trailhead sign board at the west end of the parking area and proceeds on the extension of the old road, blocked to vehicles by boulders. You quickly pass the wilderness boundary and just after you round a bend in the gravel road, one-quarter mile from the parking area, Griffith Peak comes into view, dominating the horizon. Continue to ascend mildly along the roadbed with the peak beckoning you onward. According to a trail pamphlet put out by the Forest Service, this old road was a project of the CCC (Civilian Conservation Corps) under the administration of Franklin Roosevelt. When FDR came to inspect the work, he asked the foreman of the project what was the destination of the road. When the foreman was unable to come up with an answer, FDR immediately halted construction and the progress of the road up the mountain was dead in its tracks. Continue along this old road, lined with mahogany trees, until the road does end abruptly without purpose at 1.75 miles from the trailhead, just where a steep ridge descending from Harris Mountain blocks the way.

From the end of the road, the trail (not shown on the topo) climbs moderately as it skirts hillsides where the mahogany trees give way to ponderosa pine, white fir and limber pine. The trail levels out for a short time to reach a saddle, and then makes a quick switchback before arriving at the Kyle Canyon Overlook, 2.5 miles from the trailhead. The overlook offers impressive views down into Kyle Canyon and up to the highest peaks, as well as a dramatic look at the imposing sheer face of limestone cliffs directly in the foreground.

From the overlook, the route climbs generally northward via a series of switchbacks, winding through and below limestone cliffs. A long ascending traverse leads to more switchbacks before you gain the top of the ridge in the first of a series of delightful, grassy meadows filled with wildflowers in season. Just beyond the meadow, you enter a forest of white fir and limber pine where currant covers the hillsides next to the trail. Switchback up into another meadow and over to the top of the ridge, where more views of Kyle Canyon await you. In your more immediate proximity, keen observation of some of the rocks on the ground may reveal small fossils embedded in the limestone.

The trail heads away from the ridge top and soon comes to a dry camp with a stone fire ring and a man-made windbreak. From the campsite, you continue to climb as the trail, switchbacking occasionally, makes a long, ascending loop around the upper slopes of Griffith Peak. Vegetation through this section is primarily bristlecone pine forest, intermittently broken by grassy meadows, wildflowers and currant. The long ascent eventually brings you to a saddle on the south ridge of Griffith Peak and to a crude, dry campsite. From here the gradient eases as the trail makes a traverse on the west side of the peak, descends briefly and reaches another saddle along the northwest ridge of Griffith Peak. This saddle offers fine views of Mummy Mountain—a small taste of what is to come from the summit of the peak.

From the saddle, the route follows the crest of the ridge 0.2 mile to the junction with the South Loop Trail, where a sign reads: *Mt. Charleston Recreation Trail No. 145, Charleston Peak, Griffith Peak Trail No. 140.* An older sign lying against the trunk of a bristlecone pine says: *Mt. Charleston 4.2,*

Harris Saddle 5, and *Kyle Canyon 4.3.* If you are really ambitious, strong parties can continue to the summit of Charleston Peak, a total round trip of 19 miles (see Trip 10). Next to a large, twin-trunked bristlecone pine is a campsite with a windbreak and fire ring, but without water. If the summit of Griffith Peak is your ultimate goal, as well it should be, you must first backtrack.

Head back along the Griffith Peak Trail to a point on the northwest ridge from where a faint use trail climbs up that same ridge. Climb steeply up the trail, which disappears in spots but the route is obvious, past contorted bristlecone pines to the rocky summit. The reward for your labor is a spectacular 360-degree view including Lake Mead, Las Vegas, Charleston Peak, Mummy Mountain and the desert and mountain ranges of southern Nevada. More fossils, crinoids, appear in some of the limestone rocks near the summit. If you happen to make the climb early in the season, wildflowers may grace your presence as well. You can shorten your descent slightly by heading southwest down from the top of Griffith Peak cross-country and picking up the trail as it curves around the peak.

Trip 6 🌲
NORTH LOOP TRAIL TO CHARLESTON PEAK

Trip Type: Long Dayhike or overnight backpack, Out and back
Distance: 20.2 miles round trip
Season: Summer through Fall
Access: Paved highway
Water: Cave Spring only
Map: #39, 40
     Angel Peak & Charleston Peak 7.5 minute quadrangles, 1984
       (provisional)
     Toiyabe National Forest map, Las Vegas Ranger District, 1991

Introduction: The ultimate experience of the Mt. Charleston Wilderness is an ascent of Charleston Peak via the Mt. Charleston National Recreation Trail. At 11,918 feet, the summit towers over the surrounding basins by nearly 10,000 feet and offers extraordinary views of southern Nevada, southeastern California and northwestern Arizona. Along the way are additional vistas of the deep cleft of Kyle Canyon and of the peak itself, sitting majestically above the neighboring peaks and ridges. Much of the trail passes through bristlecone-pine forest in the higher elevations.

A major advantage of the North Loop Trail is the opportunity to get water at Cave Spring, nearly 5 miles from the trailhead. Even in the fall, the spring produces enough fresh water to slake the thirst of the most parched hiker. Although climbing Charleston Peak in a long day is best, the Cave Spring area offers some limited camping for those desiring an overnight stay. Other possible spots, albeit dry, lie along the route, particularly on the ridge crest above Kyle Canyon.

Many parties shorten the climb by beginning the hike from the Trail Canyon trailhead. This steep route shaves off 2.2 miles from the climb (see Trip 8). If you have two cars, or do not mind the additional 1.5-mile hike between trailheads, you can vary your return by hiking down the South Loop Trail to the trailhead in the Cathedral Picnic Area (see Trip 10).

Trailhead: (d) Follow directions in Trip 3 to the trailhead.

Description: The first part of the North Loop Trail coincides with the trail to Mummy Spring. Follow directions in Trip 3 to the trail junction, 2.75 miles from State Route 158, where the route to Mummy Spring heads to the right (northwest) and your trail continues straight ahead.

For the next 1.4 miles, the trail basically makes a curving traverse around the slopes of the south end of Mummy Mountain, interrupted only by a moderate descent in the middle of the traverse. In a saddle on the top of the ridge, reach the unmarked junction with the trail that climbs up Trail Canyon from Kyle Canyon (see Trip 8). You can save 2.2 miles of hiking by beginning your climb of Charleston Peak from the Trail Canyon trailhead, although it is a much steeper ascent. A primitive campsite exists near the junction but the closest water is 0.75 mile ahead up the North Loop Trail.

From the junction, climb through light forest of predominantly limber pine with some bristlecone pine and sporadic white fir until you encounter a burn area where young conifers cohabitate with aspens and currant. Cave Spring, (not shown on the topo) three-quarters mile from the Trail

Charleston Peak from North Loop Trail

Canyon junction, provides the only reliable water on the entire trip. The spring receives its name from a small cave in the cliffs above containing a campsite used by backpacking parties. Additional small camping spots are scattered around the area near the cave. Young aspens and bristlecone pines surround the spring.

The next section of trail ascends, steeply at times, along the face of the steep hillside below the ridge crest, passing young aspens and dead snags to some switchbacks. Limestone cliffs, bristlecone pine and limber pine appear on the upper slopes as the trail makes an upward traverse to another set of switchbacks. You climb on rocky slopes below steep bluffs to the ridge crest, approximately 6 miles from the trailhead, where Charleston Peak comes back into view across the deep chasm of Kyle Canyon. A rock knoll provides an excellent perch with spectacular views into the canyon as well as a good opportunity for a rest or lunch.

At the crest, the most of the climb is behind you as the trail traverses along or near the crest, through widely distributed bristlecone pine. A number of campsites appear along the ridge, all with excellent views. You reach a series of switchbacks winding through steep limestone cliffs to a high point from where the trail makes a moderate descent across the head of the basin. Continue to traverse along the crest through limestone and bristlecone pine as Charleston Peak looms larger with each step. The traverse of the crest lasts approximately 3 miles, to the massive limestone cliffs of Devil's Thumb.

Pass Devil's Thumb on the south side as the trail wanders around steep cliffs and hillsides and winds over below the south face of Charleston Peak. Leave the scattered bristlecone forest behind as the trail begins to ascend long switchbacks that criss-cross the rocky face of the mountain. Some small tuffs of grass and a few tiny plants are the only living things in the rocky soil at this elevation. Four long switchbacks lead to the summit at 11,918 feet.

If smog from the burgeoning metropolis of Las Vegas does not cloud the atmosphere, the views from the long, rocky summit of Charleston Peak are spectacular. On clear days, the view can extend as far as 300 miles in all directions. Distant basins and ranges are almost too numerous to count. Las Vegas to the southeast and Pahrump to the west lie nearly 10,000 feet below. The only permanent things sharing the thin air on Charleston Peak are an antenna and some electronic equipment.

Retrace your steps back to the trailhead, or follow the South Loop Trail, reversing the description in Trip 10.

Trip 7 ✿

MARY JANE FALLS

Trip Type: Dayhike; Out and back
Distance: 3.0 miles round trip
Season: Spring through Fall
Access: Gravel road
Water: At falls
Map: #40
   Charleston Peak 7.5 minute quadrangle, 1984 (provisional)
   Toiyabe National Forest map, Las Vegas Ranger District, 1991

Introduction: A dramatic waterfall and caves are the main attractions of this hike into the upper reaches of Kyle Canyon. Spring is the best time to view the falls while the low water period of late Summer and Fall is ideal for exploring the caves. This short hike is quite popular so do not expect to be alone. The upper canyon offers plenty of off-trail exploration for those wishing to leave the crowds behind.

Trailhead: (h) Drive approximately 15 miles north from downtown Las Vegas on U.S. 95 to the junction with State Route 157, also known as Kyle Canyon Road. Proceed west up Route 157 climbing from high desert floor to the foothills of the Spring Mountains. In about 17 miles, you reach the junction with State Route 158, also known as Deer Creek Highway. Continue on Kyle Canyon Road as it climbs to the turnoff for Mary Jane Falls, 3 miles from the junction. At the beginning of a hairpin turn in the highway, turn right onto paved Echo Road for 0.4 mile, then bear left on well-graded gravel road 0.2 mile to the trailhead. Plenty of room for vehicles is in the parking area. A pit toilet is near the trailhead, as is a Forest Service sign board.

Description: The Mary Jane Falls trail starts out under ponderosa pines on the continuation of the old road, boulder-lined by the Spring Mountain Youth Camp. Occasional small stands of aspens add color in the fall. You reach the end of the road at 0.9 mile and the route becomes a bona-fide trail, which quickly switchbacks up the hillside. As you climb, you begin to see specimens of white fir. The trail continues to switchback, steeply at times, as you head up the canyon rimmed by steep limestone cliffs. Eventually the trail passes just below some vertical cliffs at it heads toward the falls. As you approach the falls, the grade steepens just before leveling out at the falls.

The falls appear in a dramatic setting at the head of Kyle Canyon, rimmed by a horseshoe bend of steep limestone cliffs. Impressive views of the canyon appear from your position half way up its headwall. During peak flow, Mary Jane Falls is a dramatic spectacle, but at other times it can diminish to just a light spray. Fall makes up for the lack of water with vivid autumn colors. The force of water thrown at the limestone face at the bottom of the cascade has produced a deep cleft back into the rock. A shallow cave with a large opening is just past the falls and is well worth the little time to reach. For the adventurous, the rest of the upper canyon is available for further exploration. There is evidence that others have camped near the falls, but those sites can hardly be recommended as they are right at the base of the falls.

Retrace your steps to the trailhead.

Trip 8 🌲
TRAIL CANYON

Trip Type: Dayhike; Out and back
Distance: 4.0 miles round trip
Season: Spring through Fall
Access: Paved road
Water: None
Maps: #40
Charleston Peak 7.5 minute quadrangle, 1984 (provisional)
Toiyabe National Forest map, Las Vegas Ranger District, 1991

Introduction: A short but steep trip up a beautiful canyon to a high ridge in the heart of the Spring Mountains awaits you on the Trail Canyon Trail. The head of the canyon, rimmed by steep limestone cliffs, contains many small caves that are just waiting for further exploration. Some of the best views of Charleston Peak occur from near the ridge crest, and you can also have a good look at the south slopes of Mummy Mountain. The main distinction of this trip, however, is that it provides a short-cut to the summit of Charleston Peak, with a round trip total of 15.6 miles as compared to 16.6 miles for the South Loop and 20.2 for the North Loop. To continue on to Charleston Peak, see Trip 6.

Trailhead: (i) Follow the directions in Trip 7 to the junction of Kyle Canyon Road and Echo Road. Turn right onto paved Echo Road and travel 0.6 mile to a hairpin turn where the road name changes from Echo Road to Crestview Drive. The trailhead is on the left side of the road. Parking is available for only a few cars along the gravel shoulder.

Description: The signed trail begins heading up Trail Canyon, following a dry wash that carries seasonal runoff along an old gravel road lined with mahogany trees. A quarter mile of moderate ascent beneath steep limestone cliffs leads to light forest of ponderosa pine, scattered white fir and aspens. Beyond the Wilderness boundary, the old road crosses the creek bed three-quarters mile from the trailhead. Currant, mahogany and spo-

Mummy Mountain from junction with North Loop Trail

radic bristlecone pines join the ponderosa pine and aspens as the road continues climbing up the canyon.

A half mile further up the canyon, the road gives way to steeper trail that winds back and forth up the head of Trail Canyon. Ponderosa pine still dominates the hillsides, and as you climb you will notice evidence of a forest fire that swept through the area some time ago, blackening the upper slopes of Mummy Mountain. Many of the older ponderosa pines survived with scarred lower trunks, but other species were not so lucky. Good views of Charleston Peak occur near the top of the canyon.

The climb ends at the ridge top where you reach the junction with the North Loop Trail at 2.0 miles from Echo Road. Near the junction, you encounter a couple of undeveloped, dry campsites perched along the ridge top. The nearest water is at a spring fl mile up the North Loop Trail toward Charleston Peak (see Trip 6). Looking north, you get a good view of the North Loop trail heading back toward the Deer Creek Road as it cuts a path into the face of Mummy Mountain's prominent south slopes. The Mummy Springs junction is 1.5 miles down that trail (see Trip 3). Charleston Peak is visible through breaks in the trees.

At the end of your trip retrace your steps to the trailhead.

Trip 9 🌲
CATHEDRAL ROCK TRAIL

Trip Type: Dayhike; Out and back
Distance: 2.8 miles round trip
Season: Spring through Fall
Access: Paved road
Water: Stream ¾ mile from trailhead
Map: #40
Charleston Peak 7.5 minute quadrangle, 1984 (provisional)
Toiyabe National Forest map, Las Vegas Ranger District, 1991

Introduction: Color, waterfalls and views are the main attractions of this trip. The Cathedral Rock trail offers a short, moderately strenuous, popular climb to one of the nicest views in the Kyle Canyon region. Spring is perhaps the best time to make the climb, when the falls and the wildflowers are peaking, although autumn is a prime time also, when the expansive grove of aspens in Mazie Canyon splashes the mountainside with a blaze of yellow color. No matter what time of year you climb Cathedral Rock, the views are always spectacular.

Trailhead: (j) Drive approximately 15 miles north from downtown Las Vegas on U.S. 95 to the junction with State Route 157, also known as Kyle Canyon Road. Proceed west up 157, climbing from high desert floor to the foothills of the Spring Mountains. In about 17 miles, you reach the junction with State Route 158, also known as Deer Creek Highway. Continue on Kyle Canyon Road as it climbs and curves to the Cathedral Rock picnic area another 3.25 miles from the junction. Turn right into the picnic area and travel up the paved road not quite 0.4 mile to the signed trailhead on your right. Paid parking is available in turnouts on the left, just before you reach the trailhead. The gate to the picnic area closes at 8 p.m. in the summer and 6 p.m. in the fall. If you do not want to pay the fee or to worry about returning before the gate closes, you can try to find a parking space along the shoulder of the highway and walk up the road 0.4 mile to the trailhead.

Description: The Cathedral Rock Trail heads past the trailhead sign board on an old road that has been rock-lined by the Spring Mountain Youth Camp, which, in cooperation with the Forest Service, provides trail maintenance and construction in the Spring Mountains. Continue up the road beneath ponderosa pine and white fir as it heads up Mazie Canyon. At a bend in the trail approximately a quarter mile from the trailhead, you reach an unsigned junction with a trail that does not appear on any map heading off to the northwest. Bear left and start climbing through an extensive stand of quaking aspens. This area is quite scenic in the fall when the

Kyle Canyon from the top of Cathedral Rock

aspens are turning and in the spring when the canyon is wet, providing plenty of water for a prolific display of wildflowers.

About midway through this vast grove of aspens, where the road curves again, a side road heads left over to a delightful waterfall that spills in three stages into small punch bowls. As one might imagine, spring is the best season to view the falls. By autumn the flow diminishes to a trickle.

Continue on the old roadbed as it winds its way back and forth up the canyon and through the aspens, until you come out above the aspens on a hillside of pines and fir. Views down Kyle Canyon begin to emerge as the road makes a nearly level traverse of the hillside. At 1.2 miles, you reach an unsigned junction in a saddle where the road continues on toward the spring above Little Falls in the next canyon. A foot trail branches off to the right, heading slightly downhill. Take the trail to the right, which after a short descent circles around to a knob, steepens and switchbacks. Heading around to the back side of the knob, the trail climbs steeply to the top of Cathedral Rock.

Cathedral Rock offers a commanding view of Kyle Canyon all the way out to the desert floor. Kyle Canyon was so named after the Kyle brothers, who operated a sawmill in the area in the 1870's and who were later murdered in 1883. While thinking about untimely deaths, please exercise caution on Cathedral Rock, as the steep cliffs have claimed lives in the past. Impressive limestone cliffs ring the gorge and you get a good look at the upper canyon toward Mary Jane Falls. Charleston Peak, the highest peak in the range, appears to the west.

Retrace your steps to the trailhead.

Trip 10 ♧

SOUTH LOOP TRAIL TO CHARLESTON PEAK

Trip Type: Dayhike or overnight backpack; Out and back
Distance: 16.6 miles round trip
Season: June through October
Access: Paved road
Water: None
Maps: #40
    Charleston Peak & Griffith Peak 7.5 minute quadrangles, 1984
      (provisional)
    Toiyabe National Forest map, Las Vegas Ranger District, 1991

Introduction: The ultimate experience of the Mt. Charleston Wilderness is an ascent of Charleston Peak via the Mt. Charleston National Recreation Trail. At 11,918 feet, the summit towers over the surrounding basins by nearly 10,000 feet and offers extraordinary views of southern Nevada, southeastern California and northwestern Arizona. Along the way are additional vistas of the deep cleft of Kyle Canyon and the peak itself, sitting majestically above the neighboring peaks and ridges. Much of the trail passes through bristlecone pine forest in the higher elevations.

The South Loop Trail offers the hiker some magnificent scenery, not only from the summit, but also on lower sections of the trail. The trip into Echo Canyon is worth the trip alone for the massive limestone face on the east side of the basin, the cascading creek (in early season) and the vivid color (wildflowers in spring and quaking aspens in fall). However, you must endure a steep 4-mile climb to the ridge. Bring plenty of water as there is none en route, unless water is in the creek during the early part of the season.

Some parties climb up the South Loop and descend the North Loop (see Trip 6) or vice versa, avoiding a return on the same trail. This option requires two cars or, if you do not mind the extra 1.5 miles, you can hike the road between the two trailheads.

Allow a full day for the climb to the summit. If you prefer an overnight backpack, there are campsites on the ridge just beyond the junction with the Griffith Peak Trail (Trip 5), but no water is available en route. The North Loop Trail has campsites with water at Cave Spring.

Trailhead: (j) Follow the directions in Trip 9. The South Loop trailhead is just 50 yards up the road from the Cathedral Rock trailhead.

Description: Begin hiking past the trailhead signboard that welcomes hikers to the Mt. Charleston Loop Trail No. 145. Initially, the trail climbs steeply amid mixed forest of white fir, aspen and ponderosa pine until the grade eases before crossing a branch of the seasonal creek draining the

The summit of Charleston Peak

upper slopes of Griffith Peak. The dense forest recedes, revealing an impressive wall of vertical limestone, laced with multitudinous caves, forming the eastern wall of deep Echo Canyon. During spring and early summer, the picturesque canyon bursts with an abundance of wildflowers, and during fall, the large stands of aspen turn the basin a golden orange.

The trail follows an old road that bears east over another branch of the creek and then turns south following the drainage. When this stream is flowing in early season, numerous cascades tumble down the steep upper canyon in dramatic fashion. Cross back over the creek and begin a series of seemingly never-ending switchbacks that begin in predominantly white fir forest. Reach the signed wilderness boundary and continue steeply up the side of the canyon. Cross over the creek near a vertical limestone cliff where the water makes a 50-foot cascade. If you are fortunate and the water is still flowing, you can quench your thirst, which certainly is exacerbated by the steep climb.

Resume climbing up the side of the canyon on switchbacks, passing through a zone of limber pine and eventually reaching bristlecone pine near the ridge crest. The arduous climb, which seems to last forever, finally reaches the top of the ridge and the trail junction with the Griffith Peak Trail, 4.1 miles and 3,050 vertical feet from the trailhead. If you survived the climb, take solace in the fact that the worst is over. The next 4.2 miles gain only another 1,200 feet. Signs at the junction read: *Mt. Charleston 4, Harris Saddle 5, Kyle Canyon 4; Mt. Charleston Recreation Trail, Griffith Peak & Trailhead*. A reasonably large campsite with wall constructed from downed timber is nearby.

The trail makes a gradual climb in bristlecone-pine forest away from the junction and then descends for quite a way through open grassy slopes. A number of campsites shaded by pines are downslope away from the trail. Continue along the ridge as the trail passes among bristlecone pines and over limestone outcrops. The forest parts now and again to allow for incredible views across Kyle Canyon and out to the valley floor. If you have the time, the limestone outcroppings provide opportunity to search for fossils embedded in the rock.

The trail makes a moderate climb up to a pass and then mildly descends to a traverse along the back side of the ridge. Bristlecone pines virtually disappear as the vegetation becomes sparse in the rocky soil above 11,000 feet. A short climb leads to a saddle below the final slopes of Charleston Peak. Follow the rocky trail as it climbs steeply to the summit along the south ridge of the mountain.

If smog from the burgeoning metropolis of Las Vegas does not cloud the atmosphere, the views from the long, rocky summit of Charleston Peak are spectacular. On clear days, the view can extend as far as 300 miles in all directions. Distant basins and ranges are almost too numerous to count. Las Vegas to the southeast and Pahrump to the west lie nearly 10,000 feet below. The only permanent things sharing the thin air on Charleston Peak are an antenna and some electronic equipment.

Retrace your steps to the trailhead, or follow the North Loop Trail, reversing the description in Trip 6.

OTHER TRAILS

Robbers Roost: A short nature trail of 850 yards leads into a narrow canyon that legend claims was a hideout for bandits in the Mormon Trail era. The canyon does provide shelter under large rock overhangs and provides a commanding view of the surrounding terrain, lending credence to this possibility. The trailhead, clearly marked, is off State Route 158, also known as the Deer Creek Road, 3.4 miles north of the junction with the Kyle Canyon Road (State Route 157).

Appendix I
A WORD ABOUT HORSES

Nevada is perhaps the one place in the American West where those on foot and those on horseback share the wilderness in equal numbers. Away from the most popular areas, a chance encounter along the trail with equestrians is as likely as one with backpackers or hikers. A number of outfitters, possessing a self-interest in preserving the backcountry, regularly use pack animals to escort paying customers and their supplies into the mountains. The great majority of people you happen to meet will be friendly and considerate, whether on foot or on horseback. Unfortunately, just as there exists a small percentage of obnoxious backpackers, there is a similar number of inconsiderate horse packers who taint the reputation for the rest. Fortunately, since the Nevada wilderness receives relatively little use as compared with other areas and the topography is well suited to the use of animals, diverse groups of recreationists can compatibly coexist by observing a few simple guidelines. To foster cooperation and mutual respect between all users we are including a list of suggested practices and regulations for parties using pack animals (horses, mules and llamas) in the Nevada backcountry:

- Backpackers/hikers should yield right of way to horses—stand quietly downslope well off the trail
- Learn and use minimum impact camping techniques
- Keep the number of stock to a minimum by carrying light weight equipment
- Scatter manure piles at trailheads and campsites
- Choose campsites wisely and tether horses well away from areas of human use
- Carry pellets or grain (clean feed) where overgrazing is possible
- Keep animals a minimum of 100 yards from any body of water
- Don't tie animals to trees or other vegetation for long periods— use a picket, nightline or hobbles. Use electric fences for temporary corrals and move them regularly

In addition to these general guidelines, some areas have specific regulations governing the use of horses, mules and llamas. Check with the local Forest Service or Park Service office for current conditions.

Jarbidge Wilderness
- No more than 12 pack or saddle stock per group
- Use of pellets or weed-free hay is encouraged

East Humboldt & Ruby Mountains Wilderness
- Pack in weed-free hay and pellets
- Use highlines or portable corrals and move stock frequently
- Scatter manure
- No camping with stock at developed campgrounds or Greys Lake and road's end trailhead

Great Basin National Park
- Pack in weed-free hay and pellets
- Horses, mules and llamas are not allowed on paved roads, interpretive trails or within developed campgrounds—allowed in undeveloped campgrounds
- All manure must be scattered
- No tying to trees or vegetation for longer than 60 minutes, less if damage would occur
- No stock within 100 yards of a water source
- Alpine Lakes, Bristlecone-Glacier, Wheeler Peak and Lexington Arch trails are closed to animals

   Note: A backcountry management plan is currently under review and new regulations may be in effect by the summer of 1998.

Mt. Charleston Wilderness
- Use pellet type feed in wilderness and prior to arrival to avoid introduction of non-native plant species
- Trails closed to stock on South Loop Trail, North Loop Trail (above Trail Canyon) and Bristlecone Trail (except on Scout Canyon Road)

   Note: Use of animals in the wilderness is under evaluation and may be further restricted if the introduction of non-native plant species becomes a more significant problem.

Appendix II
25 HIGHEST PEAKS IN NEVADA

PEAK	ELEVATION	WILDERNESS
Boundary Peak	13,140	Boundary Peak
Wheeler Peak	13,063	Great Basin N.P.
Jeff Davis Peak	12,771	Great Basin N.P.
Mt. Baker	12,298	Great Basin N.P.
Mt. Moriah	12,067	Mt. Moriah
Mt. Jefferson	11,941	Alta Toquima
Pyramid Peak	11,926	Great Basin N.P.
Charleston Peak	11,918	Mt. Charleston
North Schell Peak	11,883	Schell Creek Range
Arc Dome	11,788	Arc Dome
South Schell Peak	11,735	Schell Creek Range
Taft Mountain	11,705	Schell Creek Range
Mt. Washington	11,676	Great Basin N.P.
Lincoln Peak	11,597	Great Basin N.P.
Bald Mountain	11,562	Great Basin N.P.
Mummy Mountain	11,530	Mt. Charleston
Currant Mountain	11,513	Currant Mountain
Bunker Hill	11,464	Toiyabe Range
Ruby Dome	11,387	Ruby Mountains
Toiyabe Dome	11,361	Arc Dome
Thomas Peak	11,316	Ruby Mountains
Hole-In-The-Mtn. Pk.	11,306	East Humboldt
Troy Peak	11,298	Grant Range
Mt. Grant	11,239	Wassuk Range
Granite Peak	11,213	Great Basin N.P.

Appendix III
WILDERNESS FISHING CHART

MT. ROSE WILDERNESS

Lake, River, Stream	Trip	Fish Species
Bronco Creek	5	Brook, Rainbow, Cutthroat
Galena Creek	5	Brook, Rainbow
Gray Lake,		
W. Fork Gray Creek	1	Brook, Cutthroat
Hunter Creek	2	Brook, Cutthroat
Jones Creek	3	
Ophir Creek	6	Brook
Thomas Creek	4	Brook, Rainbow
Whites Creek	3	Brook, Rainbow

SANTA ROSA-PARADISE PEAK

Lake, River, Stream	Trip	Fish Species
Buffalo Creek	5	Brook, Rainbow
Falls Creek	4	
Horse Creek	3	
McConnell Creek	2	Brook
Rebel Creek	1	Brook, Rainbow
Singas Creek	6	Brook, Rainbow

JARBIDGE

Lake, River, Stream	Trip	Fish Species
Camp Creek	4	Rainbow
Cottonwood Creek	4	Rainbow
Cougar Creek	2	
Dave Creek	2	Rainbow, Redband, Bull
Emerald Lake	1,2	Brook
Fall Creek	3	
Fox Creek	1	Rainbow
Gods Pocket Creek	2	
Jarbidge Lake	1	

Jarbidge River	1	Cutthroat, Dolly Varden, Rainbow
Jarbidge River, East Fork	2	Dolly Varden, Rainbow
Pine Creek	1	Rainbow, Redband, Bull
Slide Creek	2	Rainbow, Redband, Bull
Three Day Creek	2	
West Marys River	1	Cutthroat

EAST HUMBOLDT

Lake, River, Stream	Trip	Fish Species
Angel Creek, South Fork	2	Brook
Boulder Creeks, First, Second, Third & Fourth	3	
Brown, Brook		
Boulder Lake	3	Brook
Clover Creek	1	
Dorsey Creek	3	Cutthroat, Rainbow
Greys Lake, Creek	1	Brook, Cutthroat
Schoer Creek	2	Brook
Smith Lake	1	Cutthroat, Golden, Grayling
Steele Lake	3	Brook
Stephens Creek	3	Brook
Trout Creek	1	Brook
Whinchell Lake, Creek	2	Cutthroat
Wiseman Creek	2	

RUBY MOUNTAINS

Lake, River, Stream	Trip	Fish Species
Castle Lake	5, 6	
Dollar Lakes	5, 6	
Favre Lake	5, 6	Brook
Hidden Lakes	1	Cutthroat
Island Lake	4	Brook
Kleckner Creek	5, 6	Brook, Cutthroat
Lamoille Creek	5, 6	Brook, Cutthroat, Rainbow
Lamoille Creek, Right Fork	2	Brook
Lamoille Lake	5, 6	Brook
Liberty Lake	5, 6	Brook
McCutcheon Creek	6	Brook, Cutthroat
North Furlong Creek	6	Brook, Cutthroat
North Furlong Lake	6	Brook
Overland Lake, Creek	6, 7	Brook

Robinson Lake, Creek	1	Brook
Smith Creek, North, Middle & South Forks	6	Brook, Cutthroat
Soldier Creek	1	Brook, Cutthroat
Soldier Lake	1	Brook
Thomas Creek	3	Brook
Withington Creek	1	Brook

BOUNDARY PEAK

Lake, River, Stream	Trip	Fish Species
Trail Canyon Creek	1	Brook

ARC DOME

Lake, River, Stream	Trip	Fish Species
Big Sawmill Creek	7	Brook
Jett Creek	6	Brown, Brook, Rainbow
Little Jett Creek	7	
Little Sawmill Creek	7	Brook
North Twin River	1, 2	Brook, Rainbow
Reese River	4, 7	Brook, Cutthroat, Rainbow
South Twin River	1, 7	Brook, Rainbow
South Twin River, South Fork	1, 7	Brook, Rainbow
Stewart Creek	3	Brook, Rainbow
Toms Canyon Creek	5	
Trail Creek	5, 7	

ALTA TOQUIMA

Lake, River, Stream	Trip	Fish Species
Bucks Canyon Creek	1	
Pine Creek	1	Brown, Brook, Rainbow, Cutthroat

TABLE MOUNTAIN

Lake, River, Stream	Trip	Fish Species
Barley Creek	2	Brown, Brook, Rainbow
Mosquito Creek	1	Brook, Rainbow, Cutthroat

QUINN CANYON

Lake, River, Stream	Trip	Fish Species
Little Cherry Creek	1	Rainbow

MT. MORIAH

Lake, River, Stream	Trip	Fish Species
Hampton Creek	1	
Hendry's Creek	2	Cutthroat

GREAT BASIN NATIONAL PARK

Lake, River, Stream	Trip	Fish Species
Lehman Creek	1, 3	Brown, Cutthroat, Rainbow
Stella Lake	1	
Teresa Lake	1	
Baker Creek	4	Brook, Cutthroat, Rainbow
Baker Creek, South Fork	4	Rainbow
Snake Creek	5	Brown, Brook, Rainbow
Johnson Lake	4, 5	Brook

MT. CHARLESTON

No fishable streams or lakes

Source: Fishable Waters of Nevada map, Nevada Department of Wildlife, 1987 and U.S. Forest Service reports.

Appendix IV
BIBLIOGRAPHY & SUGGESTED READING

Carlson, Helen S. 1974. *Nevada Place Names.* Reno: University of Nevada Press.

Charlet, David Alan 1996. *Atlas of Nevada Conifers.* Reno: University of Nevada Press.

Clark, Jeanne L. 1993. *Nevada Wildlife Viewing Guide.* Helena, MT: Falcon Press.

Cline, Gloria Griffen 1963. *Exploring the Great Basin.* Reno: University of Nevada Press.

1993-96. *Encarta 97 Encyclopedia.* Redmond, WA: Microsoft Corporation.

Fiero, Bill 1986. *Geology of the Great Basin.* Reno: University of Nevada Press.

Hart, John 1981. *Hiking the Great Basin.* San Francisco: Sierra Club.

Kelsey, Michael R. 1988. *Hiking and Climbing in the Great Basin National Park.* Provo, UT: Kelsey Publishing.

Lanier, Ronald M. 1984. *Trees of the Great Basin.* Reno: University of Nevada Press.

McPhee, John 1980. *Basin and Range.* New York: Farrar, Straus, Giroux.

Monzingo, Hugh N. 1987. *Shrubs of the Great Basin.* Reno: University of Nevada Press.

Nicklas, Michael L. 1996. *Great Basin: The Story Behind the Scenery.* KC Publications Inc.

Stone, Irving 1982. *Men to Match My Mountains.* New York: Berkeley Books.

Taylor, Ronald J. 1992. *Sagebrush Country: A Wildflower Sanctuary.* Missoula, MT: Mountain Press Publishing Company.

Twain, Mark 1962. *Roughing It.* New York: Penguin Books.

Wuerthner, George 1992. *Nevada Mountain Ranges.* Hong Kong: Nordica International Ltd.

Charleston Peak seen from summit of Griffith Peak

Trip Maps

Legend:

Access Road	▬ ▬ ▬ ▬ ▬ ▬
Trail	- - - - - - - - - - - - - - -
Trailhead Letter	△a
Trip Number	①
Campground Number	⬡1

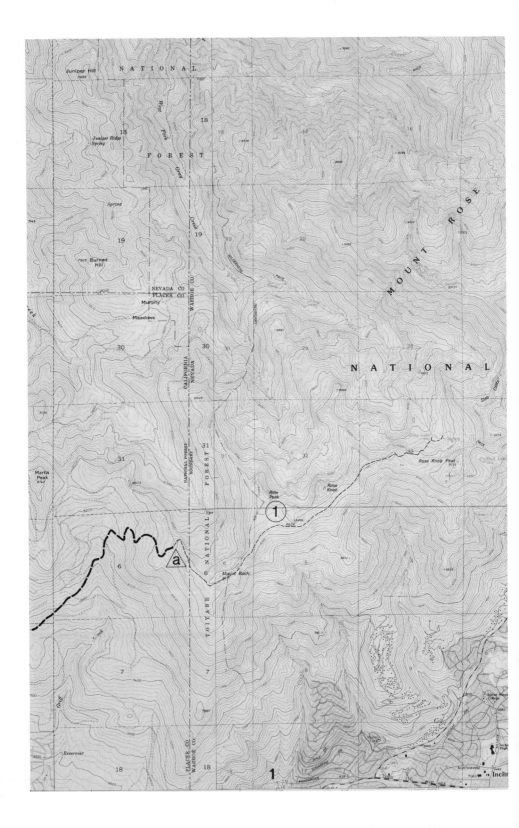

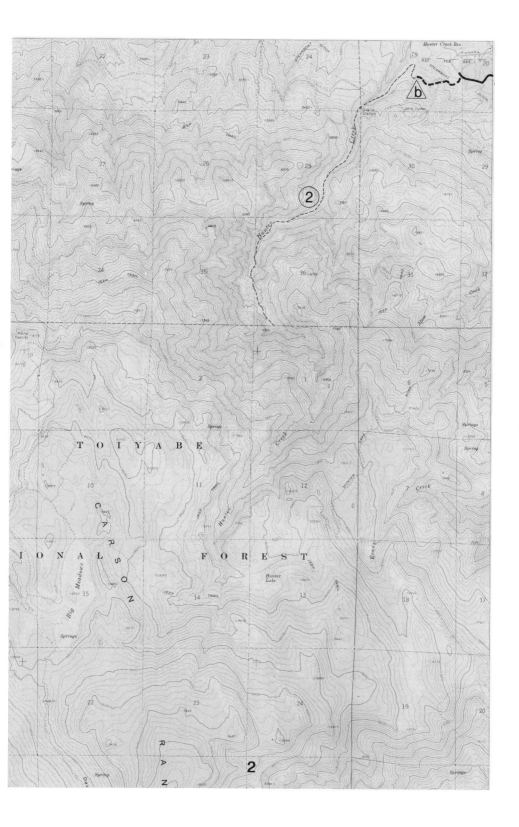

2

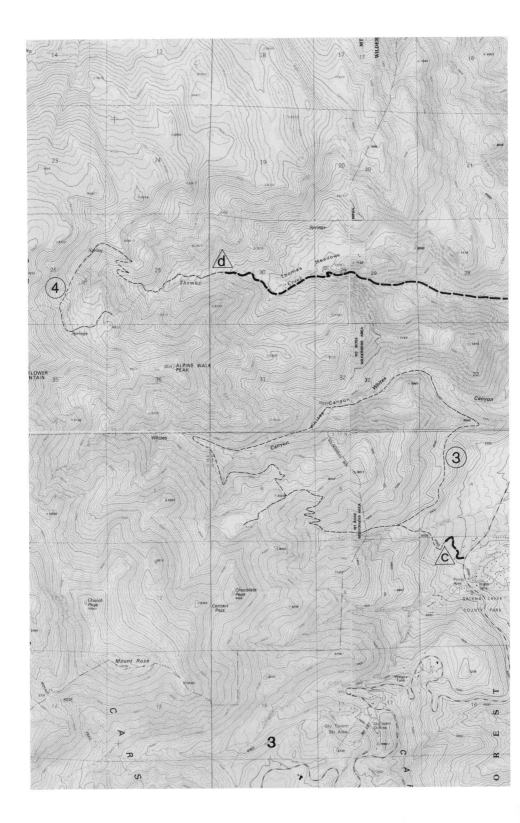

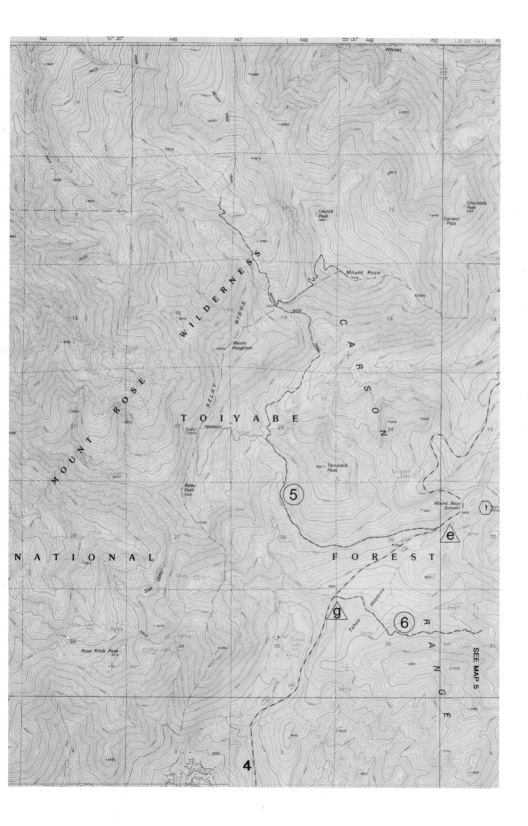

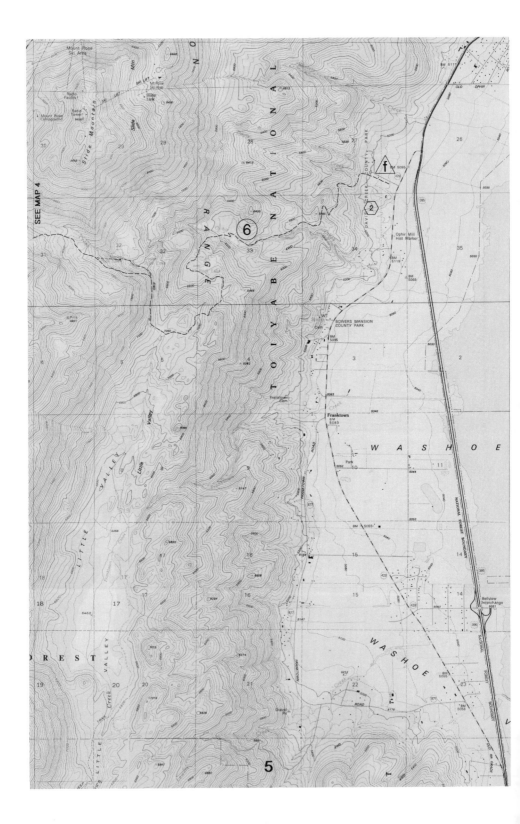

SEE MAP 4

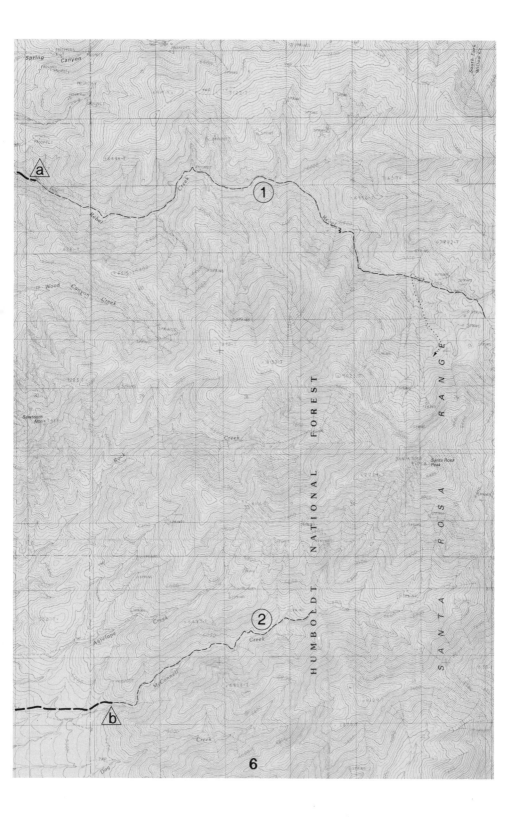

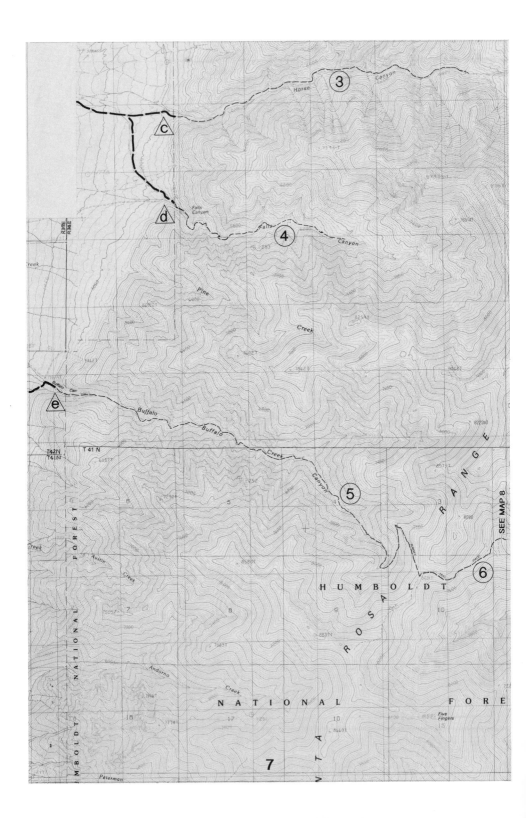

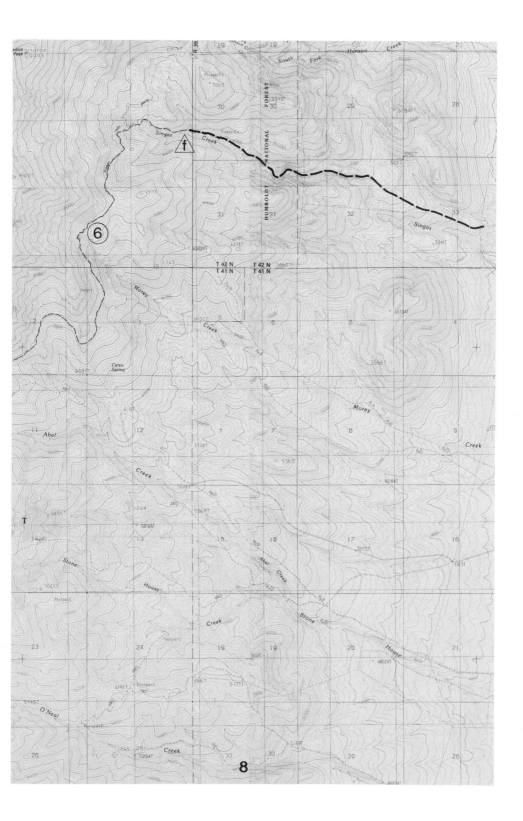

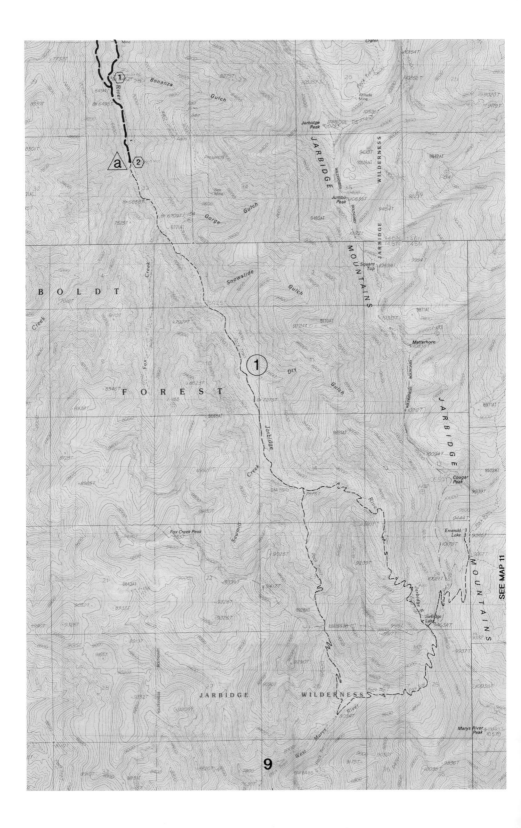

SEE MAP 11

9

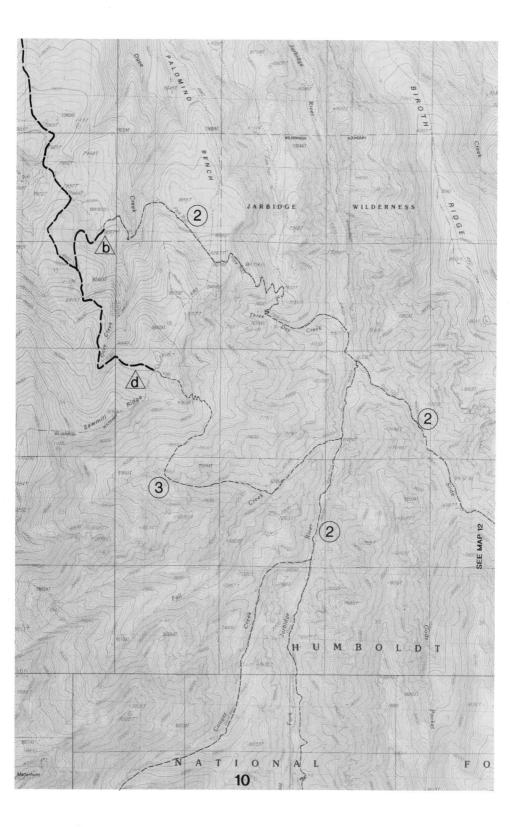

SEE MAP 12

10

SEE MAP 9

SEE MAP 12

J A R B I D G E   W I L D E R

J
A
R
B
I
D
G
E

M
O
U
N
T
A
I
N
S

W I L D E R N E S S

Prospect
Peak

Cougar
Peak

Emerald
Lake

Jarbidge R.

Jarbidge
Lake

Slide Rock Ridge

Marys River
Peak

Marys River

Camp Creek

Gods Pocket
Peak

Gold
Knob

Divide
Peak

Right Fork

Camp Creek Right Fork

North Fork Camp Creek

Springs

River

Springs

Spring

Spring

Spring

Camp
Spring

Spring

Spring

②

①

④

11

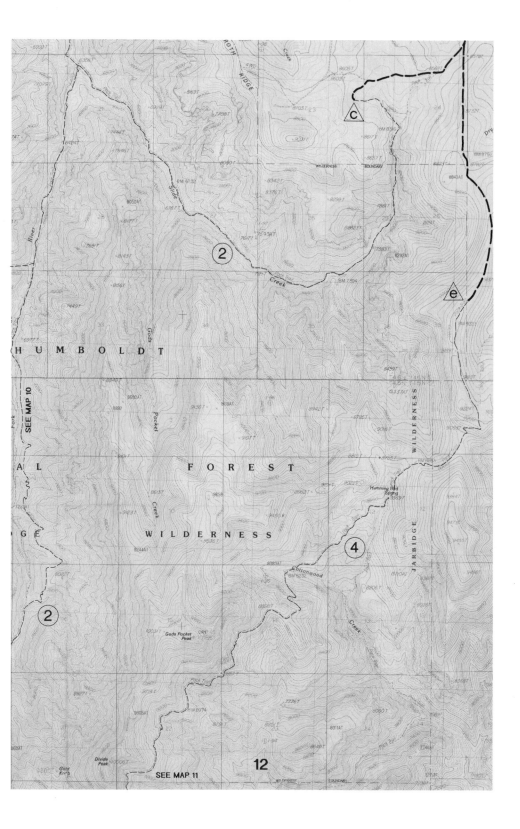

ROTH RIDGE

Creek

SEE MAP 10

HUMBOLDT

FOREST

WILDERNESS

JARBIDGE

WILDERNESS

Slide

Gods

Pocket

Creek

Creek

Cottonwood

Humming Bird Spg'd

Gods Pocket Peak

Divide Peak

Gold Knob

12

SEE MAP 11

WILDERNESS BOUNDARY

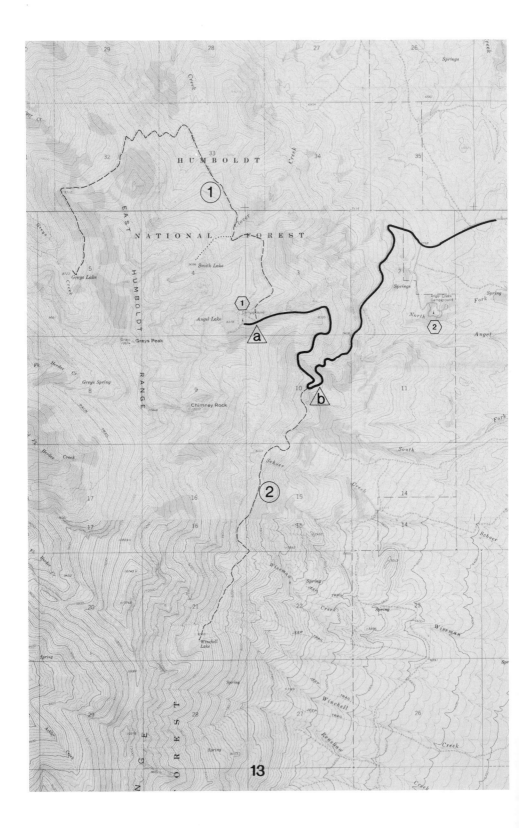

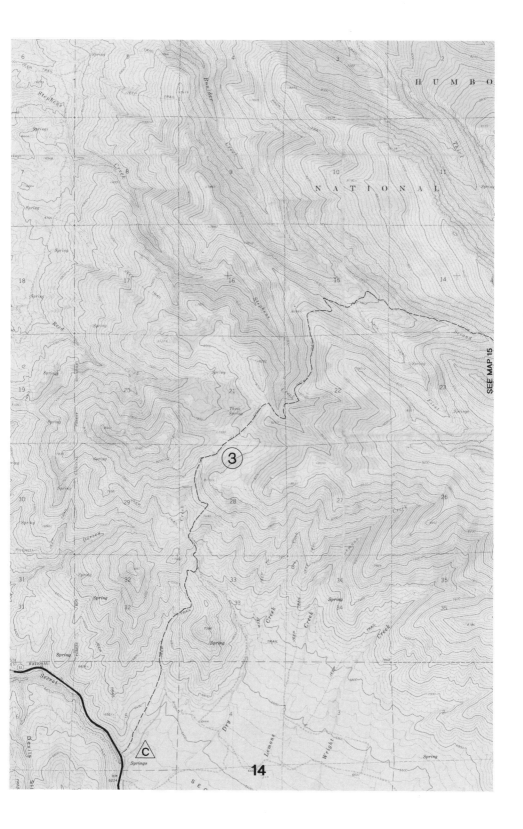

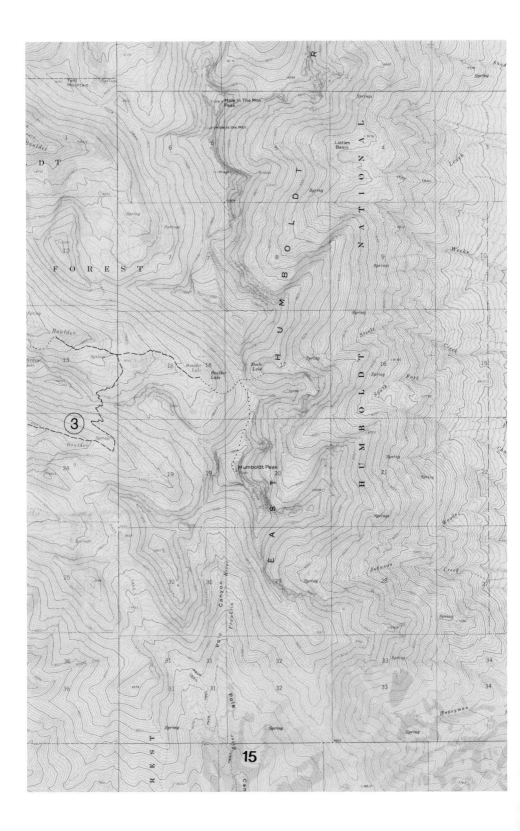

15

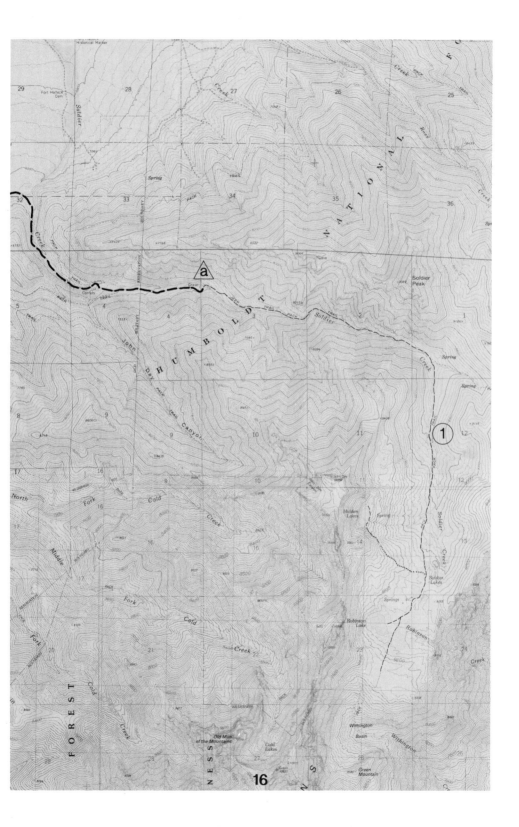

16

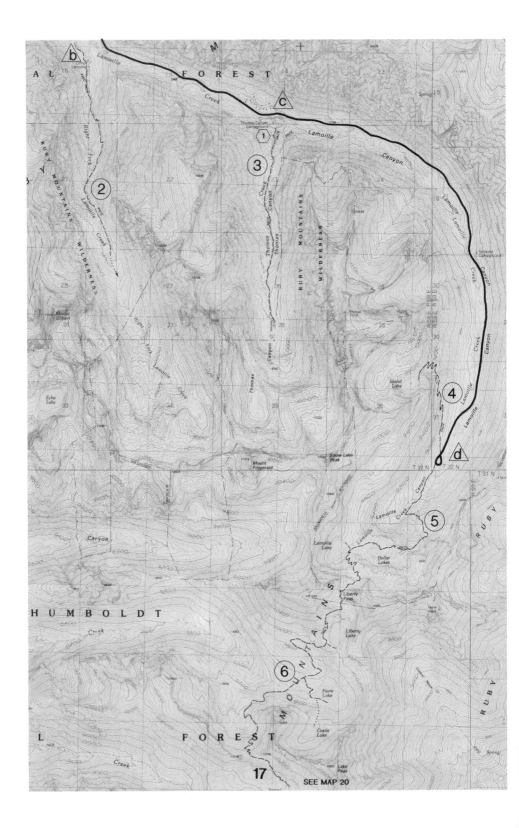

SEE MAP 20

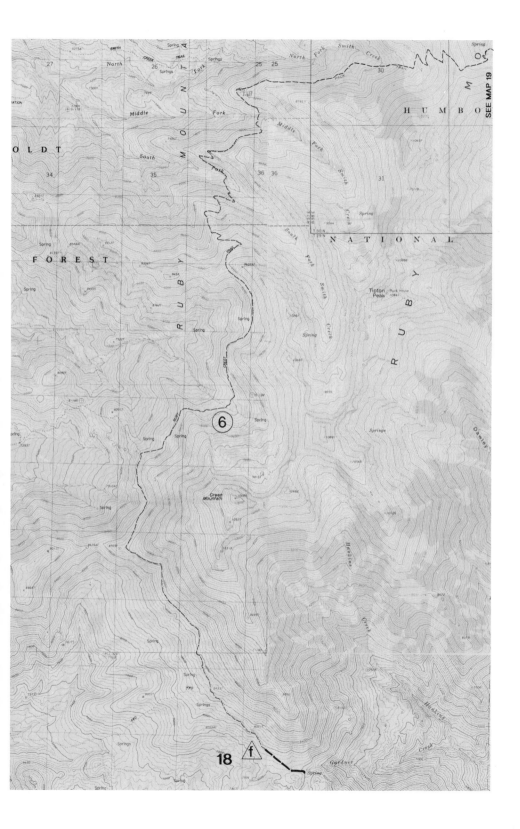

SEE MAP 19

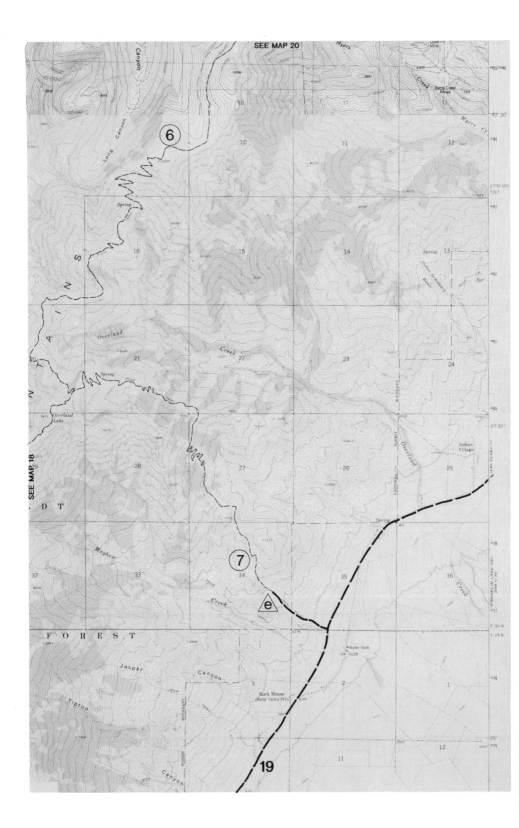

SEE MAP 20

⑥

⑦

ⓔ

19

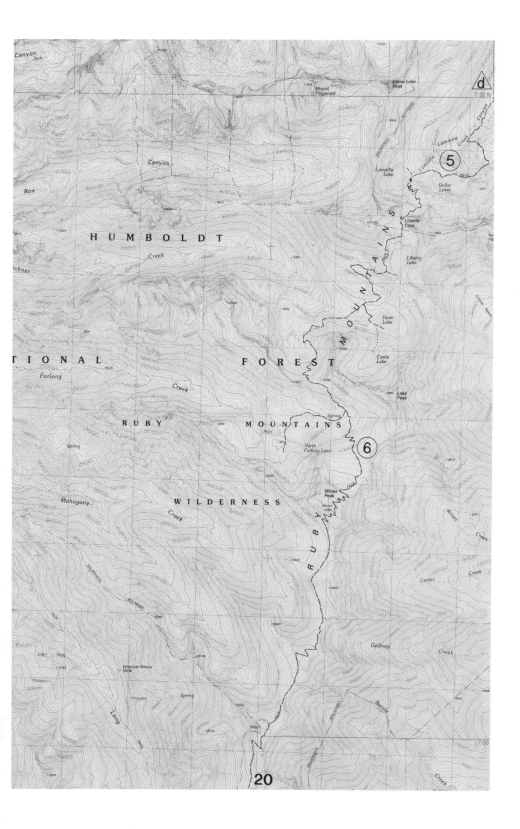

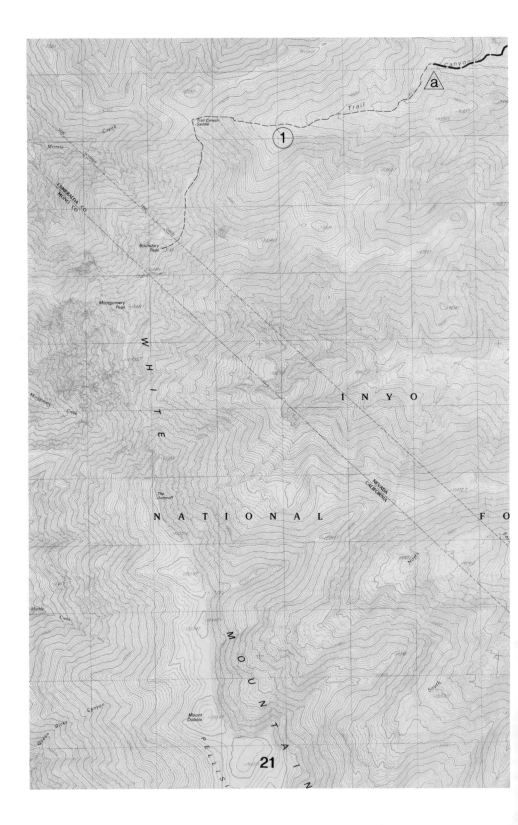

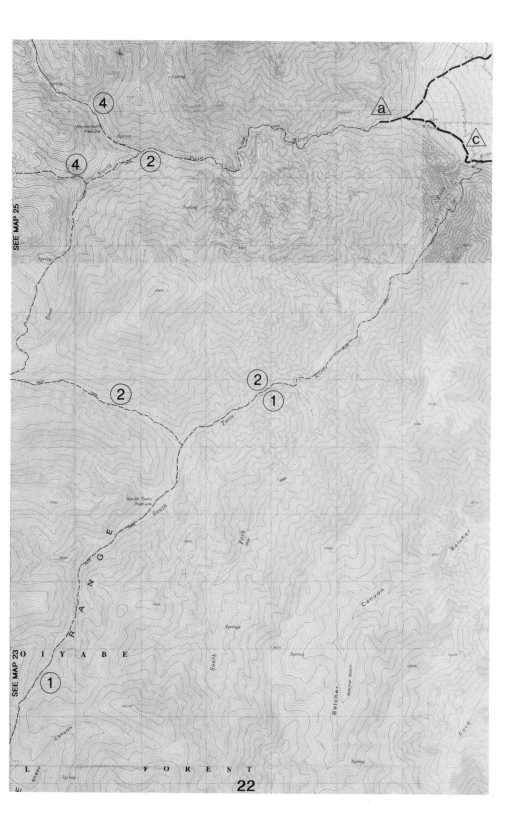

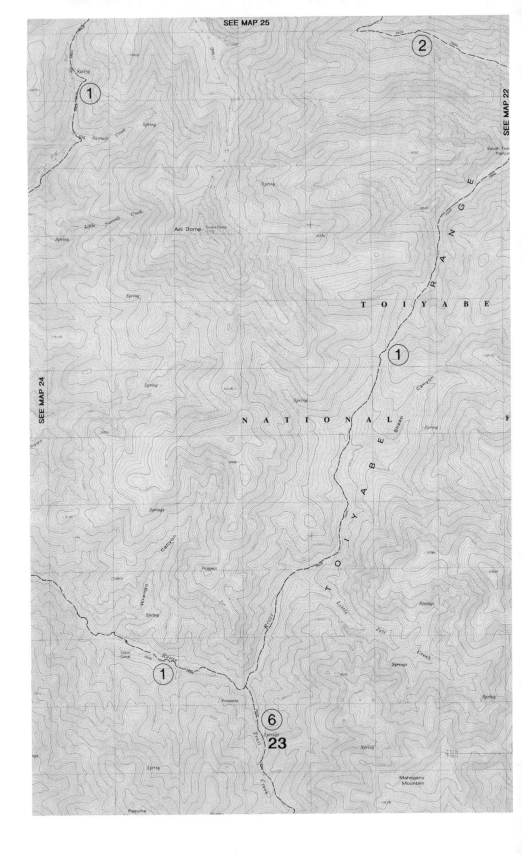

SEE MAP 22

SEE MAP 24

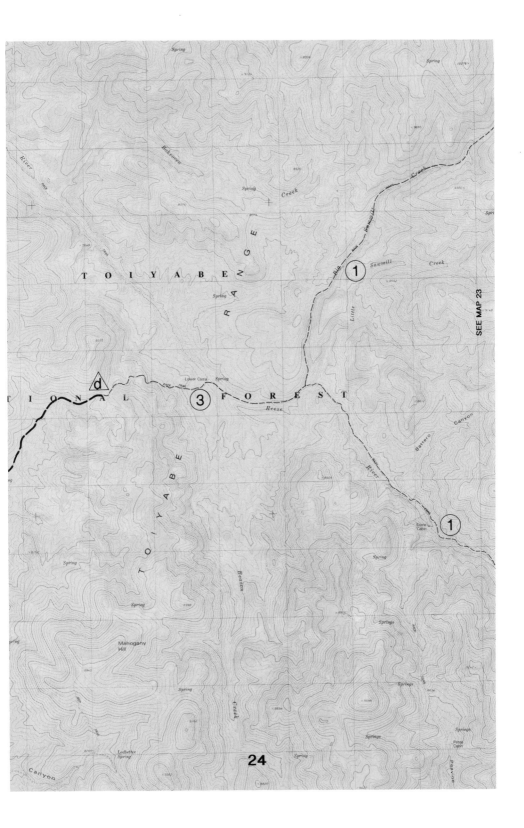

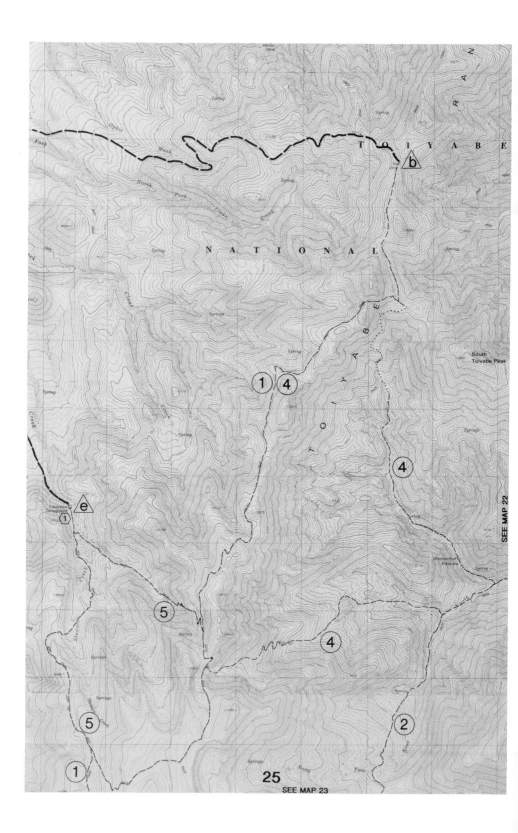

25

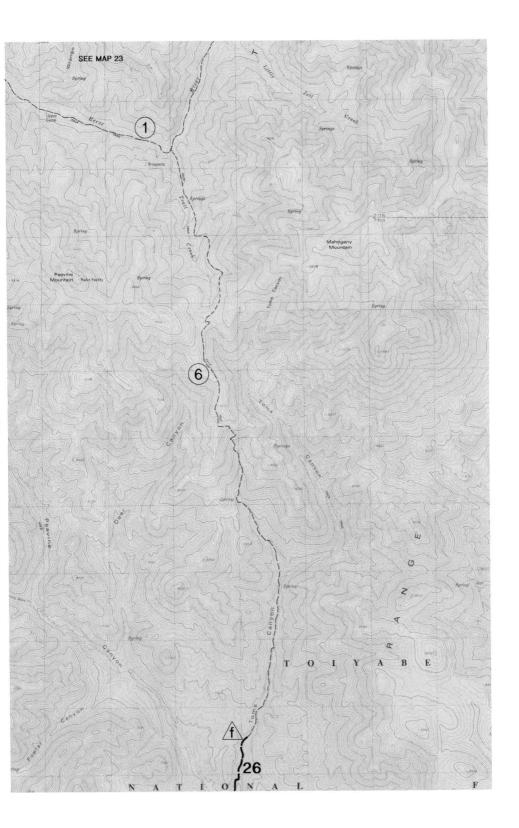

SEE MAP 23

①

⑥

⟨f⟩

26

N A T I O N A L   F

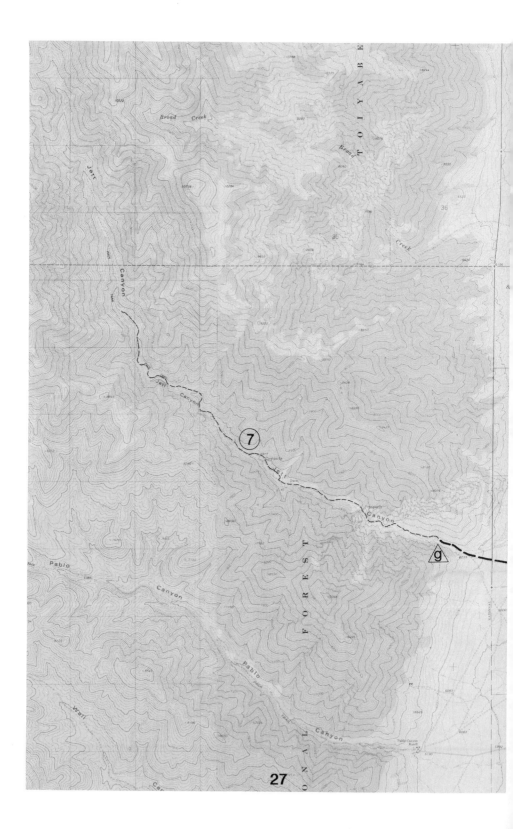

SEE MAP 29

28

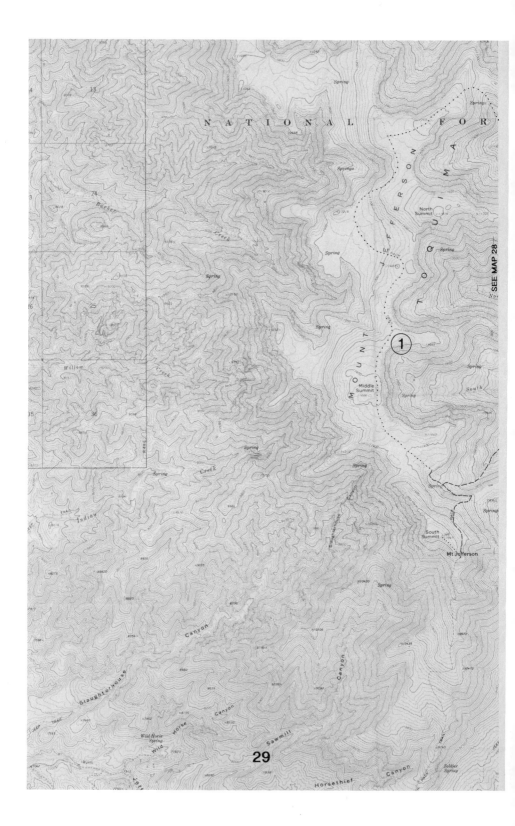

SEE MAP 28

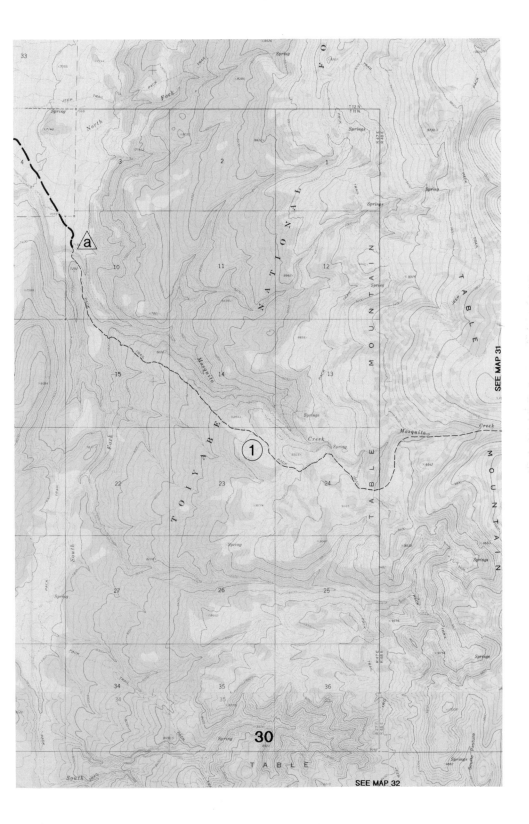

SEE MAP 31

SEE MAP 32

30

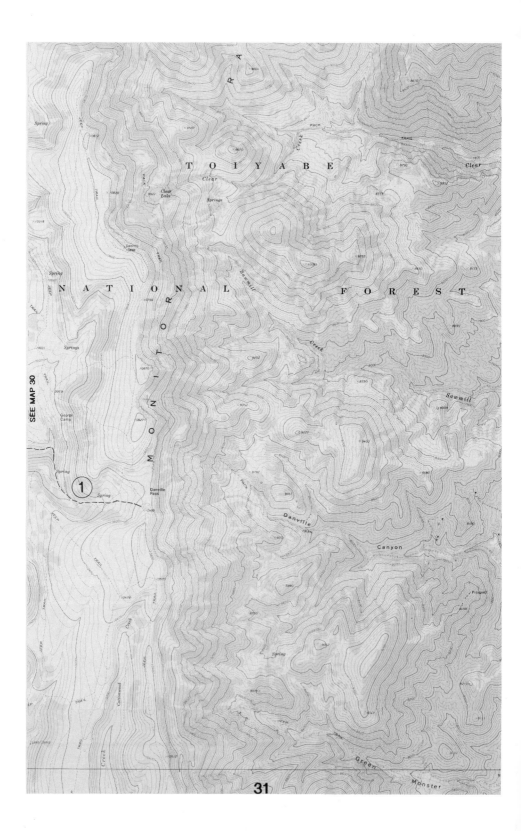

SEE MAP 30

T O I Y A B E

N A T I O N A L   F O R E S T

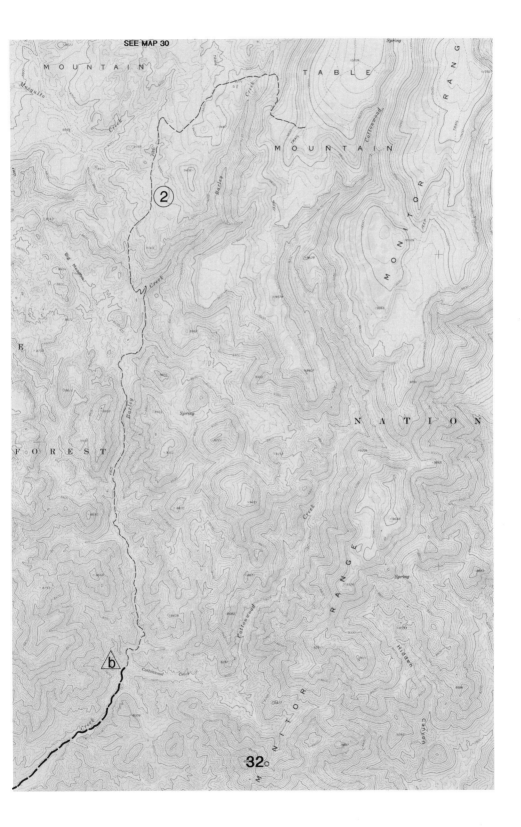

32

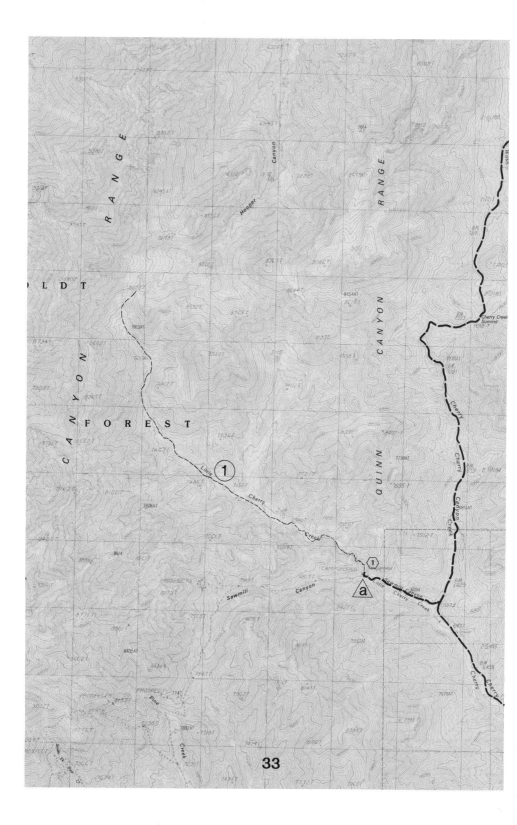

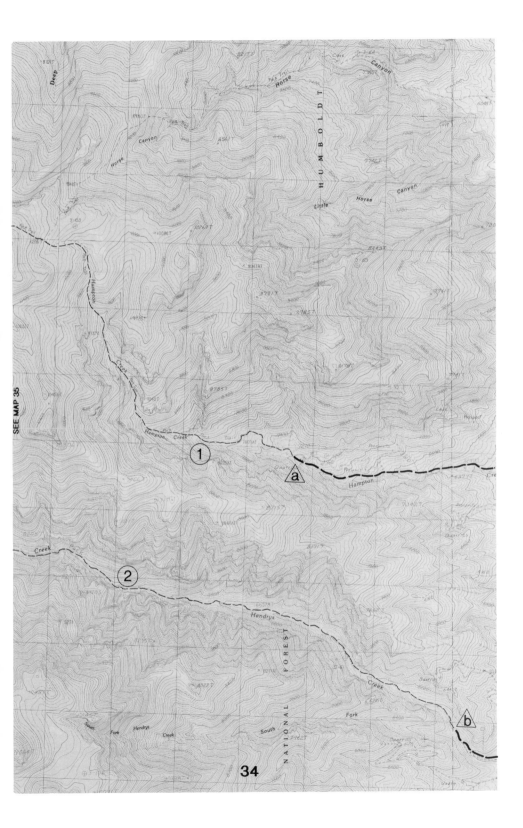

SEE MAP 35

34

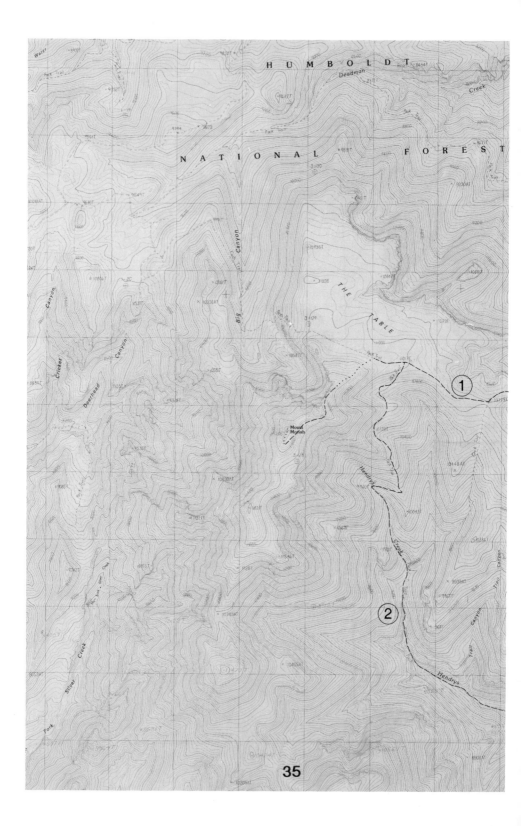

HUMBOLDT

Deadman

Creek

NATIONAL   FOREST

THE   TABLE

Big Canyon

Canyon

Cricket

Deerhead Canyon

Mount
Moriah

Hendrys

Creek

Hendrys

Silver Creek

Fork

35

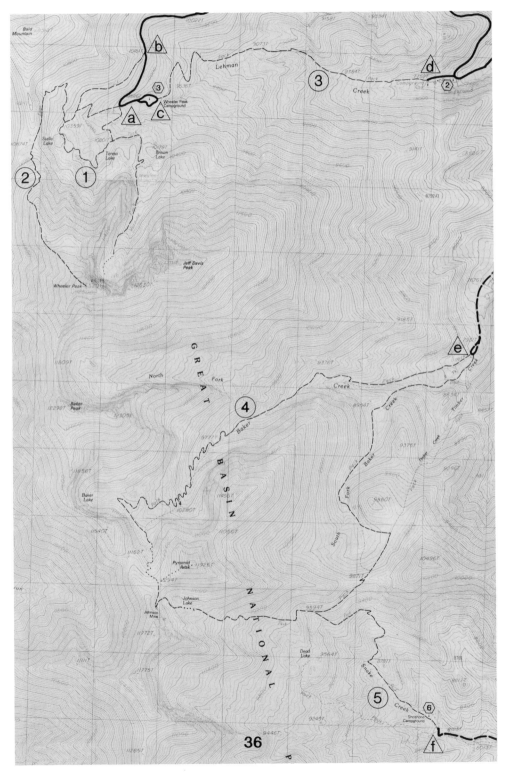

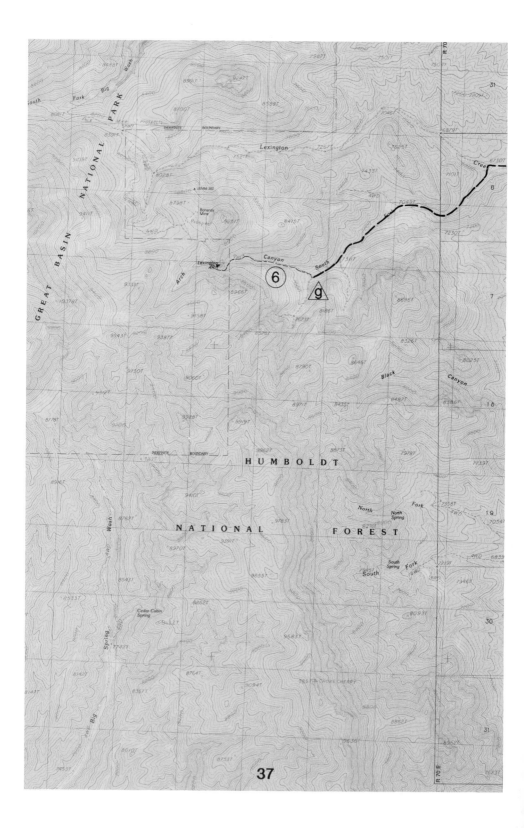

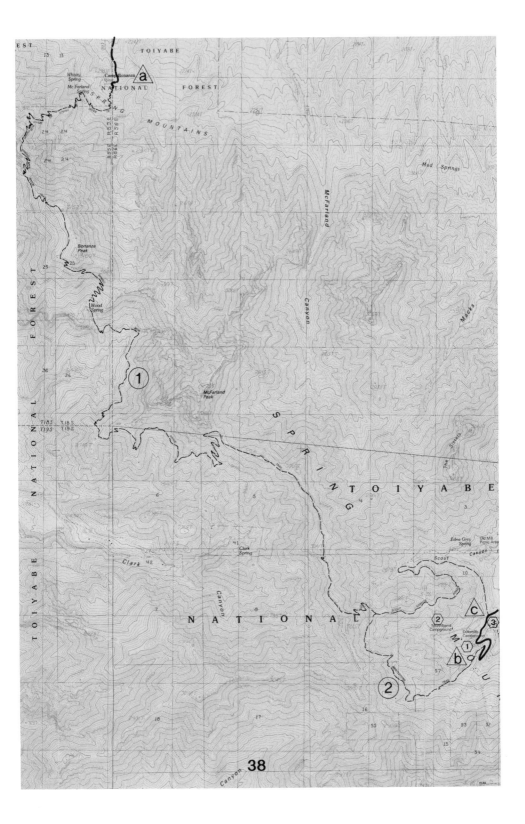

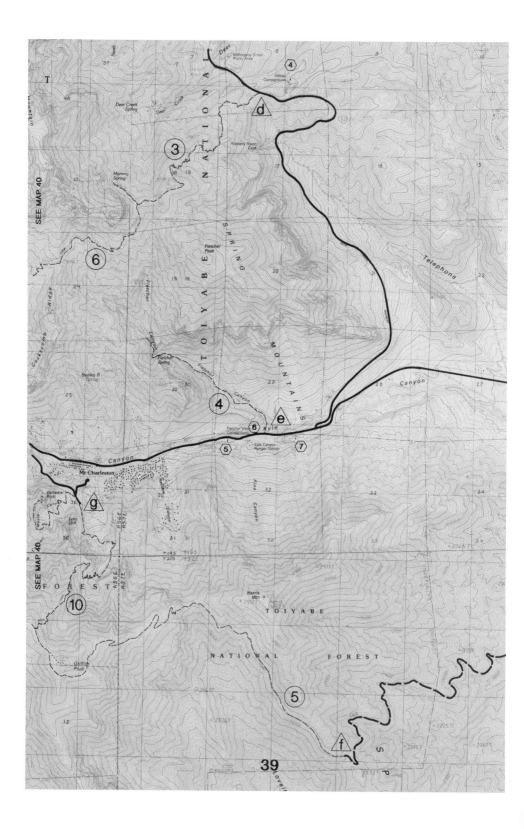

39

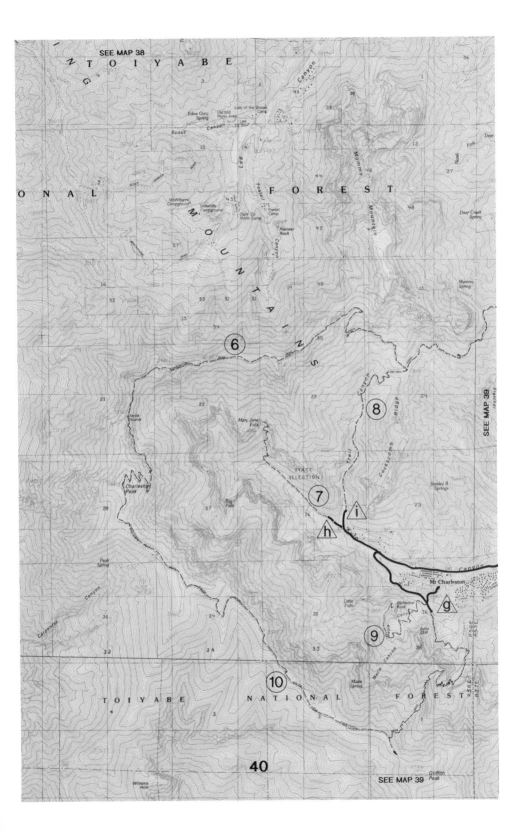

TOIYABE

ON AL

FOREST

M O U N T A I N S

Lee Canyon

Scout Canyon

Edna Grey Spring
Old Mill Picnic Area
Lady of the Snows Camp
Lee Stat

McWilliams Campground
Dolomite Campground
Clark Co Youth Camp
Forest Camp

Mummy Mountain

Deer

North Fork

Deer Creek Spring

Pioneer Rock

Mummy Spring

⑥

Devils Thumb

Mary Jane Falls

⑧

Cockscomb Ridge

Charleston Peak

STATE SELECTION

⑦

Stanley B Springs

△i

△h

Big Falls

Peak Spring

Canyon

⑨

Mt Charleston

Cathedral Rock

Little Falls

Echo Cliff

△g

Carpenter Canyon

⑩

Mule Spring

T O I Y A B E   N A T I O N A L   F O R E S T

Griffith Peak

Williams Hole

Index

ACKNOWLEDGMENTS

Many individuals have lent their assistance to this project in a variety of ways. First and foremost, I would like to thank my editor at Wilderness Press, Tom Winnett, for believing in the idea from the beginning and for his involvement throughout the process.

A number of friends granted me the privilege of their company on many of my excursions into the middle of nowhere. Their presence kept my already skewed view of reality from deteriorating any further in the midst of too much solitude. Thanks to my companions: Dwight Smith, Mike Wilhelm, Dave Peterson, Brian Gervais, John Burton, Leo Gervais and the RCF Youth Group (Ben, Brian, Danna, Daniel, David, Josh, Karen, Kristen, Peter, Rachel, Steve, Yun), Keith Catlin, Darrin Munson and Dan Whittemore.

Countless individuals in a variety of Forest Service offices proved invaluable in providing information regarding the Nevada wilderness areas. My thanks to all of them for their assistance.

Special recognition goes to Carmel Snyder, Ciera Tompkins and Mary Ann Kafchinsky for watching my two sons, David and Stephen, when I was out traipsing around and my wife was working to support the endeavor.

I would like to express additional gratitude for my wife's commitment to me over the past two years while this project grew to fruition. Her proof-reading was greatly appreciated as well.

Lastly, but most importantly, I would like to thank God for blessing me with the privileged opportunity to enjoy His creation along with the gifts and abilities to make this book a reality.

Michael White